MUCH MORE THAN A GAME

MUCH MORE THAN A GAME

PLAYERS, OWNERS, & AMERICAN BASEBALL SINCE 1921

ROBERT F. BURK

The University of North Carolina Press   Chapel Hill & London

© 2001 The University of North Carolina Press
All rights reserved
Manufactured in the United States of America
Designed by Richard Hendel
Set in Monotpe Garamond and Champion Types
by Tseng Information Systems, Inc.
The paper in this book meets the guidelines for
permanence and durability of the Committee on Production
Guidelines for Book Longevity of the Council on Library Resources.
Library of Congress Cataloging-in-Publication Data
Burk, Robert Fredrick, 1955–
Much more than a game : players, owners, and American baseball
since 1921 / Robert F. Burk.
p. cm.
Includes bibliographical references and index.
ISBN 0-8078-2592-1 (cloth : alk. paper) —
ISBN 0-8078-4908-1 (pbk. : alk. paper)
1. Baseball—Economic aspects—United States—History—20th century.
2. Baseball players—United States—Economic conditions—
20th century.   3. Baseball team owners—United States—Economic
conditions—20th century.   4. Industrial relations—United States—
History—20th century.   I. Title: Players, owners, and
American baseball since 1921.   II. Title.
GV880 .B869   2001
796.357'09'04—dc21   00-041774

05 04 03 02 01   5 4 3 2 1

CONTENTS

ILLUSTRATIONS

PREFACE

Although we prefer to see baseball as a game we play or watch for recreation, from almost the beginning it has been a labor-intensive industry whose on-field personnel constitute both the entertainment product we enjoy and men engaged in doing their job. At the very heart of this labor-intensive business has been the struggle between on-field employees and management over access to its opportunities, workplace rights, and overarching both of these, administering the industry and defining the relationship—paternalistic, adversarial, or cooperative—between the two sides. This history can be divided into three main eras. The first—examined in my previous volume, *Never Just a Game: Players, Owners, and American Baseball to 1920*—is most accurately viewed as the "trade war era" and lasted from the formation of intercity cartels, most notably the National League, in the 1870s through World War I. The two subsequent periods—the subject of this study—stretched from the 1920s to the 1960s and from the 1960s to the present day and can be described as the "paternalistic" and "inflationary" eras (see Appendix, Fig. 1). Although each era featured the general issues mentioned above, the answers reached and the labor relationship forged differed in significant ways.

In the first, or trade war, era, professional baseball emerged from its nurturing ground of northeastern Protestant villages, neighborhoods, and voluntary associations to become a fledgling entertainment business. During that process the search for the best playing talent and the demands for inclusion by the Irish and Germans led both to the modest broadening of ethnic employment and the growing separation of personnel, functions, and power between off-field managers and on-field performers. After a decade of confusion and false starts, the strongest clubs, led by the Chicago White Stockings, formed the National League and extended territorial monopolies to member franchises and strict "reserve clause" limits on the geographic mobility and choice of employment of players. Probably the most representative and influential figure in this first era was Albert G. Spalding, who followed up his playing career with leadership of the Chicago club and in large measure the entire circuit from the 1880s to the 1900s. The trade war era earned its label through a succession of economic wars for urban markets and players in which the National League either crushed its adversaries or merged with them (the most notable being the American League in 1903) in an expanded cartel. Although performers made several attempts to unionize, the frequency of trade war and the multiple suitors it temporarily created did more to give them greater workplace leverage. Even unionization itself tended to occur during times of temporary protection through trade war competition, only to collapse once the wars, and players' marketplace leverage with them, ceased. In this first era, as baseball magnates sought "order" in their industry, the search also led to efforts to standardize playing rules to strike the most profitable balance between player productivity, fan attendance, and labor-cost pressures. It also led to the dominant cartel developing working agreements with lesser leagues to secure an ongoing source of white playing talent, while systematically excluding in Jim Crow fashion baseball aspirants of color.

The second, or paternalistic, era followed the defeats of the Federal League and Players Fraternity, World War I, and the "Black Sox" scandal of 1919–20. It was marked by a semblance of stability and management-dominated order, with the NL/AL combination entrenched in the same sixteen northeastern and midwestern cities until late in the age and with a single commissioner in place to arbitrate disputes and enforce discipline upon players. Thanks in large part to a 1922 Supreme Court ruling upholding the cartel's antitrust exemption, with the sporadic exceptions of the Pacific Coast League and the Mexican League, trade war threats eased. Unionization forays were either sabotaged, as in the case of the post–World War II American Baseball Guild, or co-opted, as in the postwar representation system that subsequently evolved into the Major League Baseball Players Association. The National League and the American League, prodded by their demand for low-cost labor and by Depression-era pleas from the "minors" for economic salvation, erected vast, captive "farm systems" of clubs and players. This step further reduced the marketplace leverage of individual performers and effectively delayed serious reconsideration of supplementing Organized Baseball's playing force through racial integration. But although the industry seemed to have secured a stable monopsony over its human "means of production," and a subsequent generation of owners would look upon these years as a lost "golden age," baseball remained subject to the winds of change, whether they be the Depression's economic calamity, the rise of industrial unionism, the strains of world war, the push for civil rights, the advent of radio and television, or the demographic shift to the Sun Belt. As a consequence, baseball late in the era reluctantly reversed itself and began to integrate racially its playing ranks, and it also grudgingly adopted a system of player representation, a pension plan, and a minimum wage for its big league performers. Although the era began with the quarter-century commissionership of Kenesaw Landis, the individual most representative of the entire period and its series of labor policy adjustments was not Landis but Branch Rickey—champion of the farm system, the first big league executive to proceed with integration, and a pioneer late in the era in the scouting and recruitment of Latin American playing talent.

The third, or inflationary, era—in which we either remain or are in the painful process of leaving—began with renewed stirrings of franchise expansion in response to Sun Belt growth and the rising revenue importance of television. A new generation of players, weaned on the civil rights struggle and a new tide of youthful political activism and protest, emerged in the affluent America of the 1960s with a more questioning outlook toward authority and a fresh appreciation of the power of mobilization and collective action. Drawing strength from the ranks of the new generation of players, the Major League Baseball Players Association, now headed by Marvin Miller, transformed itself from a "company union" into the industry's most powerful force for change. The union's aggressive campaigns in Miller's first decade of leadership led not only to higher minimum salaries and greater procedural rights, including the outside arbitration of younger players' salary disputes, but even the collapse of the reserve clause and the establishment of "free agency" for veteran performers. The success of the big league players in forcing higher salaries and greater industry power inspired imitation, most notably by the umpires. In the 1980s and 1990s, owners tried with only limited success to keep ahead of the payroll surge through revenue-boosting actions such as pro-offense rules changes, franchise and territorial expansion, and aggressive licensing and television negotiating, as well as cost-restraint measures including jettisoning older big league journeymen and increasing their recruitment of cheaper prospects outside the United States. After a long series of labor confrontations that spanned three decades, by the late 1990s the two sides had battled themselves nearly to exhaustion and had risked killing the "golden goose" that had laid so many mutually profitable "eggs." As a new century loomed, baseball management and labor nervously eyed each other and wondered whether the millennium would bring a new round of combat or the start of a brighter era of enlightened partnership and global expansion.

In the process of carrying out this extended project, I have incurred so many debts of gratitude that it is impossible to cite them all. But in particular, for the access to and use of research materials my deep thanks go out to the National Baseball Library in Cooperstown, New York, especially former chief librarian Tom Heitz, research librarian Tim Wiles, and photo collection managers Patricia Kelly and Bill Burdick; the staff of the University of Kentucky Library's Special Collections, in particular archivist Bill Marshall; *Sporting News* archivist Steve Gietschier and his capable assistants; the Manuscripts Division of the Library of Congress; and the staffs of the Muskingum College and Marietta College libraries. On many occasions during the writing of both books, Rose and David Edwards have extended their love and hospitality during my research visits to Cooperstown, and I count them as cherished members of my extended family. My appreciation also goes to Muskingum College for providing me with a sabbatical during the 1997–98 year to write the original manuscript. Lewis Bateman, Ron Maner, and their compatriots at the University of North Carolina Press have been unwavering in their faith in the manuscript and their dedication to making it better. My thanks also go out to the many people who have read the manuscript at varying stages or who have endured my incessant rantings on the subject.

Last but certainly not least, I would like to dedicate this work to three individuals who in one way or another have touched me or the subject of this book. The first is Curt Flood, who sadly passed away before his time but whose courage paved the way for today's ballplayers of color to enjoy big league careers, and for all major leaguers to gain their fair bounty. To Professor Donald R. McCoy, a beloved mentor and loyal friend, I

PREFACE

offer my deepest gratitude for the times we shared and for the dissertation fund appropriately created in his honor at the University of Kansas to extend his legacy of scholarly excellence. And finally, I offer this work to Margaret, the best professor in the family and a person whose love and loyalty have sustained me in bad times and good—and with whom the latter rapidly distances the former.

PART ONE

THE PATERNALISTIC ERA

The Age of Rickey

CHAPTER 1 : A NEW ERA

1921–1929

In the decade following World War I, the United States entered a new era as a confident, maturing nation. A majority of its citizens now lived in urban areas and served as both producers and purchasers of the bounty of a revolutionary new society of mass consumption. It was in most respects a prosperous society. But it was also one in which wage inequalities and wealth maldistribution were growing. Even the most enlightened companies offered but modest "welfare-capitalism" benefits. Larger and larger firms and combinations dominated the business landscape, and they used their size and trade association networks to control industry decision making, neutralize unionization efforts, and influence politicians and the courts. Their predecessors having struggled through boom-and-bust cycles, labor militancy, and trade wars, the New Era's titans were determined not to permit a return to the old instability or to allow new threats to their dominance to emerge.

Virtually any history textbook offers such a description of the U.S. economy of the 1920s. Every part of it applied equally to professional baseball in the United States. For if the 1920s were a new era in the nation's economic life, the decade was also known, not coincidentally, as the golden age of sports. In the postwar decade, spectator sports became clearly recognizable as major entertainment businesses, and none more so than Organized Baseball. Save for a brief trough in the early 1920s, baseball enjoyed impressive customer growth and rising profits. To be sure not all clubs, whether owing to smaller markets, weaker talent, or both, shared equally in the bounty. At one end the New York Yankees generated $2.6 million in the baseball "bull market" of 1923–30. In contrast, paying a heavy price for handing over Babe Ruth to their Bronx rivals, the Boston Red Sox lost over $300,000 in the same stretch. But on average, each major league club made a $115,000 yearly profit in the 1920s. Throughout Organized Baseball, which included the white minor leagues, 1925 offered a typical gate receipt figure of $50 million.[1]

As in other industries, extraordinary productivity gains propelled baseball's growing popularity and prosperity. But what made baseball dramatically different was that its productivity and profit gains did not come from replacing workers with machines. In baseball such mechanization could not happen, since the on-field workers' labor was the entertainment product. Spurred by one noteworthy "technological improvement"—the "lively ball"—and by rules requiring replacement of dirty baseballs and prohibition of the spitball, hitting production soared to record levels. Batting averages, approximately .250 in the major leagues in 1919, jumped to .285 in 1921 and stayed in the .280s all decade. Home runs, the signature mark of the lusty-hitting batter, climbed from 338 in the 1917 season to 1,167 in 1925.[2]

In the New Era, however, such productivity gains and rising profits did not inevitably translate into wage boosts. Management, whether in baseball or more broadly, utilized a wide array of tactics to restrain employee power and therefore the benefits derived from it. The methods ranged from antiunion employer associations, blacklistings, firings, on-the-job harassment, "yellow-dog" contracts, injunctions, industrial espionage, strikebreaking, and police crackdowns to company unions, management-run grievance procedures, and limited types of welfare capitalism. In the decades before World War I, baseball players had mirrored workers in other enterprises in challenging management's hegemony over their industry. On several occasions they had formed unions and, in one instance, even a rival league, seeking greater leverage. Even though baseball trade wars usually had not been instigated by players, their periodic occurrence had offered players temporary clout with the opportunity to play off rival suitors. But the latest attempt at collective association, the Players' Fraternity, had collapsed after the failure of the Federal League challenge to the majors. By the start of the postwar decade, the performers lacked the means or circumstances to combat Organized Baseball's drive for comprehensive labor control.

Although in defeat their resistance largely has been forgotten, players of the early 1920s did not simply go down quietly. In 1921 Johnny Evers urged comrades to mobilize on "ethical" lines for procedural rights, pensions, and health coverage. Sensitive to traditional player hostility to anything that smacked of wage scales, Evers insisted his proposed fraternity would not "regulate salaries in any way." Specific incidents at the end of 1921 provoked still more player grumbling about eroding rights and inadequate benefits. On September 30 the New York Giants squad put on an exhibition game to raise over $30,000 for its disabled prewar star Christy Mathewson. When slugger Babe Ruth defied Commissioner Kenesaw Mountain Landis's ban on postseason barnstorming and drew the threat of suspension without pay, other players rallied in support of "the Bambino" and called for a union to "obtain rights." Reflecting management fears of an emerging round of postwar player militancy, the *Sporting News* cheered Landis's assertion of "law and order" on Ruth for causing "some ball players with Bolshevik tendencies [to] hesitate." As a recession reached its bottom, fears of an attendance dip in 1922 led to widespread talk among owners of salary cutbacks and release of veteran players that also promised to provoke defiance.[3]

In the spring of 1922 increasingly disgruntled major leaguers formed the National Baseball Players' Association of the United States. The membership tabbed Raymond J. Cannon, a former semipro pitcher turned attorney-agent for prizefighter Jack Dempsey and blacklisted "Black Soxer" Happy Felsch, as its leader. Setting annual dues at $20, the association drew up a constitution, chose an eleven-member board of directors, and demanded the right to voting representation in industry councils. Even Samuel Gompers, head of the American Federation of Labor (AFL), extended his public blessing to the new organization. But Organized Baseball soon counterattacked. The *Sporting News*'s Francis Richter insisted that the only real grievances the association cited were the reserve clause and the owners' prerogative to release players with only ten days' notice. Even in these matters, "the experiences of half a century prove that both are absolutely essential." "Ball players' unions are impractical," Richter concluded, "for the simple reason that the players' tenure of professional life is limited to fifteen or twenty years at most; and unnecessary because the income from playing is variable. . . . Why spend time, labor or money on a useless player organization?"[4]

Undissuaded by such arguments, the association proceeded to recruit members throughout the season. Gains proved especially strong among the poorer-paid squads of the National League. By the fall of 1922 one press account claimed that 60 percent of the senior circuit's players and 40 percent of American Leaguers had signed up. Signaling management's expectations of a hard fight, penurious Brooklyn owner Charles

Ebbets vowed he would not be "black-jacked into meeting unreasonable demands by my players" and insisted that if his men attempted to strike next spring, he would "fight them with every means at my command" and "clean house" of all malcontents. Ironically, the owners themselves almost triggered a preliminary strike during the 1922 World Series by unilaterally opting to award all game receipts from a suspended game two to charity rather than add them to the player shares pool. Union organizers conducted "fraternity sessions" the next night and found receptivity for a walkout before game three. A strike was not called, but players "went into the third game scowling," and rumors of the near-stoppage publicly surfaced. Giants field boss John McGraw counterattacked by citing the players' "fabulous salaries," and he called association members "nothing less than ingrates." National League president John Heydler, in turn, embarrassed by his earlier sympathetic comments toward the union ("I don't think the organization will hurt the game; the previous one did not, and I don't see how this one will"), seized the new opportunity to amend them and to insist no union of ballplayers was needed, since under Judge Landis, "every player knows he can always get a square deal."[5]

Using the stage of the World Series, Cannon publicly issued the union's demands: abolition of the unilateral ten-day notice of player releases, creation of an impartial arbitration board to hear contract disputes, prohibitions on waiver-rule manipulations involuntarily demoting players to lower leagues, and representation on the commissioner's advisory council of owners and league presidents. Responding to slurs in the press, Cannon insisted he had been sought out to lead the association and was not motivated by the selfish desire to secure more clients. Defending the association's reputation as well as his own, he maintained that it would not enlist crooked ballplayers. Some writers grudgingly conceded merit in Cannon's agenda and even endorsed abolition of the ten-day rule and creation of a pension fund for disabled and indigent veterans. But on the core issue of the need for the union, writers echoed management assertions that all legitimate concerns could be addressed paternalistically by the owners alone.[6]

In the 1922 postseason, owners successfully employed a carrot-and-stick strategy that eroded association support. Joining the chorus of sympathy on the need for pensions, American League owners in December indicated willingness to create a $50,000 fund for disabled players and their dependents and a pension for players who retired prematurely due to sickness. Funding, however, would come from annual World Series

THE PATERNALISTIC ERA

receipts, effectively reducing actives' series shares to pay for the plan. John McGraw backed a similar idea for a fund for a home for retired veterans, with its revenues to come from levies on current players' pay. But while major league officials talked pension, at the same time they threatened pay cuts, widespread player releases, and blacklisting of association activists. Unwittingly the union aided the management counteroffensive by clumsily floating the idea of a 10 percent strike-fund levy to be assessed on top of members' annual dues.[7]

By mid-February 1923, prospects dueled between a normal spring training and a player strike. The owners prepared for the contingency of full-scale labor war, but their fears proved overblown. Despite Cannon's public bravado in first claiming 80 percent support from National Leaguers and then a membership of 225 stalwarts (a figure that even if true only represented a little over a third of the major league playing force), his union was melting away. Only 136 men voted in the association's next election, and president-elect George Burns abruptly turned down the office. Cannon's personal credibility sustained further damage from bribery accusations against him in a nonbaseball case initiated by a Milwaukee civil court clerk. By the time Cannon won exoneration from the jury-fixing charge by a special prosecutor, the damage had been done. As association membership evaporated, veteran players retired, owner confidence in the underlying economy bounced back, and selected stars received pay boosts, the number of 1923 salary disputes and holdouts fell sharply. Abandoning the association effort, a defeated Cannon returned full time to his private practice of player clients. As "Black Sox" star Joe Jackson's attorney in a suit for back pay, however, he won his case before a jury only to have the verdict overturned by the presiding judge.[8]

Once the threat of a player union faded, the major league magnates cruelly abandoned their promises of pensions. It fell to twelve veterans of the Pacific Coast League (PCL), gathered at a Dinty Moore's diner in Los Angeles in October 1924 to collect for a destitute colleague's funeral, to take the first steps toward a modest pension program for indigent retirees. Their initial act of remembrance led to the Association of Professional Ball Players of America, which collected $5.00 membership fees primarily from ballplayers in the major and minor leagues and additional voluntary contributions from select owners. Within two years the group claimed nearly 2,000 members, and over the next forty years, receipts of roughly $240,000 provided stipends to some 5,000 needy former players. However, the yearly aggregate revenues of $6,000 represented a sum equal only to the season salary of one active major leaguer. In the first half-decade of the organization's existence its benefits accordingly remained limited to those needy members who had retired since the association's starting date. In 1930 eligibility was made retroactive, but even so, by 1933 only about 150 individuals drew modest one-time payments and 45 others received small monthly allotments.[9]

Given the fundamental insecurity of a baseball livelihood, professional players clearly needed a real pension fund. Absent that, they needed collective leverage capable of securing them basic wages high enough to enable personal saving for the exigencies of injury, sickness, and retirement. Given the failure of the association on the heels of earlier efforts, players were left with the hope that exposure of their plight might draw sympathetic political intervention. But given the dominant pro-business conservatism of the decade, it came as no surprise that players found little support in statehouses or on Capitol Hill. A few legislators with working-class roots or constituencies did attack the high sale prices owners pocketed for moving their employees without their consent or a share of the proceeds. A Massachusetts proposal in 1923 called for state regulation of baseball's workplace conditions and rights on the grounds that those who toiled in the "national pastime" constituted a category of public employees. The argument fell on deaf ears. In 1925 New York congressman Fiorello La Guardia introduced a bill to tax every club 90 percent of all contract sales over $5,000 unless the player sold received at least half of the sale price. But even though La Guardia lowered the proposed percentage to 75 in a forlorn effort to generate more support, the legislation still died.[10]

During baseball's early professional decades, the absence of a strong union or prominent political allies had not left players completely powerless. In fact, their most reliable source of temporary leverage had been neither of these circumstances but the outbursts of trade war between rival circuits and the bidding wars they triggered. The early 1920s, however, also proved less propitious for the emergence of a serious challenge to the major leagues. At the end of 1920 the Continental League, an eight-team northeastern circuit with clubs named after and ostensibly representing state markets (including Massachusetts, New York, and New Jersey), was chartered in Massachusetts. Its promoter, George Herman "Andy" Lawson, promised players no salary caps, and he even flirted with the idea of including the black Chicago American Giants team. But after Toronto replaced the Pennsylvania entry and the circuit's 1921 start was delayed from May 1 to May 20, the league folded without playing a single game.[11]

The lack of a successful trade war challenge during the rest of the decade, despite urban America's rapid population growth, owed mainly to the U.S. Supreme Court's 1922 Baltimore Federal League ruling. The lawsuit had grown out of the exclusion of the defunct Baltimore club's owners from a 1915 "peace agreement" with Organized Baseball and had produced a 1919 District of Columbia Supreme Court judgment for $240,000 that had been overturned by the U.S. Court of Appeals. George Wharton Pepper, attorney for the major leagues, maintained before the Supreme Court that baseball games were a "spontaneous output of human activity" that was "not in its nature commerce." Pepper admitted that ballplayers crossed state boundaries to ply their craft, but he maintained that the specific games themselves were local events and therefore not forms of interstate commerce. On May 22, 1922, the Supreme Court agreed. Writing for the majority, Justice Oliver Wendell Holmes Jr. maintained that "the players . . . travel from place to place in interstate commerce, but they are not the game"; that ballplaying did not constitute a production-related activity; and that professional baseball was therefore not a form of interstate commerce subject to antitrust regulation. With Organized Baseball's power, including the reserve clause, to maintain its monopolies over territory and playing labor now exempted from federal antitrust law, the Federal League ruling dealt a severe blow to any trade war challenges to the majors, and to the prospects for player economic gains from them.[12]

Without the leverage provided by a strong union, supportive political or judicial intervention, or trade war, professional players in the 1920s were left almost completely dependent on the fairness of the industry's own, unilaterally imposed administrative rules and processes. In particular, players could only look to the newly created office of commissioner and its occupant, fifty-three-year-old Kenesaw Mountain Landis, for any hint of disinterested authority. Both looking and sounding like a latter-day Andrew Jackson, the federal judge turned baseball chief executive cultivated an image of fearless championship of the common ballplayer. Like Old Hickory, Landis did much to translate his office's potential into precedents. But also like Jackson, his rise to power owed as much to powerful patrons as to his own struggles, and his concern for the "common man" proved frequently tempered by the need to preserve his personal authority over political rivals.[13]

Landis, the Ohio-born son of a Union army surgeon, spent his pre-baseball life bouncing from place to place and sponsor to sponsor. After moving to Indiana at age eight, he dropped out of school only to secure a court reporter's job in South Bend. After finishing high school at night, he enrolled in YMCA law courses in Cincinnati and then matriculated to Union Law School in Chicago. Two years later he accompanied his father's old commanding officer, Judge Walter Q. Gresham, to Washington, D.C., as his secretary when Grover Cleveland named the patron secretary of state. After Gresham's death two years later, Landis returned to Chicago to practice law and soon acquired a new political mentor, Frank Lowden. The young attorney served as Lowden's gubernatorial campaign manager, and when Lowden lost and then declined appointment to a federal judgeship, Landis stepped into the post.

As judge and, later, baseball commissioner, Landis was an opinionated, arbitrary, vindictive, and egotistical man. Reporter Heywood Broun wrote of him, "His career typifies the heights to which dramatic talent may carry a man in America if only he has the foresight not to go on the stage." As a jurist he often utterly lacked judicial temperament, but while often wrong, he never projected doubt. Although he never fought any duels while a sitting judge, "King Kenesaw" was known to order persons dragged before him without subpoena and held without warrants, plunge into prejudicial harangues from the bench and expunge them from the record afterward, and render shaky verdicts frequently overturned on appeal. In the latter category his 1907 fine of $29 million on Standard Oil for antitrust violations stood as the most famous example. Ford Frick, a successor of Landis as commissioner, offered an accurate picture of the judge as "intolerant of opposition, suspicious of reform and reformers, and skeptical of compromise."[14]

Landis loved to crusade against anything that could be depicted as radicalism, un-Americanism, or moral decay, and he saw himself a super-patriot upholding traditional American values and institutions. When a German submarine sank the *Lusitania* in 1915, he issued a legal summons on Kaiser Wilhelm demanding he answer for war crimes. Declaring that in war free speech "ceases," he presided over the trial and conviction of over 100 members of the Industrial Workers of the World rounded up in "Palmer raids" and sentenced them to pay $2.3 million in fines and

THE PATERNALISTIC ERA

Kenesaw Mountain Landis
(National Baseball Hall of Fame Library, Cooperstown, N.Y.)

issued jail sentences ranging from one to twenty years. When he similarly dispatched socialist leader Victor Berger to twenty years in prison, his only regret was not possessing the option of ordering the prisoner shot. As these examples show, Landis all too often equated labor union militancy with foreign radicalism and un-Americanism. In a 1921 building trades dispute, he slashed wages by up to 50 percent, a greater level than management had even sought. But it had been his role in delaying the 1915 Federal League lawsuit and thereby giving the magnates time to buy out their rivals that had drawn them to him as a commissioner candidate amidst the "Black Sox" scandal. It was similarly reassuring to baseball management to recall how during the Federal League trial he had railed at all courtroom references to ballplayers as "labor." Years later, when maverick owner Bill Veeck assailed baseball's reserve clause as both "morally and legally indefensible," Landis retorted, "Somebody once said a little knowledge is a dangerous thing, and your letter proves him to be a wizard." [15]

Landis's views on baseball's "political economy," like his temperament and his assertions of personal power, were reminiscent of Andrew Jackson. He clung to a nostalgic ideal of baseball as a decentralized association of separately owned businesses resembling Old Hickory's notions of the antebellum economic democracy and his hostility toward such aggregations as the Bank of the United States. Rather than permit the vertical integration of clubs into "Hydra-like" chains challenging power, Landis fought to prevent such "farm systems" and to preserve independent teams in independent leagues, linked instead only by draft processes facilitating players' reasonably paced and low-cost promotion. Baseball's proper system of labor relations — though Landis would have winced at the very phrase — was rooted in the reserve clause and its binding relationship between the individual club and player, with the commissioner serving as final adjudicator of disputes between them. He accordingly reserved for himself the supreme power to define and enforce Organized Baseball's "constitutional" relationships, and it was fitting that he insisted on having a single word emblazoned on his Chicago office door—BASEBALL. From the standpoint of a ballplayer suitor, the commissioner's assertions of prerogatives held the possibility of greater economic disinterest than those of other management authorities. But they did not reflect an underlying philosophical sympathy toward players' claims of workplace rights, especially when such assertions challenged Landis's ideal of the sport or his power in it.

Given the scandalous circumstances that had led to Landis's hiring, owners needed to show that they had given him effective authority to weed out player corruption. As a result, nowhere did he initially claim more power than in the punishment of players for violations of contract. Under the terms of his appointment and the majors-minors National Agreement of 1921, Landis became final arbiter of any appeals of monetary disputes exceeding $300 between owners or between players and owners, as well as any disputes involving a free-agency, or "liberty," issue for players. Under his newly bestowed "best interests of baseball" authority, he could suspend, fine, or banish for life any player for conduct judged detrimental to the game. Although Landis ostensibly also could discipline miscreant owners without right of appeal, the maximum possible sentence for management violations was a public reprimand and a $5,000 fine.[16]

Landis's crackdowns on player conduct, most prominent in the early years of his commissionership, concentrated on four areas of contract violations: (1) game-fixing and similar on-field corruption, (2) off-field morals misconduct, (3) unsanctioned barnstorming or other money-making activities, and (4) contract jumping. In all these areas the new commissioner's interventions enhanced rather than undermined management's monopsony power over the player work force. Crackdowns against player gambling and game-fixing not only helped cleanse the sport's tainted image from the "Black Sox" scandal; they undermined an alternative, illegitimate source of players' income and made them even more dependent on owners for economic survival. Enforcement of anti-barnstorming rules and antijumping bans served the same purpose and therefore indirectly made performers less likely to risk jeopardizing their regular income through suspension or blacklist triggered by union activism. Tighter regulation of players' moral behavior, in turn, promised to boost employees' on-field productivity and images as matinee idols in the New Era's increased marketing of stars.[17]

While the new commissioner awaited the verdict of the courts before rendering his own decision on the "Black Sox," he meted out harsh punishment to another player accused of consorting with gamblers. Landis blacklisted Eugene Paulette in March 1921 for past associations with St. Louis gamblers. The main event, however, followed five months later. After a bizarre sequence of events that included the disappearance of sworn confessions from the Chicago district attorney's office, the switching of three prosecutors to the defense team, and the dropping and then re-indictment of seven White Sox players and ten gamblers for the 1919 World Series fix, on August 2, 1921, all seven "Black Sox" were acquitted in court. Nonetheless, the next day Landis banished all seven permanently from Organized Baseball and added an eighth player not previously re-indicted. In November Landis also put Joe Gedeon of the St. Louis Browns on the ineligible list for having sat in on a meeting with the gamblers, even though he had not participated in the actual fix. Over the next quarter-century the commissioner never relented on his lifetime sentences. Demonstrating the selective nature of his justice, several other players with "guilty knowledge" of the plot received no punishment at all, nor did the longtime player/fixer Hal Chase. Landis also refused to discipline White Sox owner Charles Comiskey, likely guilty at least of jury-tampering and obstruction of justice by hiding the stolen player confessions.[18]

Given the proximity of the New York Giants to the Gotham gambling interests that had corrupted the 1919 series, it should have come as no surprise that they generated a new game-fixing controversy for the commissioner. Barely a year after the "Black Sox" sanctions, Landis banished Giants pitcher Phil Douglas, an alcoholic who had been fined for going AWOL, for a threat of baseball "treachery." Angry at being docked nearly $325, Douglas foolishly had attempted revenge by writing St. Louis outfielder Leslie Mann of his willingness to hurt New York's pennant chances by disappearing again if the Giants' rivals would "make it good" for him. Mann turned over the note to club officials, who relayed it to Landis, and the latter quickly blacklisted the hurler. As with the "Black Sox," when a sportswriter a decade later petitioned Landis to lift the banishment on the grounds of new evidence, he refused—although in a humanitarian concession he sent a personal check to the destitute Douglas.[19]

The commissioner's crusade to restore the game's integrity through his game-fixing crackdown remained selective and one-sided. Given his self-interest in limiting similar confrontations with those who had hired him, along with the more limited powers he possessed to punish them, Landis's reticence was understandable, if unfair. He refused to demand the divestiture by Detroit's Frank Navin of his financial interest in racing stables, and although he did direct Giants owner Charles Stoneham and manager McGraw to relinquish holdings in the Oriental Park racetrack and casino near Havana, Cuba, gambling kingpin and 1919 fix-orchestrator Arnold Rothstein continued to frequent Stoneham's private box at the Polo Grounds. The Giants' magnate retained his baseball position even after he was indicted by separate grand juries for perjury and mail fraud connected to the collapse of two Wall Street securities firms.[20]

In addition to the continued one-sided nature of his anticorruption campaign, another pattern quickly emerged in Landis's handling of such issues. After the initial flurry of action on scandals predating his commissionership, he showed a disturbing eagerness to sweep under the rug new charges or continuing evidence of an unredeemed industry. To admit otherwise brought his own integrity or competence into question and clouded the sport's improving image and profit picture. For both Landis and the magnates, it was a highly useful fiction to claim that the industry's evils had predated the creation of the commissioner's office and that with it corruption had now been effectively banished from the game. For similar reasons it made sense not to reopen past cases, whether in response to new appeals, new evidence, or flaws in Landis's original verdicts. By 1924, with fifty-three players already on the permanent ineligibility list, the emphasis shifted from additional reactive banishments to the preemption of new cases through covert management investigations and interventions. Landis maintained his own force of private detectives to supplement each major league club's own spies. Players who had committed preliminary or minor violations now found themselves summoned before the commissioner and warned to desist, or risk more severe punishment.[21]

Despite Landis's efforts to preempt them, new scandals continued to percolate. When Philadelphia's Heinie Sand reported that he had been offered $500 by Giants outfielder Jimmy O'Connell to "take it easy" for the sake of the latter's pennant chances, the player admitted the bribe and further implicated coach Cozy Dolan and teammates Frank Frisch, Ross Youngs, and George Kelly. When questioned by Landis, Dolan exhibited an extremely faulty memory, and the commissioner blacklisted him with O'Connell. But despite evidence of the other players' prior knowledge of the bribe, they received no punishment. Pittsburgh owner Barney Dreyfuss, whose club had finished third behind the Giants, pointed out that neither O'Connell nor Dolan by themselves could have put up the $500 — a fact suggesting a team pool or subsidization by Giants higher-ups. Adding another hint of cover-up to the whole affair, when Dolan sued Landis for defamation of character, Arnold Rothstein's lawyer represented the coach, and John McGraw paid the retainer. A furious Landis, justified in feeling that he had "gone easy" on the Giants, "conveyed his displeasure" and got the Dolan suit abruptly quashed. The how and why only surfaced later. According to subsequent revelations by baseball publisher and Landis confidant Taylor Spink, Dolan's sudden willingness to drop his suit was part of a deal in which the commissioner in turn helped scuttle a New York district attorney's criminal investigation. If the Giants had not agreed to drop their action against the commissioner, Landis had been prepared to let the full scandal break wide open and bring down Giants management en masse.[22]

Landis's handling of the O'Connell-Dolan affair demonstrated his newfound distaste for exposing player game-tampering on his watch. An even clearer indication of his desire to declare a statute of limitations on such allegations—and to insulate the game from further public taint—came in late 1926. In November the Detroit Tigers released Ty Cobb as player-manager, and a month later Tris Speaker similarly "resigned" from Cleveland. Shortly before Christmas, press reports quoted Landis as saying the two baseball giants had been "permitted" to resign in the face of long-standing game-fixing allegations dating back to the 1919 AL pennant race. Publication of the charge, however, unleashed other game-fixing claims from 1917 and 1919 against Cobb by "Black Sox" exiles Swede Risberg and Chick Gandil. The revelations in turn unraveled the commissioner's undercover resignation deal with Cobb and Speaker, who now backed out and retained attorneys. On January 5, 1927, Landis invited forty White Sox and Tiger players to hearings in the presence of fifty reporters, and he concluded that the pot of money the Chicagoans had collected for their Detroit adversaries had been a retroactive "reward" for beating Boston rather than a bribe soliciting the Tigers to lay down.[23]

Revealing his true feelings toward the entire situation, Landis complained, "Won't these God-damn things that happened before I came into baseball ever stop coming up?" A week later he issued a blanket exoneration on the Chicago charges and called for a five-year "statute of limitations" on past gambling transgressions—a step National League president Heydler admitted owed primarily to the reality that baseball could not afford to blacklist at least thirty more players. In early February Landis infuriated American League president Ban Johnson by issuing a similarly forgiving verdict on the original Cobb-Speaker allegations, rather than endure an ugly public confrontation with the two stars. Both men's old clubs reinstated and then released them, making them free agents. With the National League maintaining its ban on their entry, Cobb signed with the Philadelphia Athletics and Speaker joined the Washington Senators for 1927.[24]

The magnates finally reached the limits of their patience with both the continuing problem of game-fixing and the arbitrariness and confusion of Landis's responses. League presidents and a steering committee of three owners from each circuit drafted formal guidelines and penalties. At the 1927 winter meetings, Landis tried to preempt the effort by proposing a one-year ban as standard punishment for offering or accepting illicit gifts. But the committee upped the ante by urging a three-year suspension to anyone found guilty of giving or accepting a bribe or "going easy" on an opponent. Any attempt to improperly influence an umpire, in turn, would result in permanent blacklisting of both the offerer and the taker of a bribe. Players also would draw permanent banishment for betting on games with a direct connection, and a one-year suspension would follow bets on other contests. On December 15, 1927, the owners approved the new guidelines.[25]

The codification of formal rules and punishments on baseball game-fixing, bribery, and betting represented the forced withdrawal of Landis from his initial celebrated role as baseball's public policeman. Club officials and owners now pondered additional measures to inhibit inter-club game-fixing conspiracies and the broader "problem" of cross-club player fraternization. Giants coach Hughie Jennings proposed eliminating player visitation rights to opposing clubhouses, returning to the tradition of dressing at the hotels for games, and transporting teams to the parks only at game time to avoid precontest mingling. Clubs also continued to shadow players in an effort to secure early warning of any illicit associations. But neither the formal rules nor the covert surveillance eliminated the problem. Stars such as Rogers Hornsby and Babe Ruth continued to frequent racetracks and consort with questionable characters. When Yankee manager Miller Huggins tried to curb the gambling habit by limiting clubhouse poker bets to 25 cents a hand, the Bambino simply switched to bridge at 50 cents a point and dropped $350 in minutes. If the frequency or visibility of players' associations with gamblers diminished as the 1920s wore on, it probably owed more to the belated rise in salaries and other legitimate opportunities than to management's efforts at policing.[26]

Besides the campaigns against game-fixing in the New Era's early years, Landis and fellow officials also sought to regulate other forms of player conduct that threatened the productivity of the player or his economic dependence on his club. One form that this concern took was the increasing resort to off-season or twelve-month contracts that prohibited winter ball. In the uniform contract, management required players to maintain good physical condition, exhibit "sufficient" on-field skill, and "conform to high standards" of personal conduct on and off the diamond or risk fine and suspension for violating employment terms. Clubs also required players to gain written consent for any public appearances, newspaper or magazine article deals, commercial sponsorships, radio appearances, or participation in any other sporting activities.

These various conduct prohibitions proved far easier to enforce upon the vast majority of journeyman players than upon the game's stars. The latter not only enjoyed far more outside offers but greater marketplace leverage stemming from their fan appeal. No star of the New Era demonstrated more dramatically the industry's dilemma in establishing behavior boundaries than Babe Ruth. On one hand, Ruth and the Yankees both profited from his playing exploits and his off-field visibility. With the help of press agent Christy Walsh, Ruth's product endorsements, hospital visits, and movie appearances were orchestrated for maximum public relations benefit. But the Bambino's "unauthorized activities," including visits to speakeasies and whorehouses, put his image and potentially his life at risk. Yet baseball officialdom could not afford to punish him so severely as to lose his value as the sport's most famous attraction. It was a measure of the Yankees' estimation of his worth, and their need to protect themselves from its loss through his own recklessness, that they took out a $300,000 insurance policy on him. Throughout the 1920s, Ruth's behavior provided a barometer of how much malfeasance the magnates had to tolerate at a given time.[27]

Once he achieved stardom, Ruth wasted no time testing baseball's disciplinary boundaries. After the 1920 season, he earned $40,000 playing winter ball in Cuba only to blow it on racetrack gambling. Following the 1921 World Series, despite Landis's specific orders against postseason barnstorming by series participants, the slugger and his teammate Bob Meusel garnered $30,000 and $10,000, respectively, on $1,500 and $500 an exhibition tilt. Ruth's defiance of the commissioner sparked player rumblings of solidarity and calls for a player movement that led to Cannon's short-lived players' association. Ruth, in short, unintentionally managed to become a symbol of player freedom and a momentary rallying point for union activity, and it was both those facts, along with the blatant nature of his defiance, that led to an unusually sharp retaliation. When Ruth moved on to a vaudeville tour at $300 a week, Landis suspended both Yankees for the first six weeks of the 1922 season, fined them their series shares, and ordered their 1922 regular-season pay docked proportionally to the length of their suspensions. To gain his reactivation Ruth eventually submitted to the humiliation of an apology that included a denial of any intent of "becoming an outlaw or lending any aid to an out-

THE PATERNALISTIC ERA

law movement." Less publicized was the fact that the commissioner also was forced to step back as a price for securing Ruth's return by shrinking the length of future bans on postseason barnstorming to only the remainder of the calendar year of each World Series. By August 1922 Ruth had earned two more fines and shorter suspensions of four and five days for run-ins with abusive fans and an umpire, but Landis eased his barnstorming regulations even more by permitting tours of three players per exhibition squad after October 31 with club permission.[28]

Organized Baseball's leaders frowned on the Bambino's accumulation of outside income as a dangerous example of player financial independence tantamount to off-season contract jumping. But having helped create him as the brightest star of their new, lusty-hitting postwar game, they could hardly "throw out the Babe with the bathwater." By 1924 Ruth's contract with the Yankees already called for $156,000 over its remaining three years, which he supplemented with more than $100,000 earned through barnstorming and vaudeville appearances. A subpar 1925 season, punctuated by another showdown with manager Miller Huggins, a four-day suspension, and a $5,000 fine led to another forced apology and fresh rumors that Ruth's yearly salary would be cut to $30,000 in his next contract. But when Ruth rebounded with sixty home runs in 1927, his pay followed suit to $70,000 and then $80,000 by 1930, and his external income soared again. Following Huggins's death, the Yankees in 1929 even refunded the 1925 disciplinary fine in yet another display of Ruthian clout in action.[29]

As illustrated by baseball officials' balancing act toward Ruth, the baseball industry had become a big entertainment business in which every major personnel decision required dispassionate, hardheaded professional consideration and an appreciation of the requirements of the star system. One enduring structural outgrowth of this necessity was the rise of the general manager—the man who, whatever his formal title within the club's organizational chart, exercised the duties of a personnel director. Increasingly he not only decided roster cuts, trades, sales, and salary offers but also set and enforced the club's disciplinary sanctions. While the general manager's duties increased and his importance grew, those of the field manager, save for game strategy, diminished. "Old-school" managers complained that their postwar charges were more undisciplined, more pampered, and less respectful. Ty Cobb lamented that the new breed of ballplayer not only played solely "for the money that's in it — not for the love of it," but because it was "good business for them." According to Cobb, they also avoided injury by "not taking too many chances" on the field.[30]

The old-fashioned dictatorial manager, who could arbitrarily suspend or fine players on the spot for real or imagined transgressions and know his edicts would stick, became scarcer. The salary relationship between the field manager and his star players also represented a clear indication of, and acted to drive down further, the former's diminishing status. Early in the decade the sport's most famous skipper, John McGraw, earned a $65,000 salary that exceeded the wages of even his highest-paid players. As stars' pay began to rise significantly by the mid-1920s, payroll-conscious clubs anxious not to pay high salaries to both managers and players then improvised in the short term by choosing to combine the roles. By 1926 seven of sixteen big league field bosses performed as both players and managers, including Cobb, Speaker, and Hornsby. But within only a year's time, however, five of the seven were replaced by full-time managers. By the end of the decade, skippers consistently made less money than the star players of the teams they nominally ran. As the manager's autocracy waned, more clubs also hired an additional nonplaying coach to improve players' performance and provide a less threatening field-level monitor of their behavior.[31]

Umpires, who traditionally had suffered from lack of respect, now perceived a further erosion of their status as well. With only two umpires per game the norm in the 1920s, save for critical games or World Series tilts, the overworked "men in blue" found their salary relationship to those they supervised deteriorating. Major league arbiters generally earned about the same as an average player, while the highest-paid among them earned about $10,000. As the visibility and gate revenues of the fall classic grew, umpires demanded a raise in their series pay from the fixed $2,000 to an escalating stipend equal to the average player share. They also lamented the escalation of on-field violence and player threats as their pay in relation to that of the latter had fallen. Umpire discontent even led to rumbles of unionization. In November 1922 an International League fracas between an arbiter and two players resulted in the umpire's permanent release but the reinstatement of the players after a written apology. Outraged umpires began holding informal gatherings, and by the following May a dozen of them from major and minor leagues in the New York area had met to consider the formation of a protective association. Aware of their own vulnerability to management retaliation, the participants discussed retaining a retired veteran arbiter to head their organization. While group discussions "here and there" and formation of local "associations for mutual improvement" continued, Landis and league owners engaged in their own tug-of-war over control of the umpires. It was another sign of the growing owner defiance of the commissioner by mid-decade that the American League and the National League refused to relinquish their independent control of arbiters. After his reelection to another term in 1927, Landis did try to give the umpires some additional backing by announcing a ninety-day minimum penalty to anyone who struck one of them. The minors' National Association of Professional Baseball Leagues followed suit.[32]

If their on-field behavior actually had become more rowdy and less respectful, players in the New Era were more compliant than their predecessors in the area of contract and reserve jumping to other clubs. In the secure, monopolistic environment the major leagues essentially enjoyed in the 1920s, there were few opportunities for successful player defiance. The established majors had crushed their most recent trade war challenger, and the Supreme Court's 1922 antitrust exemption decision went far to insure that new contenders for equal status would be few and far between. The owners designated Landis as enforcer of the cartel's internal rules against contract jumping and player raiding, authorizing him to utilize the blacklist against anyone who sought refuge in an "outlaw" circuit. This primarily entailed, however, not new cases but cleaning up the backlog of 300 Federal League–era contract jumpers. Owners preferred that Landis exercise relative leniency toward those players now petitioning for reinstatement into Organized Baseball—especially those with productive years likely remaining—and crack down but selectively on the worst miscreants to deter what was a shrinking likelihood of more jumping.

It was cold comfort to those few players made early examples by the commissioner that the need for such deterrence faded as the decade wore on. In the case of Benny Kauff, the combination of his past leap to the Federal League and charges of off-field malfeasance made him a convenient example for official retribution. Hired back by the Giants after the trade war, Kauff left to enter the service in World War I. When he returned to play in 1920, authorities arrested him on charges of auto theft and receipt of stolen property. Kauff then sought the right to play while out on bail; Landis not only refused but maintained the ban even after the player was acquitted. More typical of the arbitrary selection of players subjected to harsh punishment, however, was Ray Fisher. Fisher, a thirty-three-year-old veteran whose salary for 1921 had already been cut by $1,000, refused to report to the Cincinnati Reds. He traveled to Ann Arbor to interview for a coaching position at the University of Michigan instead—with, he claimed, his manager's permission. When he was offered the job, Fisher returned to the Reds to secure his release from his major league reserve contract. Team management refused and offered instead to reduce the size of his pay cut in order to keep him. However, they still denied his demand for a two-year deal. Fisher then accepted the Michigan offer, but out of fear of being blacklisted for contract jumping he went straight to the commissioner to explain his circumstances. Landis at first remained noncommittal but then ominously put off a second request from Fisher for clarification of his status. When the ruling did come down, Landis concluded that since Cincinnati had never actually granted Fisher permission to talk to Michigan, the player had been guilty of abrogating his obligations to the Reds. Worst of all, he had also carried on covert negotiations with an "outlaw" Franklin club in Pennsylvania full of other contract jumpers. Landis then blacklisted Fisher for life.[33]

In the absence of trade war and unionization, one of the most important consequences of management's monopsony power over the playing force of the 1920s was the widening of a two-tier (or three-tier, if Ruth was considered his own category) wage system in the major leagues. While a few stars parlayed their fame and marketplace value into high salaries from mid-decade on, most players at both the major and minor league levels shared a very different reality (see Appendix, Fig. 2). Although player wages rose as owners' recession-based fears faded, they did not come close to equaling the rate of increase in industry profits. Payroll as a percentage of the clubs' operating expenses continued its decline. Players rarely received the sympathy of the average fan, since they stood among the top 5 percent of American wage earners. Nonetheless, hitters in particular rankled at the disparity between their soaring statistics and their lagging pay increases. As a Detroit beat writer noted, "Ball players have long regarded batting averages as their gauge for salaries." Owners kept a tight rein on pay through 1923, then loosened their constraints for two years, only to adopt minor drags on offense in 1926 to moderate the wage pressures. Rumors of a less lively ball surfaced throughout Organized Baseball even before the end of the 1925 campaign, and in 1926 the magnates fixed minimum fence distances at 250 feet and approved pitchers' use of resin to improve their grip.[34]

At the top of the major league pay pyramid stood Babe Ruth. The Bambino's salary, $20,000 at the start of the 1920s, climbed fourfold by the beginning of the next decade. At the end of the 1920s he earned about seventy-five times the $1,400 annual pay of the average American worker. Even Ruth, however, could claim to be underpaid. His presence on the Bronx Bombers generated for his team at least an additional $200,000 a year in direct revenue. In contrast his own 1930 after-tax pay, estimated at approximately $68,500, represented barely a third that sum. Except for Ty Cobb, however, who garnered $65,000 as a player/manager in his farewell season of 1927, the closest-paid performers of the late 1920s were fortunate to earn half as much as the Sultan of Swat. On the "Murderers Row" itself, the second-highest-paid Yankee received but $15,000, while the team mean—inflated by Ruth's pay—stood at $10,000; the median income was only $7,000.[35]

Even the stars of the 1920s versions of "small-market" clubs but belatedly received significant pay increases. Pitcher Walter Johnson still earned $12,000 as late as the 1924 season, although his salary jumped to $20,000 the next year. In 1921 only ten to twelve players made as much as $7,500 a year. Ten years later, six players claimed pay of $25,000 or more. At the start of the period, major league payrolls ranged from $75,000 to $150,000, and a decade later, $100,000 to $375,000. The major league mean salary, about $4,500 in 1920, stagnated in the mid-$5,000 area for the next three years, then climbed by roughly $500 yearly increments with pauses in 1927 and 1929. By 1930 it stood at $8,000. But because of the distorted impression left by stars' pay, most fans did not recognize that the average major leaguer, albeit a rich man by comparison with his minor league counterpart, made only a little over five times the income of the average American laborer. More to the point, the ballplayer's income each year fell further behind his employer's productivity gains and profits. In 1924 the majors took in $10 million at the turnstiles, made an estimated $4.6 million in profits, and paid out only $3 million in salaries. By 1929 payrolls had climbed modestly to $3.75 million, but they still constituted only about 35 percent of club expenditures, one of the lowest ratios of labor cost to overall expenses in American business in spite of baseball's "labor-intensive" nature. By contrast, when the National League had been in its infancy in 1878, payroll costs had been over two-thirds of total club expenditures.[36]

Given player demands for pay increases commensurate with their newly soaring performances, the New Era's early years were marked by a proliferation of holdouts. Adding to players' outrage at low pay was their frequent sale without consent for values many times greater than their salary demands. Following the initial surge in offense of 1920, the next off-season Landis's secretary Leslie O'Connor found it necessary to issue a special edict warning players that clubs would fine them and deduct the money from their current or future salaries if they refused to report for spring training exhibition games or practices. If they still failed to show up within ten days, they would be placed on the ineligible list and would have to apply to Landis for reinstatement. Undeterred, the ranks of 1921 holdouts included the White Sox' Dickie Kerr, Cincinnati's Edd Roush and Heinie Groh, Brooklyn's Zach Wheat and Burleigh Grimes, the Cardinals' Milton Stock, and the Red Sox' John "Stuffy" McInnis. Despite his club's pointed reminders of past $100-a-month wages in the Western Association, Roush initially held firm to his $20,000 demand. But after drawing a two-day suspension for violating the ten-day edict, he returned to the Reds for $15,000. Groh held out longer only to sign for $10,000 upon getting the club's promise to trade him. Even after his return, though, he continued to press for $3,000 in deducted back pay. Wheat, who demanded a $7,000 raise to $15,500, caved in for just $800 more, then brushed off his earlier demands as a "joke." McInnis, held under a reserve contract at $5,000 but denied an additional bonus for the second year, returned after being sued by owner Harry Frazee for nonperformance of services.[37]

Despite the general failure of the 1921 holdouts, salary squabbles carried over into 1922, and many involved the same personalities. Roush now demanded a $3,000 raise to $18,000 and a three-year pact. Grimes, who had held out the previous year for $12,500 only to accept $9,000, again withdrew his threat for an additional $1,000. Even Babe Ruth got into the act, demanding that Yankee owner Jacob Ruppert "double" his salary to $75,000. When reporters questioned the Bambino's arithmetic, he maintained that his figure factored in a $500-per-homer secret bonus he claimed had been paid him in 1921. According to baseball scribe Francis Richter, some forty major league stars held out that spring, with the big-market Yankees and Giants contributing thirteen to the total. Only one AL team, Cleveland, had no holdouts, while the National League had three clubs—Boston, Chicago, and Philadelphia—in similar positions. The next year, 1923, outfielder Jack Bentley unsuccessfully demanded a $5,000 share of his $70,000 sale price from Baltimore of the International League to the Giants, and Zach Wheat made his regular appearance in the ranks of salary holdouts. Spitballer Burleigh Grimes followed suit in 1924. Although the frequency of holdouts dropped by mid-decade with steadier pay raises, some keen observers still maintained that management abuses and pay disparities demanded a less confrontational, less one-sided arbitration process. Contributor Franklin W. Wilson even argued in the *Sporting News* that players deserved salaries commensurate with the gate moneys they generated. He insisted that Ruth merited every penny of his hefty pay and lamented that too many stars received inadequate incomes because they performed for poorer clubs. As a solution he called for the creation of a baseball "court of appeals" to hear salary and promotion disputes from all levels of Organized Baseball. Evidence of the lingering relevance of the issue could be found in *Baseball Magazine* in January 1926, which also devoted a feature article to salary arbitration mechanisms. But Commissioner Landis and management figures at all levels vigilantly opposed such suggestions as unnecessary challenges to their prerogatives.[38]

Rather than considering outside arbitration mechanisms, major league owners selectively tried to placate stars through special awards and incentive bonuses. Such forms of discriminative additional pay were more easily manipulated or negated through managers' actions, and therefore full payout was less certain than if stars' base salaries were simply raised. As for industrywide prizes, the American League revived the Chalmers trophy for the most valuable player (MVP) in 1922, and the senior circuit followed suit two years later. Besides Ruth's publicized homer bonus, Rogers Hornsby's 1922 three-year pact included extra pay based on his team's record, and Burleigh Grimes garnered the promise of an extra $1,000 based on the number of his pitching victories. Owners lacking deep pockets complained that while such largesse reduced the rich clubs' holdout problems, it drove up pay pressures on the rest. Under lobbying from the small-market majority, the National League in 1924 opted to ban most incentive clauses but still allowed "good behavior" bonuses. In contrast the American League, driven by its wealthier clubs, continued to utilize wider incentives to placate its stars. On the 1927 Yankee squad, for example, Waite Hoyt's contract included a $1,000 bonus for twenty wins; Tony Lazzeri's, the promise of travel by Pullman car to and from the West Coast for himself and his wife at the start and finish of the season; Wilcy Moore's, a $500 payment if he stuck with the team all year; Herb Pennock's, an extra $1,000 for a twenty-five-win campaign; and Walter Ruether's, $1,000 for fifteen victories.[39]

For the upper-division squads in both circuits, World Series shares constituted another extremely valuable source of supplementary income. The pool of available moneys grew impressively in the 1920s as gate receipts for the fall classic swelled. Helping to spread the wealth was the fact that first- through fourth-place finishers in each league shared in diminishing degrees in the bounty. For World Series participants, per-player winner and loser shares stood at $5,322.72 and $3,734.60, respectively, by 1925. But mitigating the salutary effect of these salary supplements, which amounted to as much as a typical player's entire season pay, was the continuing disparity in performance between the big- and small-market clubs in each league. Very rarely did many of the teams ever finish high enough for their players to earn an end-of-season bonus. In contrast, the Yankees, a big-market club able to pay its players top dollar regardless, failed only once between 1921 and 1946 to achieve a first-division finish, and they played in the World Series twenty-one times. Mike Gazella, a fringe player on the Bronx Bombers' 1926 squad, demonstrated the importance of postseason shares to nonstars when he formally protested his teammates voting him only a one-fourth share for having appeared in sixty-six games. Even after general manager Ed Barrow persuaded the club to up the share to one-half, Gazella pressed his full claim all the way to the commissioner, and he got it.[40]

In the New Era's star system, the emerging compensation pattern boosted star players' pay increases from mid-decade, but disparities widened between them and other performers, between the payrolls of rich and poor clubs, and between industry profits and the share of income devoted to payroll. Nevertheless, by comparison minor leaguers faced a far bleaker salary picture, save a few at the top draft-exempt levels. Even there, the circumstances that in the short run contributed to a major league style, two-tier pay pattern evaporated by the decade's end. Minor leaguers' statistical performances soared as highly as those of their major league counterparts, but their wages lagged far behind. Players in the high minors, given the draft exemption maintained by AA leagues, also found that while they made considerably more than teammates below them, their relative costliness to prospective big league

THE PATERNALISTIC ERA

buyers hindered their advance to the latter higher level of compensation. The hoarding of talent in the high minors, in turn, created logjams for the advance of players farther down the industry ladder, unless a prospect's talent shone so brightly at a tender age that an AL or NL club reached down several levels to draft him.

Then as now, minor leaguers made up most of the industry's playing talent, and major leaguers represented just the tip of the player pyramid. In 1921, despite the lingering economic woes from postwar reconversion and the loss of playing talent to industrial circuits and the military, 27 minor leagues with 151 clubs and about 2,800 players started the year. By comparison, the majors' 16 teams contributed only 400 playing jobs. Although the AA circuits (the American Association, the International League, and the PCL) did not publish team payroll limits and thereby make their salary averages known, season pay at levels D to A ranged from $790 to slightly over $1,400. The low-end D circuits employed nearly one-third of Organized Baseball's player force, despite their clubs' smaller rosters. At this bottom level, clubs seeking players advertised local tryouts in the newspapers and brought in twenty to forty hopefuls at a time at a typical net cost of $1,500. The blue-collar wage level of the local labor market, in turn, effectively set the industry's wage floor. When recession and small markets squeezed minor league revenues in the early 1920s, owners responded by lowering team payroll limits and cutting the size of rosters. The stratagem offered the advantage of not undermining a club's competitive salary position with particular players vis-à-vis outside employers, since an individual's pay could more easily be maintained within shrunken rosters. Referring to the National Association, the governing body of the minor leagues, in November 1921 the *Sporting News* observed, "Last year at Kansas City they said, 'We must raise salaries to get players, otherwise they will stick to their jobs in mills and factories.' Now in Buffalo, 'We must cut salaries or collapse.'" Minor league spokesmen justified their economies in the early 1920s by insisting that even with cuts, pay remained "better than major league salaries of 1914 in the minors now."[41]

In the early years of the decade, both roster cuts and replacement of veterans with low-priced youngsters became commonplace. Classes B (in 1922) and D (in 1923) each reduced their active rosters by one player per team for a year. Still, individual salaries rose and fell in tandem with the roster sizes and the number of minor league leagues and clubs; they gained some traction in mid-decade only to slip back at a return to hard times in the late 1920s. In Class A, individual salary averages rose to $1,720 in 1923, fell sharply in 1924, rebounded in 1925, continued the modest climb to $1,815 in 1927, and then fell off. Class B wages fluctuated in the early 1920s, jumped to a two-year plateau of $1,145 in 1924–25, peaked in 1929 at $1,440, then tumbled. Class C salaries progressed more steadily, albeit modestly, from 1921 to 1929, from $900 to $1,105, only to slump also. In the D leagues, pay seesawed, with peaks of $835 in 1925 and $860 in 1928.[42]

Over the longer term, however, the search for minor league labor economies and better bottom lines translated into a drive to locate in low-cost environments. More and more clubs and circuits, particularly those at the lower levels with the least margin for error, gravitated to the low-wage, nonunion towns of the Old Confederacy. Although none of the larger AA markets lay below the Mason-Dixon line as of 1925, thirteen of the National Association's twenty-five total circuits operated entirely or in part in the southern states. By the same token, the low-cost but small-market southern leagues were still among the most susceptible to financial collapse at the first sign of recession, despite their low labor outlays. By 1930, as the Great Depression began to exact a greater economic toll, the number of D circuits fell to six, with four in the South. Of twenty-two leagues hanging on at the start of that campaign, nine were southern-based.[43]

Despite its advantages, Organized Baseball in the New Era fell short of a management utopia. Compared with the relative chaos of the preceding fifty years, the 1920s did present a more pleasing visage, and years later, when labor strife and soaring salaries set in, owners would look back with nostalgia at the post–World War I era. But even with the decade's generally bright picture of labor docility and industry growth, magnates spent considerable time griping about the health of their businesses. Much of their discontent centered on the limited availability and high cost of acquiring talent from the minors under the 1921 National Agreement. Under that pact a player draft had been reinstated, but leagues could exempt their clubs' talent if they reciprocally surrendered their rights to draft players from lower circuits. Draft prices ranged from $1,000 for Class D ballplayers to $5,000 for AA performers. Only one player per year could be plucked from any particular A or AA club, but no restrictions existed on the number of B- through D-level draftees. Each major league club had the right to "option out" up to 8 players to minor league teams

THE PATERNALISTIC ERA

for up to two years, and they could be recalled within the option period without becoming subject to redrafting. Clubs in lesser circuits secured similar control over smaller numbers of men, with AA and A teams able to farm out 6 players each; B clubs, 5; and C squads, 3. Major league clubs gained the right to raise their total reserve lists from 35 to 40 players. The reserve clause, which enabled clubs to renew perpetually their claims on unsigned players, became a formal part of the standard contract. If a club wished to waive its rights to a player, the new agreement set the claiming price at $7,500.[44]

Almost immediately the majors resented the draft-exemption provisions of the agreement. Five minor league circuits, including the three at the AA level, chose exemption. Since the AA leagues were the most risk-free source of new talent for the majors, draft exemption meant that rather than routinely drafting the best minor league talent at low fixed prices, big league owners now had to negotiate far more costly sales prices from hard-bargaining AA owners. Although draft exemption for the high minors meant that they, too, had to negotiate the purchase of player acquisitions from below, they could recoup their higher procurement expenses from the prices they charged the majors. When criticized for their draft-exemption decisions, the AA circuits pointed out that under the 1921 draft rules they were provided only $5,000 a player in compensatory income, and therefore they had no choice but to operate outside the system.

In the early 1920s draft exemption by the high minors, combined with the majors' risk in plucking talent from still lower levels, caused the number of players actually drafted by the big leagues to plummet. In 1921 the American League claimed but 6 men and the National League, 7, at a total cost of $26,500. The next year the numbers were 21 and $36,500. In 1923, 16 major league draftees cost $49,000, and in 1924, the figures were 24 and $76,500. At the same time the cost of securing AA talent through negotiated purchases skyrocketed. In 1921 alone, the majors spent over $450,000 on minor league player sales, with 42 of the 141 men coming from the draft-exempt leagues. The final price tag also included contingency pledges of $250,000 more if the purchasees remained on major league rosters the next spring. To no surprise, many major league owners called for the end of draft exemption or at least a $25,000 ceiling on sale prices. Commissioner Landis, claiming to be motivated by concern for the upward mobility of the minor league ballplayer, also weighed in on the side of the majors.[45]

Draft exemption also cost big league clubs in indirect ways. Besides the higher cost of obtaining rookies, the bottlenecks created by exemption meant that clubs held on to veteran players longer than they otherwise might have, which in turn pushed up team payrolls. In addition, the shortage of hungry young job-seekers undercut club officials' ability to threaten veterans with job loss to induce greater on-field productivity, deter union talk, or coerce higher moral conduct. Not surprisingly clubs scrambled to find legal and illegal ways to bypass the high minors and secure more talent at lower cost. Major league organizations paid college and semipro players under the table while not listing them on reserve lists. As late as 1929 the Yankees' Jacob Ruppert admitted to the practice but insisted of his rivals, "They all do it. They are lying about it." Clubs tampered with one another's talent during the season in an effort to line up men for the next year. They manipulated the waiver rules, creating more room on the reserve list by "loaning" players to other clubs via "cover-up sales" and having the recipient teams "release" them back the following spring. They covertly negotiated "working agreements" with compliant minor league clubs to hide extra players in violation of forty-man limits. Here too, clubs with deeper pockets could better manipulate or bypass the system to gain an advantage in the player procurement game. These same organizations also bore the prime responsibility for driving up sale prices of the top AA talent. The wealthy Giants paid $75,000 to San Francisco of the PCL for Jimmy O'Connell and gave International League Baltimore $72,000 for Jack Bentley. Poorer clubs, by contrast, often had to cannibalize rosters by selling veteran major leaguers to generate revenue. The growing stakes of, and complexity of, talent acquisition only accelerated teams' development of player-personnel departments and the importance of the general manager in the baseball operation.[46]

In an effort to empower the Commissioner to protect themselves from their own manipulations, before the 1923 season major league owners moved the date at which they could no longer conduct in-season player sales from August 1 to June 15. They also authorized Landis to declare a unilateral increase in the number of players each club could option out to the minors from eight to fifteen, with the proviso that any such players optioned or released after January 10, 1923, even to a draft-exempt minor, would not be covered by draft exemption. The commissioner also discouraged the predraft purchasing of draft-eligible minor leaguers at high prices by ruling in October that a player conditionally sold during one season to a major league club had to report to the majors that same season or else reenter the postseason draft. Because of the campaign to curb the costly purchases of minor leaguers by the majors, the revenue transfer from such sales dropped by $200,000. In December 1923 the PCL and the American Association finally gave up and agreed to the modified draft, and the majors returned the yearly limit of optioned players covered by it to eight. With major league teams by 1924 now able to demote as "summer boarders" both optionees (whose rights they retained) and released players (open to redraft at the end of the season) to two rival AA circuits, the International League found itself isolated and deprived of the same talent. Accordingly, a year after the PCL and American Association actions the International League followed suit and accepted the modified draft. By 1925 draft exemption remained only for those players who had advanced to the high minors but had not yet been acquired or demoted by the majors.[47]

The imposition of the modified draft eased but did not eliminate the cost pressures from the high-priced purchase of minor league stars. Minor league stars still could become targets of bidding wars between clubs worried about losing out on the opportunity to sign them by waiting for the draft. Minor leaguers who had been bypassed earlier by the majors, only to blossom late at the AA level, still carried the draft-exempt label and the high sale prices that accompanied it. In 1925 San Francisco of the PCL still commanded $100,000 from Pittsburgh for stars Paul Waner and Hal Rhyme. Nor was the new modified draft arrangement stable. When the agreements expired at the end of the 1927 season, squabbling resumed between the majors and minors and between different levels of the latter. In the absence of a new agreement the old terms remained for the rest of the decade. But in 1929, in an effort to deter major league raids on their talent, the low minors tried unsuccessfully to impose their own draft-exemption scheme barring the majors from directly selecting players with less than two seasons of Organized Baseball experience.[48]

Despite the persistence of talent price and availability problems, the major leagues did little to broaden their sources. The magnates ignored National League president Heydler's call to create baseball academies for grooming their own men rather than depending on the minors. Partly owing to a compensatory rise in the direct signing of college players to the majors, the average educational level of the big leaguer continued to climb. According to one 1927 estimate, 107 men from 79 colleges made up nearly one-third of big league regulars. The need to find ways to bypass the supply bottlenecks in the minor leagues overrode the traditional fears that college-educated men were more likely to act as "clubhouse lawyers." But the continued overall reliance on the minors meant that the ethnic and regional composition of the major league playing force changed only modestly, and then mainly in response to the minors' shifting geographic locations (see Appendix, Fig. 4). According to data compiled by Hall of Fame librarian Lee Allen on major league rookies, the entry class of 1921 claimed less than a 3 percent share of its ethnic stock from Southern and Eastern Europe. By 1929 the figure still stood at merely 6 percent. In specific markets, clubs did try to acquire heroes for particular fan constituencies. The Giants, for example, purchased "$100,000 Jew" Moses Solomon from the Southwestern League. But by 1921 over 95 percent of the new entrants to the majors claimed British, Irish, or Northern or Western European heritage; the percentage remained high at 92 percent by the end of the decade.[49]

Not surprisingly, as Organized Baseball broadened its ethnic and regional composition only slightly, it kept its doors tightly closed to men of color. When the race issue occasionally surfaced, baseball management from the commissioner down cited the same litany of dangers: hostile white player and fan reaction, supposed inadequacies of blacks on the field, and seedy associations that popularly stereotyped the African American community. In truth, baseball's continued policies of racial exclusion stemmed, all too typically for industries of the day, from a mixture of personal and institutional racism and an instinctively conservative dread of change. For Organized Baseball to embrace integration required both a combination of acute economic crisis and an absence of any other plausible solutions. Despite the laments of major league executives about the price and quantity of entry-level talent, these complaints did not reach the magnitude of a deep systemic crisis for which racial integration was the only available remedy. As a result, only a handful of light-skinned Cubans gained entry to the majors in the 1920s.

Black professional baseball players instead toiled in their own separate and unequal world. Like the white industry, but on a smaller scale, their major leagues—the Negro National League and the Eastern Colored League—utilized a feeder system of semipro and minor circuits. Clubs at the bottom of the black baseball pyramid used the prevailing wages of African American workers in their local economies as their benchmarks. About 400 players performed in lower circuits such as the Negro

THE PATERNALISTIC ERA

Southern League and the Texas Negro League for half a year typically at $50 a month. At the major league level, pay for approximately 200 performers ranged from $135 to $175 a month, or $810 to $1,150 a regular campaign. Top stars might earn double that amount. Competition for playing talent between the two top circuits raised payroll pressures in the mid-1920s, causing the Eastern Colored League in 1927 to experiment with a $3,000-a-month team salary cap for its 15-member squads. But the circuit's collapse in 1928 undercut players' brief leverage while it underscored the value of winter ball employment in California, Cuba, and Mexico. The four-team Southern California Winter League, for example, paid $50 a month plus expenses. Play in Mexico offered $100 to $200 a month, and Cuba paid even better.[50]

The Negro majors were at least comparable to the white high minors in quality of play, if not compensation, and their stars were of major league caliber. But Organized Baseball's leadership discouraged contact with the black circuits by clubs or individual players, and the white press alternately derided and ignored "blackball." *Baseball Magazine* in 1921 claimed to favor integration but timidly added, "Through all the ages the effort to mix oil and water has failed." The *Sporting News* criticized a barnstorming St. Louis Cardinal squad for playing an exhibition with "colored players," asserting that it demeaned the former to be part of the "grand African show." By the late 1920s, Commissioner Landis, reflecting the view of Organized Baseball management that the Negro Leagues and their players were "outlaw" rivals to its teams and stars—and fearful of the embarrassment of defeat—barred the playing of exhibition games between major league and Negro League clubs. Reflecting the growing tone of official disapproval, white attendance at Negro League games plummeted. In Kansas City, where the white share of Negro League crowds was estimated at 50 percent in the early 1920s, the figure was but 10 percent by 1926.[51]

Instead of looking outside Organized Baseball to the Negro circuits for more talent, the white majors in the 1920s groped toward a relationship with their existing partners that would eliminate the latter's autonomy. Eventually independent minor league clubs and leagues were replaced by vertically integrated chains, with each run or owned outright by a major league organization free to manipulate talent up and down as it chose. In the past, sporadic attempts to create interlocking ownerships or "gentlemen's agreements" between major and minor league clubs had been resisted by the minors' National Association and struck down by the industry's ruling National Commission. But driven by the big leagues' unhappiness with draft exemption and high sale prices in the 1920s, many clubs demanded structural change. As smaller-market clubs saw it, their competitive salvation lay either in restoring a universal draft that would provide them with more equal and affordable access to talent, or in creating farm chains. Many of them preferred the former as keeping with tradition and placing less strain on their modest scouting and player assessment operations.

A few management minds, however, thought differently. More confident than their brethren in their ability to assess, sign, and promote talent from the bottom up, they did not want their superior professionalism neutralized by the leveling effect of a universal draft. As a result, not small-market clubs per se but only those few franchises with unusually shrewd and self-confident player-personnel directors were initially most likely to prefer the farm approach as ensuring survival of the "fittest" organizations. In the New Era, no rising club better fit that description than the St. Louis Cardinals, and no executive was more eager to take the industry down the farm system road than its personnel wizard Branch Rickey. Although baseball writers, borrowing a pattern from presidential scholars, have been prone to define eras by commissionerships, the dominant figure in Organized Baseball's structural evolution from the 1920s to the 1960s was not Kenesaw Landis but Branch Rickey. Although the former was commissioner for nearly a quarter-century, he enjoyed his greatest power at the outset, and by the end of his first term in 1927 his authority was already waning. It was Rickey who, if he did not invent the farm system concept, still shepherded it from its infancy to its peak of influence. It was also Rickey who, after World War II, stood first in line to recruit African Americans as the industry's new source of low-cost talent. In the 1950s it was again "the Mahatma" whose forays into Latin America presaged the ascendancy of that region's playing talent in modern times.[52]

Rickey's success as a baseball innovator in the acquisition and assessment of playing labor owed mainly to his personal knowledge of all levels of the industry. Abandoning an early career as a country schoolteacher at $35 a month, he matriculated at Ohio Wesleyan University as a combination student and athletic director, playing sports for extra money. Upon graduating in 1904, he joined the Dallas team of the North Texas League as a catcher. He was good enough to be signed by the Cincinnati Reds, but they soon released him because, according to Rickey, he refused to play on Sundays. After bouncing around for eight years in college teaching and coaching positions and playing brief stints with the St. Louis Browns and the New York Highlanders, the weak-armed backstop retired, only to contract tuberculosis. After he recovered, he entered law school and resumed his coaching career at the University of Michigan. After graduation he entered a law practice in Boise, Idaho, but when that failed, he returned to Michigan. In 1913 the Browns hired him for double duty as executive assistant and field manager. After two years as club skipper and a short stint in the military during World War I, Rickey began his career as a big league executive in earnest with the Cardinals. When Sam Breadon bought the club in 1920, Rickey stayed on as its vice-president, man in charge of daily operations, and even field manager until the end of 1925.

Rickey later claimed his championing of the farm system was a simple matter of "necessity being the mother of invention." In one respect this rare instance of modesty was justified, for he had not been the first to advance the idea. In 1913 Lee Hedges, the Browns' owner and Rickey's former boss, had propounded the multiple ownership of minor league teams. In a 1916 effort to counteract salary escalation driven by the Federal League, Cleveland's Charles Somers had actually secured minor league franchises in Eastern League Waterbury, Southern League New Orleans, and AA Toledo. When Somers had sold out, his successors had abandoned the farms. Working under the handicaps of the 1920s draft-exemption system, a number of big league clubs also had begun to build more sophisticated scouting and player assessment organizations to avoid costly talent misjudgments. What set Rickey's approach apart from that of his predecessors was his early grasp of the importance of integrating within the same parent club office the signing of entry-level talent, management of the player promotion process at all levels, and maintenance of a deliberate surplus of young talent to leverage down the major league payroll and make additional profits through sales of surplus players. In Rickey's new version of baseball "mercantilism" success lay in becoming a seller, rather than a buyer, of playing labor. He later stated that he based his system on the fundamental premise that a player initially signed by the parent organization always developed a subsequent "market value" that exceeded his minor league "production expense."[53]

As early as his first Cardinal contract in 1918, Rickey arranged for him-

The 1934 St. Louis Cardinals
(National Baseball Hall of Fame Library, Cooperstown, N.Y.)

self not only a base salary ($25,000 at first), but also a 10 percent share of the club's profits. As a result, when his farm system made the Cardinals into a talent seller, the transactions directly profited him as well as the club. After he purchased knuckleballer Jesse Haines in 1919, over the next twenty-seven years Rickey never bought a player from another organization. Between 1922 and 1942 the Cardinals, by contrast, earned over $2 million in player sales. Rickey built the Cardinals' farm empire brick by brick, beginning with the purchase of an 18 percent share in the Houston club of the Texas League. A 50 percent equity in the Western League's Ft. Smith, Arkansas, team followed in 1919, and then a quarter interest in the Syracuse AA franchise. As early as 1923 the Cardinals controlled over one hundred "farmhands." In 1925 Rickey added tryout camps in Danville, Illinois, and several other midwestern and southern towns. By 1926 the Cardinals had won their first National League pennant. Over the next twenty years, eight more followed, as well as six second-place finishes. By 1928, when the Cardinals moved their top minor league club to Rochester, they controlled dozens of grassroots tryout camps across rural America, owned seven clubs spanning all levels of the minors, and controlled 203 minor league players.[54]

Rickey's farm system was clearly the most advanced, and as other clubs launched their own forays, all drew the commissioner's wrath. In 1921 Landis "freed" a handful of players who had been demoted to minor league clubs with which the dispatching organizations held covert gentlemen's agreements. Because of these pacts the demoting clubs had illegally avoided having to secure waivers on the players or counting them toward option limits. But in the 1921 National Agreement Landis unaccountably failed to specifically bar outright major league ownership of minor league clubs as well as gentlemen's agreements, and in so doing he left an enormous loophole. As a result some owners chose to obey the letter, but not the spirit, of baseball law by substituting outright ownership for the more limited working agreements. Why the commissioner did not act swiftly to close the loophole remained a subject of speculation ever after. Rickey conceded that Landis had the administrative power at first to do so on his own, but he added tongue-in-cheek that because the commissioner had demurred, "regretfully that period of condonation left him with the disadvantage of estoppel." One theory held that Landis allies Barney Dreyfuss of Pittsburgh and Frank Navin of Detroit persuaded him that direct farm ownership would prove economically untenable anyway. Another explanation was the commissioner's hometown partiality toward the Chicago Cubs, whose owner William Wrigley had also purchased the Los Angeles PCL team but managed the clubs as separate investments. A final reason may have been that as major league differences with the high minors simmered over draft exemption, as a supporter of a restored universal draft Landis may not have wanted to prevent big league clubs from creating AA teams of reserves in order to force the high minors to cave in from the competition.[55]

Landis continued to liberate individual players bound by secret interlocking agreements. After Phil Todt was "released" by the Cardinals but refused to sign with either its Sherman or its Houston club, the commissioner upheld Todt's right to sign with the rival Browns. But whatever the commissioner's reasoning, he delayed a direct confrontation with the magnates over direct farm ownership until well into his second term. At majors-minors industry meetings in December 1928, prompted by the American Association's finger-in-the-dike effort to ban major league purchases of more teams, the commissioner demanded that magnates disclose their minor league holdings. They confessed to eighteen farms controlled by eleven of the big league organizations. Not all, however, apparently agreed that confession was good for the soul. The Browns'

Phil Ball failed to disclose his, rather than his club's, purchases of two more minor league franchises. The Cardinals also had two additional purchases pending. Even the mighty Yankees, whose big league roster as late as 1926 included only one major league player—Lou Gehrig—that had not been acquired through purchase or trade from an unaffiliated organization, admitted that while they still lacked farms, they would soon have to follow Rickey's example.[56]

Undeterred by the commissioner's public scolding, by the spring of 1929 the major league organizations' acknowledged total of farms had reached twenty-seven. National Association president Mike Sexton prophetically lamented that before long the majors would effectively control enough of his organization to run it. Landis weakly counterattacked against the farms by freeing ten players hidden by Washington, Pittsburgh, Detroit, and the Philadelphia Athletics. Citing his concerns about the integrity of pennant races in circuits where more than one club was owned by the same big league patron, the commissioner "recommended" the Cardinals sell its Dayton club in the Central League if it intended to purchase the rival Ft. Wayne entity. When Landis directly confronted Sam Breadon on the matter, however, the Cardinals owner countered with a heated defense of farming's economic logic. The Yankees' Ruppert seconded, maintaining that in the absence of farms the magnates simply could not afford the prices being charged for minor leaguers. Since the 1928 winter meetings, New York had begun constructing its own farm system by buying the Chambersburg club in the Class D Blue Ridge League.[57]

By the time Landis next convened major and minor league executives in late 1929, Mike Sexton's fears had been realized. Within the commissioner's own sight, officers of minor league clubs packed the hotel lobby begging big league counterparts to buy up their operations. With the impetus of the Great Depression, the future nature of the relationship between Organized Baseball's highest-echelon franchises and their minor league labor suppliers belonged to Rickey, not Landis. Because of the threat posed by the deepening economic crisis to the solvency of undercapitalized minor league clubs, the majors did not even have to conquer the minors by force. Instead, the latter rushed to be absorbed, trading independence for greater financial security. As a result, more than ever before the livelihoods and the rights of thousands of professional players throughout Organized Baseball lay squarely in the hands of an oligopoly of sixteen vertically integrated companies and their officers. What little benefit they had drawn from the actions of a commissioner purportedly committed to their upward mobility, and from the rivalry of competing major and minor league industry interests, now seemed likely to vanish with the fortunes of Wall Street. A grim decade for American workers — including baseball players — was about to begin.

CHAPTER 2 : WORKING ON A CHAIN GANG

1930–1940

During the 1920s, although players had possessed very little collective power, some of them had exercised modest individual leverage. Industry profitability and the star system had enabled Babe Ruth and a few others to stretch management's financial restraints and disciplinary controls. But the stock market crash of October 1929 ushered in the bleakest era of the twentieth century for baseball players. In the 1930s not even the stars were spared. With the Great Depression as the decade's dominant reality, owners strengthened their monopsonistic controls over their labor. The hegemony of the farm system broadened, management's vigilance against collective organization tightened, and both player productivity and wage compensation slumped. As industry's "stick" grew sharper its "carrots" became scarcer. Players received only what owners felt they could afford, and in the grim 1930s, rewards proved few indeed.

As if they sensed the long-term nature of the impending disaster and sought one last speculative profit bubble before calamity hit full force, the magnates "juiced up" the baseball in 1930. National League president Heydler even recommended introducing the designated hitter to his league but was rebuffed by the owners. Scoring and fan attendance jumped. Spalding's "lively ball" led to perhaps the biggest one-year explosion of offense in the game's history, with twenty big leaguers exceeding the .350 batting mark. By the end of the season, the majors had cleared over $1.5 million in profit to be banked for the leaner times ahead. As the national economic climate continued to darken that winter, however, owners abandoned the thought that extending higher scoring could shore up industry attendance and profits indefinitely, and they fretted about the salary costs of even one year's boosted offensive productivity. Accordingly, the magnates abandoned the lively ball in 1931 for a deader one with a looser cover and higher stitching. The leagues nudged down individual batting averages further by reversing a scoring rule adopted in 1920 and abolishing the exemption of an at-bat for a sacrifice fly. By mid-May of the 1931 season, Heydler confessed that the reduction in offense being achieved was "the very result of which we assumed when we adopted the new ball in February." By the end of the campaign, American League batting averages had fallen by ten points; National League levels, by 32 points.[1]

The 1931 decisions to hold down offensive productivity signaled the start of a long-range economizing strategy to meet the crisis Organized Baseball now recognized as more than temporary. In its own way it typified the old-fashioned reaction of U.S. business and government in general as each belatedly grasped the magnitude of the calamity. Belt-tightening and retrenchment were adopted as the harsh but necessary remedies for the real and imagined economic sins of the 1920s. Never mind that such approaches might actually delay the time at which businesses could grow their way out of the chasm. In baseball, certainly, the 1931 adoption of offensive reductions should not have been expected to prevent a sharp drop in attendance and profits. Gate levels plunged 70 percent from the figures of 1930 over the next two seasons, and the majors would not reach the 10 million attendance mark again for sixteen years. Major league profit margins, which had exceeded expenses by 16.4 percent at $1.5 million in 1930, plunged to 2.3 percent and $217,000 the next year. In 1932 big league clubs lost $1.2 million, a negative balance of 15 percent, and in 1933 the big leagues bottomed out at a −23.9 percent loss on gate receipts of only $10.8 million. Aggravating further the industry's revenue crisis, the federal government tried to address its own deepening deficit by reimposing a 10 percent tax on entertainment gate income.[2]

Franchise values plummeted throughout baseball. Desperate owners could not find buyers for their now unprofitable enterprises. Nine of sixteen major league clubs had changed hands in the 1920s at an average sale price of over a million dollars. In the Depression 1930s, only four such deals were struck, and at values only about two-thirds the average of the previous decade. The typical tenure of ownership rose from thirteen to eighteen years in the American League and from eleven to twenty-one years in the National League. Not surprisingly, a standing joke in the industry in the 1930s was, "How do you make a small fortune? Start with a big one and buy a ball club." As dramatically as big league fortunes shrank, those of the minors—with their tinier markets and smaller profit margins even in good times—plunged even farther. Club after club folded as major league organizations opted in the short run not to save the minors because of their own financial predicaments. The number of minor leagues, twenty-three at the start of the 1930 campaign, fell to only eleven in 1931 and recovered to only fourteen by 1933.[3]

In baseball's labor-intensive business, the player became the immediate and primary focus of management's desperate economy drive. The dead ball helped the magnates prevent statistically driven pay inflation, but it could not create the dramatic, immediate cost cuts the owners insisted they needed in the face of plunging revenues. Given the magnitude of payroll cuts needed, and the potential of the biggest savings "bang for the buck" from those with the highest salaries, even stars now faced severe wage slashing. Since the depression apparently negated even marquee players' "star power" at the gate, it made no sense to owners to continue paying them at salary levels as if their turnstile magic persisted. Babe Ruth, who had only garnered his two-year, $80,000 deal in 1930, now saw his pay tumble to $75,000 in 1932, $52,000 in 1933, $35,000 in 1934, and just $8,000 in 1935. Other stars' pay did not provide as much room for cutting as Ruth's, since it had not soared so high in the first place. But $1,000-a-season cuts in the pay of such big names as Lefty O'Doul and Pie Traynor became commonplace in 1932 and 1933. In 1931 six players and one player-manager earned more than $25,000 each in salary. By 1933 only seven players made as much as $15,000, and three of them served double duty as managers. In an unconvincing show of shared sacrifice that may have more accurately been a gauge of Judge Landis's slipping status, the magnates similarly cut the commissioner's salary in 1933 from $65,000 to $40,000.[4]

Major league owners did refuse to adopt some forms of direct payroll restraint, such as leaguewide team salary caps, but they accomplished much the same thing by paring roster sizes. Active squads were shrunk in December 1931 from twenty-five to twenty-three, although Landis and the National League overruled American League executives, who wanted an even lower twenty-two. Big league payrolls fell by roughly one-fourth, from an aggregate $4 million to $3 million, from 1931 to 1933. The average major league salary dipped from over $8,000 to slightly more than $6,000 (see Appendix, Fig. 2). Cuts continued through the 1935 season, when pay bottomed out at slightly more than a $5,000 average. Major league moguls could argue with some justification that not only had they not acted excessively or punitively, but they had behaved more charitably toward their workers than the management of most other industries. As a share of total revenues, big league payrolls actually rose slightly between 1929 and 1933 from 35.3 percent to 35.9 percent. Salaries in the majors in 1933 stood at 81 percent of 1929 levels, compared with a wage level 75 percent that of four years earlier in the U.S. economy overall. Big league baseball fared less well, however, when compared with the rest of the recreation sector, which had maintained pay at a 93 percent level. Nonetheless, because of a 25 percent plunge in consumer prices over the same time span, the "real" wages of major leaguers ironically had risen slightly.[5]

The same could not be said for minor league ballplayers. In the lower circuits both the number of jobs and the wages paid in them fell far more steeply. Although figures were unavailable for the AA leagues, 1933 pay averages at other levels ranged from $1,175 in A ball (down from $1,620 in 1929) to only $330 (down from $820) in Class D. The former represented 73 percent of 1929 wages, while the latter constituted but 40 percent of the pay of four years before. By comparison, the 1933 pay of the average worker in all of U.S. industry stood at $1,064, down from a 1929 level of $1,421. Most minor leaguers, in other words, now made less than an average U.S. worker. From 1932 to 1933 alone, the monthly pay of a typical Class D player fell by half, from $133 to $66, and from $665 to $330 for the season. While individual wages plummeted, the degree of leaguewide roster-cutting varied at the different levels of the minors. One of the ways the top circuits, with more room within their larger rosters, maintained higher individual wage averages was by cutting jobs. However, the low minors, already working with minimum-size squads, could not use the same expedient to pare payroll and had to cut wage rates more severely instead. So while A rosters fell by one person each year in 1931–34 from eighteen to fifteen, B squads shrank by just one to fourteen in 1933, and C and D teams followed suit in 1934.[6]

For some clubs in either the majors or the minors, slashing present and future salary commitments to current players proved inadequate to their economic emergency. Faced with proliferating red ink, these organizations sacrificed their on-field competitiveness (since, given generally faltering attendance, a pennant race appeared irrelevant to the bottom line) through wholesale housecleaning of their veteran talent. Of course, every organization inclined to pursue a "fire sale" strategy also needed buyer clubs willing to absorb more short-term debt themselves for the sake of on-field success. Because big-market clubs understandably were better able to take such risks, the explosion of player sales threatened to further distort competitive balance. As early as August 1931, rumors surfaced that Philadelphia Athletics owner/manager Connie Mack sought the breakup of his championship team for financial reasons. The auctions began in earnest after the 1932 season with the sale of stars Jimmy Dykes, Al Simmons, and Mule Haas to the White Sox for $100,000. Mack then shipped star pitcher Lefty Grove, with Rube Walberg and Max Bishop, to the Boston Red Sox for another $125,000. After the 1933 season the Athletics dispatched Mickey Cochrane to Detroit for $100,000 and Charles Earnshaw to the White Sox for $20,000. Having failed to force a $6,000 pay cut on Jimmy Foxx after the slugger's 1932 triple-crown season, Mack wrapped up the sell-off by delivering him and Bing Miller to the Red Sox for $200,000 in 1935.

When owner pique merged with the need for bottom-line economy, the jettisoning of baseball's human capital in the early 1930s became exceptionally heartless. Owner Joe Engel of minor league Charlotte, for example, sold shortstop Johnny Jones for a twenty-five-pound turkey. Apparently not satisfied with even that degree of humiliation, Engel then invited twenty-five writers to share the culinary harvest of his bargain. Washington owner Clark Griffith, in turn, demonstrated conclusively that blood did not run thicker than water in a time of acute industry hardship. Following the 1934 season he sold off his own son-in-law, Joe Cronin, for $250,000 and another player. Griffith, it turned out, required the immediate capital to pay off a bank debt amounting to over $124,000.[7]

After causing some initial hesitation, the major leagues' Depression-era need for economy ultimately intensified their long-run drive to integrate and subordinate the minors. More than ever, the big leagues craved a lasting way to hold down the acquisition costs of rookie talent, and lower circuits and clubs required the greater financial security and stability the majors could provide. Given AL and NL clubs' own precarious bottom lines, however, at first they preferred, if possible, to secure maximum operational control without having to spend the dollars required for outright farm ownership. Unfortunately for the magnates, that preference not only ran counter to the minors' need for a major league cash infusion, but it also brought the obstacle of Commissioner Landis back into play. Landis still had not yielded in his conviction of the illegality of

THE PATERNALISTIC ERA

majors-minors working agreements, and he was too colorful and popular for the owners simply to fire him. Nonetheless, to many owners the commissioner's views on farm systems were increasingly outmoded.

One thing Landis and his contrarian owners could agree on was the need to restore the universal draft to lower the acquisition costs of major leaguers. The minors' price of surrender was garnering higher rates of draft compensation and limitations on the majors' direct competition for amateur talent. Between the 1930 and 1931 seasons the two sides finalized a new National Agreement that accomplished both sets of aims. Yielding to the majors' threat to operate without a deal and to raid whatever lower-level talent they wanted, the minors accepted a universal, compulsory draft. The big leagues, in turn, agreed to limit draft eligibility to Class B–D players with at least two years of professional service, A-level talent with three years' standing, and AA veterans with four years. The agreement limited to just one the number of draftees that could be taken annually from any minor league club. The majors also consented not to sign any amateurs directly, save college players, leaving most entry-level professional signing with the minors. Draft prices were boosted to $7,500 at AA, $6,000 at A, $4,000 at B, $2,500 at C, and $2,000 at D. In turn, each major league club got to option fifteen players to the minors rather than just eight, and to increase the number of times they could be optioned out without losing them to another organization from two to three. Because of the interrelationship of different provisions, beginning in 1931 a big league club could manipulate its farm system to control a player for seven years in the minors without ever promoting him to the majors. And by maintaining farm clubs in the low minors as the actual initial signers of amateur and semipro talent, the major league franchise could circumvent the ban on its direct drafting of noncollege newcomers and still supplement its overall talent harvest each year.[8]

Landis viewed the new National Agreement as providing the majors with sufficient cheap entry talent without needing any further manipulations by the vertical farm chains. Given the owners' grasping for power in this and other areas he deemed his domain, the commissioner had about as much enthusiasm for farm chains as Andrew Jackson had shown for the Bank of the United States. But in this instance it was the "Biddles," led by Branch Rickey, who ultimately triumphed. During the farm system's infancy, Landis had attacked working arrangements, but he had not directly challenged the legality of straightforward major league ownership of farms because he believed the expense would prove prohibitive. In the early years of the Depression, it appeared he might be right. For that very reason Rickey's farm system vanguard particularly resented the commissioner's attacks on nonownership forms of minor league control. At the fiery December 1929 owners' meetings, Landis accused the Cardinals of "raping the minors" and disparaged Rickey as "that sanctimonious so-and-so." The following February Landis threw out St. Louis's attempt at covering catcher Gus Mancuso by "selling" him to a farm after the expiration of his two previous optional assignments. At the December 1930 meetings Rickey retaliated with his own overt threat against the commissioner, warning him that baseball was "bigger than any one man."[9]

Ironically, it was Browns owner Phil Ball, a beneficiary of a previous free agent liberated by Landis, who became the instrument for a new challenge to the commissioner's authority. In July 1930 outfielder Fred Bennett petitioned Landis for his freedom, charging that his advancement had been thwarted because the Browns had bounced his contract between its Tulsa, Wichita Falls, and Milwaukee farms. When he ruled in the player's favor, Landis then found himself the target of a lawsuit brought by Ball in Chicago federal district court. On April 25, 1931, Judge Walter C. Lindley denied the request for a restraining order against the commissioner and upheld the decision to free Bennett under the two-option limit. However, in a 5,000-word opinion the judge refused to outlaw the direct ownership of minor league clubs by the majors. A combative Landis preserved his pyrrhic victory by using a public threat of resignation to force Ball to drop his legal appeal.[10]

Even Landis's limited victory proved short lived. At the December 1931 winter meetings the owners formulated a proposal to sidestep the commissioner's supervision of the optioning process that the Lindley decision had upheld. In what they claimed was a move to shore up the lower circuits, the magnates voted themselves the right to negotiate working agreements with Class B–D minor league clubs. Under these club-to-club agreements, for the price of a single up-front payment to a cooperating farm, a big league franchise could assign players down without counting them against its forty-man reserve limits, then reclaim them later. Major league advocates of the change insisted that it helped the minors by giving them up-front financial aid before each season that represented a greater big league "stake" in their survival. But by legitimizing such unlimited working arrangements rather than remaining bound by the more restrictive option process of before, major league owners grabbed greater freedom to set the size and cost of their supplier labor pools. By avoiding optioning they also escaped the requirement of paying separate $400 fees to a minor league club every time they recalled players back to the majors. Lump-sum working agreement payments before each season promised the big leagues both far greater cost certainty and financial savings.[11]

Aware of the plan's detrimental implications for his or the minors' power to check big league manipulations of player movement, Landis pleaded with the magnates to consent to at least an additional guaranteed $100 payment per recalled player. His secretary and chief adviser Leslie O'Connor predicted that under the new rule, a parent club, by paying merely $1,000 up front to a captive organization, could promote an entire roster of minor leaguers at the end of the farm team's season. The $1,000 price would clearly constitute an unfairly low figure, given what it would have taken the same big league club to acquire a comparable number of players through purchase from an independent minor or through the option process. In addition, O'Connor correctly predicted that while the owners, for the moment, had voted for just a temporary two-year suspension of the ban on working agreements, the legalization would eventually become permanent.[12]

Some owners wanted to move at once to institutionalize the farm system in all of its possibilities. At the same 1931 winter meetings, AL magnates passed a resolution demanding the removal of Landis's power to ban any transactions between farms owned by the same major league club. When Landis again threatened resignation, however, NL owners balked. The reprieve lasted only one additional year. At the end of 1932, big league owners directly attacked the commissioner's power over all player contract assignments. The magnates adopted a resolution declaring all such assignments immune from his reversal, regardless of whether the minor league club involved was owned outright or merely controlled in its operations by a major league organization. "All assignments," the resolution stated, "shall be given, and shall have, the same force and effect," notwithstanding the nature of ownership or control exercised "directly or indirectly" by the parent club.[13]

Propelled by the industrywide financial crisis, by the end of 1932 Branch Rickey and like-minded moguls had secured the full legality under baseball law of the farm system and its procedures. They had transformed Organized Baseball from a loosely connected cartel of independently owned and operated clubs and leagues presided over by a commissioner to a tightly knit oligarchy of sixteen vertically integrated organizations led by strong-willed moguls and the professional managers they retained. In the process they had stripped away Landis's cherished powers to bar or restrict their activities, save for the right to ban interlocking financial interests between clubs in the same circuit. Henceforth, for small fixed amounts, big league clubs could draft talent from any lesser circuit in Organized Baseball. At an even lower cost they could manipulate their minor league chains to sign, develop, stockpile, and promote a swollen population of playing talent. Finally, they could retain control of players in that talent pool for up to seven years without having to risk losing any of them to rivals in an annual draft.

The vast pool of minor league talent captured in the farm system gave big league general managers an enormous hammer to hold over a professional player at any level. With so many young players hungry for a chance at stardom, a big league career now promised to be slower to attain for most, yet paradoxically harder to keep. Since the Depression had created a market environment inhospitable to rival circuits, players possessed no effective trade war leverage to play off rival suitors. The widespread joblessness and depressed wages in the general economy meant that ballplayers could not even utilize the availability of work or higher pay scales in other occupations to pressure for money or job security. Job insecurity, in turn, undermined the prospects for collective organization throughout the industry and, therefore, further guaranteed an emasculated player force and unchecked miserliness by owners.

At the lowest tiers of the minors, where pay had fallen to abysmal levels, the likelihood of long-term wage rebound was all the more dubious, given the concentration of franchises in the low-wage South. With more and more minor league clubs owned or controlled outright by the majors, their locations depended less on the profitability of a market than on their operating costs as labor farms. The big leagues' Depression-era priority on cost economy also led logically to the concentration of farms in Dixie. Southern clubs were cheaper to operate, and the region's predominantly rural, nonunion labor force provided a cheap comparative wage floor, even though the low standard of living also constrained gate receipts. At the start of the 1930s, 10 of 23 minor leagues were entirely or mostly located in the Old Confederacy. By 1935, 11 of 21 were so situated. But as the industry rebounded by 1940, 26 of 44 circuits, including 17 of 23 at the D level, were entirely or mainly within the southern states.[14]

In their push to acquire and control a larger pool of low-cost play-ing labor, baseball owners in the 1930s opened wider the doors of ethnic and regional access (see Appendix, Fig. 4). Despite the rising tide of immigration to U.S. shores in the late nineteenth and early twentieth centuries, entry by these Southern and Eastern European sons into a major league career had been bottlenecked as late as the 1920s by the draft controversies with the high minors. Ironically, it was during the anti-immigration Depression that second-generation Southern and Eastern European men belatedly reached the big leagues in greater numbers. Be-ginning in 1930 the share of the major league rookie class of the "new immigrant" heritage, led by Poles, Slavs, Hungarians, and especially Italians (dubbed the "sons of Caesar"), shot up from less than 7 per-cent to double-digit levels and stayed there throughout the decade. By 1940 the Southern and Eastern European ethnic percentage of these first-year men approached 20 percent. As the number of immigrants in-creased, most "old immigrant" categories, such as English and German, remained at traditional levels, but the percentage of major league rookies of Irish extraction plunged from nearly a one-quarter share to less than one-eighth by the end of the decade.[15]

At the same time that more Southern and Eastern European talent finally attained big league status, entry-level recruitment and eventual promotion by farms also resulted in more players from the U.S. South, Southwest, and West Coast. One additional consequence of this broad-ened ethnic and regional recruitment beyond northeastern and midwest-ern old stock communities was a shift in the educational profile of the playing force. While the percentage of major league rookies without any schooling at all continued to drop, reflecting the growing reach of U.S. primary and secondary education, the percentage of those complet-ing high school and the share claiming some time in college both fell modestly. These slight shifts in player educational levels also mirrored changes in the new entrants' economic backgrounds. It is safe to say that in the 1930s, the stereotypical new player was more likely than his im-mediate predecessors to be from a blue-collar or farm background and to hail from a new immigrant or white southern ethnic heritage.[16]

The greater ethnic and regional mixture on professional teams led periodically to the playing out of tensions and prejudices on the field and in the sports pages. Part of the reputation of the St. Louis Cardi-nals "Gas House Gang" for fisticuffs probably stemmed from its vola-tile combination not only of personalities but backgrounds. Dizzy Dean and Joe Medwick clearly loathed each other, with Dean, a product of the Ozarks, unapologetically calling Medwick "that Hungarian bastard." In 1933 an ugly on-field confrontation between the Yankees' Ben Chapman, a southerner with pronounced racist and anti-Semitic tendencies, and southern-born Jewish infielder Buddy Myer of Washington caused a twenty-minute brawl that included 300 fans and led to five-game suspensions and $100 fines for the uniformed participants. The availability of a broader range of ethnic talent from the minors, however, also enabled major league teams to tailor squads slightly more to specific spectator constituencies. Brooklyn and New York recruited Jewish and Italian players to appeal to local fans. It still helped the marketability of these players in the national press, however, if a star like Hank Greenberg did not look or sound too "Jewish" and could claim to have made good without "going into the ready-to-wear line." [17]

Over time two organizations of the 1930s — the St. Louis Cardinals and the New York Yankees — increasingly dominated the baseball landscape because of their mastery of the farm system's potential. The Cardinals best illustrated the labor economies attainable through a vast empire rooted in the South's low-cost environments. The Yankees, in turn, demonstrated the even greater level of dominance a big-market titan could achieve by using farms to procure and promote ethnic talent to supplement its traditional sources. In the case of the Cardinals, their southern- and southwestern-based empire dramatically mushroomed from 7 farms and 203 players in 1928 to 28 minor league clubs by 1937. St. Louis owned 13 of them outright and controlled the rest through working agreements. By 1940 the organization that Rickey built contained 33 clubs and 743 farmhands. The Cardinals ran at least one team in all twenty Class-D circuits by then and invested $2 million overall through their chain. Remarkably, in two cases they even held working arrangements with full leagues, the Arkansas and Nebraska state circuits, which gave the Cardinals the pick of any of the latter's players in exchange for financial subsidies.[18]

Rickey's empire enabled St. Louis not only to stock its own team with low-cost major league talent but to broker surplus players to other organizations for cash. At its peak the Cardinal system provided the majors one year with sixty-five players, nearly one of every six big leaguers. St. Louis's most lucrative sales of homegrown talent included Johnny Mize (for $52,000 and two players), Bob Bowman ($35,000 and one player), Bob Worthington and Charlie Wilson ($60,000 and one player), Nate

Andrews ($7,500), Johnny Chambers ($6,000), Don Padgett ($35,000), Lew Riggs ($20,000), Jimmy Jordan ($20,000), Frank Melton ($30,000), and Dizzy Dean ($185,000 and 2 players). Even when in a show of Depression-era frugality the Cardinals cut their general manager's base salary from $51,470 in 1934 to $40,000 in 1937, at a rate of 10 percent per player sale Rickey's "piecework" boosted his income to over $80,000, far higher than that of commissioner Landis.[19]

An organization did not have to go to the extremes of the Cardinals to be successful. But those who did not erect an adequate farm chain and professionalize their player-personnel systems accordingly paid the price. The eight organizations slowest to adopt effective farm systems — the Phillies, the Athletics, the Senators, the White Sox, the Giants, the Cubs, the Braves, and the Pirates — joined the Browns as the least successful on-field clubs over the next decade. Even the big-market members within that group found their success lagging because they failed to use strong farms to augment their advantages. If they doubted the fact, all they had to do was compare their performance with that of the Yankees. New York's farm system began in the late 1920s with owner Ruppert's purchase of the Class-D Blue Ridge League's Chambersburg club. But two events marked the organization's full-fledged commitment to building a farm empire: the purchase of the Class-AA Newark club in the International League in late 1931 and the hiring away of thirty-seven-year-old George Weiss from the Baltimore Orioles as Yankee farm director two months later.

George Weiss first became involved in a professional baseball operation in 1919 as owner of a minor league club in the Eastern League. From there he eventually succeeded Jack Dunn as Oriole general manager a decade later, only to be enticed by New York executive Ed Barrow in February 1932 to join the Yankees. More so than Branch Rickey, the dour, introverted Weiss successfully combined the player procurement techniques of the farm system with the traditional big-market methods of talent acquisition to build a sports dynasty that still has not been equaled. In his twenty-eight-year reign from 1932 to 1960 as farm director and then general manager, Weiss deployed keen-eyed scouts such as Paul Krichell to locate and sign talented prospects. By 1940 New York controlled nine clubs, with five of them operating at the lower C and D levels and the Newark Bears serving as the crown jewel at the top of the Yankee system. By combining direct college signees such as Charley Keller, Red Rolfe, and Vic Raschi with farm system products and players secured by draft, trade, or sale from other organizations, the Yankees garnered seven AL pennants in eight years from 1936 to 1943. Over the entire Weiss era, New York's farm-based dynasty eventually claimed an astounding eighteen AL pennants and fourteen World Series titles in twenty-eight seasons.[20]

As the national economy slowly emerged from the depths of the Great Depression, Organized Baseball's own early signs of recovery and its strengthened farm system labor controls led to hopes that offense and bigger gates could be reconciled with cost containment. The magnates brought back a livelier baseball in 1934 to boost scoring and fan appeal, but major league pay averages continued their decline through 1935, bottoming out at a little over $5,000 (see Appendix, Fig. 2). Although average salaries advanced roughly $2,000 over the rest of the decade, by 1940 the mean major league pay still only equaled 1927 levels and still trailed the 1930–31 peak by about $1,000. Even the Yankees, with their on-field brilliance and their large market, maintained salary discipline. Pitcher Waite Hoyt futilely tried to impress upon his bosses that better pay would produce even greater success, noting, "A winning ballplayer is motivated by two strong incentives—professional pride and the urge to make money." Nevertheless, despite winning a Triple Crown in 1934, Lou Gehrig received no raise from the $23,000 he had gotten the preceding two years. Efforts by Yankee players' spouses to stiffen their husbands' backbones or to appeal directly to the front office proved fruitless. Before the 1937 season Red Ruffing's wife, Pauline, pressed him to demand $25,000. Eleanor Gehrig lobbied Yankee brass for $50,000 for her husband. Both efforts proved to no avail. When Joe DiMaggio launched a holdout in 1938 for a $40,000 salary after two big league seasons, the club made a counteroffer of only $25,000 and forced his return to the field.[21]

The exemplars of payroll tightfistedness, however, remained the St. Louis Cardinals. Bolstered by the leverage of his extensive farm system, Branch Rickey's "negotiations" with players became the stuff of legend. When Commissioner Landis gushed to World Series hero George "Pepper" Martin, "Young man, I'd give anything to trade places with you tonight," the Cardinal performer eagerly countered, "It's agreeable to me, Judge, salaries and all!" Bill Veeck frequently told the story of Ernie Orsatti, a St. Louis outfielder who demanded a $500 raise in 1933 to $5,000. Rickey refused to budge from a frozen salary of $4,500. When Orsatti entered the Cardinal general manager's office, Rickey's telephone "rang," and the executive launched into an apparent two-way conversation with his farm operator. In a voice loud enough for his guest to hear, Rickey indicated that he might have an outfielder ready to send down soon, then hung up. The phone rang again, this time supposedly from a minor league general manager with a similar need for a soon-to-be-demoted outfielder. By the time Rickey got off the line, Orsatti's only demand was for a pen to sign the club's lowball offer sheet. Unknown to Orsatti, the telephone conversations were a charade Rickey acted out by using a foot pedal under the desk to trigger the rings of each nonexistent call.[22]

Even on the rare occasion when Rickey granted a raise to one of his suitors, he managed to find creative ways to turn the relationship to his benefit. In 1936 Dizzy Dean, who had won 96 games in his first four seasons and 58 during the last two alone, held out for $27,500, a $9,000 raise from his 1935 pay. When Rickey refused, Dean upped the ante to $40,000. Adding fuel to the Diz's fire was the fact that his brother Paul, a 19-game winner who had asked for a $6,500 boost to $15,000, had only been offered his old pay. The Cardinals forced the Deans back before the end of spring training, with the elder Dean getting a $22,300 offer that represented a $4,000 boost. Following a 1936 campaign in which Dean won an additional 24 games, Rickey put the pitcher's name on the auction block and generated offers from $100,000 to $250,000 plus other players. Aware of being shopped, Dizzy then demanded a $100,000 salary in keeping with his demonstrated market value. Even after lowering his figure to $50,000, he still received only half of that latter sum. Meanwhile, brother Paul struggled with arm trouble and saw his salary slashed by fully 80 percent. When Dizzy's own injuries curtailed his performance, Rickey cut his pay $7,500 after the 1937 season and then sold him to the Cubs for $185,000 and three players worth $65,000 in salary. By selling a player contracted for only $18,000, the Cardinal executive personally pocketed several thousand dollars more than that sum. Dean, in a desperate gambit for free agent status and needing to convince potential suitors that he was younger than he actually was, then publicly claimed that Rickey had signed him when he was underage without his parents' written consent. When Rickey retaliated by producing a copy of the player's marriage license that showed his proper age, the busted Dean could only confess, "You got me, Judge."[23]

Undergirding the owners' hard line toward veteran players' salaries was the ample number of prospective replacements toiling on minor league farms and the preciousness and tenuousness of a big league job in a country still plagued by widespread unemployment. At the same time, the ability of a major league organization to keep a player bottled up in its farm system for up to seven years and unilaterally give or withhold the initial opportunity at a big league career held down rookies' pay demands. Grateful first-timers were hardly likely to be aggressive in their requests, and their docility in turn helped set a low major league wage floor. Typical were the $3,000 salaries paid to Cardinals Paul Dean and catcher Bill DeLancey in 1934. Even popular stars, as Dizzy Dean learned, did not get salaries comparable to those of the biggest names of the previous decade, and at the first sign of decline their clubs sold them. The organization not only gained from the sales, but the team payroll dropped. One clear consequence of the power farm systems gave to baseball's personnel managers was the odd pairing of rising average ages on big league rosters with a declining percentage of long-term veterans. In other words, management now had the means to squeeze major league playing careers at both ends. By 1938 the average NL player was nearly 29½ years old, but at the same time the circuit contained only 28 ten-year veterans and 77 five-year men in its playing population of over 400. As Dizzy Dean's saga dramatized, it became more commonplace for a player to lop off two or more years from his stated age in an effort to delay his day of reckoning.[24]

The surplus of cheap playing labor at all professional levels made job insecurity an even more frightening, realistic prospect than low pay. The pain of the end of a playing career could be eased for a fortunate minority by the expansion of high school, college, semipro, and professional coaching and managing positions, scouting jobs, and by the late 1930s, broadcasting openings that accompanied the growth of the farms. The importance of evaluating and developing players and the need for experienced baseball hands to undertake such responsibilities within the farm chains provided an expanding area of postplaying opportunity within Organized Baseball. But the men who garnered the new openings in the farm empires were vastly outnumbered by the discarded ex-players who lacked such jobs or enough savings from Depression-era playing wages to fall back on. A typical example was ex-Giant Bill Wambsganss. When his playing career drew to a close in 1932 when he was thirty-eight, and subsequent scouting and managerial openings dried up, he managed a girls' softball team for four years and then turned to various odd jobs. The colorful Dizzy Dean, by contrast, proved far more fortunate. Parlaying his colloquialisms and larger-than-life personality into a broadcasting career, he also secured related work as a public spokesman for Falstaff beer at a $10,000 retainer.[25]

The shortage of jobs for baseball retirees in Depression America only magnified the inadequacies of the industry's pension system. The program for indigents created and administered by the Association of Professional Ball Players of America offered but a modicum of aid to a relative handful of ex-players and umpires. By 1933, 150 men were drawing some assistance from the fund, but only 45 received actual monthly allotments. That same year, when big league owners approved the first All-Star Game they also agreed to donate the event's proceeds to the association fund. Commissioner Landis committed another $20,000 per year from his office account. As a result the pension received an infusion of nearly $240,000 over the first eight years of the mid-season classic's existence. The sum still represented a drop in the bucket of need. Citing their own economic plight, owners refused to consider pension benefits an appropriate subject of mutual discussion or negotiation with their players, or to unilaterally establish an adequate system from their coffers.[26]

The low wages, precarious job security, and uncertain postcareer prospects of Depression-era ballplayers drove them to seek any extra money they could find between seasons. As with postretirement openings, the stars had less difficulty than the journeymen in securing what few opportunities existed. Dizzy Dean again headed the short list of players able to parlay their in-season notoriety into considerable postseason dollars. His financial statement for the calendar year 1934, for example, listed a season salary of only $7,500. But he accumulated $30,000 in additional income through a World Series winner's share ($5,389), a postseason bonus ($500), barnstorming moneys ($5,716), vaudeville appearances ($1,625), a movie short ($2,250), radio appearances ($5,000), product endorsements ($8,000), and a series newspaper column ($500). Dean's case also demonstrated the importance to a player of toiling for a first-division club and especially a pennant winner, thereby earning ample postseason shares. Given the majors' growing competitive imbalance, such supplementary income simply was not available for the vast majority. On the privileged side of the ledger sat men like Yankee Frank Crosetti, who from 1932 to 1955 collected over $90,000 in World Series money as a consequence of his team's success. Showing admirable but rare Depression-era compassion for an ex-teammate, Babe Ruth in 1932 blasted the NL champion Chicago Cubs for selfishness when they awarded mid-season Yankee acquisition Mark Koenig only a half-share from their World Series pool.[27]

The magnates' penury in the 1930s even extended to the dropping of postseason awards for individual excellence, a move that affected one of the few supplementary income opportunities open to stars on second-division teams. As one method of publicizing their stars' on-field heroics, in the 1920s major league owners in both leagues had sponsored MVP prizes. But whether out of miserliness or aggravation at having the honors thrown in their faces at contract time, both the American League and the National League jettisoned responsibility for the recognitions at the start of the Depression. The *Sporting News* picked up the ball by agreeing to sponsor their own MVP prizes, and beginning in 1931 the Baseball Writers of America assumed responsibility for selecting the winners. Similarly without financial help from the magnates, the writers belatedly inaugurated league Rookie of the Year awards after the 1940 season.[28]

Players were not the only on-field employees to endure severe salary slashing at the start of the 1930s and a painfully slow recovery after mid-decade. Umpires endured across-the-board cuts at all levels of Organized Baseball starting at the end of the 1932 season. By 1937, pay for big league arbiters ranged from $4,000 to $10,000 a year, with an extra $2,500 every five years for World Series service. The level of big league salary did place the men in blue on a rough par with most of the players they regulated. Although they still had to purchase and maintain their own uniforms and equipment, by the end of the decade they had garnered an additional $750 allowance for road expenses—though the amount only met about half of the actual costs. They also secured a tiny pension plan that paid retirees with a minimum of fifteen years of big league service $100 per annum, with a lifetime limit of $2,400. The pay picture for minor league umpires, like that of the performers they supervised, was far bleaker. By 1940 their wages in a five-month season ranged from $150-a-month starting pay in the low minors to salaries of $500 to $700 a month, plus $100 for meals and lodging, at the highest levels. No pension awaited them when their careers ended.[29]

The on-field baseball employees who arguably suffered the least from pay cuts, and who even regained a measure of lost authority, were field managers. Managers' exemptions from the harsh pay cuts of the early 1930s were a sign that they were viewed by their superiors as extensions of their authority. In a turnabout from the manager's declining economic status and practical power in the 1920s, in 1935 the five highest-paid on-field personnel, and seven of the top ten, were managers or player-managers. The Yankees' Joe McCarthy headed the list at $35,000, followed by Mickey Cochrane, Bill Terry, Connie Mack, Joe Cronin, Charlie Grimm, and Frank Frisch with $30,000, $27,500, $25,000, $25,000, $22,500, and $20,000 salaries, respectively.[30]

Although several rival managers on the salary list owed their high pay to their status as either active players or recent retirees, Joe McCarthy stood out as the emerging new model of the detached, anti-individualistic field commander. McCarthy required that his players wear coats at dining hall, and he similarly demanded team decorum on the field. Yankee uniforms, deliberately cut large to project an image of size and power, were to be kept clean between contests. McCarthy banned card playing in the clubhouse, and he disdained the rowdiness of the St. Louis Gas House Gang and other squads of the early to mid-1930s. Among the "lessons" he drew from the Cardinals' colorful escapades was a career-long skepticism of rural southern players as undisciplined and unintelligent. In contrast, with the disciplinarian McCarthy as their field boss, the Yankee squads broke with their rowdy Ruthian past and came to resemble less a collection of larger-than-life individualists than a team of resolute men in gray flannel suits—a talented unit marked not by flamboyance but by the cold efficiency with which it dispatched its opponents.

Although U.S. industry experienced a dramatic surge in union membership in the 1930s, Organized Baseball remained a nonunion business. Many factors contributed to the lack of collective mobilization within the player force. Long-standing impediments to the recruitment and maintenance of a union membership, including the geographic mobility and limited duration of baseball careers, only worsened during the Depression years. Increased ethnic and regional diversity within the baseball work force also strained group solidarity. Management's ability to exercise overwhelming control over a player's choice of workplace, employment conditions, productivity gains, and compensation stood unrivaled by any other legitimate industry. No other business could claim similar Supreme Court sanction for such monopsonistic powers as a "reserve clause" that prevented players from changing employers. The emergence of the farm system, by providing chains of ample, cheap replacement labor and anchoring them in the low-cost, antiunion South, added yet another powerful deterrent to the emergence of a baseball equivalent of the United Auto Workers. Given these factors, it becomes all too understandable why baseball failed to generate collective labor militancy when so many other industries did. When suggestions of unionization did occasionally surface, the baseball press quickly shot them down. The *Sporting News* ridiculed the very idea of sit-down strikes by men who spent much of their time sitting on dugout benches, and it raised the old bogeyman that baseball unionization would lead to standardized work schedules and pay scales and the destruction of star salaries.[31]

The same industry realities that effectively doomed unionization also precluded the need for revolutionary expansion and diversification of the player pool via racial integration. The commissioner permitted a paroled convict from Sing Sing prison, Edwin C. "Alabama" Pitts, to play in the International League. A woman, pitcher Jackie Mitchell, briefly infiltrated the Piedmont League in 1932. However, African American players remained barred from Organized Baseball. Reflecting a halting awakening to the issue, a few newspapermen occasionally commented on the industry's policy of racial exclusion. In 1931 columnist Westbrook Pegler pointed out the contrast between baseball's excuses and black participation in football, basketball, and track. At a baseball writers' dinner in New York in early 1933, Heywood Broun also raised the issue, and an informal poll taken at the event by Jimmy Powers claimed only one prominent attendee — the Giants' John McGraw — opposed to integration. But for every Broun, Pegler, or Shirley Povich, many more scribes, such as Joe Vila and Dan Parker, attacked racial integration as radical nonsense.[32]

While white sportswriters sporadically debated the merits of including African Americans, professional players of color toiled in their own circuits. Following the collapse of the Eastern Colored League in 1928, the end of the first Negro National League in 1931 left "blackball" briefly without any major league. Depression-ravaged lower circuits struggled to survive, and as in white ball, owners responded with 20–30 percent salary cuts, roster reductions, and pared-back schedules. In 1933 a reconstituted Negro National League (NNL) led by Pittsburgh numbers racketeer Gus Greenlee opened, and a rival Negro American League (NAL) followed four years later. At the lowest levels of Negro professional baseball, pay now frequently started at $40 to $60 a month. Higher up the black minors, performers in the Negro Southern League played on fourteen-member squads and earned up to $200 a month, plus meal and transportation moneys. Throughout the lesser circuits, "transportation" usually meant unglamorous bus rides; "board" indicated park benches, shelters, or fleabag hotels; and "meals" included hot-dog breakfasts. The smaller, more tenuous markets of the low Negro circuits also led to a wider variety of player contracts ranging from formal pacts to verbal or handshake deals, and payment methods varied from straight salary to per-game stipends or gate-sharing arrangements.[33]

Just as in Organized Baseball, players in the Negro circuits craved the status, pay, and greater security of their big league brothers. Rosters on the NNL or NAL clubs generally stood at seventeen or eighteen players. By 1934 an NNL rookie could earn $125 to $150 a month if he was considered a promising talent. Veteran stars drew up to $300. Clubs paid for board and lodging on the road and provided sixty cents a day in meal money. To generate more income, teams and individual players alike traveled continuously, playing barnstorming exhibitions and then hiring themselves out for winter ball in Cuba or elsewhere in the Caribbean. The Pittsburgh Crawfords played between 150 and 200 games a season, with fully two-thirds of the contests being nonleague matches against white semipros or comparable opposition. In Latin winter ball, players could amass $775 plus expenses for an eight-week season. Ironically, in contrast to exclusionary policies in the United States, high pay for winter ball was made possible by the patronage of white, U.S.-based businesses—most notably sugar and petroleum companies—in the region.[34]

The financial fragility of the Negro circuits, along with the lack of strong interclub and interleague disciplinary structures, encouraged frequent contract jumping. Players with the necessary talent to draw bidders leaped with impunity. Although both NNL and NAL contracts included a reserve clause, the enforcement mechanisms available to either league to coerce compliance held little sway. Fines and suspensions meant nothing if they were counteracted by the pay and employment offered by an outside "outlaw" owner. The need of the abandoned club or league for the deserter's services also usually meant the player was welcomed back with open arms when he returned, with all past transgressions—and their financial consequences—forgiven. As Bill Yancey, a player with the New York Black Yankees recalled, "You signed for a year . . . but if you felt like jumping the next year, you jumped."[35]

For a handful of Negro League stars, the existence of trade war and off-season and outside opportunities substantially increased their incomes and emboldened them in contract dealings with employers. No one proved the point better than Leroy "Satchel" Paige. While pitching for the Crawfords in the mid-1930s, Paige supplemented his $350-a-month salary by hiring himself out to semipro teams for an extra $100 to $500 at a time. In 1937 he refused to report after his sale to the Newark Eagles for $5,000. Instead he jumped to (or was "kidnapped" by, depending on the version of events) the Dominican Republic, where dictator Rafael Trujillo had established a summer circuit. NNL owners retaliated with a three-year suspension against Paige, but they could not enforce it. After only one campaign, the wayward pitcher jumped back to the United States. When Gus Greenlee again tried to ship Paige to Newark, the pitcher skipped to Mexico. After one more round of jumping, J. L. Wilkinson, owner of the NAL Kansas City Monarchs, secured Paige's services in 1939. Wilkinson managed to gain some semblance of control over his star by paying him a $22,000 salary. It also helped that the Monarchs' owner created a barnstorming vehicle in the form of a traveling farm team unaffiliated with the NAL, which enabled Paige to earn additional money. Newark, in turn, agreed to accept as compensation the rights to two other previously disputed players.[36]

Most professional baseball observers, who saw blacks play against and alongside white stars in countless exhibitions and winter ball, knew that many of them could succeed in the white majors. The Senators' Clark Griffith admitted in 1938 that blacks eventually would be in the white leagues and added, "The time is not far off." Gabby Hartnett maintained that if managers were allowed, "there'd be a mad rush to sign up Negroes." Reds manager Bill McKecknie, Dodger skipper Leo Durocher, and players Pepper Martin, Johnny Vander Meer, and Carl Hubbell concurred. Pittsburgh team owner William Benswanger even claimed, with dubious sincerity, that if the issue ever came to a league ballot "I'd vote for Negro players." Shirley Povich's column of April 7, 1939, stated the unfair reality when he wrote, "There's a couple of million dollars' worth of baseball talent on the loose, ready for the big leagues, yet unsigned by any major league club."[37]

If black ballplayers were that good, why did the magnates stubbornly refuse to hire them? The owners' public excuses ran the spectrum. Negro Leaguers, they claimed, had too many ties with numbers runners and other seedy black entrepreneurs. Even Branch Rickey, a more enlightened man with a sharp eye for cheap talent, nonetheless shied away for years, calling the Negro Leagues a "booking agent's paradise." Other executives, while conceding black ballplayers' "natural" gifts, disparaged a purported lack of refinement and discipline. The implication left was that training such traits into black signees was simply too time consuming and expensive. Still more management figures claimed, despite the absence of hard proof, that white players, white spectators, or both would refuse to accept black performers and react violently out of deep-seated, irreversible racial animosity. Evidence of such hate existed, to be sure. In a 1938 pregame radio interview, the Yankees' Jake Powell regaled listeners with his description of off-season police duties in Dayton, Ohio, "cracking niggers over the head." The subsequent public outcry forced Commissioner Landis to suspend the outfielder for ten days, and manager Joe McCarthy quickly barred any future pregame broadcast sessions with his men. Cardinal manager Ray Blades said owners would admit blacks only if "fans demand them," a response he did not expect. Clark Griffith, in turn, predicted "cruel, filthy epithets" from players and fans alike should the majors attempt integration.[38]

As the struggles of Jackie Robinson a decade later demonstrated, such claims did have some validity. Given, in particular, the growing numbers of white southerners and sons of Southern and Eastern European immigrants on professional teams, many Organized Baseball players might be expected to lash out at African American opponents or teammates out of a mix of prejudice and economic rivalry. Yet Wendell Smith of the *Pittsburgh Courier* insisted in 1938 that in his unscientific poll of National League players and managers, four-fifths of those asked did not oppose integration. Dizzy Dean, a product of the rural South, confessed, "It's too bad those colored boys don't play in the big leagues, because they sure got some great players." Dean's observation, however, pointed to a force in its own way as stubborn as racism in raising fears of integration in white players. For the performers whose careers had survived the bleakest days of the early 1930s, as well as those only now advancing slowly up the farm system, any dramatic moves to open wider the doors of access threatened their fragile economic opportunity and security. A marquee star such as Dean might have less reason to dread the consequences of competition from black players. But to a white journeyman, it could mean the premature loss of a career, or at least even lower wages, and the future consequence of diminished pensions and post-career financial security.[39]

The fact remained that if baseball management had wanted to integrate the player ranks even slightly in the 1930s, it could have done so. Whether or not players liked it, the men who ran Organized Baseball from its top echelons in the major leagues held such complete power over the industry by the late 1930s that they could have imposed virtually any change in labor policy they wanted. Baseball historians unwittingly obscure this reality when they focus exclusively on the role of Commissioner Landis—the owners' appointee, after all—in blocking integration. Landis and his league presidents did lie blatantly when they denied that Organized Baseball had an official policy of racial exclusion. Not only was such a policy common knowledge, but Landis even refused to legitimize the Negro Leagues as separate businesses by permitting formal competitions with his clubs or by even allowing individual players to wear their regular uniforms when playing in exhibitions with black players. When owners Sam Breadon of St. Louis and John Shibe of the Phillies encouraged a committee of prominent black leaders to appear at a major league owners' meeting in 1938, Landis refused to admit the delegation on the grounds that they had not been formally placed on the agenda.[40]

The power to grant or deny blacks' access to Organized Baseball's player ranks, however, ultimately rested with the big league owners, not Landis. As their series of triumphs over him on the farm system issue demonstrated, they could override him when they were determined enough and concentrated their efforts. But almost to a man they refused to take the lead for racial integration of their player forces. The maverick executive Bill Veeck attributed his colleagues' silence to their basic fears of the unknown. Ford Frick claimed that the magnates were simply "afraid to make a move." What both comments pointed to was the owners' deeply rooted business conservatism and their tendency to reject "risky" or radical ideas even though the competitive and financial payoffs might be enormous. The early 1930s, it was true, had presented Organized Baseball with a dire emergency that could have impelled it to accept the risk and the promise of integration. The severity of the Great Depression had destroyed or temporarily weakened many of the Negro circuits, making the selective snatching of black talent by white leagues even easier. But Organized Baseball's owners were traditionalists who, like their contemporaries in other industries, had chosen the old-fashioned path of retrenchment and cost economy rather than wage and market stimulation in response to the economic calamity.[41]

Not surprisingly, then, the white baseball industry placed its faith in the farm system road to labor-cost savings and economic recovery rather than the uncharted path of racial integration. Compared with the risks

THE PATERNALISTIC ERA

and unknowns of integrating the player force, the farm system promised significant long-term economies without requiring the industry to confront the societal institutions or the attitudinal underpinnings of Jim Crow. To be sure, the up-front expense of building a farm system chain through the outright purchase of component links had led owners early in the 1930s to pursue cheaper means of extending similar control. Those actions had led to nasty confrontations with Landis. But even with its complications and its short-run intermanagement strife, the farm system had become the remedy of choice for a labor-intensive industry's ills. As Organized Baseball gradually recovered after mid-decade and white farm systems expanded, few executives saw the integration of black players into their on-field labor forces as necessary or desirable. And the more completely the white baseball industry committed itself to the farm system form of vertical integration, and in so doing rooted itself in the segregated towns and cities of the Jim Crow South, the more it apparently ruled out any future within it for players of color.

As the white baseball industry struggled to its feet in the latter half of the 1930s, the magnates of farm system empires moved inexorably to consolidate their control over an expanded captive labor market. Too late Commissioner Landis launched counterattacks. But given the passage of the owners' resolution of late 1932 that legitimized working agreements — the core of the farm system's architecture — Landis could only fight rear-guard actions against isolated incidents that remained technically illegal; he could not strike down the farm system itself. His only hope lay in generating enough harassment to force the farms' operators to grudgingly reconsider an alternative form of industry structuring. Given how far down the farm system path the big league clubs already had traveled by mid-decade, that possibility seemed remote. Landis hardly helped his cause by launching his salvos against farm system violations of the revised National Agreement in inconsistent and arbitrary ways.

In one prominent example, in late 1936 the commissioner permitted teenage pitching phenomenon Bob Feller to sign directly with the Cleveland Indians in spite of continuing rules barring the inking of sandlotters by major league clubs. Feller and his father both claimed that because of a sore arm, the young hurler had not pitched in 1936 for the Fargo-Moorhead team of the Northern League — a team in which Cleveland general manager Cy Slapnicka maintained a financial interest. According to the Fellers, the youngster's idle connection to the Fargo team had removed his amateur status and made him eligible for signing by a major league team. To others observing the maneuverings, it appeared that Cleveland had orchestrated the Fargo arrangement to "hide" its direct acquisition of a high schooler. Even though another minor league club, Western League Des Moines, offered $7,500 for Feller, Landis sided with the pitcher and Cleveland at the end of the year rather than declaring him a free agent or requiring him to play for Des Moines. Cleveland's only price was a $7,500 reimbursement to the Western League club for Feller's rights.[42]

Even though Landis did not void the Feller signing, big league owners took steps to prevent reversals by the commissioner's office in subsequent cases. They pushed through a rules change enabling major league club representatives to contact sandlotters and, although not sign them directly, "recommend" them to minor league affiliates for signing. Three months later, in the case of Tommy Henrich, an undeterred Landis reversed his Feller precedent. Henrich, a young outfielder, complained that after his covert signing by Cleveland in 1934, he had not been promoted to the majors within the required three years. At a hearing before the judge, the Cleveland team argued that it did not control Henrich's contract since it had not directly signed him in the first place. A team scout, however, admitted to the contrary. After rewarding Cleveland's cover-up in the Feller controversy, the commissioner now assailed the practice and freed Henrich. After entertaining at least eight offers from rival big league organizations, the free agent slugger signed with the Yankees for a $20,000 bonus and a $5,000 salary. New York assigned him to its AA club in Newark, from which he was quickly promoted in June 1937 and became a star.[43]

Landis then directly targeted his primary farm system nemesis, the St. Louis Cardinals. The commissioner summoned Branch Rickey to the former's winter home in Belleair, Florida, for a direct grilling on the matter of the Cardinals' control of lower circuits. Not only did the organization have secret deals with entire leagues, but other allegations also claimed that it had violated subordinate clubs' competitive obligations by manipulating the rosters of more than one club per league. The tangled web of St. Louis farm system arrangements enabled the effective "laundering" of players to avoid per-club roster limits and the manipulation of one-player-per-team limits on draft losses. One part of the empire, the Springfield, Missouri, franchise in the Western Association, allowed Rickey to purchase any of its players for $2,500, even though the Cardinals operated Springfield's Danville, Illinois, competitor. In exchange Springfield could only accept optioned major leaguers from St. Louis. Other links in the Cardinals' chain included PCL Sacramento (owned by Rickey's friend Phil Bartelone), Cedar Rapids of the Western League, both Fayetteville and Monetto of the Arkansas-Missouri League, Newport of the Northeast Arkansas League, Crookston of the Northern League, and Mitchell of the Nebraska State League.[44]

In response to Landis's interrogation, Rickey admitted that his system of controls effectively limited the ability of individual clubs to make competitive decisions to keep or improve talent. The commissioner characterized the problem as "big as a house, isn't it?" but Rickey disagreed. Landis persisted, "I think it is as big as the universe." After the interview Landis directed chief aide Leslie O'Connor to conduct a sweeping investigation of the Cardinal system. Reporters dubbed the inquiry the "Cedar Rapids case." By spring training of 1938, rumors were flying of an imminent crackdown on Rickey's farm operation. Without presenting written charges to either Rickey or owner Breadon or providing them a formal opportunity for rebuttal, the commissioner declared seventy-four Cardinal farmhands, including star prospect Pete Reiser, free agents. Participating farms also received fines, with Cedar Rapids docked $588; Springfield, $1,000; and Sacramento, $588. In one crucial concession to St. Louis, the commissioner permitted the team and its farms the right to bid to regain the lost men. If they succeeded in resigning any of the freed farmhands, however, they could not hide a second time through transfer to an affiliate club.[45]

The ruling cost Rickey the services of Reiser, who ironically became a star player with the Brooklyn Dodgers organization the Cardinal general manager eventually joined. But the verdict could have been much more severe, and the fact that it was not probably owed to National Association president Walter Bramham. Judge Bramham, anxious to protect the Cardinals' role as subsidizer of the minors, interceded on the club's behalf. As a consequence, Landis opted not to fine, suspend, or blacklist Rickey or bar his clubs from bidding on the freed ballplayers. The biggest toll the incident took on the Mahatma was on his relationship with owner Sam Breadon. The Cardinal magnate blamed his general manager's open flaunting of farm system powers for attracting Landis's public inquiry, which in turn had exposed Breadon's alteration of financial records in an effort to conceal St. Louis's relationships with its farms.

The embarrassed Breadon, who had earlier risked himself by defending Rickey, now distanced himself from the subordinate he blamed for his humiliation.[46]

Irritating as they were to farm operators, Landis's rear-guard actions drew criticism as ineffective from a shrinking number of magnates that had held out against adopting farms and had fallen behind competitively. One of them, Washington's Clark Griffith, openly castigated the rival Yankees' system at the 1939 major league meetings. He took the occasion to demand new legislation limiting the number of clubs any major league organization could control. Landis weighed in by vetoing National Association amendments permitting more such ties. The commissioner accused the Cardinals and the Yankees, as leading major league farm operators, with orchestrating the National Association requests through their pawns. The following month Landis launched another salvo against farm system cover-ups by freeing ninety-one Detroit Tiger farmhands outright and ordering payments totaling $47,250 to five others. Unlike the St. Louis case, Landis barred Detroit from directly acquiring any of the liberated players for three years, although the Tigers were permitted to re-sign Paul "Dizzy" Trout in order to release him to a minor league affiliate. Ironically, two antifarm organizations, the Cubs and the Browns, drew $1,000 and $500 fines, respectively, for prematurely bidding on the Tiger free agents.[47]

Farm system magnates growing tired of the commissioner's sporadic broadsides and increasingly confident of winning any showdown had demanded for some time that he produce a viable alternative or else stop his harassment. One possible alternative, floated, ironically, by Tigers general manager Jack Zeller, suggested pooling all minor leaguers and distributing them in an annual draft among the sixteen major league organizations. The commissioner directed Leslie O'Connor to study the issue and prepare recommendations. Hoping to use the publicity from his Detroit ruling to generate attention, Landis issued the report soon afterward. Under his alternative scheme, all minor leaguers would exist as "free agents" in the sense of being eligible for acquisition and thereby promotion up the ranks of Organized Baseball by any club of higher classification. Minor league teams would be financially sustained not through subsidies or ownership by individual major league clubs but by a joint capital fund. All big league clubs would pay into this common fund, and graduated subsidies would be distributed from it to minor league teams based on classification level. The moneys for the fund would be generated from a tax on player sales, with selling clubs retaining only the after-tax amount of the sale price.[48]

If such a scheme for the collective subsidization of independent minor leagues had ever had a chance of adoption by either the magnates or the minors' National Association, it certainly had none by 1940. Too much of an architecture of club chains, separate subsidies, and working agreements had been erected. Too much money had been invested, and too much success had been experienced by the pioneers of farm system baseball for them to permit unraveling of their handiwork. The owners accordingly labeled the Landis plan "anarchistic" and "socialistic" at the same time. Branch Rickey dubbed the blueprint "fantastic and impractical." With the rejection of his plan, Landis had no choice but to admit defeat and execute a face-saving withdrawal from the field.

Landis's final surrender on the farm system issue took place in December 1940. It proved not to be unconditional, as the magnates extended him the consolation prize of remaining commissioner for five more years. The end of the new term coincided with the January 12, 1946, expiration of the National Agreement, which effectively denied Landis any fresh opportunity to assault farm-friendly provisions by outlasting them. The commissioner acceded to the right of the majors to erect or add farms, and to the right of any associated clubs in a chain not only to recommend but to sign players for one another. Landis even lost the right to require reporting of such transactions to him. Owners justified removing the judge from the reporting loop on the grounds of reducing paperwork. In truth, they feared that the commissioner might use a continued notification right to construe any failure to report as justification for renewed personal intervention and harassment.[49]

Although Organized Baseball's player-employees would not have entirely shared the assessment, by the end of the Depression decade the major league magnates claimed to spot the dawn of a brighter new day. More than ever before they controlled the industry's franchises and labor force at all levels. They signaled their growing confidence in the prospects for recovery, and their ability to contain any escalation in labor cost in the process, by raising their active rosters for the first time in eight years to twenty-five men in 1939 and restoring the statistical subtraction of at-bats for sacrifice flies. In the same year, minor league attendance broke old records with 18.5 million fans, and in 1940 the number of minor leagues jumped to forty-four. Major league gate attendance, only 6.3 million seven years earlier, now crossed the 10 million mark. Sales of radio broadcast rights, virtually nonexistent at the start of the Depression decade, now generated over 7 percent of major league club revenues. Night ball, viewed at first as the province of the Negro Leagues' "carnival act" and rejected by the magnates until 1935, now involved seventy big league games and twelve of sixteen big league parks.[50]

The barons of major league baseball had not only ridden out the hard times; they had used them to fundamentally restructure their labor market and their industry. They had seen their franchises plummet in value only to create more extensive and valuable vertically integrated networks. But just as they prepared to savor the fruits of their trials and their triumph, the storm clouds of war began gathering with greater and greater intensity. The magnates would discover all too quickly on the heels of constructing their farm empires that their fresh handiwork was about to be shaken to its very foundations. War and its aftermath would force a new round of choices upon them—choices that they had long dismissed as dangerously radical and which they thought had been rendered irrelevant by their decisions of the 1930s. War and social revolution lay just ahead for the baseball industry and for its captive labor force.

CHAPTER 3 : WAR AND REVOLUTION

1941–1949

By 1940 the growing specter of war had already begun to threaten a baseball industry only starting to recover from its Depression doldrums. As Nazi triumphs on the European continent left England alone to face a likely invasion, the U.S. government belatedly took steps to mobilize the nation's manpower, including mandating one year of military training for all adult males. Echoing the magnates' wishes, Joe Williams of the *New York World-Telegram* unsuccessfully urged the government to grant big league players an in-season leave of absence from such dictates. But far more disruptive orders lay ahead. Following the enactment of Selective Service and the start of registration of the nation's 16 million men ages twenty-one to thirty-eight, draft numbers were drawn in the fall of 1940, followed by a second round in early 1941 and a third that spring. Among big league stars, Bob Feller and Joe DiMaggio lucked out by drawing high draft numbers. Hank Greenberg, a bachelor unprotected by the initial exemptions for husbands and fathers, was less fortunate. Declared 1-A for service despite flat feet, the Detroit slugger traded his baseball uniform and $55,000 salary for fatigues and $21 a month on May 7, 1941.[1]

Major league executives and owners wished to convey an image of patriotic cooperation with national military priorities. Branch Rickey prescribed vitamin B-1 tablets for his charges in a show of making them more fit for their army physicals. In truth each major league club retained its own officer specifically charged with keeping players out of the draft. Washington's Clark Griffith, an acquaintance of President Franklin Roosevelt's since World War I, sought additional assurances that not more than one or two major leaguers would be drafted per club, and none if teams agreed to drill under supervision of military personnel. Similarly, Dodgers' president Larry MacPhail urged no player call-ups until October 1, and then for but a one-year duration. Although national officials refused to give such assurances, local draft boards in 1941 often demonstrated sympathy for club pleas for temporary deferments until the end of the season or were overruled at higher levels when they did not. In the summer of 1941 an entire local board and its medical examiner resigned in protest at the exemption of minor league infielder Irv Dickens for varicose veins. During the 1941 season only four major leaguers were called up, with Greenberg by far the most famous draftee.[2]

Baseball's relatively free ride abruptly ended on December 7, 1941. In the aftermath of the Pearl Harbor disaster, some men did not even wait to be called. Bob Feller set aside his 3-C deferment as his family's sole support and enrolled in the navy. Hank Greenberg, though eligible for release on December 5 under a provision that had limited the period of service by older draftees to 180 days, quickly reenlisted. With full U.S. participation in World War II now a fact, the major league owners agonized about whether they would have enough men to play a big league schedule, or whether the government would even allow the 1942 season to go forward. The fact that Commissioner Landis, a staunch Republican and enemy of the New Deal, remained about as welcome at the Roosevelt White House as the Japanese ambassador only added to the magnates' concern. FDR partially eased their fears with his famous "green light" letter of January 15, 1942, which permitted professional baseball to continue. At the same time, the government refused to exempt major or minor league players from the draft. In short, professional baseball could continue, but with no guarantee of a large enough or skilled enough playing force. By the start of the 1942 season the number of big leaguers in military uniform stood at 61, or more than 1 in 7, and 100 rookies, including Johnny Pesky, Allie Reynolds, and Stan Musial, cracked big league rosters. The following October, War Manpower Commissioner Paul McNutt reconfirmed that ballplayers were not considered workers in "essential occupations" meriting exemption from the draft."[3]

By 1943 the flow of professional baseball players into the military services turned into a flood. In anticipation of the manpower drain, the owners delayed their annual draft of minor leaguers until after the fall round of military call-ups rather than pick players only to lose them to Uncle Sam. Early in the year Commissioner McNutt signaled higher enlistments by warning that any player who left an off-season "essential occupation" job to report for spring training exposed himself to military selection. Players also continued to volunteer. Boston outfielder Dom DiMaggio, despite a 4-F rating for poor eyesight, signed up, followed by Ted Williams and Johnny Pesky. Departures of New York Yankee personnel for military service affecting the 1943 season included Joe DiMaggio and Tommy Henrich (an end-of-August 1942 call-up). By 1943 some 219 major leaguers stood in military uniform. Accordingly Branch Rickey issued a 600-word combination of defense of baseball's war contribution and complaint that ballplayers did not enjoy the same exemptions as entertainers Bob Hope and Jack Benny. Rickey's frustration stemmed in part from the fact that his organization had lost not only its share of major leaguers but also 265 minor leaguers. St. Louis placed advertisements in the *Sporting News* for replacement tryouts and wrote to 20,000 high school coaches to drum up talent. Because of the player drain, the number of minor leagues in Organized Baseball fell to nine in 1943, compared with forty-one only two years earlier.[4]

By 1944 over 60 percent of the major leagues' 1941 starters were in military service, and the total of ex–big leaguers fighting for Uncle Sam had climbed to 470. At the 1944 All-Star Game, scribes noted that 30 past All-Stars from the 1942 or 1943 tilts were unavailable due to military commitments. On the Brooklyn Dodgers, only Dixie Walker and Mickey Owen remained from a 1941 NL championship roster. More and more, professional baseball's playing ranks consisted of 4-F, underage, and overage talent or—in the case of the Washington Senators—draft-exempt Cubans. Within the ranks of the U.S.-born majority, the surge in the numbers of Southern and Eastern European descendants continued in the war years (see Appendix, Fig. 4). The share of big league rookies of such heritage jumped from 1 in 5 in 1940 to just under 30 percent by 1944, and by 1945 it still stood at about 1 in 4. While players of Polish, Hungarian, Italian, and similar ancestry grew in number, the largest declines among rookies came from "non-Irish" descendants of the British Isles. Perhaps owing to higher rates of voluntary military enlistment early in the war, "British" stock slid as a share of entry-level big leaguers from nearly 35 percent in 1940 to a wartime low of 23 percent in 1944, but it rebounded to 30 percent in the final year of the conflict. While the "Germanic" cohort of big league newcomers remained steady at just under a quarter of the total, the percentage of ethnic Irish extraction climbed from 1 in 10 in 1940 to 1 in 6 by 1943, then fell along with that of Southern and Eastern Europeans by the end of the war.[5]

As for the skill level of the men retained as professional ballplayers, broadcaster Red Barber described the scene as "a matter of playing anyone who was breathing." The clubs had little choice, for by the spring of 1945 fully 509 players from major league reserve lists and active rosters had gone to war. The minors had been hit harder still, losing a whopping 3,576 men to Uncle Sam while maintaining a shrunken work force of 1,188. The youngest major league replacement was Joe Nuxhall, who briefly appeared in 1944 at the age of 15 years, 10 months, and 11 days. More frequent was baseball's "drafting" of "senior citizens." Pepper Martin returned to the playing ranks at age forty after three years as a minor league manager, and three different clubs recycled Jimmy Foxx. A related effect was the temporary reversal of an upward trend in the level of education among ballplayers. From 1940 to 1945, according to baseball librarian Lee Allen, the percentage of major league rookies who claimed some college attendance fell by 6 percent, and the share of those who never advanced beyond high school rose by a similar percentage. As for the men classified 4-F and deemed unfit for military service, their average number per major league roster climbed to 10 by 1944. By 1945, 135 4-F's occupied roster spots in the National League and 125 in the American League, or 16 per squad.[6]

A jump in the number of Cubans also drew special notice during the war (see Appendix, Fig. 4). With the help of scout Joe Cambria, Washington owner Griffith plucked talent from the island and posted bond to counter the fears of the Justice Department that the immigrants might become "public charges." By spring training of 1944, aided by the desire of Cuban players to escape their own country's military draft, the Senators had imported eighteen men, including Gil Torres, Alejandro Carrasquel, and Bobby Estalella. Griffith's best-laid plans were nearly derailed by a Selective Service directive on April 10, 1945, requiring the Cubans to register for the draft within ten days or lose their visa status. The next month, the government extended the Cubans' visas from three to six months, only to reiterate on July 13 the demand of draft registration or deportation.[7]

By the start of 1945, war news was steadily brightening, and baseball executives prayed for a rapid conclusion to the war. But as the end of the conflict came in sight, additional government manpower directives to hasten final victory threatened to deplete the playing ranks even more drastically. On December 9, 1944, Director of War Mobilization and Reconstruction James Byrnes ordered the reevaluation of men classified 4-F to see if they could be ordered into noncombat positions or war-industry jobs. FBI director J. Edgar Hoover defended baseball by asserting there had been "few if any" cases of ballplayer shirking. Nonetheless, Senator William Langer of North Dakota introduced legislation requiring that at least 10 percent of players on big league rosters actually be amputees. Fortunately for the magnates the Langer bill did not pass the Senate, nor did a more serious national service proposal that included an ironclad "work or fight" order. Under pressure from congressmen sympathetic to Organized Baseball, including Representative Melvin Price of Illinois and U.S. Senator Happy Chandler of Kentucky, the War Department reversed Byrnes's order and suspended the 4-F reevaluation directive on V-E Day.[8]

The war exacted a heavy toll on Organized Baseball's gate. Major league attendance, which had struggled back to 18.5 million in 1939, fell to under 8 million in 1943 and only rebounded to 11 million by 1945 as veterans slowly returned to the ballfields. The minors had been more severely damaged, containing only 12 circuits in 1945 compared with 44 six seasons earlier. But in the last year of the war, the majors did manage a profit of $1.2 million despite the incomplete recovery in attendance. The main reason for the profit was the continuing freeze on professional baseball salaries in accordance with wartime wage controls begun in September 1942. As interpreted by the Treasury Department, without "special permission" from the government, no individual player's pay could rise above that of the highest-paid performer on his club as of 1942. Because of federal wage and price controls, average major league salaries remained effectively frozen at the 1942 level of $6,400 for the duration of the conflict (see Appendix, Fig. 2). Major league player payrolls, a cumulative $3.65 million in 1939, had contracted to $3.21 million by 1943, and the average individual salary was down by an average of $900. Minor league salaries remained stable over the same interval, with entry-level pay at Class D around $60 a month. But given the rise in prices from 1939 until the imposition of the federal controls in late 1942, minor league salaries had in fact endured a "real" cut of 30 percent since the 1930s.[9]

Even before the effective implementation of wage controls, owners had exploited patriotic arguments and fears for job security to browbeat their players into lower contracts. Once wage controls went into effect, management used them as justification to avoid rewarding individual players for stellar accomplishments. Stan Musial's pay at the start of his Rookie of the Year season of 1942 was only $4,250. Despite his on-field heroics that campaign, he garnered but a $1,000 raise the next year. Teammates Mort and Walker Cooper had their pay frozen at $12,000 for the duration of the war, only to see the Cardinals sell them at the end of the conflict in separate transactions for a combined $235,000 and another player. Shortstop Marty Marion, 1944 World Series MVP and management favorite, topped the team's payroll list but still only drew a 1945 salary of $15,000.[10]

In the minors, despite gate disasters and massive player shortages, clubs had generally maintained salary scales and rosters at immediate prewar levels. Payroll economizing on the farms had come in the form of dramatically fewer leagues and aggregate playing slots. For those clubs that survived the tumbling gate receipts, their payrolls as a slice of revenue doubled from 7.5 to over 15 percent. But in 1943 players only earned averages ranging from $1,530 at Class AA to $500 at Class D. While wartime major league pay remained at 85 percent of 1929 levels, and AA income stayed at 95 percent, pay at A, B, C, and D levels fell to only 67 percent, 52 percent, 51 percent, and 61 percent, respectively, of pre-Depression marks. Perhaps the most discouraging for men who managed to hold on to playing positions in professional baseball, federal wage controls, combined with the ballplayer's inability to increase his earnings by working more hours, meant a decline in relative economic status. While players' pay and hours remained frozen or worse, war had helped boost the average civilian employee's pay to nearly $2,000, compared to $1,269 at the beginning of the conflict. As a result, by the end of World War II, the average player in every level of the minor leagues, even the top circuits, no longer earned as much as the average American worker.[11]

While the minor leagues atrophied, the majors survived—in no small measure by cannibalizing their farms' remaining talent. Because of this and other temporary stratagems to fill playing rosters, the majors largely refused to take steps to find nontraditional sources of talent—with Washington's recruitment of Cubans the exception. Instead the magnates tolerated the existence of separate teams and circuits for women and blacks, rather than destroying them and then absorbing their talent—especially since, by sharing in their ownership or by garnering rental fees for providing facilities, they could profit from whatever success the segregated leagues generated.

In women's professional baseball, the Cubs' Phil Wrigley even acted as sponsor to the All-American Girls Professional Baseball League. Wrigley envisioned a female circuit as a gate attraction that would utilize minor league facilities and provide fresh income as midwestern minor league male circuits collapsed. Formed in 1943, the women's professional league sponsored four clubs in the modest-sized cities of Battle Creek, South Bend, Kenosha, and Rockford. For playing talent the circuit drew upon the nation's 40,000 women's softball teams. Despite the impressive skill level of its players, the league still marketed itself as a feminine sideshow complete with skirted uniforms and satin underpants, required player attendance at charm schools, and issued fines up to $50 on performers who appeared "unkempt" in public. Despite—or because of—its carnival aspects, the circuit drew a respectable 176,000 fans in its inaugural 108-game season.[12]

In the new women's league the circuit as a whole, rather than individual clubs, issued contracts to its players after they had won places via regional tryouts in the United States and Canada. Although no formal reserve clause appeared in contracts, the league did not permit players' free agency. Pay ranged from $55 to $150 a week plus expenses for most performers, while a few stars earned more—notably placing the female ballplayers at a salary level higher than that of most male minor league counterparts. Most of the circuit's players were young, with ages ranging from fourteen to twenty-eight. All were white. The league initially hired most of its managers, including Jimmy Foxx, and two of its four umpires from the ranks of Organized Baseball. Illustrating the short-term nature of his motives in creating the circuit, by the end of 1944 Wrigley handed over control to advertising director Arthur Meyerhoff. But rather than die off, the circuit continued to grow for another four years, reaching peaks of ten teams and nearly a million fans by 1948.[13]

As for the Negro Leagues, Organized Baseball remained content with collecting the stadium revenues generated by "blackball" rather than pursuing "riskier" strategies, such as trade war against or assimilation of black players and clubs. Consequently, while the quality of white baseball suffered during wartime, African American circuits thrived. The success at the gate enjoyed by black clubs, and their ability to sustain a high quality of play while that of white baseball suffered, eroded even further the myth of Negro inferiority. During wartime the highest black circuits retained some 200 players, or about half the total of the white majors. Lesser leagues employed about double that number. Collectively the Negro Leagues generated $2 million a year during World War II. By 1943 all but one team in the Negro American and National Leagues earned yearly profits of at least $5,000, and three clubs made over $15,000. The revived East-West All Star Game drew a crowd of nearly 52,000, and the 1944 attendance of 46,247 dwarfed the 29,589 figure recorded at the white majors' All-Star tilt.[14]

Life remained hard for Negro League players. Despite their improved economic picture, clubs showed only modest profit margins, and owners scheduled games for every available in-season date and as many as three games per club on Sundays. Black ballplayers still did not earn enough to enjoy an off-season of leisure; instead they played year-round by performing in winter ball circuits or barnstorming squads in California, Florida, and Latin America. Although the Negro Leagues utilized a smaller infrastructure of clubs and circuits and therefore were less vulnerable to devastating implosion from military call-ups, wartime personnel losses and government regulations such as temporary bans on bus transportation hampered the Negro circuits. Some of the leagues that had retained eighteen players per squad at the outset of the war had shrunk to but nine-man units by 1944. Other players avoiding military draft or searching for higher pay contracted "Mexican fever" and headed to Jorge Pasquel's Mexican League. The foreign magnate lured away, among others, Josh Gibson, Willie Wells, Buck Leonard, and Ray Dandridge. When Quincy Trouppe and Theolic Smith were denied draft exemptions by the U.S. government, Pasquel even used his official connections to arrange a "loan" of 80,000 temporary workers from his country to the United States in exchange for securing the duo's playing services. In July 1943 Mexican consul A. J. Guina appeared in Forbes Field intending to lure players Gibson, Leonard, Howard Easterling, and Sam Bankhead also to Pasquel. A physical altercation with numbers-runner and Homestead Grays' sponsor "Sonnyman" Jackson ensued. With post-scuffle bravado Jackson loudly proclaimed, "I don't care if they send Pancho Villa, they're not going to get my ballplayers."[15]

The gate strength demonstrated by the Negro majors, the reduced supply of black playing talent because of military enlistment, and the Mexican League's bidding all pushed up the price of African American stars in wartime. Given Negro Leagues owners' acquaintanceship with the concept of unreported income in their other enterprises, black stars' opportunities to leverage their services for higher pay, including under-the-table money, arguably exceeded that of their white counterparts. As early as 1942 Satchel Paige's reported income of $37,000 made him the second-highest-paid ballplayer in America, trailing only Hank Greenberg. Buck Leonard, who earned only $500 a month and 75 cents a day for eating expenses in 1941, parlayed intensified bidding for his services into a 100 percent increase the following season. Although federal wage and price controls curbed the jumps in "official" salaries after 1942, during World War II pay in the top black circuits still doubled from its 1930s levels to $400 or $500 a month. Stars garnered more than twice that much. Exhibition tilts against white major leaguers generated Negro performers an additional $100 to $500, and games against PCL white teams produced an extra $30 to $60 a tilt.[16]

The increased leverage of black ballplayers in wartime also forced owners to make concessions on the stipends they paid for All-Star Game appearances. Throughout the war years, the classic provided participants an average of $100 to $200 additional money. At the 1942 contest, West squad performers protested the lesser shares offered to them and threatened to boycott the game. In the resulting ultimatum, owners coughed up an additional $50, plus expenses. Above his teammates' demands, Satchel Paige insisted on payment of a gate share rather than a flat fee, and he, too, was bought off. The next year a similar boycott threat by Paige resulted in $800 for three innings' work, which in turn provoked his East-squad opponents to protest they had been shortchanged. Their strike threat garnered additional $200 payments apiece. In 1944 yet another bluff by Paige backfired, and he was banned from that year's contest. But in 1945 the West team won a demand for $100 shares after renewed hints of strike. In leveraging up their perks, not only did the All-Stars benefit, but gains filtered down to lesser-known compatriots. Managers and coaches selected for the game drew an extra $300, and each member club in the two circuits received $300 to divide among its non-All-Stars.[17]

Organized Baseball's white clubs benefited from the separate Negro Leagues through park rentals, concessions, and parking fees. The New York Yankees organization earned $100,000 a year from "blackball" proceeds at Yankee Stadium and at its minor league facilities in Newark, Kansas City, and Norfolk. But the magnates still denied their black tenants the use of clubhouse lockers and showers, forcing them to lodge

Leroy "Satchel" Paige
(National Baseball Hall of Fame Library, Cooperstown, N.Y.)

and dress for games at fleabag hotels or black YMCAS. However, the war against Hitler's exterminationist racism helped intensify pressure to open baseball's doors to men of color. Advocates of integration employed the new slogan, "If he's good enough for the Navy, he's good enough for the majors." In St. Louis the Cardinals and the Browns became the last major league teams to eliminate segregated seating at home games. In the nation's capital, Senators' owner Griffith conspicuously invited Josh Gibson and Buck Leonard to his office for a chat, but no offers of a tryout or a playing contract followed.[18]

Tired of official excuses from executives, supporters of the desegregation of baseball formed a pressure group called the Citizens Committee to Get Negroes Into the Big Leagues. They pointed to the support for integration even from the Negro Leagues' Effa Manley, whose Newark club was located in the home city of the Yankees' top farm team, making it a likely casualty of desegregation. When manager Leo Durocher stated in 1942 that, absent owner prohibitions, he would use black players, Commissioner Landis found it necessary, given changing wartime sensibilities, to lie about the existence of an official policy of exclusion in baseball. "Negroes," he claimed, "are not barred from Organized Baseball by the Commissioner and never have been," nor had the owners "to his knowledge" adopted their own ban. If Durocher wished to sign "one, or twenty-five" Negroes, he could. National League president Ford Frick even insisted disingenuously that he would "welcome" a black player.[19]

Although the intent of their comments was to deflect public pressure to desegregate, Landis and Frick unintentionally had thrown down the gauntlet to the champions of integration to test baseball's sincerity. The effect was to prompt big league organizations in turn to go through a charade of scouting and tryouts of black players, only to reject them on the dubious grounds that they simply did not measure up to white standards. In August 1942 Pittsburgh owner William Benswanger, having previously noted his city's black talent, agreed to allow a secret tryout for three players only to renege when the communist *Daily Worker* published the prospects' names. Negro League pitcher Nate Moreland and infielder Jackie Robinson similarly negotiated a workout from the Chicago White Sox in Pasadena, California, but despite manager Jimmy Dykes's acknowledgment of their ability, the club dismissed them without a second thought. In September catcher Roy Campanella, who lived only fifteen blocks from Shibe Park, received a favorable recommendation from Phillies scout Jocko Collins. Philadelphia owner Gerry Nugent, however, effectively scuttled a signing by indicating that the prospect would have to report to Philadelphia's C-level farm in the segregated Georgia-Florida League. Entrepreneur Eddie Gottlieb, a prominent promoter of Negro professional baseball and basketball, persuaded Jewish businessmen Ike and Leon Levy to seek the purchase of the Phillies with the aim of signing black stars, only to be thwarted by Ford Frick. In late 1942 Bill Veeck informally approached Nugent with apparently similar aims, but his efforts were nipped in the bud when Nugent instead accepted a more substantial offer from lumber dealer William Cox.[20]

With each year of the war against Hitler's Germany, pressure at home mounted on the magnates to give more than lip service to racial reform. When Clarence Rowland, president of the PCL Los Angeles Angels, first offered and then withdrew tryout invitations to Chet Brewer, Howard Easterling, and Nate Moreland, the county's Board of Supervisors and the United Auto Workers local blasted the reversal, and pickets appeared outside the team's park. In Oakland, Oaks owner Vince Devincenzi responded to similar criticism from his hometown paper, the *Tribune,* by "ordering" his manager to give Brewer and Olin Dial tryouts only to allow him to defy the edict without consequence. That same season William Benswanger, under intensifying pressure from the African American *Pittsburgh Courier,* offered Roy Campanella a tryout with so many stipulations that it did not represent a serious offer. The Pirates owner then compounded the slight by scuttling a rescheduled workout. In December representatives of the Negro Newspaper Publishers Association, accompanied by black entertainer and activist Paul Robeson, demanded access to Organized Baseball's annual joint ownership meetings, where they presented a plan for the gradual integration of the minors and promotions to the majors. Once more, the magnates refused to respond. The commissioner again obfuscated the issue with the public fiction that each club was "entirely free" to follow its own hiring practices. By saying so, however, he had once more opened the door to anyone truly independent enough to take him at his word.[21]

A year later, circumstances conspired to increase the odds that someone would break ranks and make a serious contract offer to a black prospect. Landis's death in the fall of 1944 removed the industry's most prominent opponent of racial change. In Boston, city councilman Isadore Muchnick, responding to Red Sox claims that the club had never been asked for a tryout by a black player, threatened to revoke local ordinances permitting Sunday baseball unless the team scheduled one. *Pittsburgh Courier* sportswriter Wendell Smith then selected three candidates, including recent military dischargee Jackie Robinson. After several days of stalling, the Red Sox held the belated tryout on April 16, 1945; but manager Joe Cronin refused to attend, and the club never contacted the players again. From Chicago, *Defender* sportswriter Sam Lacy had already written each major league owner in March to urge the appointment of an integration study committee. Leslie O'Connor invited Lacy to present a formal proposal to the magnates at their April 25, 1945, gathering.[22]

Nowhere, however, had the pressure for integration built up more intensely than in New York. The state legislature had enacted the Ives-Quinn statute barring racial discrimination in employment effective July 1, 1945. Under the new law a five-member commission would have the authority to receive discrimination complaints and pursue redress. In early April, under pressure from Joe Bostic of the *People's Voice,* Branch Rickey had granted a tryout for two aging Negro League veterans. Ten other, younger candidates had declined, fearing racial reprisals, and Rickey had left the Brooklyn workout unimpressed. On May 1, black Manhattan city councilman Benjamin Davis turned up the heat on all the New York clubs by demanding a formal investigation of their racial practices. Facing more inquiries and official pressure from both state and local levels in New York, the majors responded by first agreeing to Lacy's racial study commission and then appointing the Yankees' MacPhail and the Dodgers' Rickey to the panel, along with Lacy and Philadelphia judge Joseph H. Rainey. In August, New York City mayor Fiorello La Guardia, who had appointed his own municipal antidiscrimination Committee on Unity, added a baseball subcommittee, with MacPhail and Rickey once more named as members.[23]

The major leagues' Committee on Baseball Integration proved to be one more example of management stonewalling. According to Lacy, the group never even held a formal meeting because "MacPhail always had some excuse." But defense of the status quo in the form of a rigid segregationist in the commissioner's chair had gone, although the obstructionists of Organized Baseball did not yet realize it. Back in April, the owners had concluded their search for Landis's replacement by selecting Senator Happy Chandler, although his formal term would not begin until January 1, 1946. Ironically, Chandler's candidacy had been championed by the anti-integration MacPhail, who believed that the senator's effective promotion of baseball's interests in Congress during the war boded well for his capacity to protect the industry from postwar governmental assaults. One such thrust, the Yankee magnate knew, would be on racial integration, and he privately counseled the commissioner-designate to use his political wiles to thwart it. While MacPhail and Chandler's other owner employers also clearly wanted a new leader who would not be a Landis-style taskmaster, just as significant to them, as

Chandler recognized, was the fact that "I was a Southerner, and they thought I'd be all right on the nigger thing."[24]

As the integration issue swirled, the end of the war brought a different kind of labor crisis to Organized Baseball, one for which neither the new commissioner nor the magnates were prepared. After the 1945 season, player contract conflicts with management sharply escalated. Returning veterans expected to resume their interrupted ballplaying careers and believed that, as matters of both patriotic reward and law, owners were obligated to reinstate them. However, the replacement players who had filled their shoes during wartime did not expect to be thanked for services rendered by being summarily released. Under the new GI Bill of Rights, a returning serviceman was entitled to his old job in civilian life for at least one year at his prewar salary "if still qualified" for it. But did this mean *minimally* qualified, or *better* qualified than all others vying for the position? And could baseball promise jobs to all or even most of the estimated 1,000 former major leaguers and 3,000 ex–minor leaguers now demobilizing without triggering a surge of legal grievances from the wartime fill-ins?[25]

Complicating baseball's hopes for a smooth labor reconversion was the fact that wartime had seen the proliferation of government structures of mediation, arbitration, and labor conflict resolution under the National War Labor Board. In many other private industries the government had presided over the establishment of formal, bilateral labor-management mechanisms, while allowing each side to preserve its ultimate hammers of strike or lockout. But for the baseball industry, long used to management's unilateral dictation of employment terms to its workers, any spillover of such wartime procedural machinery that conveyed coequal status for labor fundamentally threatened its monopsony. And the fact that so many other industries had grudgingly accepted a new order in labor relations in the previous decade meant that more and more postwar American workers, including ballplayers, were likely to be aware of and demand greater individual and collective labor rights. In one wartime sign of this growing ballplayer "labor consciousness," in late July 1943, Philadelphia Phillies players had responded to the firing of their manager Bucky Harris by briefly launching a wildcat strike.[26]

Not only were the owners determined to resist any outside initiatives for dealing with their postwar labor grievances; they also denied their new commissioner any similar role as a labor mediator or arbitrator. Having endured the irritating, even when ineffectual, intrusions of Landis for nearly a quarter of a century on matters large and small, they were determined to avoid any prospect of meddling by the new leader. Accordingly, one condition of Chandler's selection was the deliberate narrowing of his powers under Major League Rule 22(b), which stipulated that "negotiations between player and club regarding the player's compensation under his contract shall not be referable to the Commissioner." The owners had no intention of delegating any appeals authority to anyone, not even to a commissioner they personally had hired and presumably controlled.[27]

With the owners only willing to address players' contract complaints in traditional, piecemeal fashion, one more reality of the postwar labor environment also foreshadowed confrontations between players and management. Whether wartime holdovers or returning GIs, players in general—like their fellow Americans in the first postwar winter of 1945–46—expected to be rewarded for years of patriotic restraint with substantial wage increases. At the same time, the costs of industry reconstruction in baseball, as in other businesses, and the desire of owners to use whatever immediate gate and revenue surges they received to restore their damaged profit margins and farm systems, made clubs unlikely to surrender higher pay voluntarily. The need for economic gratification by both sides, delayed and intensified by the war, now threatened to explode into confrontation, and the government's clumsy removal of wage and price controls only added to the economic confusion and inflationary pressures. As a consequence, in 1946 strikes and lockouts paralyzed 270 companies of 1,000 or more workers and cost the national economy some 25 million workdays.[28]

Faced with the requirements of the GI Bill, the owners drew up guidelines for the hiring and release of returning ballplayers for 1946. Returnees were entitled to only a thirty-day spring training trial or a fifteen-day in-season evaluation, at pay equal to or above their old salaries. At the end of the review period, the club unilaterally retained the power to keep the player, demote him, or issue him his unconditional release. If the club sent him down, he nonetheless remained eligible for his prewar pay for one year, with the parent club paying the difference between the minor league pay level and the man's previous salary. If released outright, however, the player could only claim the evaluation period pay and a "thank you" letter. Of the approximately 1,000 returning big league veterans, only about 300 regained their old jobs. Clubs seeking to rebuild and restock their extensive farm systems, such as the Yankees and the Dodgers, tried out as many as 600 to 650 men each. But even with the re-expanded personnel needs of restored farms, owners all too often considered an older veteran's outright release economically preferable to his retention in the minors at major league pay. The *Sporting News* later estimated that in retaliation more than 140 ex–major leaguers and 900 minor league veterans filed complaints demanding additional compensation on grounds that they had been illegally released or demoted in violation of the GI Bill.[29]

Although management won its share of the cases, the deluge of lawsuits nudged the owners to temporarily expand major league active rosters in 1946 to thirty. But even for those players, whether returnees or incumbents, who successfully fought to hold on to major league employment, their level of resentment had reached fever pitch that spring. Convinced that baseball owed them for their past sacrifices, veteran major leaguers resented renewed signs that owners were prepared to spend far more on unproven talent than on them. At the new commissioner's urging, in one example, in early February the magnates dropped a motion that would have prohibited the outright payment of large bonuses to amateur signees. Instead, a watered-down substitute provision required that such signees receiving bonuses in excess of $6,000 would have to be promoted to the majors no later than the start of the next season or else be subject to selection by other organizations. The new restriction barely slowed the "bonus baby" phenomenon, and veterans subject to the resumed cutthroat competition for positions and facing the risk of outright release bitterly protested contract offers they received that stood well below the money being thrown at the untested.[30]

Players infuriated at management's lack of loyalty to them discovered fresh means of retaliation in the spring of 1946: the bargaining leverage and jumping opportunities provided by trade war. A year earlier, PCL president Clarence Rowland had petitioned fellow minor league executives to back his circuit's demand for major league status. When the big league magnates rejected him, he renewed the call in 1946 and threatened economic war if the majors did not grant his circuit major concessions. As a consolation prize, Rowland's league and individual teams within it won the right to compensation if in future a big league club relocated into a PCL city, but the majors rejected his demand for a 1920s-style exemption from the majors' player draft. Commissioner Chandler and a special owners' committee also toured the league's West Coast cities only to conclude that Los Angeles and San Francisco were the lone PCL cities ready for big league status.[31]

As the PCL challenge fizzled, the majors' real trade war danger in 1946 rose up from south of the border. The Mexican League's sudden and dramatic raids on major league talent should not have caught the owners by surprise, for Jorge Pasquel and his minions had been courting Negro League stars for several years. But Pasquel now found unusually good hunting from the ranks of veterans considering themselves shabbily treated by the magnates. Although all clubs discovered players being courted that spring by the Mexican mogul's agents, the squads most affected were the New York Giants, whose players especially demanded the return of big-market peacetime salaries, and the notoriously miserly while successful St. Louis Cardinals. Eighteen major leaguers, including Lou Klein, Max Lanier, Sal Maglie, and Mickey Owen, accepted the Mexican League's overtures. Others parlayed the rival circuit's offers into better deals at home. Lanier, a seventeen-game winner with St. Louis in 1945, jumped to Pasquel for $25,000 a year for five years after rejecting a Cardinals bid of only $500 over his previous $15,000 pay. The Giants' Maglie, recipient of an $18,000 offer from the Mexicans, served as a go-between with other disgruntled players. Tom Gorman, a Maglie teammate and later an outstanding major league umpire, recalled Pasquel literally laying out $20,000 in bills in front of him on a hotel-room desk.[32]

By the time Pasquel's raids on Organized Baseball talent peaked in the summer of 1946, U.S. refugees made up nearly one-fifth of his circuit's approximately 150 ballplayers. But the haul barely missed being much larger in numbers and in famous jumpers. Stan Musial, contracted for just $13,500 a year by St. Louis for 1946, was approached by Pasquel, and the Mexican magnate produced five certified checks for $10,000 each as an up-front installment on a Mexican League salary. The wealthy magnate promised $125,000 more as a signing bonus if the Cardinal slugger would agree to a five-year deal. Although Musial rejected Pasquel's lucrative overtures, he parlayed the Mexican League's courtship into a one-time additional payment of $5,000 from the Cardinals and the latter's subsequent award of a $31,000 salary for 1947. Phil Rizzuto similarly converted courtship by the rival circuit into a hefty increase from the Yankees, and the Indians' Bob Feller, by rejecting Pasquel's multiyear deal of $500,000, parlayed the refusal into a $50,000 base-pay offer from Cleveland and incentives that pushed his income to more than $70,000.[33]

Player unrest, postwar inflation, and trade war all conspired to push salary levels in U.S. baseball sharply higher in 1946. In the minors, A-level pay rose only 1 percent, but increases elsewhere paralleled the nation's double-digit surge in consumer prices. Given the intensified competition with the Mexican League, major league pay levels especially rocketed (see Appendix, Fig. 2). In an effort to contain the outflow of talent and revenue, Commissioner Chandler threatened immediate suspensions from Organized Baseball and five-year bans on hiring by member leagues for players who contracted with Pasquel. Tempering his justice with mercy in order to encourage similar changes of heart, when St. Louis Browns shortstop Vern Stephens signed with the Mexicans for $25,000 plus a $15,000 bonus but jumped back after only two games, Chandler opted not to punish him. But when Sam Breadon prepared to travel secretly to Mexico to lure his club's deserters back with promises of forgiveness and big pay raises, the commissioner fined him $5,000 and suspended him for thirty days.[34]

In the major leagues of 1946, payrolls jumped by over $2 million to a total of $5.65 million. The average salary soared by nearly $5,000, or over 75 percent, from the preceding year to a level of $11,300. In one season the major league pay average finally leapfrogged a fifteen-year trough created by economic depression, war, and wage control to a new plateau of 150 percent of 1929 levels. Considered in such long-term perspective, the pay levels of 1946 seemed less outrageous, particularly when prices also were 114 percent of 1929 figures. And even with the overall surge, not everyone enjoyed the leverage of outside bidding or was able to translate it into comparable gains. Thirty-one American Leaguers and 11 National Leaguers still made less than $5,000. A year later, big league owners would realize with relief that the salary surge of 1946 had been more than offset by booming revenues as Americans returned to the ballparks after the war. Major league profit margins, already back up to 8 percent in 1945, more than doubled in 1946 to nearly 18 percent.[35] But in the spring and early summer of 1946 the magnates did not yet have those reassuring figures. Nor did they know that the Mexican League challenge would soon collapse as quickly as it had arisen. Instead, the magnates saw themselves besieged by economic pressures of considerable power and unknown duration, and they were not yet sure whether the encouraging early turnstile counts would prove more than just a one-year celebration of peace. The last thing any of them needed or could permit, as they saw it, was the added threat of a player unionization push.

The labor turmoil of the spring of 1946 provided both cover and context for the first serious attempt at player organization in a quarter-century. Players were unsettled, angry, and assertive, and both they and their umpire coworkers had taken note of the growth of labor rights in other industries since the 1930s. When commissioner-elect Chandler had visited an umpires' dressing room in Washington, D.C., in 1945 and had asked, "Is everybody happy?" he had been greeted by a sharp retort from veteran arbiter Ernie Stewart. The umpires' salaries in 1945 still ranged only from $5,000 to $9,000, while World Series employment generated an extra $2,500. A $750 travel and lodging allowance only covered about half of such expenses. Although umpires had gained a modest pension plan, it only applied to those with at least fifteen years of big league service and paid only $100 a year in benefits up to a cumulative limit of $2,400. Chandler naively had responded to Stewart's complaints by suggesting he consult his colleagues about forming a professional association, and the longtime umpire had done so. Furious AL president Will Harridge summarily fired Stewart as a "clubhouse lawyer" and "disturbing element" within the fraternity. Harridge saved more venom for Chandler, pointedly reminding him that the supervision of the umpires was the responsibility of the league presidents and not the commissioner.[36]

In contrast to the umpires' abortive efforts in 1945, the major league players' attempts at organization the next spring did not originate from within but from an interested outsider, labor lawyer Robert Francis Murphy. A labor relations specialist who had worked in both the nation's capital and New York City, Murphy combined formal expertise with a fan's love of sports. A Boston native, he had attended Harvard as an undergraduate and had run track and boxed. After graduation in 1932 he had attended law school at his alma mater for two years and then at Northeastern for two more. He went to Washington, D.C., as an examiner for the National Labor Relations Board (NLRB) created by the New Deal, and in the early 1940s he had opened a labor law practice in New York. Returning to Boston, he had developed an interest in ballplayers' rights through local news accounts of the personal struggles of ex-stars, in particular Jimmy Foxx.[37]

After consulting players secretly during the 1945–46 off-season, the idealistic lawyer, being between jobs, decided to attempt forming a player union. The men he talked to in Boston persuaded him that at least one or more local chapters of a player organization could become beachheads for a full-scale union that would include not only players but also trainers and coaches. On April 17, 1946, Murphy filed the necessary papers in Suffolk County, Massachusetts, to register the American Baseball Guild. At a press conference the next day, he set forth his infant union's agenda. Seeking a "square deal" for its members, the guild called for a $7,500 minimum salary for big league ballplayers, the creation of a formal arbitration system for resolution of contract disputes, the reimbursement to players of 50 percent of the value of their sale prices, the removal of the ten-day release provision, the replacement of the reserve clause with long-term contracts featuring annual renegotiable financial terms, and the creation of new spring training, insurance, and pension benefits.[38]

Both the AFL and its rival, the Congress of Industrial Organizations (CIO), quickly endorsed the new union. But while the reaction from baseball owners was just as swift, it was anything but welcoming. Clark Griffith blasted the guild agenda and specifically labeled any changes to the reserve clause "fatal" to his industry. He even recycled the assertion that any player union would result in imposition of industrywide salary scales and ceilings on individual earnings. Murphy retaliated by filing a charge of unfair labor practices against Griffith with the NLRB's Baltimore regional office. He also called on the NLRB to order a representation election in Washington to determine whether Griffith or the guild constituted the legitimate bargaining agent for the Senators players. But the NLRB refused to take up the complaint, citing doubts about its authority over baseball in view of the industry's antitrust exemption.[39]

Among major league players in general the reaction to the guild was mixed. Murphy attempted to sign up new members as each AL and NL road team passed through Boston. Both the guild and its enemies knew that a key to the union's survival lay in whether the game's stars would commit to and publicly identify themselves with the union. The stars could provide necessary cover for lesser-known players to join, and given their gate power, their allegiance also would be crucial if the guild later chose to strike to force management recognition. But it was also true that in contrast to journeymen, stars had sufficient individual economic leverage, especially that spring of 1946, that could cause them to conclude that a union was unnecessary and even harmful to their interests. Ominously, no big-name players came forth publicly as spokesmen or officers in the guild. Meanwhile, club owners covertly met with small groups of their charges to discern "what it would take" to circumvent further guild enlistments.[40]

Based partly on the failure of his Washington foray, Murphy concluded that the most promising beachhead for a representation election was Pittsburgh. The Steel City claimed a strong prolabor culture, and Pirates players were less likely to encounter grassroots hostility or fan recriminations. Just as important, Pennsylvania had a state labor relations statute and a labor relations agency, providing the guild additional avenues of legal intervention and redress. Finally, a majority of Pirate players, led by infielder Jimmy Purcell and ex-GI and reserve catcher Hank Camelli, backed the union while opponents, such as pitcher Al Lopez, kept a low profile. On May 15 the guild took the necessary first step by notifying Pirates management that an overwhelming majority (estimated at 90 percent) of its players had signed up as members. Accordingly the union demanded that the club enter into discussions to establish collective bargaining issues and negotiating procedures.

After ten days of management stonewalling followed by strike threats, Pirates owner Benswanger agreed to meet Murphy and his subordinates at a June 5 session. There the magnate and his lawyer again tried delaying tactics by urging the union to postpone a representation election and all related matters until after the season. Murphy rejected the gambit, but despite strong player support for an immediate strike to force Benswanger's hand, the guild leader foolishly agreed to a forty-eight-hour delay of the strike vote. His reasoning was that calling an immediate stoppage, given a hometown crowd of 26,000 already gathering for the day's scheduled game, would prove a public relations disaster. By giving his enemies advance notice of the guild's strike intention but delaying implementation two days, however, Murphy gave away any element of surprise and provided Pittsburgh and league management valuable time to work on Pirate players. Commissioner Chandler personally dispatched former FBI agent John "Jack" Demoise to the Steel City to serve as his "eyes and ears" and assist Pirates officials in thwarting the guild.[41]

While Murphy received the plaudits of CIO officials at a local luncheon on June 6, Benswanger quietly assembled a replacement squad for the next day's game and employed cajolery and threats to weaken striker resolve. Scabs included a prospective double-play combination of forty-eight-year-old manager Frankie Frisch and seventy-two-year-old Honus Wagner. When Pirate regulars arrived at their clubhouse on June 7 for

Robert Murphy locked out of Pirates clubhouse, June 7, 1946
(Corbis/Bettmann-UPI)

a two-hour session prior to the strike vote, security men physically pre-vented guild leader Murphy from meeting them. Although he eventually got in as far as the stadium stands by buying a ticket and entering through the turnstiles, Murphy never made it into the locker room. While the union's head languished outside, owner Benswanger personally pleaded his cause at length to the players, seconded by promanagement moles such as pitcher Eddie "Rip" Sewell and infielder Jimmy Brown (the only Pirate earning a salary over $10,000 at the time).[42]

By a 20-16 tally, a majority far short of the required two-thirds, the strike vote failed. A half-hour before game time, Pittsburgh public re-lations director Robert Price emerged from behind the clubhouse door to announce the verdict. Grim-faced regulars took the field. Conflicting sources reported opposing fan reactions, with pitcher Sewell reportedly met by cheers or boos, depending on the account. After the game, Benswanger personally thanked his charges in the clubhouse. Jimmy Brown, however, was beaten up by union sympathizers outside the ballpark as he left. In contrast, Sewell received a gold watch from the commissioner for his services to management. Years later Chandler gave both men as well as his emissary full credit when he boasted to an interviewer, "We used one man from my office, who was a former pitcher for the American Association, and Rip Sewell and Jimmy Brown, and they beat the union."[43]

In retrospect the guild's June 7 defeat in Pittsburgh was a mortal blow. Sobered by the defeat, Boston Braves players reversed their own prior vote to strike to force a representation election; instead they picked a three-man delegation headed by Billy Herman to present their grievances to team management. New York Yankee players responded similarly. The day after the Pittsburgh setback, Murphy charged the Pirates with having organized a company union to break the strike, but the NLRB threw out the complaint. The guild leader had better luck with the state labor relations board, which after several delays granted his renewed demand for a representation election and set an August 21 date. While the guild awaited the Pittsburgh representation vote, however, efforts to force similar balloting within the Boston and New York clubs failed. In Philadelphia, security men followed the example of their intrastate compatriots and denied Murphy access to the Athletics' clubhouse. On August 21 in Pittsburgh, the rescheduled representation vote was set up in a downtown hotel with the balloting set to begin at 10:30 A.M. But no one showed up for over three hours, and by the end of the day only nineteen of thirty-one eligible men had cast ballots. With one of the votes challenged and therefore thrown out, by a 15-3 tally the Pirates rejected the guild as their official bargaining agent. Adding injury to insult, in the aftermath William Benswanger exacted revenge on the union's local ringleaders. Several of its champions, including Hank Camelli, soon received their walking papers.[44]

The crushing defeat of the guild generated no shortage of postmortems. Certainly the unwillingness of stars from the start to throw their weight behind the fledgling union clearly harmed its chances. At key junctures, Murphy had demonstrated tendencies of overconfidence and naïveté and had failed to form an effective group of subordinate officers. Perhaps even more fundamentally damaging was his lack of insider

standing with most players. For his part, Yankee executive Larry Mac-
Phail opined that Murphy had erred by not launching his organizing
attempts in the minors, given their players' longer litany of economic
suffering and unaddressed grievances. But in fairness to the beleaguered
guild leader, the greater vulnerability of minor leaguers to owner intimidation or replacement posed huge obstacles to any such strategy. In fact,
with guild blessing an organizing effort had been launched within the
San Francisco Seals of the PCL, only to fizzle.[45]

Despite its abrupt demise, the guild challenge proved not a total failure. Its threat, however transitory, forced the magnates to extend concessions on player representation and economic benefits if for no other
reason than to undercut future organizing efforts. In the aftermath of
their initial June 7 victory in Pittsburgh, the owners formed a joint steering committee to review the industry's labor crisis and formulate recommendations. The study panel consisted of league presidents Harridge and Frick, AL owners MacPhail and Tom Yawkey, and NL magnates
Breadon and Phil Wrigley, with MacPhail serving as chairman. Even
before the committee completed its report, Chandler acted to undercut
any remaining possibility of a pro-guild vote in the August election by
calling upon each club to send player delegates to the owners' meeting
in late July. The MacPhail group openly acknowledged the role the labor
turmoil of the spring had played in its formation. Its report identified the
guild's "attempts to organize players" as "our most pressing problem,"
and it justified calls for modest concessions as necessary to forestall both
"attempts at unionization" and "raids by outsiders" such as the Mexican
League.[46]

The MacPhail committee announced its intent to draft a new uniform playing contract and promised to secure players' opinions in doing
so. On July 29 the group met with player delegates in New York. The
latter brought a long list of proposals, including the establishment of a
minimum salary at $5,000 to $7,500, revision of the ten-day clause to protect injured men from summary release, $5-per-day allowances for spring
training, a share of player sales prices, elimination of postseason barnstorming bans, the option of pay in either seven- or twelve-month allotments, first-class travel accommodations, locker room and park safety
improvements, an earlier contract-offer deadline, and a pension system.
To the relief of MacPhail, who along with Leslie O'Connor had fretted
privately over the legality of the reserve clause, the players meekly refused to challenge the clause but only asked for minor modifications to

it. Following the player presentations the committee reconvened a week later with a smaller group of three handpicked players from each league and scrutinized the issues raised in greater detail.[47]

On August 27 — only six days after the guild's electoral defeat in Pittsburgh — the owners' advisory committee received and approved the MacPhail panel's report. The forty-page document was as wide ranging as the player delegates' list of grievances, but it reflected only partial acceptance of those proposals. A new executive council consisting of the commissioner, the two league presidents, one owner from each circuit, and one player representative each from the American League and the National League was created. The latter would be chosen by the players' team delegates but would have no voting power and could only attend and present leaguewide grievances at two meetings a year. Each club's player delegate, in turn, could discuss internal team problems with his owner, but at neither club nor leaguewide level did players have the authority to do anything resembling negotiating or voting on proposals. A frustrated Robert Murphy described the system from outside as "the most barefaced attempt to form a company-dominated union that I have ever seen."[48]

The MacPhail report also addressed contract rights, benefits, and scheduling issues of concern to the players. The committee agreed to a thirty-day release clause to replace the old ten-day provision, limited the maximum one-year pay cut to 25 percent, granted $25 a week for spring training expenses (ironically dubbed "Murphy money" by the players) and a $500 moving allowance in the event of trade, established a minimum big league salary of $5,000, and extended the general promise of a pension plan for players, managers, and coaches. The report rejected outright, however, all player calls for arbitration machinery or the right to take salary grievances to the commissioner. Clubs retained the power to regulate their charges' off-season activities, but players were granted permission upon written clearance from the commissioner to participate in exhibition tilts for up to thirty days after the end of each season. In a compromise between traditional practice and player urgings, the owners' date of contract offers was set at February 1. In turn, a management effort by MacPhail's group to expand the playing schedule from 154 to 168 games and eliminate in-season off-days was withdrawn in the face of widespread criticism. Assessing the new benefits and contract rights extended, Robert Murphy maintained that while the players had plucked an "apple" of concessions, "they could have had an orchard."[49]

The promise of greatest interest to the players was the owners' offer to create a pension system. But the details remained to be worked out. With MacPhail and Breadon as owner participants in executive council pension deliberations, a third player attendee, the Cardinals' Marty Marion, contributed his own ideas. During a rain-out in New York, Marion, trainer Harrison "Doc" Weaver, and team captain Terry Moore had roughed out a preliminary proposal in an upstairs room of the team motel. It called for $50- to $100-a-month payouts at age fifty to major league veterans of ten years' service, with fund moneys garnered from World Series and All-Star Game profits, mid-season exhibitions, and if necessary, club and player contributions. Within the executive council's deliberations, Marion's owner Sam Breadon personified a penurious philosophy of "don't spend a dollar if you don't have to," but MacPhail appeared more genuinely convinced of the need for a pension system. Nonetheless, the Yankee owner argued for a delay in payouts until 1956, only to backpedal after complaints. When the owners floated another penny-pinching proposition before the World Series to force series participants into contributing part of their postseason shares to the pension fund, threats of rebellion by the Boston Red Sox required Marty Marion's personal intercession to head off a wildcat strike.[50]

The owners secured final approval of a formal pension plan in February 1947. Those eligible included players, coaches, managers, and trainers still in the major leagues as of April 1, 1947. Those who had completed their big league service prior to that date would receive no benefits. Even for actives, pensions could only be earned after five years of accumulated service and entitled the recipient to a minimum $50 a month, beginning at age fifty, for the rest of his life. Each additional year's service increased the benefit an extra $10 a month up to a maximum monthly stipend of $100. To build up the pension fund, All-Star Game and World Series revenues in 1947 would be supplemented with the commissioner's usual donation to the old aid society fund for indigent ex-players, and owners and players also would make yearly contributions. Players were required to provide $45.45 their first year, $90.90 the next, and so on up to $454.75 in their tenth season, thereby creating a cumulative per-player contribution of $2,500. In subsequent seasons each player would add an extra $250 annually, with employee contributions matched by the owners, bringing the latter's total share of the pay-in costs to about 80 percent. Nonetheless, with the average tenure of a big league ballplayer at less than five years, fewer than 10 percent of big leaguers being ten-year veterans, and payments delayed until 1952, the plan effectively minimized the owners' obligations.[51]

After a tumultuous year, by early 1947 players could claim a pension system, at least on paper; modest minimum salaries and expense payments; and a representation system that permitted them to raise workplace issues sporadically but not negotiate their solution. The new representation structure was a limited advance, with team delegates ostensibly elected by players but in reality often the product of owner preferences and player cynicism and indifference. Those who agreed to serve as team and league player representatives often saw such duties as stepping stones to management positions within their organizations and a nonthreatening means to promote their own economic interests. For the long-term veteran serving as player delegate, job tenure, procedural protections, safety, and pension guarantees—in other words, matters of personal economic security—were far more important issues than abstract labor rights, geographic mobility, or entry-level minimum salaries for rookie teammates. When, as usual, the self-interests of management and veteran players did not fundamentally clash, the new system promised to function in the manner the owners wanted—as a company union which channeled player concerns in deferential fashion and facilitated paternalistic co-optation of the players. But if an owner-imposed policy did happen to provoke the veteran player representatives as a fundamental challenge to their own long-term security, and that of longtime teammates, then the company union the owners had created still could become a vehicle for player defiance instead of deference.

While the series of labor storms passed over baseball in 1946, yet another was quietly building strength. Responding to growing political pressure, Brooklyn's Branch Rickey had discreetly dispatched three scouts—George Sisler, Wid Matthews, and Clyde Sukeforth—to evaluate black ballplayers. Rickey, who had left St. Louis for the Dodgers after the 1942 season, later claimed that his decision to scout and sign African Americans was a simple matter of conscience. "I couldn't face my God much longer," he insisted. He frequently recalled having coached a black player at Ohio Wesleyan who, when denied hotel accommodations in South Bend, had sobbed in frustration and had tried to rub the black pigment from his hands. Without entirely discounting his own pangs of conscience, Rickey's choice was hardly all of his own making. Moreover, his decision was consistent with his history as a man constantly innovating to acquire top talent as cheaply as possible. During World War II, he had observed Clark Griffith's efforts in evaluating Cuban players, only to conclude that African Americans presented a better immediate source of untapped talent and one that posed no language barriers. By early 1945 Rickey had told broadcaster Red Barber that a black ballplayer would soon be coming to Brooklyn. Having identified blacks as the untapped source of first-rate, inexpensive playing talent, he had concluded that they could secure pennants and profits for his long-struggling franchise while also killing off the gate rivalry posed by the Negro Leagues. To acknowledge Rickey's self-interest is not to deny the courage he still needed to take the lead in integrating a team. His own son urged him not to do so on the grounds that it would destroy the Dodgers' scouting operations in the white South. But NL president and, later, commissioner Ford Frick summed up Rickey's eventual choice best as "an answer to his own, and baseball's, shortage-of-manpower problem."[52]

To both cover and justify his pending raids on the Negro Leagues, Rickey had attacked them as "rackets" and had announced in May 1945 his intention to form a rival all-black circuit. In July of that year, after Dr. Dan Dodson, executive director of New York City's Mayor's Committee on Unity, had been denounced by the Yankees' Larry MacPhail as a "do-gooder" for pressuring club executives to integrate, Rickey privately had revealed his true intentions to Dodson. While Dodson had drawn off public attention through the Mayor's Committee on Unity, Rickey's scouts had quietly scrutinized a series of black prospects, including stars Satchel Paige and Josh Gibson, only to reject them on grounds of age or questionable private behavior. Eventually the focus had landed on Jackie Robinson, in spite of concerns about a purported hair-trigger temper, because of his unique blend of athletic ability, education, moral propriety, familiarity with interracial competition, and prime ballplaying age.[53]

Following scout Sukeforth's observation of Robinson at a Negro League contest in Chicago in late August, Rickey had summoned the young star to his office for three hours. After satisfying himself as to the ballplayer's temperamental suitability, Rickey had secretly signed him to the Montreal Royals farm team for 1946 at $600 a month plus a $3,500 bonus. In October, Rickey's scouts also had given tryouts to pitcher Don Newcombe and catcher Roy Campanella, had signed the former, and had secured the latter's pledge not to sign with anyone else before the

Dodgers could do so in the spring. With pressure growing from Mayor La Guardia to announce the signing of a black ballplayer, Rickey had then traveled to Montreal and carried out the public charade of "signing" Robinson on October 23, 1945. When cries of protest had followed from the Negro Leagues, Rickey had defended the legality of his raid by citing the black circuits' lack of binding standard contracts with explicit reserve clauses.[54]

How would Organized Baseball react to the news of Robinson's signing? Among players and managers the response was mixed, with the attitudes of white veterans and southerners the most skeptical. Pitcher Bob Feller, despite many prior exhibition appearances with Negro League players, claimed only Paige and Gibson were genuine major league material. In contrast, Brooklyn manager Leo Durocher interrupted his tour of USO bases in the Pacific to declare the news "really great." Dodger captain Dixie Walker, subsequently voted the NL players' first league representative, responded ominously to Robinson's signing: "As long as he's not with the Dodgers, I'm not worried." During the first half of 1946, as Robinson performed brilliantly for the Royals, the magnates wrestled with their other numerous labor crises. But the MacPhail committee report in August on baseball labor issues did belatedly address what it called "The Negro Question." One section of the report dealt specifically with integration, and led by its chairman, the panel came down squarely against the step.[55]

A close reading of the MacPhail report's section on race reveals that in its authors' minds, the real "race question" was how to deflect growing pressures for integration rather than how to achieve it. The document speculated that black spectatorship spurred by integration would reach a "tipping point" that would then drive away white fans and force down franchise values. It claimed that black ballplayers lacked "technique," "coordination," "competitive attitude," and "discipline" and that the Negro Leagues had failed to provide "real" professional training in on-field skills or off-field conduct. By the time the current black players received remedial instruction in the white minors, assuming they were capable of absorbing it, they would then be too old for major league duty. The report even shed crocodile tears for the fate of the Negro circuits in the event of integration, and it bemoaned the loss of rental and parking revenues from black baseball that would ensue. Demonstrating that most owners' real attitudes about integration of their player forces had not been altered by the war, the clubs voted 15-1 in favor of the Mac-Phail committee's conclusions, with Rickey's Dodgers casting the only dissent.[56]

In reality, the owners' position was unenforceable. If even one organization, such as Brooklyn, decided to sign black players to its farms and then promote them to the majors, it could not be legally stopped, especially in New York. Baseball's officialdom also found itself the prisoner of the earlier pronouncements that had denied existence of a formal exclusion policy and had purported to endorse a team's right to acquire any players it wished. Having projected this lie to deflect wartime integration pressure, Organized Baseball could not prevent a maverick club from going forward with integration if it insisted. As for their new commissioner, Happy Chandler, the hope of MacPhail and other backers that he would act as an effective obstructionist was not panning out. Baseball's new boss already had gone so far as to tell the black press that if Negroes were good enough to fight and die on Pacific beaches, "they can play baseball in America. . . . And when I give my word, you can count on it." NL president Frick found himself similarly cornered by previous public statements that he would "welcome" a Negro player in his circuit. The owners revealed an awareness of the indefensibility of their vote when they ordered the official tally kept secret and tried to gather up all existing copies of the report to prevent its public disclosure.[57]

Undeterred by the MacPhail report, Rickey devised elaborate plans to facilitate Robinson's promotion to the majors in 1947. Not only would the Dodgers play a series of exhibitions in Panama and hold spring training in Cuba rather than Florida, but the organization's four black prospects—Robinson, Newcombe, Campanella, and Ray Partlow—would be housed in a segregated hotel. By the time the club reached Panama, however, an anti-Robinson revolt already was brewing among Dodger players, led by team captain and NL player representative Dixie Walker. Backed by reserve catcher Bobby Bragan, pitchers Ed Head and Hugh Casey, infielder Eddie Stanky, and outfielder Carl Furillo, Walker circulated a petition calling for the removal of the African Americans. Dodger officials learned of the petition when pitcher Kirby Higbe, a southerner with a propensity to drink too much and talk too loudly, let the fact slip to road secretary Harold Parrott, who in turn informed manager Durocher. In a blunt early morning confrontation with his squad, the Brooklyn skipper coarsely described to the cabal what they could do with their petition and declared that Robinson's presence on the team would mean a pennant. With Opening Day but five days away, on April 10 the Dodgers announced that Robinson would be on the 1947 big league roster with a salary of $5,000.[58]

Because many of the anti-Robinson Dodgers were native southerners, their effort to sabotage him usually has been portrayed as a simple racial morality tale. Without denying the strong role bigotry played, however, the participants' motivations were more complex. The anti-Robinson players were veterans, and most were journeymen worried about their own job security and that of others like them. Those who had off-season jobs or businesses in Dixie also fretted over the financial impact of being on a widely publicized team with a black man. Walker admitted later that his action was driven partly by worries about what the implications of becoming a black man's teammate would have on his Alabama hardware and sporting goods businesses. Whether a southerner or, as with Carl Furillo, a "son of immigrants," the tendency to view a black ballplayer as scab labor taking jobs away from whites and depriving them of their hard-won pensions was understandable, if lamentable, in baseball's post-war labor climate. Ironically, whether a Dodger supported or rejected the anti-Robinson petition, he usually based his decision on individual grounds of economic security. Shortstop Pee Wee Reese, for example, a native of Louisville, Kentucky, opted not to sign the petition partly out of fear of being fired for defiance and losing the ability to support his wife and infant child.[59]

When the team returned from spring training, Rickey summoned each known anti-Robinson player for blunt personal conferences. With Furillo, simple bullying worked: either accept Robinson or be out of a job. With Eddie Stanky, the Dodger executive appealed to his loyalty by pointing out his recent pay raise. The two most intractable men proved to be Bragan, who refused to yield and was "kicked upstairs" into a nonplaying organizational job, and Walker. Walker, the popular and influential "People's Choice" in the eyes of fans and fellow players, had avoided the earlier confrontation with Durocher in Panama by leaving prematurely for the United States, citing a family illness. When Walker continued to oppose Robinson and demanded to be traded, Rickey tried to accommodate him through a proposed deal with Pittsburgh for young slugger Ralph Kiner. Unfortunately, the trade fell through, and a May 3 swap shipped out pitcher Kirby Higbe instead.[60]

Unknown to Rickey, his firmness in crushing the Dodgers' anti-integration cabal also helped scuttle a wider player action that had been planned for Opening Day. Besides having orchestrated the clubhouse petition, NL representative Walker had secretly used his new delegate network to advocate a leaguewide anti-Robinson general strike. According to veteran Cubs outfielder Phil Cavarella, all of the senior circuit's squads received communications during spring training instructing them to discuss and vote on an Opening Day shutdown. According to the plot, once participating teams received the word from Walker, either by telegram or clubhouse telephone, that Robinson had taken the field, the NL-wide work stoppage would commence. At least three squads—the Pirates, the Phillies, and the Cubs—voted to strike. On other teams, such as St. Louis, large factions had embraced the walkout idea but a formal majority had not yet voted to join it. Rickey's action, however, placed Walker on notice of Dodger management's scrutiny, and consequently the planned strike fizzled.[61]

Despite the collapse of the Opening Day strike plot, however, NL players remained free—and in some cases received encouragement from clubhouse leaders or management—to embark on their own anti-Robinson actions as a team or individually. The continuing hope behind such efforts was that by demonstrating their unyielding defiance and making the newcomer's presence a living hell, they would either drive Robinson out from fear for his life or provoke him into a retaliation that would trigger his disciplinary expulsion. Following two relatively uneventful road series in New York and Boston at the start of the regular season, the Dodgers returned to Ebbets Field to host the Phillies. Philadelphia's bigoted manager, Ben Chapman, led his men in a chorus of gutter-level verbal abuse, and players even pointed their bats at Robinson as if aiming rifles. When the incident unleashed a torrent of public criticism of the Phillies' behavior, Commissioner Chandler and league president Frick reprimanded Chapman and his squad but refused to issue any suspensions.[62]

The next crucial juncture in the anti-Robinson vendetta occurred in the first week of May. With St. Louis scheduled to open a series in Brooklyn and with Robinson struggling to emerge from a batting slump, Cardinal players plotted their own teamwide wildcat strike to drive him out of the circuit. According to Dick Sisler, then a St. Louis rookie, seven teammates including veteran leaders Marty Marion, Terry Moore, and Enos Slaughter agreed to sit down. Ironically, the same St. Louis team had raised no objection earlier when trainer Doc Weaver had retained an African American assistant and passed him off before southern train conductors during spring training as a Cuban. But to many of the Cardinals a black ballplayer presented a different picture. By the morning of game day, May 6, rumors of the intended strike had leaked to Cardinals owner Sam Breadon, probably from team physician Robert Hyland. Breadon called NL president Frick, who immediately traveled from his New York office to Ebbets Field and threatened the plotters with lifetime suspensions. In support of his threat, Frick declared, "I don't care if it wrecks the National League for five years!" Anticipating similar job actions elsewhere, the NL chief sent the same message to other NL clubhouses by telegram, effectively squelching them.[63]

For decades participants and outside contemporaries with knowledge of the strike plot issued vague denials or displayed curious memory lapses. Marty Marion, the Cardinals' clubhouse leader, insisted long afterward that no organized boycott had ever been contemplated — "as far as I can remember." But revealing a residual anti-Robinson hostility, he maintained that the black Dodger had been the recipient of special favoritism in 1947 from the NL office through its crackdown against on-field abuse. Stan Musial, who to his credit had refused to aid the boycott, nonetheless later protected his teammates by disclaiming knowledge of anything beyond "rough and racial" clubhouse talk. But revealingly, one prominent person with firsthand knowledge of both the strike plan and the steps taken to crush it — Ford Frick — conspicuously never contested the basic accuracy of reporter Stanley Woodward's May 9 account of the incident in the *New York Herald-Tribune*.[64]

The collapse of the player strike against Robinson did not end the efforts to harass and threaten him out of the majors. When the Dodgers visited Philadelphia on the same day Woodward's story appeared, Phillies officials tried their own gambits to keep him out of the City of Brotherly Love. Owner Robert Carpenter threatened to pull his team from the field if Robinson played. General manager Herb Pennock telephoned Rickey to demand he not "bring that nigger" to Shibe Park, only to be reminded that if the Phillies refused to show up, the game would be forfeited. At Pennock's urging the Benjamin Franklin Hotel refused Robinson lodging, leading the entire Dodger team to relocate to the Warwick. A furious Rickey protested to Commissioner Chandler, who again dispatched Jack Demoise to shadow the black Dodger for his safety. Chandler also threatened Pennock, "If you move in on Robinson, I'll move in on you." The obstructionism then reverted to on-field intimidation, prompting another call from Frick to manager Chapman and a hastily arranged "photo opportunity" with Robinson and Chapman awkwardly standing together. The staged pose showed the two holding a bat rather than shaking hands because the Phillies skipper adamantly refused to touch his adversary.[65]

When the Dodgers moved on to Pittsburgh, Pirate players took the field seemingly without incident. Unknown to spectators, however, was the fact that they had been issued a five-minute ultimatum to play or else forfeit the contest. In Cincinnati the death threats against Robinson were so numerous and credible that FBI agents checked rooftops of surrounding buildings for snipers prior to his appearance in Crosley Field. Within the Dodger organization, yet another planned trade of Dixie Walker fell through, this time because the benched outfielder suddenly became essential insurance when starter Pete Reiser sustained a serious injury. When the Dodgers met St. Louis again, Enos Slaughter deliberately spiked Robinson at first base. When the latter confessed to Stan Musial his desire to "punch the SOB in the mouth," the Cardinal star admitted, "If you did, I wouldn't blame you." In a Cubs game, Chicago's starting pitcher knocked Robinson down on four consecutive pitches to start the contest. When shortstop Len Merullo kicked Robinson during a confrontation later in the season, the Dodger newcomer literally caught himself in mid-punch and restrained himself from retaliating.[66]

Although he was hit by pitches six times in his first thirty-seven games in 1947, and the spikings and abuse continued to rain down on him long after, Robinson did not sit out a single game until September 7. More and more of his teammates saw his value to their pennant hopes, and they grew to admire his courage and self-discipline. After the Merullo incident, pitcher Ralph Branca even called a whites-only Dodger player meeting in which they pledged to tackle Robinson and cover him in the event of any on-field brawls so that no opponent could draw him into a suspension-triggering fight. By the second half of the 1947 season Robinson was no longer the only African American in the majors, which helped diffuse the hostility toward him. On July 5, Bill Veeck announced Cleveland's signing of Newark Eagles slugger Larry Doby. The St. Louis Browns then inked Hank Thompson and Willard Brown from the Kansas City Monarchs and took out a thirty-day option on Birmingham's Piper Davis. By the end of August, nonetheless, all three Browns' signees had been released. Brooklyn, however, won the NL pennant, and Jackie Robinson earned Rookie of the Year honors. That off-season Dixie Walker belatedly sought to withdraw his demand to be traded. An unforgiving Branch Rickey nonetheless shipped the People's Choice out of Brooklyn to the more hospitable environs of St. Louis.[67]

Thanks to the determination shown at crucial moments by Rickey, Frick, Chandler, and above all, Robinson himself, playing employment at even the top level of Organized Baseball no longer remained off-limits to African Americans. But save for Robinson's determination, the impulse to integrate had not been driven primarily by a crusading zeal for racial justice. The Mahatma, Branch Rickey, had been motivated above all by the imperative to make Brooklyn a contender on the field and at the gate by employing untapped bargain talent. Chandler and Frick belatedly had understood that whatever their personal prejudices, integration could not be blocked once a fellow member of the management fraternity crossed the color line. Their decision also had been dictated by the need to set the important broader precedent of standing up to any form of player collective action that challenged club management's prerogatives. Most crucial of all, the overdue decision to enforce rather than obstruct the start of player integration had been ratified by the public at the turnstiles. The gate impact of Robinson had been anything but the disaster foolishly predicted by the MacPhail committee, and attendance records had been set even in St. Louis and Cincinnati. As a result, Rickey's decision was certain to be emulated, albeit with varying speed, by the rival organizations that had once unanimously opposed his gambit.

The revolution of 1947 had opened Organized Baseball's top floor to African American playing talent, but the pace of the subsequent progress depended on the individual decisions of each organization's management. Lifting the color ban did not result in the rapid or comprehensive integration of all teams and leagues (see Appendix, Fig. 4). While some organizations pushed ahead, many others refused at first. By the end of the 1940s, observers detected a quota system at work in which only the Brooklyn and Cleveland organizations demonstrated the will to move beyond outright exclusion or tokenism. In the big leagues, the first 5 black arrivals in 1947 were followed by 2 more in 1948 and 4 others in 1949. By the end of the decade, Organized Baseball had retained thirty-six black players, including at least one man in every AAA and A circuit. But of the 36 pioneers, 26 belonged to either the Indians or the Dodgers. The two key AA leagues of the South, the Southern Association and the Texas League, maintained exclusionary policies that bottlenecked all but the best black signees able to leapfrog to AAA. By 1949 only the New York Giants had joined the Dodgers, Indians, and Browns as employers of black major leaguers. In marked contrast, Connie Mack's Philadelphia Athletics not only still refused to sign a black player but went so far as to subsidize a racist heckler to follow Larry Doby around the American League.[68]

Combining the Athletics' shameful record with the documented racism of the Phillies, Philadelphia justly earned a reputation in the black press as the city with the most prejudiced major league organizations. But the City of Brotherly Love had close competition. The New York Yankees squad, despite political pressure it received as the only big league organization in Gotham without a black signee, held fast to its segregationist ways. General manager George Weiss even dispatched a known bigot from his scouting system to ensure an unfavorable report on prospect Willie Mays. Justifying the rejection of two other black hopefuls, Weiss proclaimed he would never allow a Negro to wear Yankee pinstripes because "box holders in Westchester" would not "sit with niggers." He added in a statement he surely knew better than to believe, "There isn't an outstanding Negro player that anybody could recommend to step into the big leagues and hold down a regular job." Reflecting similar attitudes, the Boston Red Sox signed no African Americans, nor did the Detroit Tigers.[69]

The limited early degree of racial integration in Organized Baseball did, however, deal the top Negro circuits a death blow by skimming off their best talent. When Branch Rickey had signed Jackie Robinson in late 1945, the black leagues had belatedly tried to prevent more player jumping without white compensation by belatedly issuing standardized written contracts. But even when white organizations showed black clubs and owners respect by buying rather than stealing their stars, the bottom-drawer prices they paid, ranging from $1,000 to $5,000, were a pittance compared with the sums given white bonus babies. As talent drained away, the Negro Leagues finished in the red in 1947, and the outflow became a torrent in 1948. Newark, the black circuits' main competitor to the white New York teams, saw its attendance fall in 1947 from the previous year's 120,000 to less than half that number. The NNL closed down entirely after the 1948 campaign, and the NAL limped along with only its Kansas City and Birmingham clubs showing a profit by 1949.[70]

After its challenge of 1946, the Mexican League also collapsed as a gate and talent competitor to the white leagues. Commissioner Chandler had issued edicts that summer imposing five-year bans from Organized Baseball for contract jumpers and three-year sanctions on reserve jumpers, along with smaller suspensions and fines on anyone who played with or against them. But the magnates' victory over Jorge Pasquel eventually owed more to the rival circuit's own internal flaws. Since the Pasquel family was virtually the sole financial underwriter of the Mexican League, imported players found themselves constantly transferred from one club to another to shore up each franchise. Although Pasquel had promised not only higher pay but also free housing, medical and dental care, and cars, the reality proved to be long-distance bus rides, unmet pay deadlines, and unsafe playing conditions that even included railroad tracks across one park's outfield. As the circuit's money dried up, rumors of pay cuts of 50 percent or more for 1947 spread. When Pasquel's own attentions wandered elsewhere, major league refugees soon scrambled for lifelines out of Mexico.[71]

Sensing victory, Chandler and the magnates refused to lift the sanctions and reinstate the jumpers. As Cubs general manager Jim Gallagher put it, "The spectacle of Mickey Owen languishing on a Missouri farm will do more to keep players from jumping this winter than anything Mr. Rickey or the rest of us could do." Minor league clubs followed suit, refusing to re-sign returnees for fear of big league retaliation. Abandoning Mexico, refugees Max Lanier, Lou Klein, and Fred Martin played winter ball in the Cuban Professional League. In retaliation, major league owners then facilitated the use of their players by a rival circuit, the Cuban Baseball Federation, only to see it fail to complete its schedule. A year later in 1947, the magnates shut firmly the Cuban League door by negotiating the latter's promise not to employ jumpers, in exchange for the services of a limited number of minor leaguers from the United States. Similar agreements with the Panama Professional Baseball League the same winter, the Venezuelan and Puerto Rican circuits in 1948, and the Quebec Provincial League in 1949 tightened the economic noose around the exiles. By March 1949 Chandler had even inked a deal with Pasquel's Mexican League successor, Dr. Eduardo Quijano Pitman, that formally ended the trade war by barring the use of jumpers by either side and respecting each other's contract and reserve agreements. In the meantime, desperate for work, the exiled Lanier in 1948 had organized a touring team that also included Sal Maglie. Owen organized his own semipro team in South Dakota, but Organized Baseball sanctions barred both squads from playing in any of its parks.[72]

The adamance of the commissioner and the owners, however, triggered dangerous new lawsuits challenging the reserve clause, something Chandler's predecessor had consistently and successfully maneuvered to prevent. By 1949 four exiles from the majors had filed actions against Organized Baseball. The most dangerous was initiated by Danny Gardella, a former player with the New York Giants who had been unsigned when he fled to the Mexican League in 1946 and, therefore, was a reserve rather than a contract jumper. With the help of New York attorney Frederick Johnson, Gardella had charged in federal district court that baseball had violated his employment rights, and his lawyer had asserted that the reserve clause constituted an illegal restraint of trade and a violation of both the Sherman and Clayton Anti-Trust Acts. The plaintiff demanded $100,000 in lost wages, which translated to triple damages of $300,000. After the original trial judge had died in February 1948, a second judge had dismissed the action on the grounds that he lacked jurisdiction to overturn a Supreme Court ruling. In the fall of 1948 Johnson had appealed his client's case to the Second Circuit Court of Appeals, and in a 2-1 margin provided by jurists Learned Hand and Jerome Frank, the suit was reinstated for consideration by the U.S. Supreme Court.[73]

Faced suddenly with the alarming prospect of a high court challenge to his industry's antitrust exemption and reserve clause, Chandler covertly signaled three other prominent former jumpers—Owen, Martin, and Lanier—that they would be reinstated along with Gardella if they could persuade the latter to drop his lawsuit. The gambit nearly backfired completely when, after Gardella rebuffed their approaches, Lanier and Martin themselves opted to sue Chandler. Fortunately for the commissioner, a federal court threw out the action of Lanier and Martin in mid-April 1949. Owners still staring down the barrel of the Gardella case blasted the ex-player and his lawyer as "communists," but the anger only revealed their growing state of panic. On June 5, 1949, claiming to have been inspired by the urge to "temper justice with mercy," Chandler suddenly announced an amnesty to all Mexican League jumpers who had violated Organized Baseball contracts or reserves. In early October, barely one month before the scheduled trial date, baseball reached an out-of-court settlement with Gardella that included the Cardinals' purchase of his Giants playing contract and a $60,000 payment to Gardella and his lawyer. A visibly relieved Chandler confessed, "If I were a drinking man, I think I'd go out and get drunk."[74]

The last-minute resolution of Gardella's lawsuit marked a fitting end to a decade of tumultuous labor relations in baseball. By the fall of 1949, owners could look back with wonder at what had transpired and feel fortunate that they had survived and prospered. They had seen the gutting of their labor supply by war, the attendant chaos of its return, a costly trade war, a union challenge, a racial revolution, and legal threats. Not only had their major league operations bounced back robustly, so, too, had their minor league dependencies. Major league attendance had hit a new high in 1948 at 21 million. Cleveland alone had drawn over 2.6 million fans, a record that would stand for thirty-two years. By 1949 the minors had mushroomed to 59 leagues, compared with but 10 five years earlier, containing nearly 450 teams, 9,000 performers, and 42 million spectators. At the same time, salaries had stayed modest, with upper levels averaging $3,000 and A- to D-level pay capped at $750 to $1,600. Although the pay of big league players had not regressed from the surge of 1946, the rate of increase had significantly moderated. Major league incomes now ranged from the new $5,000 minimum up to six-figure levels claimed by Joe DiMaggio and Ted Williams, but the average stood at only about $13,000 (see Appendix, Fig. 2). In fact, by the end of the decade the major league payroll bite of the magnates' incomes had fallen to barely one-fifth of revenues, compared with one of every three dollars twenty years earlier.[75] Having successfully withstood the shocks of war and revolution, Organized Baseball now settled in for what it anticipated would be an overdue "summer" of prosperity and tranquility in the 1950s.

CHAPTER 4 : MEN IN GRAY FLANNEL SUITS

1950–1965

Throughout baseball's paternalistic era, each time the owners weathered one storm and anticipated an extended period of peace and profit, the unexpected plunged them into renewed crisis. At first glance, the 1950s did not appear to promise a repeat of that troubling pattern. The Mexican League rivalry had been successfully repelled. The player union threat had been crushed and its company union substitute steered into nonthreatening channels. Racial exclusion within the playing force had been replaced by gradual, piecemeal desegregation. Little seemed to remain to pose a serious hazard to management's goal of a cheap, plentiful, docile on-field labor force and the industry profits it would generate.

What management failed to anticipate was a crisis not in costs but in revenues, an extended era of sluggish growth that prompted them to squeeze their players even harder and set the stage for bitter future labor confrontations. Starting in 1950 the baseball industry's revenues began to hemorrhage badly. The adverse trend affected all forms of professional baseball, including the women's circuits, the remnant of the Negro Leagues, and the minors as well as the majors. Only six years after attracting nearly a million fans, the All-American Girls Professional Baseball League collapsed completely in 1954. The minor leagues' National Association reported that following profitable seasons in 1939–42, 1944–47, and 1949, 29 of its 40 D-level circuits were losing money in 1950. Over the next fifteen years the number of minor leagues plummeted from 58 to 19, playing slots shrank by over 70 percent to 2,500, and attendance shriveled from 40 million fans to half that total. As more farm chain "links" became unprofitable, major league sponsors pulled out even more financial props and accelerated the collapse.[1]

The magnates maintained that, given their own profit problems, they had no choice but to allow the attrition of the minors. After an attendance peak in 1948 of 20 million fans, major league turnout slumped to 14.4 million by 1953 and did not reach 20 million again until 1960. The American League felt the crisis the worst, given the Yankees' dominance and the circuit's laggardness in signing African American talent. AL attendance dropped from 9.1 million in 1950 to 7.3 million by 1958. In 1950, big league profit margins suddenly slumped 7.5 percent to only 2 percent on net revenue of $65 million. By 1956, revenue had shrunk $5 million more, and the average club profit stood at but $30,000. Reflecting baseball's decline relative to other forms of recreation, the industry's share of the U.S. entertainment dollar, sixty-eight cents in 1948, slipped to forty-nine cents as early as 1950 and kept falling.[2]

The causes of baseball's revenue stagnation were varied and interrelated, but the industry's reaction to them demonstrated its persistent backwardness and obsession with cost control rather than innovation. One major contributor to the crisis, without question, was television—and the magnates' hesitant, confused reaction to it. TV's impact on the minor leagues in particular was devastating. Back in 1946, big league owners had adopted rules barring broadcasts of their games beyond a fifty-mile radius of their ballparks. The old rules had generally protected minor league games from TV competition, but they invited legal challenges from potential viewers, advertisers, broadcast networks, and the government. In the face of Justice Department threats, in 1949 the magnates modified their policy to permit telecasts into minor league cities except during game times. The compromise satisfied no one, and in 1952 the Liberty Broadcasting System sued. The next year the owners gave in completely and allowed each club to set its own local broadcast policy. The American Broadcasting Company contracted for Saturday afternoon games to be blacked out in major league markets but not in those of the minors. At their December 1955 meetings, the magnates rejected the minors' pleas for a ban on such telecasts into their areas and instead endorsed Dodger owner Walter O'Malley's push for another Saturday Game of the Week telecast on the Columbia Broadcasting System, again blacked out only in big league cities. AL owners even killed the senior circuit's tentative offer to share some of the television revenue with the minors as compensation. In December 1957 the majors added a Sunday national telecast.[3]

Although the magnates proved quite willing to sacrifice their minor league dependencies on the twin altars of cost control and television profits, they still remained inept at anticipating or fully capitalizing on the potential of televised sports. In their negotiations of the late 1940s and 1950s they drove anything but hard bargains. Commissioner Chandler inked the majors' first World Series TV deal with Gillette in 1949, a six-year pact at $1 million annually. Showing what a bad deal baseball had struck and what a good one Gillette had brokered, the latter resold the rights to NBC at $4 million a year. Cardinals owner Fred Saigh dubbed Chandler the "bluegrass jackass," and he combined forces with the Yankees' Dan Topping to oust the commissioner and replace him with Ford Frick. Even after Chandler's ouster, however, the magnates fumbled their collective negotiations with the networks, and their individual local broadcast deals often turned out no better. In the early 1950s, a New York Yankee fan could see every home game on "free" television. As of 1950 the majors had garnered about $1.2 million in national broadcasting money, with the per-club local average less than one-tenth that amount. Ten years later the totals had risen only to $3.3 million and $200,000. While broadcast income's share of major league dollars nearly doubled to almost 20 percent, the relative rise spoke more about declining gates than owners' mastery of TV.[4]

Another contributor to Organized Baseball's revenue woes was the demographic shift from northeastern central cities to the suburbs and the South and West, which in turn was due to the growing impact of highway and expressway construction and economic migration to the Sun Belt. The Korean conflict also temporarily harmed baseball rosters and attendance. A bigger long-term challenge, however, was the rise of other sports industries, most notably the National Football League (NFL). Glaring problems with competitive imbalance and inadequate revenue sharing between clubs also compounded baseball's crisis, and each exacerbated the other. With the 1950s accelerating trends that already existed, NL visitor gate shares, 21 percent in 1929, slid to under 14 percent. AL visitors' take, fully 40 percent when the junior circuit had first pushed its way into major league status in 1901, had dropped to 21 percent by 1953 and continued to fall. But when maverick owner Bill Veeck proposed that AL owners boost the figure back to 40 percent, the motion failed to receive the necessary two-thirds margin by one vote. The owners even refused to share national broadcast revenue equally among themselves, instead allocating it on the basis of the frequency of a club's TV appearances — a decision that aggravated competitive imbalance further in favor of big market "haves" such as the Yankees. By 1959 the latter had pocketed an extra $1 million a year from broadcast revenue, while the struggling Washington Senators received only $150,000.[5]

Whatever the relative importance of baseball's multiple causes of stagnation, their impact was magnified by hidebound industry attitudes on the comparative importance of growth versus cost control. Most clubs in the 1950s remained the property of local businessmen who viewed themselves as civic "sportsmen." These men ran their organizations in an increasingly detached fashion but still maintained ownership of them as paternalistic enterprises or expensive hobbies. By the 1950s, ownership turnover occurred, on average, once every fifteen years. When Phil Wrigley remarked, "Baseball is too much of a business to be a sport and too much of a sport to be a business," he was, in effect, confessing his inability to master the increasingly complicated and changing demands of baseball success on the field and on the books. Even club general managers still generally followed a Depression-era organizational tradition and apprenticeship that emphasized payroll penny-pinching over broader economic vision or the modern arts of marketing.

New York's George Weiss offered one striking example of a general manager who was apparently oblivious to the marketing side of his operations. When aides suggested that the club sponsor a cap day at Yankee Stadium, the personnel genius exploded at the thought of giving away free merchandise: "Do you think I want every kid in this city walking around with a Yankee cap?" Demonstrating management's continued preoccupation with cost control over revenue stimulation, executives also hesitated to do much tinkering with playing rules to boost offense and attendance. In 1950 they modestly shortened the strike zone from the shoulder and the bottom of the knee to the armpit and the top of the knee. But when the one-quarter-run-per-game increase that year failed to raise attendance immediately, rather than attempt a bolder change, the clubs stood pat. Instead, in 1958 owners established a minimum fence distance of 325 feet in all new ballparks, which effectively barred the creation of a new generation of home-run-friendly facilities in the tradition of Yankee Stadium and Fenway Park.[6]

One of the clearest signs of management's continued emphasis on cost control in the 1950s and early 1960s was the stagnation of player salaries (see Appendix, Fig. 2). Despite general prosperity in the United States, baseball's payroll and job retrenchment trends hearkened back to the grim days of the Depression. For the ballplayer the contrast between his low pay and job insecurity and the affluence of "Happy Days" America made this second round of hard times doubly difficult. In 1951 testimony before a congressional subcommittee, new commissioner Ford Frick admitted that the average professional player earned less than the average skilled workman. At the major league level, the 1950 mean salary sat at $13,288 (roughly equivalent to a $70,000 income in the late 1990s), but the median was closer to $11,000. Baseball officials regularly cited the Korean War and flagging attendance for their lack of wage progress. But even as late as 1962, salaries remained no higher than those a decade earlier. A 1957 survey revealed that three-fourths of major leaguers made between $10,000 and $25,000 a year, and since the average big league career lasted less than five years, a majority of them would not even qualify for retirement benefits. By the mid-1960s the average pay of $16,000 still represented only a $2,500 gain in fifteen years. Minimum salaries did climb belatedly to $6,000 in 1954 but remained there for over a decade.[7]

Because of the impact of the high salaries of a handful of stars on affluent teams, the economic well-being of most big leaguers was dramatically overstated overall. In 1978 the *St. Louis Globe-Democrat* provided a more accurate retroactive snapshot of one "unnamed" (although clearly the Cardinals) major league club's payroll over a twenty-five year span. On this particular team, the mean salary in 1954 stood at less than $10,000. Although the figure jumped to $12,880 the next season, it never surpassed that new level until 1962, when it reached $13,840. By 1965 the club mean was $16,240, virtually identical to the overall big league average despite the fact that the Cardinals were coming off a World Series triumph. Across the majors, pay ranges rose from $5,000–90,000 in the early 1950s to $6,000–125,000 by the late 1950s, but they went no higher in the early 1960s. By the mid-1960s, although Willie Mays had cracked the $100,000 circle, big league salary and pension costs generally had shrunk to 18.5 percent of club revenues, compared with more than 22 percent in 1950.[8]

In a new era of economizing, players cherished any supplemental income. As in the past, however, only the wealthier and competitively successful clubs were positioned to provide it with any consistency. New York Yankee players earned an extra $40,000 each in World Series money for the years 1949–55, although George Weiss tried to use that fact to hold down pay raises comparably. In 1955 the victorious Brooklyn Dodger squad split 30 full shares at nearly $10,000 apiece and 10 partial allotments, while the defeated Bronx Bombers divided 34 full amounts of

THE PATERNALISTIC ERA

over \$5,500 each and 12 lesser awards. Second-, third-, and fourth-place teams in each league also garnered an extra \$1,500, \$1,000, and \$500, respectively, per man. But as with salaries, series shares did not increase significantly over time. By 1960, wining and losing shares actually stood at \$8,418 and \$5,125, lower than those of five years earlier. During the 1952 fall classic, a pair of Brooklyn stars demonstrated just how much extra money mattered even to them. Jackie Robinson and Gil Hodges launched into a public argument in the Dodger dugout between innings after Robinson had fielded a pop-up. It was later revealed that during the regular season Hodges, because of his trouble fielding infield flies, had paid his teammate \$5 apiece to catch them for him. For the series, however, Robinson suddenly had demanded a postseason fee of \$10. The two eventually compromised at \$7.50.[9]

Other sources of additional player income included testimonials, endorsements, autograph fees, and promotions sponsored by local businesses. Television spots also provided an emerging new source of player money. Willie Mays, for example, earned \$15,000 that way following his 1954 World Series heroics. By mid-decade, players increasingly demanded nominal payments for postgame radio and TV appearances. In 1955 men on eight clubs charged a standard \$50, while Washington Senators players asked \$25; seven teams still offered their services for free. Even the high-end figure was hardly outlandish, for television paid other on-air performers on a union scale of \$70 minimum for a fifteen-minute show. Nonetheless, even the best players still found it necessary to work off-season jobs. The Phillies Robin Roberts sold cardboard boxes at \$75 a week, while Carl Furillo labored as a hardhat, Yogi Berra and Phil Rizzuto sold men's clothing, and Jackie Robinson worked in an appliance store.[10]

At the minor league level—as had been true in the Depression 1930s—the players' economic situation was far worse, since low wages coexisted with a shrinking number of teams and jobs. In 1950, AAA monthly salary means were \$978 in the PCL, \$832 in the International League, and \$759 in the American Association, translating into a seasonal pay of about \$4,000 in the top minors. At AA the averages ranged from \$613 in the Southern Association to \$665 in the Texas League, or about \$3,100 to \$3,325 a year. A-level pay of \$350 to \$432 a month translated into annual salaries of \$1,750 to \$2,160. Figures for B- and C-levels were not available, but D clubs reported means of \$192 a month, or less than \$1,000 a year and less than one-third the pay of an industrial worker. The AA player earned about the same as the latter, while a AAA performer drew about $1,000 more. Major leaguers, by comparison, made slightly more than physicians. While big leaguers received a month's pay if they were released, minor leaguers had no rights to either advance notice of releases or severance pay or pensions. If injured and then released, a player received only two weeks of additional salary. Although many circuits imposed team salary caps, at the other end minor leaguers were not guaranteed minimum salaries. Even before the worst rounds of job cuts later in the decade, a National Association report of 1950 revealed that the average minor leaguer endured five trades, demotions, promotions, releases, sales, or other changes of employment status a year. By the mid-1960s the number of professional ballplaying jobs below the major league level had contracted by fully 60 percent.[11]

Players at all levels of Organized Baseball could do little about owner miserliness, since the industry refused to implement any formal system of pay mediation or arbitration. In 1950 Commissioner Chandler violated an earlier promise to the magnates and intervened in behalf of pitcher Al Widmar, resulting in Widmar obtaining a "considerable raise." Players such as Pee Wee Reese then sought similar interventions. Former player Cy Block testified before Congressman Emanuel Celler's House judiciary subcommittee in support of a three-man arbitration team consisting of the club owner, the league president, and a player representative. But when Chandler expressed sympathy for the idea of player arbitration rights before the same House panel, he put another nail into his commissionership's coffin. In contrast successor Ford Frick, despite the public pronouncement that a commissioner should represent the players, the public, and the owners in that order, consistently acted as if he had reversed the priorities.[12]

In the absence of outside arbitration processes, team general managers exercised unilateral economic power over their charges. Day-to-day baseball operations resided with executives who had literally or figuratively learned their craft at the tightfisted hand of Branch Rickey. National Association president George Trautman was a Rickey protégé, as were rising management figures Bill DeWitt, Bing Devine, Warren Giles, and Buzzie Bavasi. Clubs refused to make individual salary information public, and as a result players often had only their general manager's word as to how their pay compared to that of teammates or opponents. Executives loved to relate their sporadic acts of paternal generosity, whether extending $100 to a player to take his wife to dinner or providing a few hundred more to help square away debts to creditors. But better wages would have made these gestures unnecessary, and general managers continued to inject special provisions into player contracts that effectively limited off-season earning prospects and intruded upon private behavior. On the positive side, clubs now retained physicians with higher professional credentials than the old "rubbers" of prewar days, but their management status and their cronyism with owners frequently created conflicts of interest in their diagnoses and medical advice. On rare occasions, daily contact with ballplayers by a member of management caused a shift in loyalties. When Yankee road secretary Frank Scott refused George Weiss's orders to spy on certain performers and was fired for "disloyalty" after the 1950 season, for example, he became Yogi Berra's booking agent.[13]

For most of the 1950s and early 1960s, baseball players remained largely nameless, replaceable links in their industry's chains. Only by 1959 did player surnames even appear on the backs of big league jerseys, with Chicago White Sox owner Bill Veeck the innovator. Nor was it only players who were expected to fit the colorless, standardized mold. The Dodgers, demonstrating the trend toward "company men," even jettisoned Branch Rickey for his unwillingness to toe Walter O'Malley's line, as well as announcer Red Barber and manager Leo Durocher in favor of the young Vin Scully and Walter Alston. Baseball kept the "dirty linen" of its stars, such as Mickey Mantle's extramarital liaisons, vulnerability to blackmailers, and unsavory gambling associations (which had been recorded in a confidential FBI file), well out of public view. As maverick Bill Veeck saw it, baseball had gone too far and become a tired show of "good, gray ballplayers, playing a good, gray game." "Where," he pleaded, "are the drunks of yesteryear?"[14]

Veeck himself did not hesitate to treat his players as cold machinery in one respect, however. He pioneered, and other owners soon copied, the tax-saving technique of writing off player contracts as depreciated capital expenses. Basing his accounting innovation on an obscure 1935 Internal Revenue Service (IRS) ruling involving the Pittsburgh Pirates, Veeck claimed that an owner who bought a club, reorganized its management structure, and maintained a 75 percent ownership share could attribute most of the club's purchase cost to its player contracts. Then the owner could deduct the contracts from his taxes in stages over a period of several years (2½ to 5, based on the asserted average career of a major leaguer and the IRS's acceptance) as capital depreciation. To take full advantage, the club owner would claim an operating loss by subtracting the amortized cost of his player payroll, then applying the loss to his other income to reduce his tax liabilities on it until the player-depreciation amount had been completely used up. When asked if the practice constituted tax evasion, Veeck sarcastically quipped, "Look, we play the Star-Spangled Banner before every game. You want us to pay income taxes, too?"[15]

The foundation of the ability of baseball clubs to retain multiyear control of players for both tax purposes and payroll restraint remained the reserve clause. By 1951 only eight of 8,000 minor league contracts lacked its formal restrictive language, and all big league pacts included it. Technically when the standard player contract had been revised in 1946 as part of the MacPhail committee's recommendations, the reserve clause had been replaced with a renewal clause or unilateral owner option on the player's contract for the next season. Baseball management, however, still interpreted the clause as authorization to renew player services perpetually rather than for just one additional year, even in the absence of a signed contract. George Edward Toolson, a former Yankee farmhand, eventually filed suit for triple damages, challenging the legality of the reworked reserve clause. According to the plaintiff, the reserve had effectively prevented him from fairly moving up the professional ladder by keeping him from shopping his services to other organizations. Instead the Yankees had demoted him from their top farm in Newark to Birmingham of the Eastern League. When he had refused to go, New York had retaliated by refusing to either release Toolson or trade him to another organization.[16]

As the Toolson case inched up the federal appeals system in 1952 and 1953, many major league owners nervously anticipated the outcome. Phil Wrigley, remembering the advice of past industry stewards O'Connor and Landis never to let such a reserve clause case reach the federal courts, expected defeat and accordingly advocated loosening the farm system's control of its players. Fellow owners overwhelmingly rejected the idea. To the magnates' relief, on November 9, 1953, the Supreme Court by a 7-2 margin refused to overturn baseball's antitrust exemption and reserve clause. The justices restated that it remained for Congress, not the courts, to decide whether or not to apply antitrust law to the industry and its internal regulations and practices. Ironically, a year and a half later the high court contradicted itself and declared both professional boxing and the legitimate theater industries properly subject to federal antitrust statutes. Although Congress held antitrust hearings regarding the baseball industry in 1951 and again in 1957, no action followed to repeal professional baseball's monopoly status or to dismantle the reserve.[17]

Without government intervention on behalf of their labor rights, major leaguers depended on the new player representation system the owners had allowed as an alternative to an adversarial union. The magnates scarcely expected frequent or bitter exchanges with the representatives, given the tremendous leverage they exercised over their selection process. National League player representative Marty Marion, for example, who succeeded Dixie Walker in 1948, regularly sought out owner Fred Saigh's counsel before acting on labor issues concerning players. The St. Louis shortstop eventually relinquished his representative position for a field manager's job and was succeeded by Ralph Kiner in 1951 and Robin Roberts in December 1954. In the American League, Johnny Murphy's term was followed by those of pitcher Fred Hutchinson of Detroit, Boston outfielder Dom DiMaggio, Yankee hurler Allie Reynolds, and in 1955, Bob Feller of Cleveland.[18]

Neither owners nor players saw the new representation system as an independent union or claimed to want one. To the veteran team delegates, a union meant confrontations, strikes, job insecurity, and an economic leveling that clashed with their aspiring, individualist values. They faithfully relayed grievances they shared with their younger, more anonymous brethren, such as doubleheaders after night games, spring training night tilts, ballpark safety hazards, inadequate road allowances, and clubs' refusal to provide accident and health insurance. Periodically they even voiced the more narrow concerns of younger teammates, such as increasing the minimum salary, but they rarely questioned the reserve clause. Above all else, however, one issue ranked as preeminent to them: the pension. The veteran delegates' preoccupation with it owed partly to the fact that because of the shrinking minor league pool, the reserve's barriers to mobility across teams, and the impact of Korean War military call-ups, major league rosters were filled by older players. By 1953 NL teams contained 30 ten-year veterans, up 2 from fifteen years earlier, and 88 five-year men, a gain of 11 over the same span. By the end of 1955 the number of NL ten-year men had climbed to 60, and 40 more had at least eight years' service.[19]

The pension system had been started in 1947 with an initial fund of $675,000, including a $150,000 annual contribution from a three-year All-Star Game and World Series broadcast pact and all net proceeds from the mid-season classic. Matching player and owner levies added to the pool. Payouts, however, were not scheduled to begin until 1952. Tragedies such as the sudden death in September 1949 of ten-year vet Ernie Bonham at age thirty-six, which left his wife penniless, dramatized the consequences of the time lag. Another flaw in the system was that it commenced payments to retirees at age fifty as long as the recipient had played five years and had been active as of April 1, 1947. As the number of such retirees expanded between 1947 and 1952, they threatened to create an initial "back-service" payout strain on the program.[20]

Recognizing the pension plan's insufficient starting revenue base, Commissioner Chandler hastily negotiated a deal in 1950 with Gillette that promised $1 million a year in broadcast fees for 1951–56. He urged that all of it should go into the retirement fund. But owners quickly registered their opposition to both the amount and the exclusive use of the money envisioned in Chandler's scheme by firing him. The owners estimated that by 1954 they would still face $2.3 million in immediate back-service obligations that Chandler's contract could not meet. What the magnates demanded in light of their stagnant gate revenues was a television bonanza that would provide millions of dollars more than any pension payouts. But given the shortcomings of the television deal, they could either try to live up to both the letter and the spirit of their pension promises and probably still fall short, with no money left over for their dwindling profit margins, or they could play fast and loose with the pension by skimming off revenues. The players would be denied the financial details of this shell game, for if they learned about them, they might become emboldened to utilize recent legal precedents, such as the Supreme Court's Inland Steel decision of 1949, to seek collective bargaining rights over the pension and possibly other issues as well.[21]

As early as 1950, even before the Gillette contributions began, Chandler and the magnates had solicited legal advice on how to siphon off money for other needs rather than commit it all to the pension fund. Consultants had suggested that contributions be placed initially in an omnibus central fund under the commissioner's control, rather than directly in the pension fund. Then the commissioner could remove 15 percent up front for his office expenses and another $10,000 for his central fund's "administrative costs" before calculating the 60 percent of the remainder dedicated to pension insurance contracts held by the Equitable Life Assurance Society. That year alone the skimming resulted in a pension fund contribution of $290,000 rather than $350,000. Underscoring management's bad faith, while they covertly were designing these methods of skimming they called upon NL representative Marion to prevent yet another potential player walkout at the 1950 World Series. Yankee and Phillies players had threatened not to perform when told that their series shares were to be reduced to shore up the pension fund.[22]

Not surprisingly some owners privately proposed scrapping the pension plan outright at the end of its first five-year term, paying out not a cent, and simply pocketing the proceeds. But fearing legal action, a majority opted for renewing the plan for another five years in 1951 and beginning payouts on schedule, while they secretly continued to raid fund revenues and deny players the right to see the books. By 1953 Commissioner Frick could proclaim that contributions to the pension fund, over and above player and club allocations, amounted to $1,387,000. But the owners refused player representatives access to the central fund records and continued to withdraw revenue for the commissioner's office, other administrative costs, and even the tax liabilities on their pension contributions. They also continued to rebuff annual calls by the players for increases in the benefit levels.[23]

During the first of their two permitted meetings with the magnates in 1953, player representatives Ralph Kiner and Allie Reynolds at the All-Star break set forth proposals that included a boost in the minimum salary, permission for major leaguers making less than $10,000 to play Latin American winter ball, and above all, pension modifications. They asked for an accounting, increasing monthly benefits to $80–150, and lowering the age of eligibility to forty-five. The two spokesmen "got a lunch" but nothing else from their hosts. Frustrated at the stonewalling, Kiner, Reynolds, and their team delegates then screened a series of thirty candidates and selected lawyer J. Norman Lewis to become a new legal counsel to the players and formal liaison/watchdog between them and the owners. Demonstrating how naive they were about such matters, the man they hired actually came from a law firm that had represented New York Giants management and had coauthored an article in the *New York Law Journal* in 1945 describing major league salaries of $5,000 as "enviable."[24]

Reynolds insisted that the players' move to hire Lewis was no signal of an intent to convert the representation system into an actual union. He maintained, "I would be as much opposed to a labor boss in baseball as would be the owners." Kiner echoed, "All we want from Lewis is legal advice." The owners, however, did not want anyone familiar with pension law seeking access to their financial records. Boston's Tom Yawkey derogated Lewis as an "outsider" and suggested the players hire one of their own, Dom DiMaggio, as a liaison. Yankee general manager George Weiss effectively registered his disapproval by intoning, "It certainly does not sound like something Allie Reynolds would do." Walter O'Malley even tried directly lobbying Lewis into relinquishing his new assignment on the grounds that he was "an owner's man." Baseball even trotted out former player representatives Johnny Murphy and Dixie Walker to criticize the hiring. Other players, at their bosses' urging, complained that Reynolds and Kiner had not consulted them first. Reynolds called his critics' bluff by indicating a willingness to put himself up for a vote of confidence by team delegates.[25]

With the owner-instigated campaign against Lewis thus temporarily quelled, the new counsel traveled to the owners' August executive council meeting only to be denied a formal audience. At the winter meetings in Atlanta the magnates similarly refused to allow him to present player calls for an $8,000 minimum salary and a new series of pension proposals. The player delegates then held separate contemporaneous meetings and solicited the support of ex-commissioner Chandler, who was eager to strike a blow at those who had dismissed him. By the spring of 1954, the player delegates reluctantly had concluded that in order to force the owners' respect of their right to see pension records and decisions, they would have to reconstitute their representation system as an independent professional association, to be called the Major League Baseball Players Association. At the 1954 All-Star break the players openly proclaimed their organization's new title and status. Ironically, given the Players Association's later triumphs, the AFL-CIO refused to enlist the newly constituted organization in the federation on the conclusion that major league ballplayers were an insufficiently cohesive work force to ever be able to carry out the collective actions necessary of a member union.[26]

Despite the AFL-CIO's pessimism and the players' denials, creating an outside union was exactly what the owners now accused the players of doing. Allie Reynolds rejected the charge, but in fact leaving the impression that the players were building a union was useful in scaring baseball management out of its dismissive attitude toward the players' pension demands. A gleeful Chandler added to the pressure on Frick and the owners by publicly accusing them of raiding the pension fund. Frick was forced to issue a printed report that admitted to the executive council's detouring of revenues via the central fund. Frick justified the practice by claiming that the entity to which contributions were first assigned, and from which pension pay-ins came, had never been designed, even under Chandler's reign, exclusively as a pension collection fund.[27]

As the Players Association and the magnates squabbled first over whether the latter would permit Lewis access to its sessions and then over which side would pay his salary, the owners scrambled to come up with a bigger revenue source capable of fulfilling both their pension promises and their other purposes. Allie Reynolds maintained that since the new organization was not a union, the owners legally could and should pay Lewis's retainer. Owner Frank Lane countered that his colleagues should not be expected to pay for "legal help against themselves." Given the owners' intractability, the Players Association agreed to pay Lewis his $30,000 salary and expenses to November 1954 out of the commissioner's central fund—a concession that effectively reduced the pension pool by that same amount. Despite Reynolds's earlier repugnance at the idea of "an organization with dues-paying members which would smack of a union," the Players Association again picked up the tab in 1955 for Lewis's services with a $15,000 contract.[28]

In 1956 the financial pressures behind owner obstruction on the pension eased with a new $3.25 million annual pact with Gillette. With the need for penury and secrecy lessened, the owners finally came to terms with Lewis and the Players Association. Although the owners tried to trick the players into accepting a flat $1 million contribution rather than a percentage of what promised to be a growing television revenue pot, Lewis secured 60 percent of the All-Star Game proceeds and All-Star and World Series national broadcast revenue to the pension. The new deal boosted benefits to $88 a month for retired five-year vets at age fifty, $175 for ten-year pensioners, $225 for fifteen-year men, and $275 monthly for twenty-year vets. Widows received pledges of payments until death or remarriage. Life insurance now could be acquired, conditional on length of service, up to maximums of $6,000–20,000, as well as family hospital and disability coverage. The Players Association even garnered a belated increase in the minimum salary to $6,000. Other modest concessions included reducing to eight years the service time necessary for major league demotees to gain free agency, establishing January 15 as the deadline for contract offers, and jointly studying the issue of reimbursement of player sales prices.[29]

Given the players' gains through newfound assertiveness, they might have been expected to become even less deferential. But instead the modest progress led to renewed apathy. Having agreed to pay their legal counsel's $15,000 annual fee, many players now failed to pay their dues intended for that purpose. The new association's president, Bob Feller, formed an executive council with Stan Musial as vice-president, Jerry Coleman as secretary, and additional members Eddie Yost and Ted Kluzewski, but the rank and file drifted farther from active engagement in the organization. When Commissioner Frick informed the player delegates that management had unilaterally decided to authorize one-year salary cuts of over 25 percent if affected individual players agreed, the association meekly acquiesced, despite the clear potential for intimidation in the policy. When Feller strayed from a "company line" during congressional testimony in 1957 by calling the reserve clause a form of "peonage" and owners "arrogant," management abruptly canceled his scheduled Los Angeles clinic for youngsters. The next year, when the star hurler advocated creation of a salary arbitration system to resolve contract disputes, and recently retired Jackie Robinson called for a 5- to 6-year limit on the reserve clause, owners recruited compliant players to trumpet the status quo. Ted Williams, for example, claimed incredibly that he had never heard a single "gripe about salary" in his twenty-two years in professional baseball.[30]

Attorney Lewis did try his best to represent the interests of all his player constituents, not just the better-paid veterans who dominated the representation ranks. But the players generally felt little personal bond with him. He had never been a player, and he compounded the problem by not taking the time to "touch base" with the membership regularly at spring training or elsewhere. The counsel found himself pulled in other directions by competing and lucrative clients, including one New York television personality who made $25,000 a week. Although in 1958 Lewis secured another boost in the minimum salary to $7,000 for players who remained on rosters beyond the first thirty days of each season, more ambitious demands for a 20 percent guaranteed share of club revenues for player salaries and a 25 percent portion of all national TV money for the pension fund infuriated the magnates. When they counterattacked, Lewis found that his backing within the ballplaying fraternity had eroded. Veteran stars equated his calls for aggregate payroll percentages with wage leveling and industrial-style salary scales and blamed Lewis for making a radical, risky proposal they had never been consulted about. Sealing the counsel's demise was a rumor early in 1959 that associate Gary Stevens had been dispatched to organize International League players, and that he had advised them not to sign new contracts unless their owners agreed to grant them a pension plan. Fearful of being called upon by Lewis to strike in behalf of minor leaguers poised to take their jobs, Players Association delegates deposed their counsel in February.[31]

Frank Scott, the former Yankee road secretary turned agent, became the association's new emissary to the owners. The Association hired Judge Robert C. Cannon as its new legal counsel and contract expert. A Milwaukee municipal jurist and the son of Raymond Cannon, the earlier player rights crusader, Cannon might have been expected to offer a re-invigorated leadership. But in his case the apple had rolled far from the tree. The new counsel craved the magnates' respect and approval and even hoped to use his new post as a stepping-stone to the commission-ership. Under the compliant Cannon the major league minimum salary did not budge from the $7,000 attained by Lewis. When the higher pen-sion benefit levels also secured by Lewis proved to need more revenue, the owners refused to boost the percentage of their contributions and instead imposed the disastrous experiment of a second All-Star Game for three years to raise additional moneys.[32]

With Cannon's blessing and over the opposition of AL player represen-tative Eddie Yost, owners in 1961 even "refunded" themselves $167,400 of the previous year's pension pay-in on the grounds that under the original 1947 plan they were only required to make *tax-deductible* contributions. Because the increases in owner broadcast revenues had pushed some of the magnates over their income limits for tax deductibility, they now made retroactive overpayment claims on the pension fund. In the later words of a New York state insurance examiner, the withdrawal consti-tuted a "rape" of the fund and an open violation of law. With player grumbling increasing, the owners sought to buy off trouble and shore up Cannon's standing the next year by increasing the benefits. Payments for future retirees rose to $125 a month for five years' service at age fifty and $250 for ex-players of the same age with ten years' standing. But for the first time since the creation of the pension plan, a benefits increase was not extended to those already retired. Some 300 of them, led by longtime Yankee player and coach Frank Crosetti, retained J. Norman Lewis as their attorney but lost their suit. Cannon also did nothing to extend help for the surviving pensionless veterans of the pre-1947 period. The num-ber of dues-paying members of the old Association of Professional Ball Players of America had fallen from over 5,000 in 1951 to three-fifths that number a decade later. Although the commissioner's office continued to make annual $50,000 contributions and all major league and some minor league clubs provided $260 each, only about 50 needy men a month received stipends, and contributor shortages led to the abandonment of aid to widows or dependents of the pre-1947 players.[33]

Cannon served his active membership little better. Despite the owners' refusal to share any of their regular-season broadcast revenue with the players, the association counsel told a congressional committee in 1964, "We have it so good we don't know what to ask for next." Under Cannon, club general managers actually were invited to observe association spring training meetings. When franchise expansion increased the number of insured players by 25 percent in 1962, Cannon stood by while management unilaterally stuck the players with the full increase in coverage charges. Players exercised no voice in the decision to expand season schedules from 154 to 162 games either, even though it increased their workload and travel burdens at the gain of but a few dollars a day in meal money. The magnates in similar unilateral fashion altered playing rules with clear salary implications by expanding the strike zone and raising pitching mounds in 1963. By 1964 Baltimore Oriole player delegate Steve Barber had to admit that the Players Association he represented offered major leaguers little practical leverage, and that they were effectively on their own in dealing with management. A year later the association's assets had dwindled to but a single beat-up filing cabinet and $5,400 in funds.[34]

The birth of the Players Association and the related issue of the pension were not the big leagues' most troublesome labor headaches in the 1950s and early 1960s. That dubious honor went to the majors' relationship with their captive minor leagues. Big league executives complained that the costs of maintaining extensive minor league systems had become too high, while the minors' attendance declines and franchise contractions threatened a shortage of low-cost talent for the majors to pluck. As revenue at the major league level grew sluggishly, the owners took a hard second look at their farm systems and generally concluded that in emulating empire builders Rickey and Weiss, they, like the rail barons of a century before, had overbuilt. With all big league clubs now possessing extensive farms and providing them with financial subsidization, no one organization could exclusively exploit the rest by selling off its surplus talent.

By 1950 even a latecomer to farm building such as the Cubs team

THE PATERNALISTIC ERA

spent $1.2 million on salaries and expenses of scouts, related management expenses, and bonuses to amateur free agent signees. That same year the Cubs estimated their per-player development costs of producing major league talent at nearly $114,000. They also calculated their "combined team replacement expense" at over $450,000, a sum considerably higher than their big league payroll. For wealthier organizations with bigger farm systems, the price tag was even steeper. Yankee per-player development costs stood at over $200,000, and from 1946 to 1960 the club spent $1.22 million on scouts and baseball schools, $615,000 on amateur bonuses, and over $4 million on "team replacement" (i.e., development) expenses. In 1950 Brooklyn controlled 25 clubs, and a year later the Dodgers claimed to have 637 players in their system, including Korean War call-ups. By 1952 the majors owned outright 195 of 364 minor league teams. Despite some economizing by 1956, the average AL team that year still controlled 289 players, and the typical NL organization managed a whopping 391.[35]

Not surprisingly, given their own revenue dilemma, the majors in the early 1950s began to pull out more and more of their financial props from the minors. They demanded that minor league dependencies become more self-sustaining and defied the latter's pleas for greater subsidies or increased draft prices. As attendance fell by 50 percent from 1949 levels by 1956 and 75 percent by 1963, the minors' cries for relief became more shrill. But as long as the big leagues' immediate needs for talent continued to be met, they frowned on providing subsidies beyond those necessary to maintain that level of supply. Only the PCL's franchises could seriously threaten trade war as leverage to force greater financial concessions. In both 1950 and 1951 the circuit again threatened to withdraw from Organized Baseball if it did not receive such support. Under Commissioner Frick, the majors did grant the PCL a new AAAA classification in which only one player with a minimum of five years in professional ball per team could be drafted annually by the majors at a $15,000 price. The magnates also boosted draft prices paid to other leagues to $10,000 at AAA, $7,500 at AA, and $6,000 at A, and they likewise limited team losses to one player per team per year. B-, C-, and D-level draft prices rose as well to $4,000, $2,500, and $2,000, respectively.[36]

As part of their new arrangement with the minors, Frick and his colleagues implied that at least four of the PCL's teams would be brought into the majors. The subsequent criteria, however, included a market of 15 million fans, a stadium that could seat over 25,000, and attendance figures over three years of more than 3.5 million. Outraged, the PCL in 1952 tried to block the majors from optioning demotees to its circuit for up to three years, a move that only deprived the league itself of quality players. The majors also managed to evade the higher draft fees they had pledged by drafting fewer men, which also contributed to the "aging" on big league rosters. The number of direct major league draftees, 28 in 1950, fell to 10 by 1955. Another stratagem involved organizations loading up their top minor league talent on a single club and effectively limiting both draft losses and draft fees. In the process of concentrating their talent on a minimum number of clubs, the big league organizations worsened the minors' talent maldistribution and accelerated the minors' financial contraction.[37]

By the mid-1950s the majors themselves had begun to migrate to address their gate problems. In 1953–54, baseball fans saw the Boston Braves relocate to Milwaukee; the Philadelphia Athletics, to Kansas City; and the St. Louis Browns, to Baltimore as the Orioles. Even more dramatic was the rapid-fire migration of the Brooklyn Dodgers and the New York Giants to Los Angeles and San Francisco, respectively, after the 1957 campaign. Besides shoring up the majors' attendance revenues, the moves snuffed out the lingering trade war threats from the PCL. Meanwhile, with the increased per-player draft prices not translating into any greater net subsidization from the majors, minor league clubs and leagues folded with alarming regularity. From 1951 to the start of 1957, the number of minor league teams plummeted from 207 to only 38. Because the majors desired consolidation, not complete collapse, of their minor league systems, in 1956 the majors injected a "stabilization fund" of $0.5 million into the low minors. Each major league club's bill was a modest $31,500, however, while the National Association was forced to add $100,000.[38]

One additional reason the magnates refused to provide greater financial help to the minors was their inability to control their appetites for top-drawer amateur and outside talent. Free agent bidding for bonus babies devoured moneys otherwise available to possibly shore up the minors. Big spending on bonus babies had been evident even before Pearl Harbor, as fears of roster losses triggered by war had led to a wave of bidding. In 1941 Detroit had paid Dick Wakefield $52,000 and had seen him go on to eventually win a batting title. At the end of World War II the competition had renewed as clubs scrambled to stock their rosters. Despite the 1946 adoption of a rule requiring any signee valued over $6,000 to be placed on a big league roster or forfeited in the next year's draft, the under-the-table bidding had continued. In 1947 alone the Phillies anted up $65,000 for pitcher Curt Simmons, and the Boston Braves paid $75,000 for Johnny Antonelli. In 1949 the Tigers paid out $68,500 and two cars for catcher Frank House.[39]

The bidding for bonus babies took a giant leap upward in 1950, however, when the owners repealed even their weak earlier restrictions. Some of the new signees amply justified their owners' investments. But for every Dick Groat, Harvey Kuenn, or Robin Roberts, there were also expensive "busts." In 1951 alone, the aggregate $4.5 million spent on bonuses to amateur signees almost matched the total outlays for big league salaries. Under new restrictions passed in December 1952, bonus babies signed for over $4,000 had to be assigned to the major league club for a full two years or else be exposed to drafting. Spending slowed but did not stop. Fourteen prospects garnered $0.5 million in 1953, including outfielder Al Kaline, and seven more the next year received $285,000, among them slugger Harmon Killebrew. Of the majors' 100 bonus babies of the 1950s, 37 were acquired in 1955 alone. Admitting defeat, the magnates once more scrapped their bonus rules in 1957, although carryover signees such as the Dodgers' Sandy Koufax remained subject to the two-year big league requirement. Again, bonus payments surged. St. Louis added Ray Sadecki and Tim McCarver, and in 1961 Kansas City owner Charley Finley inked pitcher Lew Krausse for $125,000.[40]

The majors' failure to rein in their competitive appetites left them even less willing to take more costly steps to shore up the minors. Although they agreed to raise draft prices for top-level minor leaguers to $25,000 and to remove the one-per-squad limit on draft-eligible players, the magnates gave themselves an out by allowing draft eligibles to be "promoted" to the majors and then optioned back down while retaining their draft-free status for four years at AA or higher, three years at A, and two at B or C. Ironically, the minor leagues' continuing implosion and the majors' bonus baby costs led Cleveland owner Frank Lane to propose resurrecting Judge Landis's prewar scheme to dismantle the farm systems, return all signing rights to amateur talent to independent minor leagues, and provide the majors universal draft access to the latter's talent at low, fixed prices.[41]

Rather than adopt Lane's radical departure, the owners instead settled for patchwork alternatives in the form of more stabilization moneys to the captive minors and renewed efforts to curb the hunger for bonus babies. In 1959 a new stabilization plan established a $1 million fund for development and promotion of minor league players. Two years later, triggered by the Krausse signing, a big league study committee on the bonus problem headed by Lee MacPhail (son of the former Yankee power broker) recommended limiting each club to one protected bonus baby in the minors and requiring any others to be kept on the big league roster for two years. Again the measures slowed, but did not stop, the signing of expensive amateurs and did too little to arrest further franchise collapses in the minors. The International League, wounded by the loss of its Havana franchise because of the Fidel Castro revolution, saw its Montreal team fold and migrate to Syracuse, its Jersey City team also relocate, and its Puerto Rican franchise fail after only one season. At the end of 1961 the circuit cut back the rosters of its surviving clubs by one player apiece and shortened the "payroll season" by eliminating off-days and thereby compressing the length of the season. The International League's Syracuse club also arranged to serve as a AAA farm team for both the Yankees and the Senators.[42]

By early 1962 the majors and minors finally agreed on the basic outlines of a settlement to define their relationship more permanently. On balance it better reflected the majors' demand for cost control and talent price stability than it did the minors' need for revenue. In exchange for the majors' pledge to continue their sponsorship, the minors accepted their shrunken dimensions as irreversible. As outlined by a twelve-member committee chaired by the Pirates' John W. Galbreath, the plan consolidated the minors from seven classifications to four. The three AAA circuits were reduced to two with the folding of the old American Association, while the old AA and A leagues merged in a new AA category, surviving B through D circuits consolidated in a new class A, and a new rookie-level classification was created. Under the restructuring plan, the majors agreed to maintain a minimum of twenty clubs at the new AAA level, twenty at AA, and sixty overall in the A and rookie circuits.[43]

In response to the minors' pleadings, the plan also featured a new player development contract that authorized player salary reimbursements from the majors for minor league players' pay in excess of $800 a month at AAA, $150 a month at AA, and $50 at A or rookie level. The majors also agreed to pick up the tab for their dependencies' spring training expenses and manager salaries up to a $7,500 maximum at AAA. Save for the majors' four new expansion franchises — the New York Mets, the Houston Colt-45s, the Washington Senators (replacing the team of the same name after its migration west as the Minnesota Twins), and the Los Angeles Angels—each major-league club committed itself to maintaining at least five farms. For the minors and the multitude of small towns that had sustained them, stabilization came at a steep price. By the end of 1964, one estimate placed the number of communities that had lost professional baseball since the minors' heyday at 320.[44]

The magnates' drive to consolidate the minors, painful though it was, proved easier to implement than curbing their own appetites for bonus babies. But triggered by fears of a new wave of high-priced signings after the Angels' $205,000 payment to collegiate outfielder Rick Reichart in 1964, they acted. Guided by the recommendations of yet another Lee MacPhail study panel, over the objections of six big-spending opponents a majority of owners voted in December 1964 to establish an amateur player draft. Beginning in June 1965, AL and NL teams would alternate picks in reverse order of their previous season's finish for the exclusive negotiating rights to amateur players. Any such player still unsigned by the following January would then become eligible for "reentry" selection. Each big league club could only pick one player directly in each draft, but its AAA team could make two selections; its AA club, four picks; and A franchises, as many as they wished.[45]

With the first overall selection of an eventual 814 players picked in the inaugural draft, the Kansas City Athletics took Arizona State University outfielder Rick Monday and signed him for $104,000. The high price proved necessary to prevent owner Finley from losing his pick to reentry, but it still remained well below the Reichart predraft standard. In contrast to Monday, the University of Southern California's Tom Seaver balked at the hometown Dodgers' offer and stayed in school, to be drafted and signed the third time around by the New York Mets. Seaver, too, failed to crack the Reichart barrier. The $205,000 sum for an amateur signee remained unsurpassed for another sixteen years, until the Mets broke it in 1980 with their acquisition of outfielder Darryl Strawberry.[46]

It was a major irony of professional baseball in the 1950s and early 1960s that in the effort to hold the lid on player procurement costs, the magnates dismantled large chunks of the system they had created in the interwar years to achieve similar goals. In the deconstruction process they also unwittingly triggered a cultural revolution within player ranks that would eventually help undermine their monopsony. In the years before World War II, following the lead of Branch Rickey they had built extensive, southern-based farm systems. Because the host region's Jim Crow customs militated against integration, the owners had effectively refused recruitment of nonwhite players and had rooted the industry in conservative, white, small-town America. But in the postwar era, ironically again led by Rickey, the industry had reversed itself on the issue of racial integration, and the change was accompanied by the deterioration of much of the minor league structure, especially its southern-dominated lower circuits. It was as if without directly choosing to replace one system of generating cheap talent with another, the magnates had radically changed course and opted for an expanded multiracial player base as their future long-term key to controlling labor costs — after having rejected the same option by constructing their elaborate white farm chains two decades earlier. What the magnates painfully would learn was that in diminishing the role of the white southern farms in professional talent recruitment and development, they paved the way not only for a more diverse work force but also for a more independent one.

At the major league level the 1950–65 period saw a significant expansion of African American and Latino employment in the playing ranks (see Appendix, Fig. 4). In 1950 only nine U.S.-born blacks and four Latin-born players toiled in the majors. But by 1956 African Americans constituted 10 percent of the big league rookie crop and 17 percent by 1963. The black share of all major leaguers climbed from 7.5 percent in 1954 to 12.5 percent as early as 1958, and by 1965, 86 African Americans played in the American and National Leagues. In similar fashion, the share of foreign-born or U.S. players of Hispanic ancestry among big league rookies rose to 17 percent in 1960 and leveled off at about 10 percent of each year's new class through the mid-1960s. By 1965, 54 Latinos held big league roster spots. The combined percentage of black and Hispanic rookies jumped from 8 percent in 1950 to a pre-1965 peak of 28 percent in 1960 and held at approximately one in five by the mid-1960s.[47]

Some clubs continued to trail in minority recruitment, and they paid the competitive price for their delay. In the early 1950s the Dodgers, the Giants, and the Indians continued to lead the pack in hiring minority players. At the other extreme, the St. Louis Cardinals, the Philadelphia Phillies, the Detroit Tigers, and the Boston Red Sox each signed but one black player to their organizations by 1952, and as late as September 1953 only six of sixteen big league clubs claimed an African American on their rosters. The Red Sox team was the last to promote a black player to the majors when it elevated Elijah "Pumpsie" Green to its squad in 1959. Although the New York Yankees continued to dominate the American League and the World Series, baseball analysts increasingly deemed the National League the superior circuit, largely because of its greater incorporation of nonwhite talent. At the start of the 1957 season, NL rosters contained eighteen black players; AL teams, only eight.[48]

Because of the Yankees' visibility, their stubborn resistance to nonwhite ballplayers attracted the most scrutiny. The aversion to hiring blacks and Hispanics came straight from the top. General manager George Weiss explicitly instructed scout Tom Greenwade, a former Rickey bird dog, not to "sneak around down any back alleys and sign any niggers." The Yankee organization deliberately passed up the chance to secure not only Willie Mays, but also shortstop Ernie Banks of the Kansas City Monarchs. When slugger Vic Power, a dark-skinned Hispanic star signed by New York in 1952, led the American Association in hitting, the Yankees not only refused to promote him but released him for possessing "unsuitable" temperament. The Yankees then tabbed Elston Howard, the 1954 International League MVP, as their first black major leaguer because the soft-spoken catcher possessed better "manners." New York's organizational philosophy against nonwhites began to change seriously only with the "retirements" of Weiss and manager Casey Stengel after the club's surprising 1960 World Series loss to Pittsburgh, an NL leader in Hispanic recruitment.[49]

Clark Griffith's Washington Senators had been the early front-runners in the pursuit of Latino talent. Building on his wartime Cuban forays, Griffith had established a B-level minor league franchise in Havana and "promoted" it to the International League in 1954. Soon, however, the Pirates, the Giants, and the Dodgers entered the competition. Cuba and, to a lesser extent, Puerto Rico constituted the main hunting grounds until the 1960s, when the Castro revolution and American diplomatic and economic isolation closed access to Cuba. Scouting then shifted to the Dominican Republic, Central America, and Venezuela. When Branch Rickey left the Dodgers for the Pirates, his Latin American scout Howie Haak made Pittsburgh a rising force in Hispanic recruitment. By inking directly or by raiding other organizations' signees in the draft, the Pirates garnered such stars as Roman Mejias and Roberto Clemente. By the early 1960s the San Francisco Giants had emerged as Pittsburgh's biggest rival, and the two organizations vied for the Alou brothers, Orlando

Cepeda, Jose Pagan, and Juan Marichal. Even the Philadelphia Phillies proved willing to sign and promote Latinos, obtaining Ruben Gomez in 1959 and Juan "Pancho" Herrera and Tony Taylor in 1960.[50]

By the mid-1960s, earlier organizational reputations had changed. Some clubs that had been pioneers in racial recruitment now retreated as front-office leadership changed, while others surged to the front. Notable in the latter category were the Cardinals. Under owners Breadon and Saigh, the Redbirds had maintained a predominantly white southern image while eschewing blacks, Hispanics, and Jews. But following purchase of the club by the Busch brewing family, St. Louis belatedly added black stars Bill White, Bob Gibson, and Curt Flood. When the Cardinals met and vanquished the Yankees in the 1964 World Series, reporters noted that New York still had but one black starter—Howard—while the Cardinals fielded four. While St. Louis's racial reputation dramatically improved, that of the Dodgers turned in the other direction. Although Los Angeles stepped up Hispanic recruitment in the 1960s in keeping with its shifting fan base, its pursuit of African American players dropped off—a trend some observers linked to the prejudices of owner Walter O'Malley.[51]

African American and Latino major leaguers continued to be racial pioneers in the United States in the 1950s and 1960s. On the regular-season circuit, black players forced the lifting of barriers to integrated hotel facilities in the mid-1950s. In 1953 Jackie Robinson forced the Chase Hotel in St. Louis to extend lodging to blacks in exchange for not utilizing its dining room, nightclub, or pool. Robinson continued to stay at, and pressure, the facility during road trips for the next two years. In 1955 the Chase—the last segregated hotel in the big leagues—finally lifted its remaining restrictions. Southern communities hosting big league spring training squads, however, proved more stubborn in the maintenance of segregation. In many cases, Florida towns did not relent until the 1960s. Although Branch Rickey created "Dodgertown," a massive spring training complex on the site of a leased naval air base in Vero Beach, partly to avoid racial harassment, players still faced discrimination when they went into the city. The Dodgers played exhibition games before integrated audiences in Atlanta and Miami, but segregated crowds remained the law in Jacksonville, Montgomery, New Orleans, and Savannah for years.[52]

A handful of clubs moved their spring training operations to Arizona when confronted with massive resistance in the South. Players in other

Jackie Robinson and Branch Rickey
(AP/Wide World Photos)

organizations, however, continued to meet the challenges head-on. In 1961 Bill White led black Cardinal teammates in a successful campaign against a whites-only player breakfast in St. Petersburg. Confronted by housing segregation, a Busch family friend bought a local motel and leased it to the Cardinals for a six-week stretch to guarantee integrated accommodations. On the Milwaukee Braves of the late 1950s, the black outfield trio of Hank Aaron, Wes Covington, and Bill Bruton found that because of segregation in the club's spring training home of Bradenton, Florida, they were forced to reside in a small apartment over a garage while white teammates stayed at the Manatee Hotel. The Braves traded Bruton after the 1960 season; but in 1961 Aaron and Covington forced the removal of racial seating designations from the Braves' Florida ballpark, and the club promised integrated housing for all team members by the next year. Milwaukee ultimately accomplished its pledge by moving the entire team to a hotel outside the Bradenton city limits. Only the passage of federal civil rights legislation in 1964 truly guaranteed the end of Jim Crow in public accommodations in the South.[53]

Minority major leaguers at least could escape the worst segregation and terror once the regular season began. Minor leaguers faced far greater peril. Not only were their spring training facilities in the South, but so were many of their clubs and leagues. Prospects faced the possibility of years of toil in such adversity before cracking the majors. Big leaguers could offer their prominence to help their juniors in the spring, but from April on, minor leaguers of color battled alone. At the start of the decade, thirty-two of fifty-eight minor leagues operated entirely or in part in the states of the Old Confederacy. Ironically, one discovery of the nonwhite prospect was that as many leagues foundered, clubs became more and more dependent on his talent not only to win pennants but to attract fans and maintain financial viability. Nonetheless, when the Pork Hill, South Carolina, team in the Tri-State League tried to use black outfielder David Mobley in 1952, the circuit's officials barred him after one appearance. The Cotton States League attempted to expel its Hot Springs franchise for a similar racial transgression. The local chamber of commerce in Jacksonville excluded blacks from the city's Florida State League team. But that same season the Texas League began to integrate, and by the following year most circuits in the Southwest, Florida, and the border South followed suit. For those that stubbornly held out, the consequences often were fatal. By 1965, of a total of nineteen minor league circuits, only seven operated in the South. At the same time, ironically, three circuits included clubs in Mexico.[54]

Life during the season presented a frightening struggle for minor league prospects of color even once a league or club grudgingly agreed to integrate. Willie Stargell once had a shotgun raised to his temple while he walked the streets of Plainview, Texas, and the holder warned him not to play that day if he valued his life. Bill White remembered pleading with the New York Giants, his original organization, in 1953 to assign him to a lower minor league rather than to its affiliate in the Carolina League. When they refused, White became an unwilling pioneer as the circuit's first African American. On one occasion the first baseman and his teammates had to use their bats to fight their way to the team bus after a game. Curt Flood, who followed White into the league, bitterly recalled sitting and crying in his room many nights and hating his own teammates for treating him as subhuman. Billy Williams similarly became so dispirited that he left his San Antonio team and returned home to Mobile, Alabama, only to be talked into returning by friends and family. Dodger catching prospect John Roseboro even experienced nightmares of the mutilated black teenager Emmett Till when his club traveled through Mississippi.[55]

Two high-ranking circuits, the South Atlantic "Sally" League and the Southern Association, constituted the "flagship" leagues of Dixie. As massive resistance rose in many southern states after the *Brown* decision, they became the flash points of baseball's struggle to integrate the minors. The Southern Association "successfully" held the line against black players but paid the price for it. Only one African American, Nat Peoples of the Atlanta Crackers, managed a single at-bat in 1954, but the circuit folded at the end of 1961. In the Sally League, Hank Aaron's heroics prompted one admiring scribe to quip that he had "led the circuit in everything except hotel accommodations." Nonetheless, Aaron and teammate Felix Mantilla routinely faced death threats, racial slurs, and humiliations. Only one city in the league, Montgomery, even had a hotel within its city limits in which the two ballplayers could stay. The league president, a former Happy Chandler employee, evoked the memory of the earlier protective surveillance of Jackie Robinson by having a subordinate "sort of keep a lookout" on Aaron.[56]

As growing numbers of black and Hispanic players fought their way onto Organized Baseball's rosters, they ran into other, subtler barriers. One was financial, for besides their talent and gate appeal, their low price tag attracted owners. While magnates offered white prospects six-figure bonuses, blacks signed for $5,000–15,000 advances and salaries of $5,000. Latinos could be gotten for as little as $300–400 in bonuses. Hank Aaron, a $200-a-month player in the NAL at age nineteen, jumped at the Braves' offer of $2,500 for an initial thirty-day trial and $7,500 more if he stayed. Although Roberto Clemente initially inked with the Dodgers at $10,000, the Giants secured Juan Marichal from the Dominican sandlots for only $300. As of 1959, while twenty-six white prospects had received signing bonuses of $20,000 or more, no African Americans had. From 1959 to 1961, forty-three more whites and only three blacks added their names to the list.[57]

At the major league level, the black pioneers also earned far less in salary than white players who were less talented. Despite a fan appeal rivaling or even exceeding that of Ted Williams, Ralph Kiner, or Stan Musial, Jackie Robinson drew a peak salary in 1957 of $42,000, less than half that of his top white contemporaries. According to one estimate, the low cost and high return of nonwhite major leaguers in the 1950s resulted in an average "differential revenue product" to their employing clubs of over $55,000 per man. From 1953 to 1961, black hitters batted twenty points higher than their white counterparts, and the differential widened to over twenty-one points from 1961 to 1965. In the 1950s blacks received 8 of 10 National League MVP awards. In the ten-year period ending in 1962, the figure was 9 of 10. At the 1960 All-Star contests, 7 Latinos made NL or AL squads, and by the 1965 game the figure was 8. Both circuits' batting champions in 1964, Roberto Clemente and Tony Oliva, hailed from the Caribbean.[58]

With this success, however, also came the establishment of unofficial racial quotas, management claims of squad "tipping points" that would trigger adverse gate effects, and prejudicial positional stacking. When it appeared likely that Dodger infielder Billy Cox would lose his starting position in favor of African American prospect Jim Gilliam, he lashed out to writer Roger Kahn, "How would you like a nigger to take your job?" As early as the mid-1950s, big league reporters whispered about the existence of a five-man minority limit on teams to avoid white player or fan backlash. One way of minimizing this "problem" that reinforced ugly racial stereotypes of the mental and physical characteristics of blacks was "stacking" them in outfield and first baseman positions. By 1965 blacks constituted 50 percent of big league outfielders, but only 16 percent of infielders and 9 percent of pitchers. The positional prejudice, which could be found from entry level upward, also effectively thwarted the hopes of even minority stars to continue in baseball as scouts, coaches, and managers. Of eighty-eight big league managers from 1947 to 1967, only 12 percent were outfielders, while two-thirds were catchers or infielders other than first basemen. Lou Brock recalled that when former Negro League member Buck O'Neill scouted him for the Chicago Cubs, he was the only African American scout in the Deep South. By 1962 O'Neill was the only black coach on a big league team. In testimony the *Sporting News* tellingly praised as "superb," Commissioner Frick excused baseball's sorry record in minority advancement by asserting that because the game had "evolved in slavery days," blacks had fallen fifty years behind whites in their mastery of the game. Accordingly, it would be another fifty years after the start of integration in baseball before minorities would become "important in the organizational baseball picture."[59]

In another form of continued racism in baseball, by the mid-1960s black and Hispanic players were starring on the field but regularly still had to deal with bigotry at the hands of coaches and managers. In many cases the latter were products of the all-white leagues and playing force of the 1930s and 1940s, with all their regional and cultural prejudices against nonwhites. During Hank Aaron's minor league years, one of his managers, a native of Mobile, Alabama, wrote of him, "Nobody can guess his IQ because he gives you nothing to go on." What passed for praise included the comment, "The kid looks lazy, but he isn't." Bill White's hitting instructor in St. Louis, Harry Walker, helped him refine his skills but at the same time stereotypically described blacks as undedicated and irresponsible. On the San Francisco Giants, manager Alvin Dark's tirades against Hispanic players included banning the speaking of Spanish on the team bus and accusing them of malingering. Orlando Cepeda recalled playing with a severe case of the flu out of fear that his skipper would accusing him of "jaking." The Giants' clubhouse atmosphere briefly improved in 1965 with Dark's replacement by Herman Franks, but following an ugly act of on-field violence by Juan Marichal against Dodger catcher John Roseboro, San Francisco unloaded many of its Latin stars to other organizations.[60]

The experiences of minority players as they climbed the professional ladder left them hardened to prejudice and more skeptical of management authority figures and their intentions. They were part of an even broader, subtle change in player outlook that led to a more aggressive, assertive player posture in the years ahead. Not only by race, but also by ethnicity, region, education, and social class the player force was changing (see Appendix, Fig. 4). The ethnic share of Southern and Eastern European descendants, Germans, English, Irish, and Scandinavians all dropped, as did the proportion of players hailing from the rural South. A 1963 survey of big leaguers by home state also showed the five biggest contributors of players were, in descending order, California, New York, Pennsylvania, Illinois, and Michigan. The same study showed that fewer than one-third of major leaguers came from states south of the Mason-Dixon line and west to Texas. And of them, a growing share were African Americans.[61]

Reflecting the rise of the middle class in the United States after World War II, more and more professional ballplayers also claimed better economic backgrounds and education levels than either their predecessors or their supervisors. The *Sporting News Baseball Register* in 1963 indicated that over 40 percent of current big league players had attended college for at least one semester, compared with only 30 percent of their coaches and managers. Data on rookies compiled by Hall of Fame librarian Lee Allen indicated an even higher level of education among new major leaguers. Forty-four percent of rookies of the 1946–50 period had attended college, and the figure for the 1961–65 group was 15 percent higher.[62] By many measurements, a new breed of player was rising up the ranks. He was more skeptical of authority, expected higher material reward, and whether from formal education or a Jim Crow "school of hard knocks," was more assertive in seeking control of his own career. All that this new generation of players needed to pose an unprecedented challenge to Organized Baseball's traditional prerogatives was someone with the expertise to show them the way.

As the baseball industry entered the 1960s, it persisted in being its own worst enemy. Every time the magnates seemed to embrace expansionist strategies, they followed up with retreats. Prodded by pressure for new franchises in New York and Washington, D.C., the threat of federal antitrust legislation, continued population growth in the Sun Belt, and the bonanza promised by expansion fees and higher broadcast revenue, in August 1960 the majors voted to add four new teams. Partly to accommodate the majors' expansion to twenty teams, the two leagues lengthened their schedules to 162 games beginning with their newcomers' first seasons. Existing clubs protected their top twenty-five men and still garnered $75,000 from the new teams for each player selected in a special draft. TV revenue also grew. By 1960 the total big league annual broadcasting pool had expanded by over $10 million in a decade to $12.5 million. Five years later it had doubled again. Construction of ballparks such as the new Dodger Stadium in 1962 also signaled a wave of baseball modernization. Over the 1960s ten new parks were built, and seven were in the National League. In its new facility Los Angeles attracted an average of 2.5 million spectators a year in the first five years, generating annual profits of $4 million.[63]

Yet the owners could not break completely free from their traditionalist, cost-obsessive mentality. Nor did they appear capable of thinking of the best interests of the entire industry rather than just their separate agendas. Even as new stadiums promised a more appealing fan experience and higher gate and concession revenues, their price tags (ranging from $18 million to $38 million, with an average of $25 million) engendered caution, selfishness, and retrenchment. When expansion temporarily diluted pitching and, combined with the longer schedule, led to offensive records such as Roger Maris's sixty-one home runs in the 1961 season, Commissioner Frick devalued the accomplishment with an asterisk in the record book. Rather than viewing the offensive surge as a brief aberration at worst and a boon at best, the owners responded by curbing batting. By raising the pitching mound and expanding the strike zone to 1887 dimensions in 1963, the magnates ushered in a half-dozen years of crippled offense. From 1950 to 1962 the composite major league batting average had stood at a modest .259. Within a year of the rules changes it fell to .246, and to .237 by 1968. As might have been predicted, AL attendance, which peaked in 1961 at 10.2 million fans, slid to 8.9 million by 1965. The National League hung on more gamely, aided by the addition of the big-market Mets, but attendance figures of 15 million in 1966 slumped to less than 12 million by 1968.[64]

The majors' gate woes, especially when compared with the booming popularity of the NFL, put even more pressure on the industry's broadcast revenue to boost profits. But although the television pie gradually increased, more and more of it came in the form of national contracts that only skewed the benefits more in favor of the big-market clubs, especially the Yankees. Local rights payments that each club negotiated and kept leveled off beginning in 1963, as the game's excitement and fan attendance diminished. In 1964, in a move that underscored the national networks' concert of interest with big-market clubs at the expense of the rest of the fraternity, CBS bought the Yankees outright for a record $11.2 million. As a consequence, New York received roughly two-thirds, or $895,000, of the national TV moneys paid out by the network for its Game of the Week broadcasts. CBS, in effect, paid itself. The other clubs retaliated in December with a $5.7 million pact with rival ABC, generating $300,000 for each franchise. Without the Yankees in the package, however, ABC not only refused to pay a higher sum but then dropped the deal entirely after just one year. In a belated effort to mend fences between the Yankees and their AL brethren through greater revenue sharing, the league raised visiting teams' share of after-tax gate receipts back to 20 percent, but the change excluded receipts from luxury boxes or concessions. On the TV front, NBC—holder of World Series and All-Star Game rights—raised its payments by 65 percent and picked up the regular-season Saturday package, along with plans for a Monday prime-time offering. But it refused to boost its own per-club compensation above ABC's earlier level.[65]

If the owners' backwardness and bickering caused them to squander opportunities, they at least claimed general labor peace and payroll restraint. Even on the labor front, however, storm clouds had begun to gather, not from the players but, instead, from the umpires. For years the men in blue had endured low pay and inadequate pensions. By 1950, entry-level big league arbiters earned $5,000 a year and $15 a day for expenses. World Series work brought in $2,500 more, and All-Star Games paid $100 plus expenses. The circuits also subjected their umpires to intrusive regulation of moral conduct, fraternization, and outside earnings. In 1953 the umpires received a modest pay boost that elevated minimum salaries to $6,000 and series pay to $3,000, but both major leagues still provided no medical insurance coverage. Rather than being included in the same pension plan with the players, managers, and coaches, the arbiters had been forced to maintain a separate plan since 1951 with the Equitable Life Insurance Company. Under the plan's limited benefits, a retiring umpire earned annual payments of $100 at age fifty for each year of big league service, but only men with fifteen years of big league service were eligible. In 1957 the owners' refusal to raise umpire pension contributions from All-Star Game proceeds triggered a round of protests by arbiter Joseph Papanella and his colleagues at the mid-season classic.[66]

By 1963 the umpires of the National League concluded they had endured enough. Augie Donatelli, the Italian American son of a western Pennsylvania coal miner and veteran of twenty-four big league seasons, launched a union recruiting effort among fellow arbiters and crew chiefs. Initial enlistees included the legendary Jocko Conlan, who was nearing retirement, and Al Barlick, who, like Donatelli, was the descendant of pro-union coal miners. Insisting "all we need is half-a-dozen" more signers, Donatelli prompted his recruits to seek more members from their respective crews. As a result, Ed Vargo, Henry "Shag" Crawford, John Kibbler, Tom Gorman, and Chris Pelekoudas soon joined. When Conlan's hope of retaining a friend and Chicago judge as the group's legal representative fell through, the men hired John J. Reynolds, the veteran umpire's personal attorney and an ex-arbiter himself. During an off-day in the Windy City the pro-union arbiters, about two-thirds of the National League's total force, elected Barlick, Conlan, Gorman, Crawford, and Donatelli to the board of directors of the new National League Umpires Association.[67]

When NL president Warren Giles and league owners discovered the organization's existence, they fought back to "bust the union." The cir-

cuit demoted Donatelli from crew chief and assigned him to a recon-
structed Al Barlick crew as part of an effort to consolidate and isolate the
"troublemakers." Following repeated attempts by Reynolds to schedule a
meeting with Giles and the NL executive board, management responded
with a proposed session in Chicago that meant, because of other umpires' work commitments, only the Barlick crew could attend. Reynolds
warned the four men, who included Stan Landes and Mel Steiner, that
they risked being singled out and fired if they went ahead with the meeting. Bravely, they accompanied Reynolds to the appointment and presented their proposal to boost NL umpire pensions to $500 for each year of
service up to a maximum $15,000 payout. They also pressed demands for
salary and expense increases and fringe benefits. Although league harassment continued, economic gains slowly came. As a result of the efforts
of the National League Umpires Association, arbiters in the senior circuit began to garner higher pay than their AL counterparts, a fact that
only hastened the day the latter would follow their brothers' lead. By the
late 1960s, minimum salaries of NL umpires had climbed to $10,000, and
their top-end pay of $26,500 compared with only $17,000 for AL senior
arbiters.[68]

Changes were coming whether or not the magnates liked or were prepared for them. As Ford Frick stepped down as commissioner in 1965
after two terms, even he appeared to grasp that fact, though he had done
little to prepare his employers for the new day. In his farewell address,
he chided them for their refusal to "look beyond the day and the hour,"
their unwillingness to "abide by the rules they themselves make," and
their rejection of "sound judgment" in favor of "expediency" in policy
decisions.[69] Events would soon test the willingness of the stewards of
Organized Baseball to take such admonitions to heart, or whether by
persisting in their backwardness and outmoded paternalism they would
fail to appreciate, and thereby lose the chance to mold, the economic
revolution about to send shock waves through their sport.

PART TWO
THE INFLATIONARY ERA
The Age of Miller

CHAPTER 5 : MILLER TIME
1966–1972

By the middle of the 1960s, Americans found themselves buffeted by powerful winds of change. The civil rights movement that had gathered momentum in the 1950s and early 1960s and produced remarkable legal gains for blacks now confronted white backlash, lingering poverty in the ghettos, and rising violence. What had once seemed a distant minor conflict in Southeast Asia had become a war demanding the sacrifices of hundreds of thousands, but it lacked clear objectives or the prospect of a quick conclusion. The new generation responded by taking to the streets to question their elders' political authority. On the cultural front, too, the young were challenging older conventions regarding sexuality, abstinence from illicit drugs, and other forms of traditional morality. All the while surging material growth and consumer demand, spurred by the "guns-and-butter" spending of the Great Society and the Vietnam War, threatened to push the U.S. economy into inflationary peril. Indeed, a new era of inflation—of hopes followed by disillusionments, passions leading to public violence, and prices presaging stagnating living standards—was beginning.

Baseball was swept along in the tide of social chaos, and particular manifestations transformed its labor relationships. Although the magnates had not taken adequate advantage of it, rising U.S. wages and recreational spending pointed to new growth in baseball attendance and television ratings, but also to accelerating costs, including payrolls. Baseball's changing playing force also represented an alteration of the owners' economic environment. The players' "radicalization," however, remained in its infancy and, as yet, had not created the collective focus and direction to challenge the performers' imbalance of power with management.

Nonetheless, a few leading ballplayers spotted emerging changes in the baseball economy. They were determined not to allow the impending revenue opportunities to pass the players by, as they largely had done in earlier growth periods. The visionaries included former NL player representative Robin Roberts and Philadelphia Phillies team delegate Jim Bunning. Both men had grown concerned that the owners would hoard virtually all of the industry's pending television bonanza for themselves rather than increase the share going to the players' pension system. The last agreement, negotiated early in the decade by Judge Cannon, would expire in March 1967, and it had excluded revenue from the majors' increasingly lucrative Game of the Week package. Bunning had also noted that the purchase of the Yankees by CBS signaled an era of cozier financial relationships between sports leagues and broadcasting entities that could all too easily leave the players out in the cold. The two player leaders also recognized that the television era offered expanded visibility for baseball's performers, but the latter needed more professional representation to capitalize on opportunities for individual and group licensing and marketing. The Players Association glaringly lacked the full-time professional staff capable of such toe-to-toe bargaining with the magnates and with outside merchandisers.[1]

Not all association leaders shared Roberts's and Bunning's conviction that new blood was needed. NL representative Bob Friend, for example, had asserted publicly in 1963 that "during the thirteen years I have been in the major leagues, I know of no player who has been exploited." Friend had even gone along with Cannon's consent to the retroactive removal of pension funds by the owners. Not surprisingly, when the association in late 1965 decided to seek a nominee for a new position at the top of their organization, an executive director, Friend lobbied for the judge. The association's executive board, however, selected a four-person search committee of Roberts, Bunning, Friend, and Harvey Kuenn to pick a nominee to place before the membership. Roberts then contacted George William Taylor, a Philadelphia-based labor expert and professor at the Wharton School of Finance, for his recommendations. The man Taylor suggested, forty-eight-year-old Marvin Julian Miller, was an outsider to baseball but a former colleague on the War Labor Board and an economist with the United Steelworkers of America.[2]

Marvin Miller, who would take the Players Association from a position of dormancy to become the dominant economic force in major league baseball, significantly was the first professional unionist to lead a baseball players' organization. That difference—in ideology, training, and professional experience—would prove telling. Miller, the son of an outgoing Orthodox Jewish garment salesman and a schoolteacher, grew up in Brooklyn during the Great Depression. As a youngster he drew from both parents an instinctive sympathy for society's underdogs, strong prolabor sentiments, and fervent support of the New Deal. He resented, however, his father's attempts to constrain his own activities, restrictions rooted in Alexander Miller's religious convictions and in complications during Marvin's birth that left his right shoulder permanently crippled. In one symbolic act of rebellion, although his father was a Giants fan, young Marvin adopted the Dodgers. Determined to prove his virility, Miller covertly played sports and took up the "masculine" habit of tobacco. The emerging young man demonstrated a superior intellect, an untypical awareness of the larger world, an initial caution in interpersonal exchanges, strong class and civil libertarian convictions, an instinctive mistrust of restrictive paternalists, and a driving personal ambition.[3]

After he graduated from high school at age fifteen, Miller attended New York University. From there he hired on as a caseworker for the city's welfare department; in the process he joined his first union—the State, County, and Municipal Workers—and served on its grievance committee. Ineligible for World War II military service, he was hired by the National War Labor Board as a staff economist and graduated to hearings officer, where he adjudicated various labor-management disputes under George Taylor's supervision. After the war, Miller bounced from the U.S. Labor Department's Conciliation Service to the International Association of Machinists and the United Auto Workers. In 1950 Miller, thirty-two years old and married with two young children, received the key break of his career when another wartime colleague, Otis Brubaker, hired him as an economist for the United Steelworkers of America.[4]

Miller's tenure with the Steelworkers proved a valuable learning experience. He became one of that massive union's leading technicians under flamboyant, detached president David J. McDonald and "shadow president" and general counsel Arthur Goldberg. When Goldberg eventually left the Steelworkers to assume new duties as President John F. Kennedy's secretary of labor, Miller ascended to the position of chief union economist and assistant to McDonald. But in 1964–65 the union's secretary-treasurer, I. W. Abel, successfully challenged McDonald for the presidency, ushering in a series of major staff reshufflings. Accordingly Miller fielded offers from the Carnegie Endowment for International Peace to head a conflict resolution study and a visiting professorship tendered by Harvard academic and fellow Kaiser Committee member John Dunlop. Both, however, promised to take him out of the stimulating atmosphere of labor relations battles for the dusty, quiet halls of academe.[5]

While attending a Kaiser session in San Francisco in December 1965, Miller was approached by George Taylor about Robin Roberts's overture. Intrigued at the untapped potential of the baseball union, Miller allowed his old boss to arrange a meeting with the Players Association search committee. The session did not go well. Friend was still pushing Cannon's candidacy and did not even attend the interview. Harvey Kuenn displayed the traditional coolness of many players toward anyone with a "hard-core" union background. Even Bunning favored another lawyer friend. Other candidates under consideration included former leader Bob Feller, Giants executive Chub Feeney, and John Gabel, a Cleveland-based actuary to the pension fund. Only Roberts backed Miller, and even he suggested pairing him in a divided leadership with former vice-president Richard Nixon serving as legal counsel. Despite the risk to his candidacy, Miller pointedly opposed the idea, citing Nixon's conservative leanings and likely 1968 presidential candidacy, and the association's need for one clear leader.[6]

When the search committee gathered in early 1966 to pick a nominee, only Roberts was still squarely in Miller's corner. A plurality actually voted for Judge Cannon. Cannon then squandered his advantage through a demonstration of laziness and greed. He informed the association that he would not accept the new post without extra perks, including the union matching his judicial pension in addition to a $50,000 salary and a $100,000 office account. Signaling that despite his desire for full-time pay he did not intend to be a full-time leader, Cannon also insisted that the association office be transferred to his home city of Milwaukee rather than remaining near management offices in New York. Even when the players added compensation and offered a compromise location of Chicago, Cannon still held out for more. Frustrated and angry, the search committee then withdrew its offer. On March 4, 1965, one day before the union executive board's scheduled session to issue a new recommendation, the magnates belatedly tried to restore Cannon's candidacy through a thinly veiled carrot-and-stick proposal. At the judge's private urging, the owners' pension committee offered to provide the new union officer's salary and expenses out of the central fund, thereby relieving the players' need to finance the reorganization but violating Taft-Hartley Act provisions against company unions. At the same time, the new commissioner, William D. "Spike" Eckert, reminded the players that any boost in player pension benefits in the next agreement would depend on the association's fostering management's goodwill through its choice of a leader.[7]

In a demonstration of both good faith and naïveté, the players' executive board invited Eckert (an obscure former army procurement officer whose appointment led incredulous sportswriters to dub him the "Unknown Soldier") and aide Lee MacPhail to its March 5 meeting in Pittsburgh. Although a hard core of conservative delegates, led by the Cubs' Larry Jackson, pleaded for "anybody but Marvin Miller," the majority voted to place Miller's name before the membership for ratification at spring training. Although Eckert's reaction gave nothing away (his moods were said to range from "stoicism to constraint"), the commissioner was concerned with the result. Even more alarmed were the magnates, who had already witnessed the spectacle of a joint contract holdout by star Dodger pitchers Sandy Koufax and Don Drysdale. Labeling their move a collective bargaining action and demanding three-year, no-cut pacts at not less than $166,666 apiece annually, the pair sought to force the Dodgers to treat them as "coequal partners to a contract." Faced with the possibility of an extended holdout and the claim of the pitchers' agent to have arranged a made-for-TV movie offer for them, owner O'Malley was forced to give each pitcher a one-year deal for $130,000 and $115,000, up substantially from the $70,000–75,000 range the two had earned in 1965.[8]

Alarmed and angered at the assertiveness of both the Koufax-Drysdale holdout and the Miller nomination, the magnates swung into action to scuttle the latter's election. Rumors spread that the nominee was a mob-tied "labor boss" who would employ "goon squads" on opposing players. In response Robin Roberts unsuccessfully counseled Miller to shave his pencil moustache to counter management's caricature of him as a shiny-suited Jewish hireling of gangsters. When Miller arrived at Cactus League parks to meet players before the vote, he found orchestrated harassment from managers, coaches, and even some player delegates. Cleveland manager Birdie Tebbetts, who admitted being egged on by his management, openly insinuated that Miller was a communist. Throughout the sessions managers rather than players ran the meetings and barraged the nominee with hostile questions. Before the Los Angeles Angels meeting, delegate Buck Rodgers even ushered out the rookie players and then openly renounced Miller in front of the remaining teammates. Rodgers also had "written" an anti-Miller petition for the *Los Angeles Herald-Examiner,* although the document's specific demand for a different candidate possessing a "legal background" and owners' "respect" bore the stamp of Judge Cannon. At clubs' expense Cannon also printed up and distributed some 500 copies of the Rodgers petition to association voters. Given this orchestrated anti-Miller effort, it was not surprising that the actual vote from early Sun Belt "precincts" of the Indians, Cubs, Angels, and Giants repudiated the search committee's nominee by a 102-17 margin.[9]

Management operatives in Florida tried similar strategies to assure Miller's defeat. Joe Reichler, former sportswriter turned commissioner's hireling, circulated among the players and cautioned them to be "very, very, *very* careful" before considering any vote for Miller. Houston manager Leo Durocher hit fungoes into an outdoors Houston team meeting with the nominee in an attempt to disrupt it. But in Florida, in marked contrast to Arizona, player representatives led by Roberts worked hard to bolster their candidate. Miller also became more relaxed before the players, demonstrated a willingness to listen to them, and offered a pragmatic approach visibly at odds with management's caricatures. Of 506 votes cast in the decisive Florida "precincts," all but 34 backed Miller. Five of 16 squads—including coaches, managers, and trainers—endorsed him unanimously, and 3 others contained but one negative voice apiece. In Florida, of 96 nonplayer voters in the association's election, 62 also endorsed Miller. By a 489-136 overall margin Marvin Miller passed his first and possibly most crucial test and became the new executive director of the Major League Baseball Players Association. The owners, although stung by the outcome, remained determined to erect more roadblocks in the days and weeks to come.[10]

Having marshaled their initial opposition to Miller too clumsily and too late, the magnates now compounded their early failure through crude efforts at intimidation. Judge Cannon, a "lame duck" but technically still the union's legal counsel, drafted an employment contract for the man who had defeated him that would not take effect until January 1,

1967—*after* the new pension benefit package had already been imposed by the owners. The draft document also contracted Miller's services for two years instead of five, thus ending before the new pension plan could come up for renegotiation. Other provisions allowed only $20,000 for office expenses and no accounting requirements. The latter represented a trap to entice Miller into incurring undocumented expenses, which his enemies then could use as grounds for dismissal. Reinforcing that interpretation of the provisions' intent was a clause that permitted the association's executive board to fire the executive director upon the mere accusation of improper conduct. Miller cleverly blocked Cannon's gambit, and at the same time promoted an image of solidarity with his new membership, by countering with substitute conduct language identical to that in the players' own standard contracts. On the advice of legal adviser and former Steelworkers colleague Richard M. "Dick" Moss, Miller also demanded a July 1, 1966, start date; a two-and-a-half-year term, with termination only after thirty days' written notice; and procedures to compensate documented expenses up to $20,000. At the 1966 All-Star break, the union's executive board ratified the revised contract. Later in the fall, after interviewing Richard Nixon out of courtesy to Robin Roberts, Miller retained Moss instead as union legal counsel.[11]

The owners then tried to starve the union of operating funds. Eckert's deputy Lee MacPhail proclaimed that the owners belatedly had realized that their earlier offer to finance the new association position violated Taft-Hartley provisions and had to be withdrawn. Having scheduled a rare in-season meeting for June 6 with player representatives to discuss the pension, the commissioner then tried to bar Miller from the session because, in large part due to Judge Cannon's machinations on management's behalf, his contract had not yet been finalized and therefore his term had not officially begun. The union called Eckert's bluff by refusing to go ahead with the meeting without Miller, and Eckert relented. In an obvious insult to the union's new leader, however, pension committee chairman John Galbreath did not show up for the meeting. At the session, when Eckert's legal adviser and former Office of Price Administration head Paul Porter reiterated that the owners could not provide central fund moneys for the union, Miller countered with a surprise offer to make the player pension "non-contributory" and to apply the $344 annual premium as union dues instead. Unprepared for the proposal, flustered owners stonewalled, leading White Sox delegate Eddie Fisher to shout angrily, "Not a single thing has been accomplished!" In an apparent act of retaliation, six days later the star reliever found himself traded to Baltimore.[12]

A week later Eckert reported back to Miller the owners' acceptance of his union funding proposal. The magnates did so assuming that many players would balk at routing moneys once designated for their pensions to union coffers. Miller also recognized the danger and saw the players' willingness to support the union from their paychecks as an early test of his leadership. Nonetheless, the dues payments would not start before the spring of 1967, leaving the union still in the position of having virtually no resources to conduct business, including the pension negotiations. In September Miller asked for membership endorsement of the dues checkoff. All but two players voted their support. At the same time he dispatched Frank Scott to put together quickly a group licensing deal to shore up union finances. Scott managed to work out a two-year, $60,000 annual pact with Coca-Cola for rights to players' pictures on bottle caps, and another $20,000 to players in exchange for public appearances in behalf of the company. When the owners learned of the union's marketing negotiation, they tried to scuttle it by denying permission to use team logos in the player pictures unless they received licensing fees. The union thwarted the holdup by having the team insignias airbrushed from the players' portraits.[13]

While Miller and the Players Association fought these early skirmishes with management, their policy attention remained fixed on the pension. For months the owners acted as if, as usual, no two-party negotiating would take place. At most the players would be allowed to present their ideas, and then a new agreement would be handed down from on high. When the magnates convened in June to discuss the progress of their new television negotiations, given the latter's pension implications Miller flew to the Windy City in hopes of participating. But when he arrived, he found NL associate counsel Bowie Kuhn describing as accomplished fact a new two-year pension deal assigning a flat $4 million annual payment to the fund and scrapping the precedent of 60-40 pay-in percentages from All-Star and World Series broadcast revenues. Whether through malice or obtuseness, Commissioner Eckert had even scheduled a press conference to announce the "done deal." Miller rushed to head him off in a hotel elevator and browbeat him into canceling the announcement, since no collective bargaining had occurred to produce such an agreement and announcing it would constitute a clear, actionable violation of labor law.[14]

THE INFLATIONARY ERA

By the time the association's executive board assembled at All-Star break, Miller himself had concluded that the union would have to agree to scrapping the percentage-formula precedent. The membership did not have the strength yet to fight all out for a percentage high enough to generate big benefit increases, and the owners' actual delivery on past revenue-percentage promises had been impossible to verify anyway because of their secrecy and money shifting. Miller similarly suspected the magnates of deliberately lowballing their rights fee demands to the networks on All-Star Game and World Series contracts in exchange for higher Game of the Week payments not subject to division with the pension. Miller also knew that any formula did not constitute a binding precedent for the future but only applied for the length of the particular contract.[15]

Miller and the player representatives again were stonewalled by the owners at the All-Star break, and with no new meeting scheduled until December, management appeared ready to wait the union out in hopes it would crumble. But the September player vote for the dues checkoff and the bargain with Coca-Cola sent the message to owners that delay might be strengthening, rather than corroding, the association. In November the New York State Department of Insurance dealt the magnates another blow when it released its findings of malfeasance in the owners' past "refunding" of pension payments. Possessing new economic and legal leverage, Miller now proposed that the owners add $200,000 to their earlier $4 million proposal. The union would consider it principal and interest on the amount illegally withdrawn earlier, thereby lifting management's legal liability. Faced with the prospect of court judgments if they held out, the lure of $6.1 million and $6.5 million in 1967–68 from their new television deal, and the imminent deadline for a pension pact, the owners agreed to raise the benefit contributions to $4.2 million. More immediately impressive to Miller's player constituents, monthly pension and disability payouts doubled under the new three-year agreement. Ten-year veterans now received $500 a month at age fifty and $1,300 a month if they initiated their payments at age sixty-five. Although some ex-players, most notably Bob Feller, criticized the deal for abandoning a revenue percentage in favor of a fixed amount, to the overwhelming majority of current players Miller had proven his mettle.[16]

Miller's performance in his first year of stewardship was absolutely vital to forging solidarity within the Players Association and ultimately to the victories that stemmed from it. The immediate tangible gains were essential, but just as critical was Miller's skill in creating an engaged rank and file with heightened collective pride and consciousness. Admittedly, achieving such solidarity stood a better chance with a union membership numbering merely in the hundreds and increasingly made up of a generation of players who had not usually been, in the words of pitcher Mike Marshall, "big men on campus" with prima donna egos to match. But just as important, and in marked contrast to his predecessors, Miller met every player at spring training, listened to and educated team delegates and league player representatives face-to-face a minimum of four times a year, talked to them by telephone innumerably more often, and invited players to visit his New York office. The clear new message being sent was, "This is *your* union." [17]

Miller also shrewdly defused the "union" label as a frightening term to players, and he encouraged players' self-image as an elite group of professionals deserving to be treated and paid accordingly. While he infuriated old-line owners in bargaining sessions by referring to his membership as workers, in public statements and press releases he consistently addressed his constituents as the Players Association, a title that underscored their professional standing. Miller regularly drove home the point to his members, "Together, you are irreplaceable. . . . *You* are the game." As Baltimore delegate Brooks Robinson observed, the players also learned over time that their leader was a man who did not intentionally lie or mislead them. Miller made sure that the union's bargaining positions first had the clear support of the membership before he put them forward, and as part of a deliberate strategy of self-effacement he often projected less militance in front of the players than he actually felt. As pitcher Jim Bouton noted, "Marvin was always the least gung-ho of anyone in the room." And no player's concern was publicly belittled as trivial or irrelevant. At a meeting of team representatives in Mexico City in December 1967 Miller encouraged each man to write down anonymously on slips of paper every conceivable player grievance, large or small. The union then checked into them all, even gripes about inadequate clubhouse outlets for hair dryers. [18]

Besides Miller's own doing, however, his success in establishing a beachhead for the union in his first year owed to the combination of arrogance, confusion, and indecisiveness shown by management. The magnates—though it might sound contradictory at first—were both too reactionary and too lethargic in dealing with an energized challenger. While Miller presented an infuriating public persona of reasonableness

THE INFLATIONARY ERA

at odds with the face he gave the magnates behind closed doors, they crudely lashed out at him both publicly and privately in language that only served to rally the players to him. As Dick Moss characterized it, owner rhetoric and issue positions evoked images of a "labor-relations scene from the Thirties in the mid-Sixties." Jim Bouton maintained that if the magnates had merely demonstrated a degree of reasonableness by offering to boost minimum salaries to $10,000 with yearly $1,000 raises for the next twenty years, provide decent pension increases, and extend cost-of-living adjustments to meal money, they could have cut the ground out from under Miller. Instead, as the executive director described it, the owners became "my best allies."[19]

If the owners' unreasonableness prevented them from killing the association through kindness, their disunity and ineptness kept them from simply crushing the upstart. U.S. Steel executive Bruce Johnston recalled that in past negotiations with his company Dick Moss had been but a secondary player on the Steelworkers legal team, and Marvin Miller had seemed a competent union hand but no more so than "2,000 other guys." But in contrast to baseball executives, he added, they had been "trained in that [modern industrial relations] system, then turned loose on an industry that was, in terms of labor relations, naive and illiterate." Johnston described the baseball owners as a "loose amalgam" of independent entrepreneurs rather than a cohesive, hierarchical management team. As such, they constituted "the worst people in the world to deal with labor . . . impatient, egocentric, and exasperating to represent," as well as "very poor at cooperating in the face of unified opposition" because of their rampant egoism.[20]

When the owners next met the Players Association in a major bargaining confrontation, they already faced a more unified and competent adversary. In January 1967 Miller formally demanded a start of negotiations on nonpension issues, especially an increase in the $7,000 minimum salary. When the magnates not only refused but declined to share payroll information as a statistical preliminary, the association filed suit for the data and confidentially polled its members at spring training to generate its own figures. The union found that the mean salary still stood at only $19,000, and the median was an even lower $17,000. Thirty-five players did not yet receive even $7,000 but were paid according to a two-month "rookie" scale of $6,000. At a time when the average U.S. worker made $8,000, fully a third of the players earned $10,000 or less, and over 40 percent of them made $12,000 or less. Based on the findings, Miller proposed a minimum salary of $12,000. The owners, who at the advice of Harvard consultant James Healy had belatedly created a bargaining panel called the Player Relations Committee (PRC), consisting of the two league presidents and three owners from each circuit, countered with an offer of $8,500.[21]

Hoping to bluster management into a more serious offer, despite private doubts Miller floated the threat of a "superunion" of professional athletes from baseball, football, basketball, and hockey. When that failed to motivate the owners, Miller grabbed their attention by expanding the scope of the bartering to include virtually all conceivable contract issues save individual pay as prelude to a comprehensive "basic agreement." The negotiations now encompassed scheduling rules, season length, grievance procedures, official recognition of the association as the players' collective bargaining representative, limits on salary cuts, spring training and in-season allowances, moving expenses for traded players, standards for hotel and travel accommodations, curbs on management's power to change playing rules with an economic impact on the players, reserve clause modifications, and much more.[22]

Overwhelmed by the flood of bargaining issues raised by the union, less than a week later the magnates notified Miller that the PRC had retained its own professional negotiator, a twenty-one-year veteran of labor disputes named John Gaherin. Gaherin, the candidate of AL counsel Jim Garner, claimed a list of past clients that included the Scripps-Howard newspaper chain and had served as president of the Publishers Association of New York, the city newspapers' bargaining arm in negotiations with their unions. Miller immediately introduced his adversary to the character of his new employers by handing him a *Sports Illustrated* article on Buzzie Bavasi's player contract negotiating tricks. Gaherin soon learned on his own that his sponsors were "backroom negotiators" who refused to attend collective bargaining sessions directly but argued with each other and him and issued conflicting, frequently changing marching orders. Given that the owners' own "boss," the commissioner, was specifically barred from a direct labor negotiation role, Gaherin found himself not working for anyone in particular but for "everybody in general"—an arrangement unlikely to produce management clarity or decisiveness in negotiations.[23]

Although Gaherin's presence added needed decorum and professionalism to the talks, management's fuzzy chain of command led to more stonewalling on specifics. Before one midsummer bargaining session,

Dick Moss jokingly advised one player representative to throw up on the table as a useful dramatic gesture should Gaherin stall again by re-issuing a blatantly unrealistic offer. Nonetheless, given the additional new revenue from television and the moderation of the union's monetary proposals, the owners' negotiator reported in December 1967 that many issues had been substantially resolved, including boosts in travel allowances and spring training Murphy money and a $10,000 minimum salary. Although Miller argued for changes in the reserve to permit veterans greater movement and for reductions in the playing schedule, he appeared willing to assign the issues to joint study committees through which the owners could effectively delay action.[24]

What emerged instead as the stumbling block to a final agreement was Miller's call for a formal, independent grievance procedure to resolve future disputes over individual players' contract rights. Gaherin, familiar with such processes throughout private industry, advised his employers to offer concessions, only to be shouted down. Walter O'Malley, furious at any suggestion of outside arbitrators, crudely bellowed, "Tell that Jewish boy [Miller] to go on back to Brooklyn." The owners then refused to schedule the regular December joint session with the union's executive board. Miller threatened unspecified "action," probably an NLRB complaint; instructions to players not to sign 1968 contracts; and a strike vote at spring training. Backing Miller, the union executive board quickly voted to tear up his old contract and replace it with a three-year extension at a $5,000 raise. Shortly after New Year's Day, Gaherin publicly signaled a renewed willingness to cut a deal. A final Miller threat to seek outside federal mediation failed to dislodge the magnates' opposition to grievance arbitration, and the two sides concluded their pact on February 19, 1968.[25]

Among its landmark features, the first Basic Agreement contained the boost in minimum salaries to $10,000, spring training meal money of $12 a day, in-season meal allowances of $15, and Murphy money of $40. Owners agreed to provide moving expenses for promoted or traded players and first-class road hotel and air travel accommodations. The agreement even provided for salary continuation for players serving National Guard or Reserve duty—an important feature in the Vietnam era—and lowered maximum one-year pay cuts to 20 percent. The new pact also made both sides parties to scheduling rules for 1968–69, prohibited noncharity exhibitions during the All-Star break, and created joint committees to study the length-of-season and reserve issues, with reports due at the end of

1969. In a less trumpeted but significant provision, article 7 included the requirement that the union be formally notified in the preceding off-season of any changes in playing rules and that their consent be secured in the case of any such change potentially affecting player benefits—a clause later asserted by the union in the case of such provisions as the designated hitter. As for outside arbitration of player contract and procedural rights grievances, however, Miller had to wait for another day. The Basic Agreement did establish a grievance procedure, but it designated the commissioner rather than an independent arbitrator as adjudicator. As Dick Moss later noted, the issue of impartial arbitration had not yet achieved the necessary standing with the players for them to "go to the mat."[26] Miller clearly had gained both credibility and concrete benefits for his membership. But to win even bigger prizes ahead, he still had educating to do.

The Basic Agreement of 1968 marked the start of a new, more adversarial relationship between owners and players. Despite the limitations of the pact, no longer could general managers hoodwink players with impunity over contract provisions. Both to test the new grievance procedure and to educate the membership, the Players Association encouraged its troops to file actions whenever any possible reason arose. Curt Blefary of Baltimore was the first filer, lodging a grievance against a fine for playing in an off-season basketball game. Blefary lost, but the union's next two complainants won. Typical of the reaction of clubs to the new reality, the Orioles abruptly halted financial tax counseling to their players, claiming that the old familial relationship had been irrevocably shattered. The association similarly skirmished with Cincinnati owner Bob Howsam over his team's practice of bumping players from first-class air accommodations in favor of reporters, broadcasters, and coaches. When the union won the case, Howsam traded away Reds player delegate Milt Pappas. In December 1968 the owners went out of their way to antagonize the union by unilaterally declaring that not only could a player's salary be suspended because of an injury sustained off the playing field, but even on-field injuries had to be certified by club physicians and the league president before pay would continue. Miller denounced the statement, issued in the midst of the new round of pension talks, as a "vicious anti-player action."[27]

Despite owner harassment, the union continued to grow stronger, a trend that neither escaped the magnates' notice nor improved their mood. For years the Topps Company had extended one-sided deals to players for rights to their images on trading cards. While a player was still in the minors, Topps paid him $5 for his rights and promised $125 a season for five years once he reached the majors. Two years into each major league deal the card manufacturer extended a renewal with a $75 bonus. By the late 1960s such reimbursements fell far below "market value," but Sy Berger, Topps's liaison to the players, kept them "on the reservation" through merchandise and other favors in the fashion of modern shoe company hustlers. Following repeated rebuffs at union calls for renegotiation, Marvin Miller decided to call the company's bluff during spring training in 1968 by advising players not to sign renewals with Topps. With remarkable speed company president Joel Shorin yielded to Miller's muscle flexing, and the two sides reached new terms by the fall. Topps doubled per-player pay to $250, plus an 8 percent royalty on sales up to $4 million and 10 percent on those above that level. In the first year of the new pact, royalties totaled $320,000 — an impressive perk and a war chest in the event of future collective bargaining strife.[28]

With the 1967 pension agreement scheduled to expire in March 1969, the owners eyed their adversary's rising strength with a palpable frustration. But confusion and disunity continued to plague them. At the end of spring training in 1968, the refusal of some players to play on the day of the Reverend Martin Luther King Jr.'s funeral had been met by a compassionate gesture from Commissioner Eckert calling for no penalties. His action, however, drew scorn from management firebrands who did not want to show the players any leniency. When Robert F. Kennedy died in June, the commissioner turned 180 degrees and refused to upset the regular-season schedule, drawing sharp condemnation not just from players but from the press and the public as well. By that winter's meetings, the magnates were ready to jettison the ineffectual Eckert but were squabbling over franchise expansion and offense-minded rules changes, as well as who would succeed the deposed commissioner and what powers he would have. Young Turks pushed for a special committee to draft proposals for executive reorganization and lobbied for Yankees and CBS executive Mike Burke. Traditionalists opposed major structural changes and backed Chub Feeney. After a two-month deadlock, the two sides wearily settled on a compromise interim choice sponsored by powerful Walter O'Malley, NL associate counsel Bowie Kuhn.[29]

Adding to management's chaos on how to tackle the Players Association, ironically, was the growing television revenue stream, which undermined the sense of emergency necessary to forge and maintain an un-compromising line. In 1968 local and national broadcast income broke through the $30 million mark, and in 1969 the figure reached $37 million. National TV moneys alone had risen by more than 40 percent since the last network pact. Franchise expansion, in turn, offered NL owners an additional $20 million and AL clubs $11.2 million in entry fees from the new San Diego, Montreal, Seattle, and Kansas City teams. In short, the owners had much more than enough money to meet reasonable pension demands from the players' union.[30]

From the association's standpoint, expansion meant one hundred or more new members to be provided for in the new agreement. In view of the revenues available and the enlarged ranks to be covered, the Players Association's pension proposal in mid-season 1968 was more ambitious than it had been two years earlier. The union called for a 44 percent increase in the owner contributions to $5.9 million, a reduction in the major league service time required for eligibility to four years, and the retroactive application of all changes to veterans of 1959 on. Because of the owners' disarray, they not surprisingly delayed a counteroffer until the off-season. The stalling only pushed the onset of serious negotia-tions closer to both the old agreement's expiration deadline and the start of a new season. When the magnates did respond, their offer clearly represented an opening gambit driven by hard-liners. It provided for an increase of pay-ins to only $5.1 million—barely enough to cover the additional personnel mandated by expansion with no increase in benefit levels—and kept the eligibility standard at five years. The owners also ruled out Miller's call for the reestablishment of a guaranteed minimum revenue percentage.[31]

Having sensed as early as September that the owners planned a hard line, Miller had begun preparing his membership for the likelihood that they would have to counterattack through refusing to sign new 1969 con-tracts or report for spring training. The executive director's reading of the reserve clause convinced him that it bound a player for only one reserve year after the expiration of a previous contract. Therefore, by sitting out a year, a player could become a free agent available to the highest bidder. He calculated that if the union could remain united be-hind a holdout strategy, the specter of a delayed or canceled 1969 playing season and massive free agency in 1970 would impel the magnates into a reasonable agreement. In December association representatives and the membership approved the strategy. Even retiring superstar Mickey

Mantle agreed to delay his retirement announcement in order to include his name among prospective holdouts.[32]

At first the owners maintained that the union would not be able to keep its members out of camp. In the previous negotiation the union had, after all, shied away from launching a strike for the sake of impartial grievance arbitration. Miller privately entertained similar doubts about whether his membership was ready for its first real test of solidarity. He staged a "pep rally" for his player representatives and some half-dozen other members per team at New York's Biltmore Hotel in early February and reminded them that the union's proposal only asked each current club to increase its annual individual pension contribution from $205,000 to $212,500. Well-paid stars, including the flamboyant Richie Allen, gave strong testimonials in support of the union's stance. Nonetheless, when camps opened in mid-month, defectors surfaced. Catcher Russ Nixon reported, followed by Jim Palmer, Pete Rickert, and Clay Carroll. Mets catcher Jerry Grote signed a new contract in defiance of the union, as did—more damagingly—Tom Seaver. By February 19, nineteen of thirty-one Baltimore Orioles had reported. PRC negotiator John Gaherin grew increasingly confident that association solidarity was beginning to break apart. Reflecting that confidence, he repeated management's old offer as his "last, best" proposal. Privately hard-liners boasted they now had Miller and his union "by the balls."[33]

The breakdown of the Players Association was not to be, however, primarily because of the intervention of the television networks. When the camps had opened with most players absent and without contracts, worried NBC executives had stepped up their pressure on interim commissioner Bowie Kuhn to ensure a deal that would enable the regular season to start on time. One network official insisted that his company would not pay "major league" prices for "minor league" games but would try to escape its rights-fee requirements. Kuhn, seeking ratification as Eckert's permanent replacement, recognized that his brokering a deal and "saving the season" would raise his as-yet microscopic stature and force his coronation upon the magnates. Kuhn called Gaherin and made it abundantly clear that a delay of the season because of a player holdout was no way for a new commissioner to start his tenure. When Gaherin abruptly summoned a new bargaining session, Miller knew that his adversaries had blinked. New PRC proposals upped management's financial offer an extra $200,000, to $5.3 million. The next week the two sides came to terms. Under the new pension pact, contributions rose to $5.45

million, about halfway between each side's original positions. The agreement still rejected fixed percentages of broadcast revenues for the pension plan, but the union gained the lowering of vesting requirements to four years as well as $10-a-month benefit increases for each service year and retroactive application of provisions for service since 1959. The pact did not place particular hardship upon the owners, but because of their initial hard-line stance, it represented a clear defeat. Owner Paul Richards of the Atlanta Braves—who had labeled Miller a communist during the standoff—threatened team delegate Joe Torre with a 20 percent maximum salary cut and then traded him two weeks later to St. Louis.[34]

The association's pension victory had demonstrated the potential of union collective action, the owners' overriding hunger for television revenue, and the new commissioner's egotism. It had also proven that baseball management did not want to risk a direct test of its interpretation of the reserve clause. Not just Miller had become convinced of the reserve clause's illegality beyond a single option year, but so, too, had Gaherin and NL chief attorney Lou Carroll. During that same spring of 1969, following the end of the union's mass holdouts, Yankee pitcher Al Downing persisted in refusing to sign a club offer sheet and had his services unilaterally renewed by general manager Lee MacPhail at a 20 percent cut. Downing intended individually to test the reserve clause by not signing a new deal and declaring himself a free agent at the end of 1969. Miller cautioned him that under the 1968 Basic Agreement, any such player contract dispute with management over the reserve clause would still be heard not by an independent arbitrator but by the owners' employee, the commissioner. When Downing then abandoned his challenge and signed with the Yankees, the club quickly traded him to Oakland before the start of the season.[35]

After the campaign, however, another veteran picked up the baton. Curt Flood, the St. Louis Cardinals' star center fielder, was a twelve-year veteran of the major leagues drawing a $90,000 salary in the aftermath of his team's second straight World Series appearance in 1968. But following a slumping 1969 season, the club notified him that he would be traded to Philadelphia, a franchise with a history of racial bigotry. The move promised to uproot him from the team he had been part of for eleven years and from long-cultivated local off-field opportunities. Desperate to contest the trade, Flood contacted Miller, who as he had with Downing, warned him that the commissioner would deny his suit. If he subsequently pursued and even won a court challenge, the lengthy appeals process would exhaust his playing career, and his defiance would shatter any hope of future employment in the industry. Reluctantly, however, because he could not oppose the principle of a worker's right to choose his employer, Miller recommended that the union pay Flood's legal and travel-related expenses, if not his living expenses. Even that degree of union financial backing came only after player representatives satisfied themselves as to Flood's motives. Los Angeles player delegate Tom Haller bluntly posed the question, "Are you doing this simply because you're black and you feel that baseball has been discriminatory?"[36]

After the grilling, the executive board voted unanimously to back Flood's case. Miller, in turn, arranged for him to be represented by his former Steelworkers superior and U.S. Supreme Court Justice Arthur Goldberg. Goldberg's offer to accept the case pro bono eased a potential drain on the association's cash reserves. On Christmas Eve 1969, Flood wrote Commissioner Kuhn to demand his freedom. "After twelve years in the major leagues," he asserted, "I do not feel that I am a piece of property to be bought and sold irrespective of my wishes." When Kuhn, as expected, rejected his demand, Flood's legal team filed suit in federal district court in New York charging baseball with conspiracy in violation of interstate commerce to deny him employment, sought an injunction enabling him to play for the Cardinals in 1970, and called for triple damages.[37]

The Flood lawsuit provided the backdrop for the next potentially contentious round of collective bargaining over a new Basic Agreement. The joint study committees on the playing schedule and the reserve issue had, as expected, produced nothing but separate recommendations from each side's members. Having failed to secure independent grievance arbitration the first time around, Miller and the association could be counted on to make it the central objective now. And in contrast to his interjection into the pension talks, Commissioner Kuhn, having removed "interim" from his title, might be expected to show more restraint, particularly since any yielding on the grievance arbitration would lessen his own authority. Nonetheless, Kuhn still suffered from a severe case of "commissioneritis," the belief that despite owing his job to management, the commissioner somehow exercised a dispassionate, evenhanded patriarchy over all of baseball's constituencies. Kuhn had even crashed association meetings and executive board sessions during spring training, only to be cold-shouldered by union officials and players.[38]

By the spring of 1970, after he again presented an initial unacceptable offer as a "take-it-or-leave-it" proposition, John Gaherin reported to the PRC that, as in 1968, the two sides were near agreement on the monetary issues. Both parties had settled on a minimum salary boost to $12,000 for 1970, with gradual increases the next two years of the contract. They had agreed on a 30 percent maximum pay cut over two years and longer severance pay to sixty days. Proposed language also reiterated the union's status as official collective bargaining spokesman and gave formal sanction to players' use of agents in individual negotiations. The clear stumbling block, however, was impartial grievance arbitration. Gaherin advocated flexibility on the issue, but this time Commissioner Kuhn strenuously opposed any reduction of his authority as a betrayal of the legacy of Landis. Without the replacement of the commissioner with an outside arbitrator, however, Miller and the union would not ratify any new pact. Underscoring the point, in May the membership overwhelmingly rejected management's offer by a 505-89 tally.[39]

Now it was Gaherin's time to turn the tables on Kuhn and force him to accept the terms necessary for a deal. The PRC negotiator enlisted the commissioner's trusted friend and legal adviser, Harvard-educated Lou Hoynes, to draft a proposal that would remove Kuhn from most potential arbitration areas while preserving his office's authority in matters involving the "integrity of the game." When Kuhn insisted upon slightly broadening the language to include "public confidence" matters, Gaherin then had to reassure Marvin Miller that the change would not undermine the new independent arbitrator's range of powers. Gaherin also noted to his bargaining adversary that the union could still seek to narrow the commissioner's authority through negotiation once Kuhn had left that office, or it could reopen the Basic Agreement or even strike if Kuhn intervened in what the association considered an improper manner to preempt the arbitrator.[40]

After the necessary stroking of the commissioner's ego, a deal was struck by June with provisions made retroactive to the old agreement's December 31, 1969, expiration date. Under the pressure from the Flood lawsuit, the magnates had wanted to show an image of reasonableness on issues of player contract interpretation, and accordingly they had acted to remove their commissioner from having final say in virtually all such cases. Instead of a management employee acting as ultimate arbiter of disputes involving contract rights, such cases now would be decided by the majority on a three-member panel consisting of union and management representatives and the key "swing-vote"—an independent professional arbiter chosen with the blessing of both sides. At the magnates' insistence, an item was inserted into the 1970 Basic Agreement that stated it did not address the matter of the reserve system's legality because of the parties' "differing views." Baseball viewed the wording as preventing any reinterpretation of the meaning of the reserve clause by the new arbitration system. The union disagreed, although it pledged not to initiate such separate actions to challenge the reserve pending final resolution of the Flood lawsuit. In Marvin Miller's view, the language meant that the *wording* of the reserve clause could not be modified or overturned except through collective bargaining, but the new arbitration system remained free to *interpret* the current clause to define its real meaning. The union executive director was confident he already knew the answer to that question. What he lacked was a player willing to provide the test case.[41]

By 1970 major league baseball franchises had begun to resemble automobiles whose drivers, after being repeatedly passed by faster traffic, had finally decided to step on the accelerator. More revenue "fuel" now flowed to their engines, and the cars/clubs were gaining momentum, but at the cost of higher rates of "fuel consumption" and operating expenses. Expansion, offense-boosting rules changes, new stadiums, and rising TV ratings all were generating more gate and advertising money. At the same time, the new arenas, such as Cincinnati's Riverfront Stadium, Pittsburgh's Three Rivers Stadium, and Philadelphia's Veterans' Stadium, cost $50 million and more to build. After the disastrous six-year experiment with lower offense from 1963 to 1968, the magnates had lowered pitching mounds to ten inches and shrunk the strike zone back to 1950 dimensions to inject more excitement into the game and bring more fans into the stadiums. But with expansion, rules changes, and consequent rising offensive productivity and attendance came elevated salary demands (see Appendix, Fig. 3). In 1970 the average big league pay climbed to over $29,000, nearly $5,000 more than the year before and 83 percent higher than the average in 1965. The number of players making more than $50,000, only nine in 1965, jumped to fifty-six by 1970.[42]

In past eras offense-minded rules changes and other revenue generators had not inevitably led to rapid cost escalations. In the absence of trade wars or player unions, owners had been able to respond to temporary rises in on-field productivity with selective generosity to stars and compensatory economies on the rest of the team. But things were different now, and the biggest single reason was the presence and growing clout of the Players Association. The union's power, exercised across a broad front for higher minimum salaries, better pensions, and free-agency market leverage, was a rising tide intended to lift all player "boats." During the Flood hearings that spring, Marvin Miller offered evidence of a crucial turn in the history of the baseball economy. After two decades of stagnant wages and benefits for players, bringing them to but 18.5 percent of major league costs by 1965, the percentage now was rising again, to 20.5 in 1969. Managers and coaches also, ostensibly members of management but also of the association, had seen their pay climb even more sharply in percentage terms, with the former now drawing from $30,000 to $75,000 and the latter averaging $15,000 or more.[43]

Even grievance arbitration, precluded from use in individual salary impasses, was proving a useful tool to boost player income. After the majors introduced divisional playoffs in each league in 1969, Miller and the association filed a grievance demanding retroactive increases in post-season player shares on grounds that the owners de facto had not complied with the guaranteed minimums of the Basic Agreement. Despite their participation in an additional round of league championship series, World Series players earned no additional postseason money; it remained at $15,000 total for the winning squad and $10,000 for the losers. In addition, although the magnates had extended playoff shares to an additional, sixth team in each league (three teams per division), the $1,200 offered to divisional runners-up actually came to less than the 1968 guarantees for third- and fourth-place league finishers. On June 22, 1970, arbitrator David L. Cole concurred with the union, boosting World Series shares and awarding over $82,000 in retroactive balances to players on the four divisional runners-up.[44]

To appreciate fully the difference the Players Association had already made, it was necessary only to compare its constituents' gains with the continuing plight of nonmember baseball employees and pensioners. In the minor leagues of 1970, nearly two-thirds, or 2,100, of 3,700 players toiled at the bottom rookie and Class-A levels making $115 a week plus $3 a day in meal money. Even at AA and AAA levels, the former's 475 men earned but $5,500 to $6,000 a season and $6 for meals, and the latter's 525 got only $8,000 and $9. Managers drew $14,000, or about a quarter of their major league brethren's pay, and coaches earned far less. Umpires made only $500 a month, and scouts, even with twenty or thirty years' tenure in the profession, typically received $9,000. Current and former minor league employees also made up most of the 4,501 members of the struggling Association of Professional Ball Players of America. Despite annual contributions of more than $50,000 from the commissioner's office, the organization's scarce resources limited it in 1970 to payouts of less than $55,000 to fewer than fifty pre-1947 players and dependents.[45]

Thanks to the Players Association, its men did not face such prospects. The key to that success had been Marvin Miller's ability to forge with remarkable speed a solidarity that substantially bridged otherwise dangerous fissures of status, seniority, education, region, ethnic background, and race between members. Latin American–born players alone now numbered about 10 percent of the total big league player population. According to baseball librarian Lee Allen, African Americans made up 10 to 15 percent of each year's rookie crop between 1966 and 1970 (see Appendix, Fig. 4). At the same time, according to Allen's figures, the percentage of first-year men with at least some college experience rose still another 6 percent to surpass three-fifths of the rookie population. Given the growing numbers of college men on major league squads, in matters both serious and silly, big league clubhouses increasingly took on the atmosphere of fraternity houses.[46]

Miller had recognized the need to speak the language, figuratively if not literally, of his membership, and he had solicited black and Latino players' specific grievances, including continuing housing and travel discrimination, unequal endorsement and off-season opportunities, and positional stacking. Although his leverage in the latter area proved limited, he utilized the new grievance process to ensure at minimum that all of his players received their full benefits and treatment entitled to them under the Basic Agreement. As a consequence minority stars such as the Dodgers' Maury Wills agreed that "the black and Latino ballplayers are eager to support this union." The association also carefully and skillfully promoted the interests of rookies, journeymen, and stars alike through its wide-ranging economic positions. As adversary John Gaherin enviously admitted, "Miller understood that you had to have a contract that applied to the least and the most." In the negotiations the executive director solicited the active help of the game's brightest rising stars and encouraged in them a greater willingness to provide their clout in behalf of collective and not just individual aims. As a result, articulate heroes such as Joe Torre, Don Baylor, Tom Seaver, Mike Marshall, Reggie Jackson, Ted Simmons, and Bob Boone assumed increasingly visible roles in the association's battles with the owners.[47]

In the case of African American players, their faith in Miller's willingness to "go to bat" for one of their own, even when the cause was unpopular, was rewarded by the union's defense of Alex Johnson. Johnson, reigning 1970 AL batting champion of the California Angels, exhibited increasingly erratic behavior the next season, and the club responded in disciplinary rather than therapeutic fashion. After fining Johnson twenty-nine separate times, the Angels placed him on the suspended list without pay or service credit. The Players Association filed a grievance in Johnson's behalf, and arbitration hearings were held later in the summer. On September 28, 1971, panel chairman Lewis Gill upheld the $3,750 in fines that the club had levied prior to the suspension, but he ruled that the latter action had been improper in light of Johnson's documented emotional illness and constituted a violation of his rights under the Basic Agreement. Accordingly the arbitrator restored both the player's $29,000 salary and his lost service time.[48]

If the union's unquestioning advocacy of its members' economic interests and rights to due process was understandable, even justified, in view of the industry's past abuses, it did include its myopic aspects. With the collapse of the old management paternalism that had existed toward players, authority figures from owners on down no longer could exercise the same unrestrained power to spy on or discipline wayward charges. One unfortunate consequence was that players could not as easily be preempted from consorting with dangerous associates or becoming entangled with new forms of substance abuse beyond baseball's traditional plague of alcoholism. Denny McLain, a thirty-game winner for the Detroit Tigers in 1968, provided perhaps the most conspicuous example. In 1970 a grand jury in the Motor City heard testimony of the hurler's long-term partnership in a Flint bookmaking operation sponsored by organized crime. Three years earlier, McLain's failure to pay $46,600 in debts had led an enforcer to dislocate several of the pitcher's toes, and the injury had forced him to miss two stretch-run starts. Additional information linked McLain to wagering against the Tigers on his start on the last day of the same season, which he lost. Although Commissioner Kuhn suspended McLain before the beginning of the 1970 season, he lifted the ban on July 1, and the pitcher continued to engage in questionable behavior that included threatening a parking-lot attendant, dumping ice buckets on two reporters, and toting a gun aboard a commercial airliner. McLain drew two more suspensions. By 1972 the one-time Cy Young Award winner had fallen out of baseball entirely, but his troubles with the authorities followed him. In 1985 a Florida jury convicted him of racketeering, loan-sharking, extortion, and possession of cocaine, from which he won a appeal after thirty months in prison only to be rearrested and found guilty of several of the charges a second time in 1988.[49]

Whatever its members' excesses or lapses, the gains made by the Major League Baseball Players Association in the areas of wages, pensions, and employee rights had not escaped the notice of other industry workers. In 1969 players in Puerto Rico formed their own Professional Baseball Players Association, and vice-president/catcher Woody Huyke threatened to strike the island's winter league in December in behalf of higher pay, per diems, and meal allowances. In Mexico the following spring, that nation's Confederation of Workers announced plans to organize professional athletes, including baseball players, in response to new union-friendly laws that, despite sanctioning the use of the reserve clause, banned sales of players without their consent and guaranteed them 25 percent of sales prices and an additional 5 percent for each year of Mexican League service up to a 50 percent maximum. U.S. baseball officials nervously pondered whether these developments outside their borders would complicate their continued ability to assign players from American minor leagues or major league demotees.[50]

The biggest aftershock from the success of the players' union, however, came from major league umpires. Although NL arbiters had been organized since 1963, those in the junior circuit had hesitated to follow suit. Shortly before the end of the 1968 season, AL president Joe Cronin fired Al Salerno and Bill Valentine for "incompetence," only to trigger voting by umpires in Cronin's circuit to join their unionized NL brethren. Hoping to quell the uprising, Cronin reinstated the two men, only to fire them again when they retained attorneys and sued the league for damages. When Salerno and Valentine again sought backing from the Umpires Association, however, many of their compatriots felt they had been manipulated earlier by the two "militants." Only eleven of fifty attendees voted to support them again, while fifteen others walked out of the session altogether, and over twenty more voted against backing their lawsuit. Cronin further undercut support by indicating willingness to take the two men back if they accepted temporary demotions to the minors, but they refused.[51]

Despite the controversy in the umpire ranks created by the Salerno-Valentine imbroglio, the AL arbiters' earlier vote to join their NL colleagues in common representation stood, pressuring Cronin to accept the NL umpires' attorney, John Reynolds, as negotiator for the men of both circuits. Because AL officials still blocked an NLRB-certified election by all umpires to select a single bargaining unit, the 1969 contract negotiations still led to separate pacts. Salaries of umpires in the junior circuit, which had lagged behind those in the NL, now jumped 27.5 percent to a range of $10,000–17,000. To the grumbling of the better-paid arbiters in the senior league, their pay actually rose a smaller 10 percent for those making under $15,000, 7 percent for men earning between $15,000 and $17,000, and 5 percent for senior umpires with pay ranges from $17,000 to $26,500. To dampen its umpires' newfound discontent, the National League granted an additional $500 each. In December 1969 the long-awaited NLRB election took place, and all big league arbiters subsequently claimed membership in the retitled Association of Major League Umpires, their consolidated collective bargaining agent.[52]

Despite the unification of NL and AL umpires under common representation, the two leagues continued to try to play off each cohort against the other by maintaining separate agreements. Both presidents insisted that a single set of interleague negotiations and a unified pact with common benefit levels represented diminution of the leagues' separate traditional authority over their employees. Baseball managed to hold out against a comprehensive pact with common pay levels until 1977. In early 1970 negotiations, NL umpires became outraged anew at management proposals to boost the pay of rookies by $2,500 but of senior men by only $1,500, with no additional money for crew chiefs. AL arbiters, by contrast, were being offered raises of $4,000, $6,000, and $1,000. NL management countered by pointing out that the senior circuit umpire payrolls still exceeded those of the American Leagues by $5,000.

By the fall of 1970, however, a new dispute unified the two leagues' umpires in common cause. Throughout the season umpires' association head Reynolds had fought official stonewalling in behalf of a Basic Agreement similar to that secured by Marvin Miller and the Players Association. It called for an increase throughout the big leagues in minimum salary to $11,000 and in average pay to $21,000; increased expense allow-

Major league umpires on strike, October 3, 1970
(AP/Wide World Photos)

ances, pensions, and widow's benefits; and of most immediate effect, higher playoff and World Series pay. In the first year of divisional formats and additional playoffs in 1969, arbiters had received $2,500 for working the league championships and $6,500 for the fall classic. Now with the 1970 postseason looming, Reynolds demanded raises to $5,000 and $10,000 for his men. After first securing the backing of the Teamsters and Building Services unions, on October 3 the umpires struck the first game of the 1970 playoffs.[53]

Shaken by the arbiters' one-day walkout, a management negotiating team lead by NL president Feeney resisted a broader pact but gave in to higher All-Star Game, League Championship Series, and World Series pay. The men in blue of both circuits garnered $1,000 for the mid-season classic, $3,000 for playoff assignments, and $7,500 for duty in the fall classic. They also received $40 per diem and $300 for incidental expenses related to their extraseason service, up to a $10,000 group maximum. Finally, they secured the establishment of a rotation system for postseason eligibility that guaranteed playoff or World Series work each year for eighteen men (six different men for each playoff series and the World

Series) and ensured every association member an opportunity to work a league championship at least every fourth year and a World Series every eighth. In recognition of these and subsequent gains to come, it was fitting that when John Reynolds retired as leader of the umpires' association in 1972, his membership hailed him as their own Marvin Miller.[54]

The magnates increasingly blamed their own irresolution for failing to crush the Players Association and emboldening other employee groups in the industry. In his first two sets of negotiations for pensions and basic agreements, Marvin Miller had stood up to them and beaten them soundly. Even though pay and benefits for major league players still barely measured a fifth of clubs' operating costs, the upward trend galled the owners. The share of the industry's expenses allocated for player payrolls provided a symbolic measure of the owners' power over their employees, and management's past unquestioned dominance seemed to be eroding. Although to a dispassionate outsider the slippage hardly seemed to have reached crisis proportions — by comparison, labor costs in the steel industry amounted to twice their share in baseball — the long-term direction signaled by newly rising payroll percentages fed a management mood that approached panic.

No other context adequately explains the suddenness and bitterness of the new confrontation over pension funding. By 1972 Commissioner Kuhn had surrounded himself with a coterie of experts that included Cleveland and former AL lawyer Alexander "Sandy" Hadden as secretary-treasurer and Thomas Dawson as broadcast negotiations counselor. Despite Kuhn's staff expansion, however, the PRC had no intention of including the commissioner in the forthcoming talks with the union. They recalled bitterly how Kuhn's inaugural intervention in the 1969 pension talks had forced them into concessions. This time, a hard-line majority of owners did not plan to concede anything. Creating both the need for early negotiations and the potential for owner obstinacy was accelerating price inflation in the U.S. economy, which by late 1971 had already eaten into the "real" value of pension accumulations by 17 percent and had forced a doubling of annual premium costs in the players' insurance plan.[55]

Marvin Miller had added still more fuel to the owners' fire by using the threat of an NLRB lawsuit to force them to reveal the details of their new network contract with NBC. Based on the increased annual TV payments of $18 million, the Players Association chief in late 1971 called for renegotiated, higher pension contributions by the magnates a year in advance of talks to set new benefit levels. Miller also tweaked the owners' sensitivities by chastising their regular poor-mouthing about revenues and pension costs. Aware of how national broadcast revenue represented the industry's income future, Miller challenged the magnates to let the players have it as their sole source of salaries and pension, and in turn they would leave all other forms of revenue to management. All too aware as well of the industry's financial future in television, the owners railed at Miller's public grandstanding at their expense.[56]

When he reopened discussions on the pension agreement contribution levels, Miller failed at first to sense the depths of the owners' determination for a showdown with his union. To cover the effects of inflation in 1969–71, he called for a 17 percent boost in club pay-ins to $6.5 million. As an olive branch to ease the impact of this increase, Miller suggested applying $800,000 in unanticipated existing surplus accruals toward the premium increase. The union also called for comparable increases in moneys for the health care plan to cover its inflation in premiums. Although the requests were substantial, they were readily achievable from the higher revenues in the owners' TV deal. Even the PRC's John Gaherin initially suggested a half-million dollars more in health insurance contributions, although he refused to make a formal counteroffer to Miller's proposal.[57]

Although progress remained slow into the early weeks of 1972, the pattern did not seem markedly different from previous negotiations. Miller did not even bother to mention the possibility of an owner impasse, or a player strike to break one, when he began his annual spring training visits. But while preparing for a routine session with Chicago White Sox players, he learned to his surprise that at PRC insistence Gaherin had unilaterally taken his earlier health insurance offer off the table and replaced it with one $100,000 smaller. The action was a clear signal that management had decided on full-scale confrontation rather than quick agreement. The owners' new offer for the pension fund, an extra $372,000 for the next three years, also came nowhere close to offsetting the inflationary erosion of the preceding three years. Having already visited seven squads, Miller was forced to backtrack and brief them on the new, ominous developments before bringing the other seventeen teams in Florida and the Sun Belt up to speed. From each he now sought votes authorizing the union's executive board to call a retaliatory strike if necessary, with March 31, 1972, the deadline for a final decision.[58]

A look at the composition of the PRC revealed the impetus behind the choice to play hardball over the pension negotiations. The panel was dominated by a majority of "hawks," most of whom were from small-market (especially as measured by local broadcast revenue) clubs. The cast included Cincinnati's Francis Dale, the Kansas City Royals' Ewing Kauffman, St. Louis's Busch-surrogate Dick Meyer, Minnesota's Calvin Griffith, and Pittsburgh's Dan Galbreath. Besides directing Gaherin to adopt a deliberately provocative line in the negotiations, the hard-liners had also displayed their taste for revenge on the union by retaliating against player representatives. Between the spring of 1971 and 1972, clubs cut or traded away fully two-thirds, or sixteen, of the twenty-four team player delegates on the union's executive board. Countering the owners with their own show of resolve, the players voted 663-10 to empower their representatives to call a strike, with eight votes against the resolution coming from just two clubs, the Red Sox and the Dodgers.[59]

The overwhelming tally in support of the union's board failed to reassure Miller. The association had never seriously contemplated a regular-season strike in which players would have to go without their normal paychecks. Befuddled at management's destructive rigidity over "peanuts," Miller conveyed his dismay to Walter O'Malley at a private party only to be reassured by the latter, "Oh, well, don't worry. There's not going to be a strike. We'll resolve this." The Los Angeles owner added cryptically, "A lot can happen in two weeks." O'Malley's words, however, were either a deliberate effort to deceive Miller or a reflection of his own misreading of the situation as a big-market owner. This time, in contrast to 1969, O'Malley's man in the commissioner's office — Bowie Kuhn — was seen as persona non grata by the PRC. At its March 22 session, the group instructed Gaherin to hold firm and offer no concessions. Leaving the meeting, firebrand Gussie Busch foolishly boasted to the press, "We're not going to give them another cent. If they want to strike — let 'em!" The defiant declaration immediately became Players Association bulletin-board material in clubhouses around the country.[60]

Each side prepared with varying levels of enthusiasm and misgiving to try to call the other's bluff. Two days before the union's strike decision deadline, Miller revealed his side's unease by proposing unsuccessfully that the two sides submit the deadlock to binding outside arbitration by a prominent figure of management's choosing. Among the names he offered were President Richard Nixon, former president Lyndon Johnson, and former chief justice Earl Warren. Gaherin and the two league presidents, Feeney and Cronin, continued to label the union's idea of applying the surplus $800,000 to premium increases as "imprudent" and insisted it remain untouched as a reserve. As they finalized arrangements for a union executive board meeting for March 31, Miller and Dick Moss pessimistically forecast that the union would have to perform a graceful fold. The two men even drafted a resolution to lift their strike threat while offering to bargain through the 1972 season. If no progress was made, the association would then seek to blend the unresolved pension issues into the next Basic Agreement talks in early 1973, or if the owners refused that, the union would seek legislative relief from Congress.[61]

On the flight from Arizona to Dallas, the union leaders found themselves in the company of Oakland Athletics' team delegate Chuck Dobson and alternate Reggie Jackson. To the surprise of Miller and Moss, the two stars breathed defiance and unshakable determination to press forward with a strike. At the executive board session, other members echoed the resolve of the Oakland men. Ironically, for one of the few times in his stewardship of the association, Marvin Miller had underestimated his membership almost as badly as his adversaries had. By a 47-0 vote with only Dodger delegate Wes Parker (later "impeached" by his teammates) abstaining, the board voted to strike. In a demonstration of shared sacrifice with constituents who faced lockout from team facilities and denial of their incomes, Miller and Moss took themselves off the union payroll for the duration of the struggle.[62]

Surprised and furious owners maneuvered behind the scenes to coax their respective players into breaking ranks and returning to action. Philadelphia's Bob Carpenter unsuccessfully tried to entice Phillies' delegates Tim McCarver and Tom Harmon to launch an anti-Miller movement. The Orioles' Jerry Hoffberger, a more moderate PRC member, held private sessions with groups of his players, only to have Miller put a stop to the clandestine meetings. The union chief warned his troops that such discussions hindered the union's negotiators by giving the owners hope of victory without needing to make serious proposals at the bargaining table. To shore up the morale of the financially vulnerable younger players, veteran Twins pitcher Jim Perry lined up free housing for them with wealthier veterans, and they trained at high schools or other makeshift facilities in anticipation of an eventual return. A potentially serious crack in player solidarity surfaced when Dodger veteran Maury Wills was cited in the press as leader of a group of thirteen teammates intending to play in the club's April 7 home opener with or without a deal.

Miller responded with a "pep-rally" of the executive board at New York's Four Seasons restaurant. Offering particularly inspiring testimony at the gathering was veteran star Willie Mays. Mays had only become the Giants team representative after two predecessors were traded away, and he had chosen to sacrifice a six-figure salary by backing the strike.[63]

Through March and early April the players took a beating in the press as "pampered," "spoiled," and irresponsible to the fans. By the end of the first week of the strike, however, cracks began to show in the owners' ranks. Contributing to the growth of owner dissension was John Gaherin's introduction of Philadelphia employee-benefits specialist John Able. Able explained to skeptical magnates that the union's proposal to transfer the surplus $800,000 posed no danger to the pension fund's soundness. Owners familiar with such procedures through their backgrounds in the insurance industry, such as the Braves' Bill Bartholomay and the Athletics' Charles O. Finley, now claimed more ammunition with which to lobby recalcitrant colleagues. Big-market mogul O'Malley woefully predicted Dodger losses of $1 million for each weekend the strike continued. Privately even some of the hard-liners previously the loudest at saber-rattling now begged for a settlement. When Gaherin informed Calvin Griffith, for example, that if he truly wanted to break the union he and the others had to be willing to keep the players out until May 1, the Minnesota magnate weakly lamented, "What will the press do to us?" As the PRC's negotiator recalled later, "Everybody wanted to shoot him [Miller] but nobody wanted to pull the trigger."[64]

On April 8, over a week into the strike, Gaherin gave the first public indication that owner resolve had crumbled. Having reiterated to Miller only two days earlier that he would not raise his offer even a penny, the PRC negotiator now boosted his pension proposal by $400,000, with the funds coming from the surplus accrual as the union had advocated. In another sign that the ice had broken, the White Sox, the Pirates, and the Phillies defied league strictures and opened their facilities to striking players for workouts. On April 11, Gaherin restored his original suggestion for boosting player health care pay-ins and proposed future cost-of-living adjustments to pension benefits. The only key issues remaining, ironically, were those the deadlock itself had created—whether to reschedule lost games and, if not, whether players should be paid and receive service time for days lost. In a public relations gesture, Miller had proposed early in the strike that any lost games be made up by free contests from which neither owners nor players would be paid. Now he offered a compromise in which lost games would not be made up, and the players in turn would not recapture lost wages but would be credited with service time.[65]

On April 13, 1972, the two sides announced an agreement. If the owners had accepted the same deal only three days earlier, they could have reduced the number of canceled games by nearly half. Instead the strike wiped out 86 contests. Because of unequal schedules created by the cancellations, some teams played 153 games, others as many as 156, and the difference eventually cost Boston the AL East pennant to Detroit by a half-game. The owners' insistence on provoking the showdown had cost them $5.2 million in revenue, while the players had sacrificed $600,000 in salary. Vindictive owners such as Gussie Busch attempted to extract compensatory savings and risked new grievances by eliminating players' single road accommodations. A few self-absorbed stars grumbled at the lost wages in the strike's aftermath. One of them, Pete Rose, insisted, "If there's another strike . . . the Players Association will not get my support." But on balance, Marvin Miller could claim more than the usual reasons for celebrating on his fifty-fifth birthday, April 14. His members had won $500,000 in additional owner pension contributions, to better than $5.9 million, and comparable boosts in health insurance offerings. More important, the union had shown the owners, the public, and above all, itself that it could endure the pain of a regular-season strike to win a major victory. It was a lesson the owners had hoped the Players Association would never learn. Ironically, because they had forced the showdown in their effort to break the union, only to be the ones to cave when the going got tough, the magnates had been the most responsible of all in teaching their players the value of solidarity.[66]

Hovering in the background throughout the pension battle, the Curt Flood lawsuit approached its conclusion before the U.S. Supreme Court. Flood's challenge to the reserve clause had first been heard in federal district court in May 1970, before Judge Irving Ben Cooper. The plaintiff's case had hinged on five main arguments. First, the reserve clause functioned as a collusive agreement between clubs to suppress salaries below fair market value. Second, the reserve constituted a form of involuntary servitude that violated the Thirteenth Amendment. Third, the blacklisting employed by owners to enforce the reserve represented an illegal labor practice barred by the Wagner Act of 1935. Fourth, trading a veteran player against his will exacted significant personal and financial hardship and destroyed his roots in his community. Finally, the reserve denied second-string and fringe players the opportunity to advance through switching clubs.[67]

At both the district court and the appeals levels, Flood's supporting witnesses included Jackie Robinson, Bill Veeck, Hank Greenberg, and ex-pitcher and author Jim Brosnan. Management's defense team retained as experts league presidents Feeney and Cronin, Commissioner Kuhn, and ex-player turned broadcaster Joe Garagiola. In retrospect, given the particular arguments Flood's team employed, a less prominent, more financially disadvantaged player might have stood a better chance. For example, although Flood's lawyers claimed that their client had suffered direct salary harm from the reserve clause and from his involuntary trade, the defense pointed out that the Phillies' 1970 offer represented a $10,000 raise from his Cardinals pay the year before. While Brookings Institution economist Robert Nathan testified that the reserve clause generally held down big league salaries, he was unable to provide any specific estimate of either its overall impact or its effect on Flood. As a consequence he provided the courts no reliable figure on which to base damages. When Jim Brosnan took the stand and described how the magnates had used the threat of blacklist to quash his off-season personal appearances and writing activities, the testimony only suggested that the witness himself might have been a stronger litigant.[68]

Organized Baseball countered with claims that the reserve did not constitute a form of slavery, since a player could always leave baseball for another livelihood. Although they did not contest the fact that Flood's trade had disrupted his life and prospects in St. Louis, the claimant and his lawyers had not pressed that issue hard or asked for damages from the loss of the player's photography store in the city. As for Flood's argument that the reserve crippled advancement by journeyman players, once more the argument would have better fit someone less successful. As Bill Veeck noted, a ten-year AAA veteran without a dime in future pension claims would have made a more sympathetic victim. Instead—perhaps the necessary price of Flood's reliance on legal help sponsored by the Players Association—the case presented a broad, general attack on the reserve rather than a well-focused delineation of an individual litigant's own victimization. In fairness, Flood's lawyers did force the defense into its share of damaging tactical decisions, not least of which was to argue that the complaint was not an antitrust matter but an issue within the scope of baseball's collective bargaining system. By saying that, management's lawyers effectively aided Marvin Miller's later argument that a reserve clause test could be brought before the grievance arbitration process secured in the 1970 Basic Agreement.[69]

In his ruling of August 12, 1970, Judge Cooper had sided with baseball that the Supreme Court's 1922 antitrust exemption invalidated Flood's suit. Cooper had urged both sides to seek a nonjudicial modification of the reserve through either negotiation or arbitration. The chances that the owners voluntarily would agree to either course were virtually nonexistent. During a 1970 bargaining session, when player representative Jim Bouton had asked tongue-in-cheek whether the magnates would consider allowing a player to become a free agent once he reached age sixty-five, Lou Carroll had refused "because next time you'll want it reduced to age 55." After Arthur Goldberg had filed his appeal of Cooper's ruling, Flood had left the country for Denmark, but in October the Phillies had traded away their rights to the expatriate outfielder to Bob Short's Washington Senators. Because of his mounting financial difficulties and assurances from his lawyer that belated acceptance of big league employment would not harm the litigation, Flood had accepted Short's $110,000 offer. After less than two weeks of the 1971 regular season, however, Flood had found his ballplaying skills irretrievably eroded and had given up his comeback. Multiplying his setbacks, that same April the appeals court had rejected his claim. Goldberg then had appealed the case to the Supreme Court. In October 1971 the high court had agreed to hear the case and render a final verdict in its 1972 spring term.[70]

Given the disappointing outcome of Flood's litigation at district and appellate levels, the Players Association did not expect a favorable result in the Supreme Court. Although they had given their blessing and limited financial backing, both Miller and Moss already had judged that the union's best chance to dismantle the reserve lay in finding a player willing to play out or sit out a season without a signed contract and then seek his freedom through a grievance arbitration test of the reserve clause's renewability. To deter the prospect the owners, in turn, for years had employed the combination of regulations called Major League Rule 3(c) and Section 10(a) of the Standard Playing Contract. As the magnates interpreted Section 10(a), a club could unilaterally renew its exclusive rights to an unsigned player each season after March 1. Under such a renewal the general manager could cut the player's salary by up to 20 percent of the previous year's level. But if the player tried to serve out his reserve year as an active performer despite having no signed contract, Rule 3(c) barred him from doing so. Under 3(c) an unsigned player could not suit up or play for his current club or anyone else. The "double-whammy" of the two regulations effectively pressured the player to sign a low salary offer from his current club, thus ending the holdout, or else stay home and risk having his skills and marketplace value erode from idleness. Even then, the owner still asserted the right to apply his reserve claim the following spring on the dubious grounds that the reserve could be perpetuated indefinitely.[71]

Every spring training since he had been named union executive director, Miller had read Section 10(a) to assembled groups of players and given them his interpretation of it. To him it was clear that the reserve clause bound a player for only one additional year and that after that, the performer became a free agent. In support of his reading of the clause, he cited the 1967 lawsuit by National Basketball Association (NBA) star Rick Barry against the San Francisco Warriors. Barry had sought to jump to the rival American Basketball Association (ABA), and a federal judge had ruled that while under his sport's own reserve clause Barry could not switch employers for a year, the clause was not renewable beyond one season. In baseball, however, the New York Yankees in 1969 had used 3(c) and 10(a) in classic fashion to torment Al Downing. When the hurler had threatened to play out his reserve year and secure free agency, club player-personnel director Johnny Johnson had notified him that under 3(c) he would be locked out of spring training. Downing had given in and signed, only to be traded away.[72]

By the spring training season of 1972, however, a new test case of the reserve clause had emerged. Twenty-one-year-old catcher Ted Simmons, a former two-sport high school hero, had been drafted and signed by the Cardinals at a $50,000 bonus in 1967 and had reached the majors by 1970. Having made just $14,000 the year before, in 1972 the rising star demanded a raise to $35,000. Citing Nixon administration wage and price controls in defense of its hardball stance, the club refused. Simmons then reported to spring training without a signed contract. Needing their young backstop and fearing that a show of unreasonableness might be viewed negatively by the courts in the Flood litigation, the Cardinals reluctantly permitted Simmons to continue playing despite Rule 3(c). Since the Cardinals had opted not to lock him out, Simmons now feared that the club would trade him, as it had done with pitchers Jerry Reuss and Steve Carlton when faced with their salary demands. But no other clubs were willing to take the unsigned catcher off the Cardinals' hands and risk their own subsequent contract showdowns and possible reserve clause challenge. Looking toward the imminent Flood verdict, John Gaherin, in turn, pressed St. Louis to do whatever necessary to sign Simmons and thereby eliminate a new test of the reserve.[73]

As the Simmons impasse dragged through the regular season, the Supreme Court issued its decision on the Curt Flood appeal. On June 19, 1972, by a 5-3 margin the justices ruled against the ex-outfielder and on stare decisis grounds upheld the judgments of the lower courts. Two of the dissenting justices, however, William O. Douglas and William Brennan, maintained that if the majority had been willing to look at the baseball industry with a clean slate, the antitrust exemption would not have withstood legal scrutiny. They pointedly added in reference to the high court's 1922 ruling, "The unbroken silence of Congress should not prevent us from correcting our own mistakes." In the aftermath of Flood's defeat, the union and its leaders privately second-guessed virtually every aspect of his case. Marvin Miller questioned the impact of Nixon appointees on the court's composition, and he even criticized his old boss's performance, wondering if Goldberg's decision to run against Nelson Rockefeller for the New York governorship after giving prior assurances to the contrary had distracted him. As for the Nixon justices, Lewis Powell had absented himself because he owned Busch company stock, but William Rehnquist, Warren Burger, and Harry Blackmun had voted against Flood, with the latter authoring the majority decision. In truth, even a more "favorable" decision might well have been carefully limited to either overturning the antitrust exemption while retaining the reserve as part of the industry's collective bargaining agreement, or remanding the case to Judge Cooper for reconsideration.[74]

The one favorable consequence of the conclusion of Flood's lawsuit was that it released the union from its earlier pledge not to initiate a fresh reserve challenge while the case remained active. If Ted Simmons and the Cardinals remained in their respective positions through the end of the season, the union could file a grievance on his behalf before baseball's arbitration panel. Aware of Lou Carroll's earlier stricture, "Don't ever let them [the union] try that renewal clause," John Gaherin continued to pressure the Cardinals to sign Simmons whatever the price. Following a federal pay board ruling that declared professional athletes exempt from Nixon administration controls, St. Louis abruptly dropped its hard line and offered the catcher a two-year deal for a combined $75,000. Unable to refuse, Simmons signed in the second week of August.[75]

The owners had managed to dodge two bullets aimed squarely at the reserve—one from Curt Flood, the other from Ted Simmons. But John Gaherin reminded the magnates that all they had won was a temporary reprieve. Barring some negotiated compromise with the union, they still faced the possibility of congressional legislation or, much more likely, a union grievance before the industry's arbitration panel. Trying to argue reason to owners deafened by their temporary success, Gaherin urged his clients to bargain modifications to the reserve for long-term veterans. "Fellas, this is the twentieth century," he pleaded. "You can't get anybody, drunk or sober, to agree that once a fella goes to work for the A&P, he has to work for the A&P the rest of his life!"[76] The magnates, however, remained obstinate in their defense of just such a system as long as they could.

CHAPTER 6 : STAR WARS

1973–1979

By the end of 1972, major league owners could still claim possession of the reserve clause, but they had been regularly beaten at the negotiating table by the Players Association. Led by John Gaherin and new PRC head Ed Fitzgerald of Milwaukee, some magnates belatedly favored compromise to avoid losing the reserve clause entirely. Those backing a deal with the union wanted alternatives that would retain the reserve's hold on most players but lessen holdouts, permit stars modest salary advances, and give long-term veterans a chance to change employers at least once in their careers. The hard-liners still placed their faith in league lawyers who continued to tell them the courts would sustain Organized Baseball's position. In the middle, wanting to yield as little as necessary but grudgingly prepared to compromise to avoid a season-threatening work stoppage, were Commissioner Kuhn and patron Walter O'Malley. Few in any camp, however, really wanted a second confrontation like that over the pension anytime soon.[1]

As one sign that the magnates wanted a quieter negotiation and a quicker deal in the next Basic Agreement talks, the PRC had been streamlined by two owners, and the moderate Fitzgerald had been named its new chairman. The owners also had lowered the ratification margin necessary for a deal from a concurrent majority of each league's clubs to a simple overall majority. Although Commissioner Kuhn and aide Sandy Hadden remained barred from direct negotiations, the two men clandestinely monitored developments through Gaherin's office, to the mixed horror and amusement of the union. Aware of Kuhn's self-perception as defender of all in baseball, Miller considered the commissioner's secret comings and goings to PRC headquarters acts of hypocrisy rather than obtuseness. Accordingly, when the commissioner attempted to establish similar back channels with the players, Miller treated them as infiltration attempts and refused to reveal any bargaining hints.[2]

From the start of the new negotiations in the fall of 1972, Miller probed management's flexibility on the reserve. In September he suggested to Gaherin that players have the right to test their value as free agents at least once. He also proposed that men with three years of service making less than the major league average salary, and five-year men at less than 1½ the mean, be eligible for free agency. Seven-year, twelve-year, and seventeen-year veterans could test the market whatever their pay level. The club signing a free agent would have to pay compensation to the losing organization equal to half the lost player's most recent salary. For weeks Gaherin offered in return only another three-year study of the issue. But on November 29, the owners trotted out Commissioner Kuhn to announce a new position to the press. Under the new proposal five-year veterans under $30,000 would be eligible for free agency, as would eight-year men under $40,000. Ten-year veterans would not have unrestricted free agency but would gain the power to veto trades. In order to finance these minimal modifications to the reserve, the owners demanded that each club's reserve rosters be reduced from forty to thirty-eight men.[3]

Although Miller had always questioned the commissioner's claims of impartiality, the latter's new role in pushing owner proposals infuriated him, as did the subtle penury of the plan. The union calculated that under the scheme only 5 of 960 players would qualify for free agency. At most the proposal indicated the magnates' willingness in principle to modify limitations on the reserve. At the same time, because the union had made so much progress since 1966 on issues such as the minimum salary and the pension, these now assumed "back-burner" status. The PRC proposed a boost in the minimum salary to $15,000 by 1975, while the union called instead for an immediate jump to $15,500 and $17,500 by the later date. On the central issue of the reserve, Miller continued to demand that all major leaguers receive free agency at the end of a specified length of service. But he concluded privately that while a hard line on free agency and the threat of a strike could not force the owners to make immediate direct changes, it might still be useful in nudging the owners to a less "radical" means of boosting players' pay leverage — outside salary arbitration. Salary arbitration could build on the grievance arbitration process the union had already secured and could be applied to big leaguers with as little as two years' service. Ironically, the PRC's Gaherin had been urging the same concept to his bosses since the late 1960s as a way to reduce holdouts and divert the union from attacks on the reserve clause.[4]

Through the winter of 1972–73, the owners wrangled among themselves over salary arbitration. Hard-liners already had concluded that Gaherin was a hired hand who did not understand their industry and was too willing to strike a deal for its own sake. In their view Gaherin too often defined "victory" as a negotiation that gave the players "only 90 percent" of what they asked for. Fitzgerald likewise received criticism as an industry newcomer naive to the danger posed by Marvin Miller. While Kuhn, O'Malley, and Montreal's John McHale sided with Gaherin and Fitzgerald, St. Louis's Busch, Oakland's Charley Finley, and Cincinnati's Bob Howsam led the opposition to any concessions on either arbitration or free agency. At the start of 1973 Kuhn announced that the owners would not accept any more alterations of free agency beyond their own November proposal. But he signaled greater flexibility on arbitration by stating that the magnates' main objection to it was the fear that outside arbitrators would "split-the-difference" between player and management bids and thereby push salaries sharply higher.[5]

Miller then sweetened the union's offer by dropping the routine demand to shorten the playing season, suggesting an additional year of study on the reserve, and proposing the use of "either-or" final-offer salary arbitration in which the arbitrator would have to select one side's final offer. When confronted with the union's rapid reply, the PRC tried to bluff for additional concessions by instructing clubs not to permit players to report to spring training without a deal. But the lockout order soon lost its potency when two clubs refused up front to go along. By the end of the first week of February, the owners' new counterproposal finally appeared. In exchange for a three-year rather than one-year moratorium on negotiations of the reserve system, they suggested final-offer arbitration to veterans with three years of service. Eligible players could use the process, however, only every other year. Sensing a deal nearing, Miller still rejected the PRC proposal on the basis that if a player received salary arbitration only once every two seasons, after a "defeat" a vengeful owner could compensate the next year by cutting his pay up to the 20 percent maximum.[6]

Hard-line owners attacked the PRC plan from the other direction, claiming it gave too much to the union. Charley Finley railed against the consequences of outside arbitration, warning, "You'll have guys with no baseball background setting salaries." But other owners anxious to avoid a repeat of the 1972 impasse inched toward a deal. O'Malley, who could be counted on to abandon a hard line once it threatened Dodger regular-season revenues, weighed in, and to no one's surprise Kuhn echoed him. Finley's counterattacks lost credibility when his colleagues remembered that he had more to lose from salary arbitration in 1974 than they. Finley had justly earned a miser's reputation for the low pay he extended his players, and that combined with his team's on-field brilliance made him more likely than anyone else to face a rush of hearings under the new procedure. With only Finley and Busch holding out, the owners endorsed final-offer arbitration in principle and granted PRC flexibility in reaching an agreement.[7]

On February 17 talks resumed, and it immediately became clear that the ice had been broken. Eleven days later the two sides finalized their pact. The owners agreed to the right of players with two seasons' experience to request salary arbitration after the expiration of any signed contract, with hearings to begin in early 1974. The union and the PRC would select a pool of arbitrators from lists drawn up with the help of the American Arbitration Association, and one would be assigned to each pay dispute. Prior to the start of the new process the owners would provide comprehensive salary data to the union to enable players to prepare their cases. Claims would be filed between February 1 and 10 of each season, and each arbitrator would hear arguments from both sides within a week and issue a verdict within seventy-two hours after that. No salary could be cut more than 20 percent in one year. In addition, ten-year vets with five years' continuous service with their current team could block trades, and five-year men could protest demotions to the minors.[8]

Although its other provisions received less attention, the 1973 Basic Agreement also continued the string of union advances on its broad front of compensation and workplace issues. Minimum salaries rose to $15,000 immediately and to $16,000 by 1975. World Series shares were bumped upward to a $20,000 individual minimum on victorious squads. Based on higher owner pension contributions, benefits to players, widows, and dependents all rose. The monthly pension of a ten-year veteran at age fifty climbed $110 to $710, five-year pensioners garnered $919, and ten-year men received $1,813 monthly at age sixty-five. The eligibility deadline for the college scholarship plan stretched to two years after the end of a big league career. Road meal allowances climbed to $19 a day and Murphy money rose to $57 a week, with cost-of-living adjustments for 1974 and 1975. Three-year players secured the right to live outside their club's spring training facilities while still receiving $16 in daily meal money and $10 a week in supplemental allowances. Moving expenses also were liberalized, and players could demand single-occupancy rooms on the road as long as they agreed to pay half of the double-room rate. Spring training could not start earlier than March 1 or ten days before the second Saturday of that month, whichever came first. Beginning in 1974 the pact also barred doubleheaders on "getaway" days, and clubs could not waive existing rules to reschedule contests unless the players affected formally approved by majority ballot.[9]

Still, the attention of virtually everyone involved in or covering the baseball industry centered on the new salary arbitration procedures. Having agreed to the new process, the magnates now tried their utmost to undermine it or mold it to their advantage. In October 1973 Miller accused them of deliberately withholding salary information in order to scuttle upcoming hearings. Chief among the instigators was Finley, who anticipated as many as eleven arbitration cases. It was not until mid-February, after players had already filed formal hearing requests, that under threat of an NLRB judgment the owners released the 1973 pay data. Although the subsequent arbitrations did help raise payrolls by approximately 12 percent in 1974 — about double the previous rate — the immediate consequences did not live up to hard-liners' worst nightmares. Fifty-four players filed for salary arbitration, but 25 settled prior to hearings. Of the remaining 29, the clubs "won" 16 times; players, 13. Fairly typical were the results secured by the Baltimore Orioles, who won two of three cases and ended up $28,000 "worse" in payroll than what the club had originally offered. Even Finley's A's lost only an extra $87,000 in 1974 salaries from its nine cases.[10]

If salary arbitration initially was not the monster its opponents feared, neither had it derailed Marvin Miller's determination to gut the reserve clause. In retrospect, the PRC's Fitzgerald and negotiator Gaherin both underestimated the resolve of the Players Association on the issue. Years later Gaherin conceded that by the time the 1973 Basic Agreement was negotiated, Miller had already decided to "dynamite the reserve clause." But he still maintained, "If we'd started salary arbitration earlier, we might have forestalled him." In truth the union's leader could never have been dissuaded from a challenge. At most, his membership might have been enticed at the start by preemptive concessions to try to restrain their boss's fervor. But with every passing day and new success by the union, that possibility had evaporated. Instead Miller continued to search for one or more players willing to play out their option season and test the renewability of the reserve before the grievance arbitration panel.[11]

In 1973 five players had started the season without contracts, but by the end of the campaign four had been signed and the fifth released. In 1974 seven more unsigned men started the schedule. All but two — Yankee relief pitcher Sparky Lyle and San Diego outfielder Bobby Tolan — re-upped by mid-September. Lyle, presented with an immediate $7,500 raise to $87,500 and $92,500 for 1975, signed with only two weeks to go. But Tolan remained a strong candidate for free agency. The Padres' disgruntled outfielder was disparaged privately by John Gaherin as a man unable to "write his name twice and spell it the same." But Tolan was both talented and a union loyalist. The Players Association had earned his loyalty by challenging a prior series of suspensions and fines levied by the Reds against his high socks, long hair, sideburns, and mustaches. Cincinnati had subsequently unloaded Tolan to San Diego after the 1973 season, where his demands for a pay raise had run straight into the obstacle of general manager Buzzie Bavasi, a graduate of the Rickey school of contract negotiations.[12]

By late September, with one week left in the 1974 season and Tolan still unsigned, Gaherin and NL president Feeney pleaded with the club not to let the outfielder become a free-agency test case. On the campaign's last day, Padres owner and McDonald's hamburger titan Ray Kroc anted up a two-year contract at $100,000 a season, plus a substantial loan to facilitate Tolan's purchase of a new house in the San Diego area. To Gaherin's relief and Miller's frustration, the player signed. Once more the owners had dodged a formal demand for free agency. But before they had time to congratulate themselves, they faced a new suitor, this time in the person of one of the game's premier pitchers.[13]

James Augustus "Catfish" Hunter was the cornerstone of an Oakland Athletics pitching staff that captured three consecutive world championships from 1972 to 1974. Signed by Charley Finley out of American Legion baseball as a teenager for $75,000, by age eighteen Hunter had reached the majors, and in 1968 he hurled a perfect game. By the time the Athletics reached the World Series stage in the early 1970s, he justly claimed a status as one of the best, if not *the* best, pitcher in baseball. Hailing from a humble North Carolina background, he had encountered both the good and the bad sides of his mercurial owner's temperament.

Besides the pitcher's signing bonus and even his nickname, Finley had bestowed upon the star a $5,000 salary raise after his perfect game and had advanced him a $150,000 loan with which to buy 300 acres of Carolina farmland in 1969. But after Hunter had borrowed the money, Finley had become overextended from poor team revenues and unwise investments in National Hockey League (NHL) and ABA franchises. Within weeks he had demanded immediate reimbursement in full. Ultimately the pitcher had been forced to sell all but thirty acres of the land to meet his owner's demands, only to see the purchaser of his acreage win awards for the crops raised on it. For the hurler who had been led to believe that he enjoyed a special relationship with his owner, the loan recall was a searing lesson in Finley's capacity for meanness and hypocrisy. Not surprisingly, when Finley found himself on the short end of a financial obligation to Hunter, the latter seized the opportunity to play his own form of hardball.[14]

For 1974 Hunter had signed a new two-year contract with Oakland at $100,000. In order to reduce his tax liability, he arranged to have Finley pay half of the salary in the form of payments on an insurance annuity the pitcher had arranged with a North Carolina insurance company. Either because of cash flow problems or because he simply wanted to claim the full $100,000 as tax-deductible salary on his club ledgers, Finley failed to make the required annuity installments. After repeated written notifications by Hunter's attorney, J. Carlton Cherry, Finley's continued failure to pay, followed by Hunter's grumblings to teammates and the press, caught the attention of Marvin Miller and Dick Moss in September. Under the 1968 Basic Agreement, a player's right to mutually agreed deferral of salary had been formally recognized, and the 1970 agreement had created the arbitration machinery to challenge Finley's continued right to Hunter's services in view of the owner's apparent breach of contract.[15]

To Miller's delight, Hunter and his attorney agreed to cooperate in a challenge, with the union formally representing Hunter in the grievance. In mid-September, Moss sent the Oakland owner formal notice of the asserted violation and cited Section 7(a) of the Uniform Playing Contract. The provision stated that as of ten days after a written notification, either party to a contract could unilaterally declare the pact terminated. Moss even gave Finley more than the required ten days to rectify his delinquency, but when Finley continued to stall, on October 4 the union lawyer dispatched the termination notice and declared Hunter to be a free agent. As the controversy swirled in the midst of the fall classic between the A's and the Dodgers, Finley publicly dismissed the dispute as a "misunderstanding" that would be rectified as soon as the series ended. When AL president Lee MacPhail and the PRC finally impressed upon Finley the gravity of his predicament, he belatedly tried to scotch the complaint by directly offering Hunter a check for $50,000. Following the advice of both attorney Cherry and the union that such a taxable gift was not an adequate substitute for the promised payments on a tax-free annuity, Hunter refused the money and again demanded the sum be paid directly to his insurance company. Again, Finley refused.[16]

After the World Series, as a formal courtesy to John Gaherin the union notified him of its intention to press for Hunter's free agent rights through the grievance arbitration process. Gaherin then tried valiantly to coach Finley for his testimony before the three-person panel. PRC counsel Barry Rona, the National League's Lou Hoynes, PRC chairman Fitzgerald, and AL counsel Jim Garner joined Finley in his hometown of Chicago. The subsequent meetings, however, only convinced all but the cavalier owner of his legal vulnerability and of the likelihood that he would be a loose cannon on the witness stand. After the session Gaherin, referring to the upcoming hearing, confessed to Hoynes, "It's a tough one to prepare for. . . . We'll never know when he [Finley] is telling the truth."[17]

On November 1, 1974, the arbitration hearing commenced. Chairing the session was Peter Seitz, a longtime veteran of labor-management deliberations and a man with the appearance and preferences for literary allusions of a college professor. Because of the black-and-white nature of the facts, and Seitz's earlier role in NBA and ABA free-agency rulings, Miller privately maintained great confidence in the eventual verdict. Complicating his side's presentation, unfortunately, was the intervention by an extra participant, agent Jerry Kapstein. Kapstein, who had previously represented several other Oakland players in contract negotiations, had been retained by Hunter on the eve of the hearing. Miller had little respect for the agent's legal knowledge or negotiating skills, and he viewed him as a rival for the loyalty of star players. Miller demanded and got assurances that Kapstein would play no active role in presenting Hunter's case. As the hearing unfolded, Gaherin's fears about Finley's credibility proved amply justified, as the owner tried to claim he had never received the annuity paperwork in either February or June from Hunter's attorney. Finley even purported to have been surprised

THE INFLATIONARY ERA

in August at the pitcher's demand for full payment of the $50,000 premium. Baseball attorneys were no more credible in claiming that Finley's late offer to pay the sum in cash, despite its adverse tax implications for Hunter, met his contractual obligations. Nonetheless, Jerry Kapstein declared to the press his assessment that Hunter would lose the case. A furious Miller and Cherry used the unwelcome, unauthorized comment to persuade their client to dismiss him from his legal team. In truth, it was Finley who was in big trouble. Swing-voter Seitz clearly telegraphed his leanings following the owner's testimony by commenting to fellow panelist Gaherin, "John, you know your client's a liar." The PRC's director reported the troubling observation to his superiors and prepared for the worst.[18]

Seitz handed down his decision on December 13. Before making his official presentation, he showed a draft copy to fellow panelists Miller and Gaherin. The union head suddenly noted with alarm that the statement ordered Finley to make the annuity payment and terminated Hunter's extant contract with the A's, but, intentionally or through oversight, it did not explicitly state that he was officially a free agent. Fearful that the omission might embolden Organized Baseball to claim that the pitcher remained under Oakland's option control, Miller pointed out the error. After a brief recess Seitz reemerged with a revision that contained the explicit declaration of free agency. After the arbitrator announced the verdict, Commissioner Kuhn blasted the ruling, claiming it gave "a life sentence to a pickpocket," and he tried to negate its impact by directing major league owners not to bid for Hunter's services. When Miller then threatened to file suit against him for collusive restraint in violation of the Basic Agreement, however, Kuhn was forced to back down. Finley also lost a last-ditch appeal of Seitz's ruling before the California Supreme Court.[19]

Following the repulsion of baseball's futile counterattacks, the bidding for Catfish Hunter began in earnest on December 19. Fearful that he might snap at the first serious offer, Miller urged the hurler and his attorney not to accept any bid as small as $200,000 a season, even though that sum still represented a doubling of his salary. The association leader need not have worried. Within days every club except the A's and their Bay Area–market rival, the Giants, had made Hunter initial bids by phone, telegram, or personal messenger. Opening antes fell in the $2 million range over five years, followed as early as the afternoon of December 19 by an offer of $3 million from the Boston Red Sox. The next day, San

Diego—whose general manager Bavasi had initially forecast a $400,000 *total* price tag to owner Ray Kroc—offered nearly $4 million. The Phillies presented their own multimillion-dollar package, as did Angels owner Gene "The Cowboy" Autry. Other clubs not as willing or able to bid as high attempted to exploit personal ties to entice Hunter's signature. Cleveland dispatched fellow hurler and North Carolinian Gaylord Perry to lobby him, while Milwaukee sent former teammate Mike Hegan to accompany Ed Fitzgerald and colleague Bud Selig.[20]

As the bidding continued, clubs assembled creative financial packages to appeal to Hunter's individual, family, and even horticultural interests. The Pirates proposed $750,000 a year for five years, $1 million in annuities, $400,000 in other tax-deferred income, and limited partnership in five Wal-Mart outlets. The Kansas City Royals offered an $825,000 annual package for six years that included farm equipment, $5,000 annual college annuities for Hunter's children, and a guaranteed $50,000 retirement income until age seventy. It was a sign of the heady new leverage Hunter enjoyed that, prophetically, given his later death from Lou Gehrig's disease, he privately crossed the Royals off his list because they neglected to include provisions for his wife in the event of his premature passing. Until the last minute, it appeared that the club with the largest overall financial offer, San Diego, would win the Hunter sweepstakes. But then a new bidder entered the fray—George Steinbrenner's New York Yankees. When Steinbrenner's ownership group had purchased the Bronx Bombers in 1973, he had paid a total of $10 million. Now the flamboyant novice prepared to offer a single player nearly 40 percent of that amount over five years. The Yankee bid, $3.75 million in total salary, did not match those of either the Royals or the Padres. But it did include an immediate signing bonus of $1 million, a $1 million life insurance policy, $500,000 in other deferred money, $50,000 in college annuities for the children, and $200,000 in attorney fees for Cherry. Steinbrenner also shrewdly dispatched as a personal emissary the man who as a bird dog for Finley had signed Hunter to his first professional contract, Clyde Kluttz. Hunter, now wearying from the process, finally ended the suspense by inking with the Yankees on New Year's Eve 1974.[21]

Ever since his retention as Players Association leader in 1966, Marvin Miller had privately speculated just how much one of his stars could command in a truly free and open marketplace. The Hunter decision, though it had not involved a direct challenge of the reserve but the simple breach of a player's contract by an employer, nonetheless had provided him with his answer. From a single set of negotiations with multiple suitors, Catfish Hunter had increased his annual salary more than seven-fold. Now Miller and his membership alike knew precisely what was at stake in their challenge of the reserve. If no player previously had been willing to stay out long enough to generate a formal challenge to Section 10(a), the potential bonanza now awaiting a victorious claimant virtually ensured that someone finally would go the distance, and sooner rather than later.

John Alexander "Andy" Messersmith was a native of Anaheim who had attended the University of California at Berkeley and became an All-American pitcher there. Signed by the hometown Angels in 1966, he had reached the majors in just three years. After four solid seasons for that struggling team, he had been dealt to the Los Angeles Dodgers and had blossomed into one of the best starters in the National League. As a star hurler on a team that reached the World Series, Messersmith had every reason to expect the Dodgers to express gratitude though an amicable negotiation, a handsome pay increase, and a guarantee of his future as a fixture on the ball club. It did not happen. Unable to come to terms with personnel director Al Campanis, Messersmith began the 1975 season without a new contract. Although the two sides remained apart on salary, money proved not the main snag. In the absence of a new pact the Dodgers still agreed to pay the pitcher a $115,000 salary. But citing "organizational philosophy," Dodger officials refused to extend Messersmith a multiyear contract with either a no-trade or a trade-approval clause.[22]

By August 1975 Messersmith remained the only active major league holdout out of six who had started the season. Now, Marvin Miller came calling. Frustrated and embittered at Los Angeles's refusal to grant him job security, the pitcher gave the Players Association conditional permission to file a grievance in his behalf at the end of the current campaign. Late in the season the Dodgers revealed their awareness of the rising danger of a grievance arbitration filing by Messersmith and significantly upped their monetary offer. The club extended a proposal for a three-year pact with salary levels of $150,000, $170,000, and $220,000. But Campanis and his boss O'Malley, urged on by the National League's old-line Chub Feeney, continued to reject any no-trade contract language. The Dodgers owner even claimed that Feeney and the league office were forc-

Andy Messersmith
(National Baseball Hall of Fame Library, Cooperstown, N.Y.)

ing him not to extend such an offer by threatening retaliation. Marvin Miller doubted the validity of O'Malley's excuse, however, noting that the National League lacked the authority to ban no-trade contracts.[23]

In past crises, such as the Hunter case, individual clubs and owners had needlessly provoked player challenges through double-dealing and hardball tactics and had been further goaded by league officials and lawyers. John Gaherin and a minority of management moderates had urged cutting a deal, but their advice had fallen on deaf ears. The same scenario once more played out. During the 1975 season both the PRC's negotiator and its chairman sought the owners' permission to preempt any post-season free-agency suits by initiating negotiations for a modified reserve system. Gaherin cautioned against the folly of letting reserve challenges reach an arbitrator or the courts, noting that "Marvin [Miller] can afford to lose a hundred times as long as he wins once." Ed Fitzgerald stressed the positives of a deal, expressing optimism that talks with the union could secure the clubs' hold on players for an eight- or possibly ten-year span. Although a few traditionalists later claimed to have seen the merit in such arguments, at the time they remained in the background as the most vocal diehards, led by Busch and Howsam, assailed any idea of negotiations. As a consequence there would be no preemptive talks about limiting the reserve, nor any pressure on the Dodgers to abandon their traditional stance against no-trade contracts.[24]

For his part, Marvin Miller could not fathom the magnates' intransigence. They appeared willing to risk the complete survival of the reserve over a matter as trivial as a no-trade clause in one player's contract. Convinced that the Dodgers would yet come to their senses, the union scanned the lists of other 1974 players unsigned in 1975 and came across the name of Dave McNally. The veteran left-hander, a mainstay of Baltimore pitching staffs from the mid-1960s through the early 1970s, had been traded to Montreal after the 1974 season. Early the next spring, however, arm problems, age, and ineffectiveness had led him to return to Billings, Montana, where he owned a Ford dealership. McNally had always been a union loyalist and even served as a team player representative. Because his career probably had reached its end anyway, he also possessed the virtue of being practically immune from magnate retaliation. Miller proposed to him that as insurance in the event Messersmith came to terms with Los Angeles, McNally should be prepared to file his own grievance for free agency from the Expos for 1976.[25]

Once again, in its solicitation of McNally the union drew upon a player's resentment of management's bad faith. In the ex-Oriole's case, as a "10-5" man (one with ten years' major league service and the last five with the same club) he had enjoyed the right under the Basic Agreement to approve or veto any trade. McNally reluctantly had accepted his being dealt to Montreal on the promise of Expos chief executive John McHale that he would get a guaranteed two-year deal at $125,000 a season. Once the trade had been consummated, however, the Expos had reneged and offered only a one-year pact at $115,000. When a panicky John Gaherin now learned of Miller's recruitment of McNally, he summoned McHale and pleaded, "For Christ's sake, get the bastard drunk and sign him." On the shaky pretext of "passing through" Billings on a trip, the Montreal owner courted McNally hoping he would sign a new contract. He promised the pitcher a guaranteed $25,000 signing bonus just for showing up at 1976 spring training, and a $125,000 salary if he lasted the season. McNally rejected the outdated overture. "McHale wasn't honest with me last year," he stated confidentially. "I have no intention of playing, and it wouldn't be right to take the money." [26]

McNally's enlistment in the union's free-agency war carried two important consequences. First, it ensured that at least one grievance challenging the reserve's renewability would be filed no matter what the fate of the Messersmith negotiations. Second, because of that fact, the Dodgers also no longer had any reason to reverse themselves and offer the latter a no-trade clause in order to keep him out of arbitration. The PRC reiterated to O'Malley to stand firm, and in early October the Players Association filed grievances in behalf of both Messersmith and McNally. According to the union's reading of Section 10(a), which had been incorporated into the collective bargaining agreements, the two men were entitled to free agency for having served the required single option year without contracts. Baseball management then filed suit in federal court in Kansas City to enjoin the arbitration process. According to the owners' lawyers, the interpretation of contract renewal procedures lay outside the grievance arbitration system. But although Judge John Oliver allowed baseball to seek judicial relief after the fact if it felt the arbitrator exceeded his authority, he refused to grant the preemptive injunction. [27]

One other key issue remained for the PRC before the two cases went to arbitration. Should they, as was their right, dismiss Peter Seitz in favor of a new third panelist? Marvin Miller privately expected the owners to do so, for even before Seitz had been hired in 1974 to replace the retiring Gabriel Alexander, union staff research had unearthed his support of the 1969 Rick Barry free-agency verdict against the NBA. Nonetheless, at that time the owners had not blocked his appointment, a development Miller attributed to their failing to have "done their homework." But by now baseball management not only should have discovered what the union had long known about Seitz's background; they had witnessed his ruling in the Hunter case. Behind closed doors, NL lawyer Lou Hoynes argued strenuously for Seitz's removal, as did Commissioner Kuhn. John McHale relayed NBA commissioner Walter Kennedy's judgment of Seitz as a "players' man." Based on his own earlier professional experiences with the arbitrator, steel negotiator Bruce Johnston derided him as "a poet, not an analyst" and also urged letting him go. But ironically, the majority of PRC owners, having consistently rejected John Gaherin's previous advice to get rid of the reserve issue through a negotiated compromise, now inexplicably chose to obey his counsel and keep Seitz in place for the upcoming hearing. The PRC negotiator indicated his preference for dealing with "the devil you know" rather than a newcomer, and with only one dissenter—McHale—the PRC voted not to make a change.[28]

A few days before Thanksgiving the Messersmith-McNally hearings began. They ran to three days and filled 842 pages of testimony transcript before resting in the hands of Seitz, Gaherin, and Miller. The owners' brief, argued by Lou Hoynes, contained both a procedural and a substantive tack. On the first line of argument, the NL attorney contended, as he had before Judge Oliver, that the panel lacked jurisdiction to hear the matter—hardly an ingratiating approach. On the second issue of contention, Hoynes maintained that because baseball's historic structure depended on the long-standing precedent of the right to control players in perpetuity, limiting that power to a single option year would reduce the industry to chaos and collapse. In effect, as baseball economics writer John Helyar later dubbed it, the second parry was the "but we've *always* done it this way" argument.[29]

On the second day of the hearings Bowie Kuhn tried to inject himself as an "impartial witness" to underscore management's "gloom-and-doom" argument. At the union's insistence, however, he was forced to appear in the identity of an owners' witness. Association counsel Moss proceeded to poke holes in the commissioner's testimony in a merciless cross-examination. In a plea ringing with hypocrisy, given the magnates' refusal to negotiate the issue, Kuhn urged resolution of the differences via collective bargaining rather than either the arbitration process or the courts. In the process, however, the commissioner effectively revealed not only his doubt about the immediate outcome before Peter Seitz's panel but any appeal before Judge Oliver's court. In his closing arguments, attorney Hoynes again cited baseball tradition and court precedent to warn that if the industry lost, "the baseball world . . . will be turned upside down."[30]

Countering over the three days, Dick Moss constantly refocused the hearing participants on the narrow question of the language of Section 10(a) and its meaning in light of similar wording and case histories from other professional sports. By doing so, Moss also clearly reminded Seitz of his keen familiarity with those same rulings. In what was probably his single most effective moment during the hearings, the association counsel in closing argument quoted the words of one of the magnates themselves to reinforce the accuracy of the union's reading of the reserve. From a March 5, 1974, article in the *Minneapolis Star,* Moss quoted Twins owner Calvin Griffith as saying that if his star hitter Tony Oliva refused to sign a new contract, he would cut the player's pay the allowable 20 percent, but that "*he* [Oliva] *would then be playing out his option. At the end of the season he would become a free agent.*" The two sides then adjourned.[31]

After several weeks of deliberation, the swing arbitrator revealed to both camps his desire to have them take the decision out of his hands by entering immediate collective bargaining. Shortly before the owners' winter meetings Seitz presented his request to both Gaherin and Miller in an eight-page letter. Years later he commented, "I begged them [the owners] to negotiate," but like "the French barons in the twelfth century," they continued "too stubborn and stupid." While Miller indicated the union's willingness to negotiate if the two sides pledged to reach an agreement before next spring's exhibition schedule and player contract negotiations, the PRC still refused. Gaherin, recognizing in Seitz's request the desire not to impose a verdict but 'the reluctant willingness to do so, again pleaded with his superiors to authorize new negotiations, but to no avail. Instead the PRC bumped the decision upstairs to the full owner fraternity, and with league lawyers still predicting a 50 percent or better chance of any adverse ruling being overturned in the federal courts, the magnates rejected the idea of talks. Conspicuously and hypocritically silent during the entire debate was Bowie Kuhn, who had testified before Seitz on the desirability of a negotiated resolution.[32]

Bearing the countenance of a condemned man, Gaherin glumly delivered the owners' refusal to negotiate to Miller and Moss, then informed Seitz. On December 23, 1975, the panel chairman returned with his expected ruling. To the union's satisfaction the verdict came down squarely in favor of Messersmith and McNally. Although Seitz protested afterward that he was not, nor claimed to be, "a new Abraham Lincoln freeing the slaves," he had dealt the mortal blow to baseball's century-long version of employee captivity. Gaherin had anticipated Seitz's verdict, and as soon as it was delivered, he fired his colleague with the words, "Peter, I'm sorry . . . I love you dearly, but you're out." Upon hearing the ruling at a holiday party, Calvin Griffith could only manage to blurt out, "Oh, shit!" John McHale, whose intransigence had helped instigate the grievance and whose subsequent advice to fire Seitz had been overruled, dubbed the verdict a "disaster."[33]

Now the magnates would find out if their lawyers' faith in the federal courts as saviors had been justified or folly. To their dismay Judge Oliver upheld the Seitz ruling, as did the federal court of appeals. In references particularly pleasing to Marvin Miller and painful to the owners' legal team, Oliver and the appeals court both cited as precedents a group of 1960 Supreme Court rulings, dubbed the "Steelworkers Trilogy," to sustain the grievance arbitration panel's procedural jurisdiction over the Messersmith-McNally suit. In that earlier set of cases, which had occurred while Miller had served in the Steelworkers union, the high court had upheld as sound policy the use of arbitrators rather than jurists as specialized adjudicators of labor rights disputes. The justices had concluded accordingly that such arbitrators' judgments should only rarely be reversed, and only then on narrowly limited grounds. Given the unambiguous and rapid verdicts in support of baseball's arbitration system, even the most diehard management attorneys now conceded the futility of any more appeal of the Seitz ruling to the Supreme Court.[34]

With Messersmith and McNally as their personal vehicles, big league ballplayers had won the right to free agency. For McNally it had been strictly about principle, since he had never entertained serious thoughts of personally exercising the right by returning to the game. But for Messersmith the outcome presented him, as it had Catfish Hunter a year earlier, the dizzying prospect of multimillion-dollar offers. Upon hearing the news of his freedom, his first response was an understandably foggy "Great! What do I do next?" Once more Kuhn and the owners tried to enforce nonbidding on the pitcher despite its dubious legality under anticollusion language in the Basic Agreement. Then fresh rumors of suspect origin circulated claiming Messersmith suffered from a debilitating arm ailment, which Miller quashed by threatening Al Campanis into issuing a public statement to the contrary. Finally Ted Turner, one of the new, deep-pocketed management mavericks with little or no baseball background, defied Kuhn by offering the pitcher a $1.75 million, multiyear deal to sign with Atlanta. The offer proved so enticing that Messersmith agreed despite a contract clause limiting his future free-agency rights by giving the Braves "right of first refusal" to match any later offer. Citing Basic Agreement language that prevented players, knowingly or not, from signing away rights they had as a result of collective bargaining agreements, Miller prevailed upon NL president Feeney to have the offending clause stricken from Messersmith's new contract.[35] With the final confirmation of Andy Messersmith's lucrative deal, the nail had been driven into the coffin of the clubs' long-standing power to limit a player's compensation through restricting his geographic mobility. What remained undetermined was what kind of new system could jointly be constructed by owners and players to take its place, and how well it would work.

With the 1973 Basic Agreement scheduled to expire at the end of 1975, the Messersmith-McNally arbitration ruling had backed the magnates into a corner. They long had known of the Players Association's intention to make replacement of the existing reserve system the central issue of the new negotiations. Because of the Seitz verdict, the owners now faced a hard fight in the collective bargaining arena just to minimize their losses within the requirements of a new system. Should they seek genuine accommodation with the union in the upcoming talks, or should they adopt a "scorched-earth" stance via a lockout? If the owners opted for the latter strategy, they faced several risks. Would they, as before, prove unable to withstand the pain of an industry stoppage? If the big-market magnates, capable of paying the higher salaries of a new, free-agency environment, chose to break ranks and force a deal, would not the other owners' sacrifices just be wasted? Another danger with adopting a hard-line approach lay in the prospect that if no 1976 deal resulted, the consequent wide-open free agency for *all* players who served out their option year that season promised massive roster disruptions. A few owners, most notably Oakland's Charley Finley, argued that opening the "Flood-gates" was preferable as it would drive down the price of individual free agents through an excess supply. But most clubs and general managers saw unlimited free agency as a prescription for team chaos and a remedy worse than the disease.[36]

Privately the union also feared that its adversaries might opt for unlimited free agency. Marvin Miller also fretted that under his reading of the Basic Agreement of 1973, nothing in it prevented the owners from engaging in collusion not to bid. Although he talked the language of a labor rights ideologue, the executive director remained first and foremost an economist concerned with maximizing his members' financial return on their labor. A minority on the union's executive board, led by pitchers Mike Marshall and Jerry Reuss, advocated pure free agency on libertarian grounds. But the vast majority argued for the maximization of earnings for many over complete freedom of movement for all. As board member Bob Boone noted, "If you came in behind it [free agency] with salary arbitration, then everybody was artificially high." Large contracts garnered by a limited quantity of older free agents would peg the value for performers at each position regardless of seniority, which in turn would ratchet up arbitration awards to young players. Added to the continuing push for higher minimum salaries for the entry-level major leaguer, the rising salary tide would lift all boats.[37]

For the union, the question was where to draw the line on free agency. Any new system, the leadership argued, should have a service-time threshold high enough not to flood the labor market, yet attainable enough that most players would have at least one chance during their careers to avail themselves of the process. Preferably the threshold would also be timed to match the typical player's period of top performance and thus maximize his bonanza. Suggesting that the union had not yet done the research, in his initial bargaining proposal in June 1975 Miller suggested free agency to players after five years of professional service (in the majors and minors *combined*) and an option year. He had also presented the idea of limits on the number of free agents any team could lose, and compensation for them, to address owners' concerns about damage to competitive balance. But by the winter of 1975, the association's internal actuarial studies indicated that with a player eligibility of six years of *big-league* tenure, the odds of qualifiers lasting for ten seasons jumped dramatically, which meant that many veterans in such a system could even qualify twice during their careers. That threshold also would make most first-time free agents players in their late twenties — their ballplaying, money-maximizing prime.[38]

While the union did its homework, the magnates stalled. At the end of the year, still hoping against hope for salvation through the judicial process, the PRC instructed John Gaherin to announce the unilateral termination rather than extension of the 1973 collective bargaining and pension agreements while talks continued. On the free-agency issue, Gaherin's presentation proved to be about what the union expected. The owners proposed free-agency rights to only ten-year veterans (nine years under contract plus the option season) whose teams refused to offer contracts of $30,000 or more. The plan also limited to eight the number of clubs that could bid on any one player. When Miller predictably rejected the offer, the PRC then announced the owners' intention to lock out all but nonroster players from spring training camps. Since a lockout carried the accompanying threat of replacement squads, the union retaliated by instructing all 350 unsigned veterans not to agree to new contracts but to use 1976 as their option year for free agent eligibility. Miller was calling the owners' bluff, calculating that they would not prove willing to persist in their hard line at the risk of wide-open free agency and roster chaos a year hence.[39]

When spring training began with the lockout in place, Miller called publicly for an intervention by Commissioner Kuhn and threatened formation of a rival league run by the players. Privately, he remained uncertain about his members' resolve on the complexities of free agency. Players' spirits were buoyed by news of the appeals court ruling sustaining the Seitz decision, only to be deflated when maverick Baltimore star Jim Palmer defied union strictures and signed a multiyear pact. On March 11 a joint assembly of the Players Association executive board and the PRC in a Tampa airport auditorium enabled each side to vent its frustrations but accomplished no substantive progress. Although Miller never conceded the point, Gaherin believed by then that despite the owners' setback in the appeals court, they had turned the tables through a public carrot-and stick negotiating strategy. As the lockout had dragged on, the PRC negotiator had offered a slightly modified proposal that, while still unacceptable to Miller and the majority of player delegates, had managed to split off four delegate dissenters.[40]

The PRC negotiator held to his hope of ultimately securing a free-agency system limited to eight- to ten-year veterans. On March 15 he made a new, purportedly final, offer that recognized the Messersmith-McNally decision, provided for the right of 1976 optionees to free agency after the season, and proposed an eight-year threshold for subsequent free agent "classes." Although the union executive board rejected the package, the opposing majority shrank further to 17-5. With the regular season only two weeks away and nervous players practicing in ad hoc workouts, Gaherin believed that if the owners could hang tough until late April or early May, they could salvage a respectable remnant of a reserve system that seemingly had been lost altogether during the previous fall and winter.[41]

To Gaherin's and the PRC's shock and dismay, Bowie Kuhn once more exercised his interventionist powers to destroy the lockout. Behind his action lay the fact that while player unity had frayed around the edges as the impasse dragged on, the magnates' solidarity also had weakened. Under renewed pressure from the television networks and key owners O'Malley and Steinbrenner, Kuhn ordered the opening of spring training facilities to regular players effective March 17. The commissioner later admitted the influence of the powerful Dodgers and Yankees in his decision by confessing that the two clubs' magnates had been "troubled by the lockout." O'Malley also had convinced himself that a profit-threatening lockout was not necessary to bring free agency to heel, but instead a firm negotiating position backed by owner collusion not to offer bids. However, in view of the self-interest in his stance, O'Malley's faith in his colleagues' capacity for solidarity in rejecting free agents seemed questionable. After Kuhn, O'Malley, and Steinbrenner cut the ground out from under the PRC, Baltimore owner Jerry Hoffberger prophetically warned that the players would never again take an owner lockout threat seriously.[42]

Having lost its leverage by forfeiting the lockout, the PRC floundered for a month and a half without making a new proposal. Trying not to completely waste the time, the union steered the talks to other, less controversial subjects such as the pension and minimum salaries. The association's executive board did contemplate a mid-season strike to move the talks along, but at Miller's advice the players dropped the idea as a likely public relations disaster. A postseason strike seemed more feasible given the lesser economic impact on players, but even it carried the risk of fan backlash and required membership solidarity that the leadership still doubted it had. A promising sign finally emerged by May when Gaherin suggested streamlining both sides' negotiating teams. Daily bargaining sessions resumed at the "neutral" location of New York's Biltmore Hotel.[43]

In the meantime, Oakland owner Charley Finley already had concluded that his days of retaining a championship-caliber team had ended along with the lockout. Gaherin's own latest proposal would cost him many of his stars, for they already had chosen to play out their options rather than ink new pacts for 1976. Outfielder Joe Rudi had demanded a three-year, no-cut contract at $125,000 a season. Relief ace Rollie Fingers had held out for a similar pact at a total of $435,000. Finley had offered each man first one-year pacts at $100,000, then multiyear deals without guaranteed money. When the two refused, and three other A's led by Reggie Jackson followed, Finley imposed 20 percent cuts and begun shopping for the best trade offers. He succeeded in dealing Jackson and pitcher Ken Holtzman to Baltimore for two stars embroiled in similar disputes with the Orioles, outfielder Don Baylor and pitcher Mike Torrez. But efforts to trade Rudi, Fingers, pitcher Vida Blue, first baseman Gene Tenace, and third baseman Sal Bando all fell through.[44]

Unable to trade most of his stars before the June 15 deadline, Finley then negotiated a series of player sales. The Oakland owner offered Rudi and Fingers to Boston and Blue to New York for a combined $3.5 million, only to see Bowie Kuhn step in to void the sales. Citing his "best interests of baseball" powers, the commissioner nullified the player auctions supposedly to protect competitive balance and Oakland's fans, although others wondered if his move actually was revenge for an earlier, Finley-led "dump-Bowie" movement. Regardless of the action's merits, Kuhn once more also was carrying out the wishes of Walter O'Malley. The Dodger magnate resented the prospect Finley's sales offered for poorly run yet wealthy franchises to buy pennants and bid up payrolls at his club's competitive expense. He also hoped that Kuhn's voiding of the sales on the grounds of baseball's "best interests" would forge a precedent for the commissioner's exercise of power to similarly block upcoming free agent signings. A furious Finley, however, blasted Kuhn as a "village idiot" and filed a $10 million restraint-of-trade lawsuit, only to see the courts uphold Kuhn's action.[45]

Viewed from the union's perspective, the commissioner's voiding of Finley's fire sale had to be either irrational vindictiveness or a gambit to create precedents for later voiding free agent signings. Otherwise, all Kuhn had done was enable the Oakland owner to show players their real monetary value through their negotiated sales prices, while preventing him from reaping the financial return on the deals. To guarantee that Kuhn could not unilaterally nullify any free-agency process negotiated with the PRC, Miller demanded that the new agreement include specific language prohibiting the commissioner's interference with its stated provisions. The new issue joined two others—whether the pact's free agent eligibility threshold should be applied to the current year's class, and at what level of service the long-term threshold should be—as the major remaining obstacles to a settlement. As for the 1976 free-agents-to-be, Miller had promised them early in the year that he would hold out for eligibility for all of them. At the time he had made that promise, the 350 potential eligibles had threatened to flood the market and drive down the average windfall. But once Kuhn had lifted the lockout, Miller had freed his players to sign new contracts, and by the end of spring training the figure had dropped to 150. The ranks continued to shrink throughout the season as clubs upped their offers to prevent the losses of key players. By the start of the summer, Miller could keep his promise to the remainder of the 1976 free agent optionee group without causing adverse consequences to their prospects. But Gaherin and the PRC still insisted on making any new service-time limits on free agent eligibility apply to this first group as well as future optionees.[46]

With veteran executive and AL president Lee MacPhail serving as a draftsman, the two sides inched toward a deal in early July. The owners not only gave up their opposition to free agency for all 1976 optionees, but in an amazing oversight they continued to place little emphasis on the type or amount of compensation paid to clubs that lost free agents under the new system. On the issue of the service-time threshold, Gaherin lowered his position to seven years, and Miller pretended to make a similar sacrifice by raising his offer from a two-year to a four-year big league requirement. In truth the union wanted the four-year threshold, and it used its "concession" on the free-agency service requirement to preserve salary arbitration for younger players. In the end, the two sides settled on a six-year service-time standard—the very level the union had covertly concluded would generate, in conjunction with arbitration, the maximum earning power for its members. As player representative Phil Garner recalled the moment, union bargainers pretended "not to grin and you're trying to say 'Ah, Christ, this is going to kill us.' Meanwhile, inside you're going, 'Yes! Yes! Yes!'"

The last item to be cleared up was the issue presented by Kuhn's voiding of the Finley sales. The commissioner had to be barred from similarly interfering in implementation of Basic Agreement provisions, including the new free-agency process. Gaherin once more found himself shuttling back and forth between the bargainers and a petulant Kuhn until the latter finally relented to the limitation on his power. On the eve of the All-Star Game, the two sides announced a tentative settlement. At the union executive board session, player representatives easily approved the pact by a 23-1 vote. Gaherin, MacPhail, and Feeney had a much tougher sell, but by an uncomfortably narrow margin of 17-7 the owners also ratified the agreement.[47]

The 1976 Basic Agreement increased owner contributions to the players' pension fund by nearly $2 million, boosted minimum salaries to $19,000 for 1976–77 and $21,000 for 1978–79, and retained the salary arbitration system for veterans with two to five years of big league experience. But the new reserve system with its free agent opportunities for older veterans represented the pact's most dramatic new feature. In November all unsigned players who had completed their option season would have their names placed in a pool, with teams in each league from worst to best alternating selections. Up to a dozen teams besides a player's old club could draw the right to bid for his services. Each team that lost a free agent would be compensated with a pick from the signing club in the next amateur draft. After the first year, unsigned veterans with six or more years of big league service would constitute the pool of free agents, and once a player had participated in the process, he could not reenter before another five years of service. Players with signed contracts and five years' tenure could demand to be traded and designate six teams they would not play for. If by the following March they still had not been traded, they also became free agents. If a five-year veteran exercised his right to a trade, however, he could not reassert the right again for another three seasons.[48]

In language with enormous significance for the future, the 1976 Basic Agreement contained specific anticollusion stipulations barring either side from conspiring against the unfettered operation of the free-agency process. Ironically, the owners also had insisted on the clause, fearing that the union or a powerful player agent with multiple clients would orchestrate "separate" negotiations like a puppeteer. Management figures' own tampering violations toward free-agents-to-be, however, forced Commissioner Kuhn to issue a directive threatening transgressors. Atlanta's Ted Turner still made no secret of his lust for San Francisco outfielder Gary Matthews, and even St. Louis's Gussie Busch let slip publicly his desire for Fingers and Rudi. Late in the season Don Baylor received an on-field courtship from Yankee first-base coach Elston Howard, acting on behalf of boss George Steinbrenner. For their respective forms of illegal public salivation, Busch drew a $5,000 fine, and

Turner got a one-year suspension, although the Braves were still allowed to sign Matthews. But the feeding frenzy had begun, and the individualism that had prevented magnates from maintaining a common front in March now went on display as a wholesale bidding war for playing talent.[49]

By November twenty-two men remained available for free agency. Over seventeen rounds of drafting, thirteen were drafted by the maximum number of suitors, and only Cincinnati refused to participate. Before nightfall the first free agent signed: Minnesota relief specialist Bill Campbell to a five-year, $1 million deal with Boston. Of Finley's deserting stars, Tenace and Fingers migrated to San Diego for five years and $1.8 million, and six years and $1.6 million, respectively. Gene Autry signed two more ex-A's, Baylor and Rudi, for $1.6 million and $2 million spread out over six and five seasons. Bert Campaneris, despite being thirty-two years old, received a five-year pact from Texas for nearly $1 million. Oakland's biggest star, Reggie Jackson, topped the list at nearly $3 million over five seasons from George Steinbrenner. Even bottom-tier Cleveland entered the frenzy, shelling out $1 million over ten years for starter Wayne Garland. Since many of the eligibles were clients of Jerry Kapstein, the agent also pulled down a reported $1 million. Stunned at the sudden outpouring of six-figure annual salaries and multiyear contracts on not only the great but the merely good, Reggie Jackson asked the question on virtually everyone's mind. "Do you think," he posed out loud, "there will ever be a million-dollar ballplayer?"[50]

The 1970s saw the arrival of baseball as a mass-televised entertainment industry. Over the same decade Marvin Miller and the Players Association dragged the sport into the modern realm of labor relations. Big-money performers, agents, and a formalized industrial relations system with negotiated work rules and procedures had replaced the old paternal order's one-sided, informal practices. In baseball's new order elaborate agreements, enforced by the countervailing scrutiny of management and union watchdogs, defined the distribution of rewards, the mobility of workers, and the regulation of the workplace. Individually and collectively, major league ballplayers enjoyed more power over their economic lives. But greater power carried with it heightened responsibility for self-policing conduct and contributing solutions to the game's problems.

Whether measured by increases in minimum salaries, final-offer arbitration victories for two- to five-year men, or free-agency bonanzas for the six-year-plus veteran, major leaguers' boats were being lifted by a rising tide, although the gains were not being distributed equally (see Appendix, Fig. 3). In 1977, the first year of widespread free agency, the average big league salary jumped nearly 50 percent to $76,066. Even when adjusted for inflation, real wages registered a 39 percent rise and went up another 31 percent the next season. By 1979 the mean major league salary stood at $113,558, more than double the pay since the inauguration of free agency. At the top end of clubs, the New York Yankees starting lineup averaged nearly $200,000 a man. Although lesser median salaries in baseball reflected growing pay inequality, they, too, climbed from $34,000 to $80,000 from 1975 to 1979.[51]

Increasingly, attention focused on the migratory and inflationary effects of free agency. With six-year or senior men constituting about two-fifths of major league players, free agency had a major impact—but not always in the ways expected. Press accounts dramatized the jumps in the top individual salary, from Reggie Jackson's $600,000 contract in 1977 to Nolan Ryan's $1 million deal in 1979. But although baseball's richest "mercenaries" drew the lion's share of fan expectation and scrutiny, more often than not free agency did not produce migration from old clubs to new. Instead, it provided stars with greater leverage to force lucrative pacts with current organizations. The free agent drafts of 1976–78 did result in 80 of 106 free agents leaving their old teams. But more frequently players struck multiyear settlements in advance of the draft. In 1977 alone, 281 men inked such deals. Back in 1975 only one major leaguer, Catfish Hunter, had garnered a multiyear contract. By 1980 over 40 percent of 650 big league performers held guaranteed deals of two or more years.[52]

Free agency also proved less responsible on its own for the death of management frugality than its effect on the pay of the greater numbers of players eligible for arbitration. Two- to five-year veterans actually constituted the core of most major league rosters. Salary arbitration proceedings allowed each side to debate a player's past-season and career statistics, his physical or attitudinal qualities, his salary compared with other big leaguers, and his team's recent record. Off limits, however, were considerations of the player's or the team's financial state, press testimonials or criticisms, prior demands or club offers, or cross-sport salary comparisons. The most important data proved to be comparative major league salary figures, broken down by service time, position, and club and provided to each arbitrator. When clubs had grudgingly signed on to the process, they had assumed that relative seniority would become the main basis for pegging arbitration awards. But as early as February 1975, when NL batting champion Ralph Garr saw his salary virtually double to $114,500 despite his limited big league tenure, management's expectations evaporated. Instead, hefty free agent salaries of older veterans set the market for younger players at the same positions and exhibiting comparable recent statistical performances. In order to avoid even higher arbitration awards, more and more clubs then extended to younger stars preemptive multiyear deals. From the 1974 start of salary arbitration through 1979, 95 of 165 cases were settled before the conclusion of hearings. Of the rest, owners actually "won" ten more than they "lost." But since even the clubs' final offers usually represented significant raises from previous salaries, even losing players came out ahead.[53]

Because of the mutually reinforcing nature of the system the union had negotiated, even grievance arbitration bolstered pay levels and hampered club efforts to impose cuts. In 1979 the Atlanta Braves tried to slash holdout third baseman Bob Horner's pay by the maximum 20 percent. According to the Braves, since the player's previous base salary had been only $21,000, the club was entitled to reduce it to $16,800. But arbitrator Raymond Goetz overruled the Braves and decided that in calculating the 20 percent reduction the club had to include all 1978 payments to Horner regardless of how they were categorized. In other words, a club could not load up a contract with performance-based or other incentives in one year, then not count them in the base when cutting pay by a fixed percentage the next. As a result of the judgment, Horner's 1979 pay was restored to more than six times the amount Atlanta originally had intended to provide.[54]

The collective bargaining agreements secured by the Players Association also produced a host of other new or increased benefits. Based on a formula of guaranteed minimums and 60 percent of the gate from the first three games of each League Championship Series and the first four games of the World Series, world champion squads drew at least $640,000 and 36 percent of postseason gates. Fall classic "losers" were assured $320,000 and 27 percent. Second-place finishers in each league could count on $160,000 and 25 percent, and second- and third-place teams in each division garnered $128,000 and 9.5 percent and $32,000 and 2.5 percent, respectively. World Series individual winner and loser shares jumped from $18,216 and $13,688 in 1970 to $28,237 and $22,114 by 1980. Pension benefits also rose with each negotiated boost in owner contributions, and a union-operated scholarship plan enabled players to pursue college degrees in the off-season. Licensing revenues, just $400,000 in 1969, rose to $700,000 by the late 1970s. Even Fleer's successful 1978 antimonopoly suit against Topps and the Players Association, ironically, resulted in a proliferation of card companies with which the union then negotiated separate licensing deals.[55]

The list of perks and guarantees enjoyed by a big league ballplayer by the late 1970s defied quick recitation. Teams were required to carry regular-season active rosters of twenty-five men until August 31, then forty until the end of the season, and twenty-five in postseason play. Players still drew pay during in-season National Guard and Reserve obligations. They enjoyed free parking at home games and on practice days. Cost-of-living-adjusted allowances covered road lodgings, meals, and first-class airfare, as well as travel to spring training at the start of the year and back home at its end. No player could be forced to report to camp until March 1, and married players with sixty days of major league experience or single men with three years' service time could use out-of-camp spring housing. Disabled players still received full meal allowances if they stayed in their home city's motels, and a lesser amount if in their own houses. Men selected for the All-Star Game earned free accommodations and travel expenses for themselves and a guest for three full days. Clubs could not unilaterally assign players to any new team outside the United States or Canada. Even men who were traded or released received first-class accommodations and meals en route to their new destinations, reimbursement of family moving expenses, and lump-sum payments ranging from $300 to $1,200 depending on the number of time zones crossed. If cut during spring training, unless the action was disciplinary a player drew thirty days' severance pay, and if he was let go during the regular season, he received the full balance of his year's salary. If he refused a contract offer from another club, however, he forfeited severance pay equal to the value of the latter bid. Players disabled from baseball-related injuries also received the full balance of their wages, minus worker's compensation benefits paid by their home states.[56]

Backed by detailed contract provisions and the union's clout, big leaguers also claimed expanded procedural rights. During spring training the union had the right to hold meetings with each squad at ten days' notice to management, with a ninety-minute time limit. Player contracts contained a standard nondiscrimination pledge. The length of the playing season constituted an ongoing issue of collective bargaining requiring mutual agreement, and clubs could not demand winter ball. Players could prohibit day-night doubleheaders and one-day road trips, and provisions limited the maximum number of in-season exhibitions to two per team. Mutually enforceable scheduling rules also barred night contests before day doubleheaders and any day game before 1:00 P.M., except on holidays. Even then no team could schedule more than six games a season starting between 10:30 A.M. and noon. Rules banned night games on "getaway" days if the traveling squad faced more than a 1½-hour journey to the next day's contest. Players played no more than nineteen consecutive days before an off-day, with no travel permitted on the latter, and a maximum of three twi-night doubleheaders. In order to promote player health and safety, a joint advisory committee met at least once a year. Any individual member could call the panel into session, although its power was limited to issuing nonbinding recommendations.[57]

Although clubs retained some disciplinary powers over their workers, they were now more narrowly circumscribed. They could limit public appearances through individual contract provisions and could similarly bar participation in other sports or "dangerous activities" during or after the season. They could ban player barnstorming save for a thirty-day window following the season, limit to three the number of men from the same team on such squads, and prohibit a player from subsequent participation in a winter league. Players remained subject to paltry fines of $50 to $100 for participating in exhibitions with ineligible men. Clubs could also still demand that players submit themselves to physical examinations by team doctors. But management attempts to constrain their players' off-season opportunities were largely futile, given the risk of union grievances and the skill of agents in skirting such regulations. In disciplinary matters Marvin Miller also was pushing the envelope of association members' rights. In 1977 he challenged the power of umpires to issue fines for on-field violations. Demanding that all fines be automatically reviewed by an arbitrator before being assessed, he added that if the men in blue did not like it, they could "move to Communist China."[58]

In baseball's new order, management could not roll back any of these employment provisions or even change playing or scoring rules without the notification and the formal or practical approval of the union. If clubs wanted to change work rules, they had to notify the Players Association and then agree to negotiate the matter, with the union equally able to reopen issues of its choosing. The owners not only had to provide advance notice of intention to the union for any changes in playing rules, but in addition the association could veto any moves that threatened its members' contractually guaranteed benefits—a standard it defined liberally. Even if a rules change did not affect benefits, it could not be implemented until after completion of the next full season after its proposal. Even franchise expansion, since it affected the number of big league jobs and pension beneficiaries, entitled the union to reopen existing collective bargaining agreements with ten days' written notice to address the impact.[59]

Star players could—and some did—live the lifestyle of Hollywood entertainers or rock musicians. But like others who were rich and famous, ballplayers relied more than ever on financial managers and agents to handle their business. Although its motives were somewhat self-interested, based on a fear of influence from competing agents as well as the desire to protect members, in 1977 the Players Association began a push to certify player agents. Marvin Miller cited examples of what he considered fee-gouging, incompetence, and conflict of interest by agents such as Jerry Kapstein, who eventually married Ray Kroc's daughter and became a Padres executive. Although the union failed to fully implement the certification process until 1988, it pressed for maximum representation fees of 4 percent and required agents to fill out lengthy questionnaires kept on file for members' reference. Looking to his own retirement and fearful of being followed by the "wrong kind" of leadership in the new big-money environment, Miller also maintained a policy of restraining his staff's own salary growth. The union did boost his pay modestly in 1974 to $100,000, with annual cost-of-living adjustments afterward. But the lure of higher income and the skepticism toward many agents led Miller aide Dick Moss to leave the union in 1977 after ten and a half years to join the ranks of player representatives.[60]

The union proved more hesitant to address the image and safety problems posed by individual recklessness and decadence within its membership. Perhaps understandably, given his memory of the McCarthy era and his recent experiences with the baseball owners, Miller tended to reject automatically on civil libertarian grounds any external or internal policing of players' personal behavior, and to view accusations of impropriety invariably as inspired by management self-interest. Nowhere was this habitual union rejection of self-regulation of members' conduct more harmful to the players themselves than in the area of drug abuse. In the wake of college and professional football scandals, Commissioner Kuhn had introduced a halfhearted educational campaign, but the effort had quickly faded from attention. By the late 1970s, besides baseball's traditional problem of alcoholism, the use of prescription and performance-enhancing drugs, from amphetamines to steroids, and the abuse of so-called recreational drugs, especially cocaine, had risen sharply. As expansion increased the need for players and because the minors remained contracted, more young men reached the majors at an early age. They proved highly susceptible to outside influences, sometimes of a dangerous nature, although not well informed of the risks, and they possessed much higher discretionary income with which to indulge themselves than newcomers of an earlier day.[61]

Despite the nondiscrimination clause in player contracts, the union's power also failed to translate into an effective assault on baseball's barriers to minority advancement. Mirroring a comparable slowdown in civil rights progress nationally, even the African American population playing in the big leagues, which had peaked at 26 percent in 1974, slipped to 20 percent by the end of the decade. Both the combined overall share of black and Hispanic major leaguers and that of such rookies also leveled off at about one-third of the total population of each category (see Appendix, Fig. 4). Because of new IRS restrictions, the number of Latin Americans allocated visas for U.S. baseball employment became curtailed to about two dozen annually per organization (including all major and minor league clubs of each). Frustrated magnates fought one another even more fiercely to secure that limited supply, for Latino recruits still could be signed at bonuses of only $4,000, compared with the six-figure awards given to top U.S. amateur prospects.[62]

Institutional inertia toward racial progress in hiring, compensation, promotion, and recognition persisted at the top as well as the bottom of the baseball pyramid. Nine days before his death in 1972, Jackie Robinson chose the forum of the All-Star Game to highlight the continued lack of African American managers. When Hank Aaron broke Babe Ruth's career home-run record in 1974, Commissioner Kuhn was not in attendance. By 1975 baseball had been shamed into hiring Frank Robinson as Cleveland's manager, and Aaron entered Atlanta's front office the following year. But the "old-boy" network, rooted in racial positional stereotyping and stacking throughout the industry, still blocked opportunities for all but a token few. By 1976 blacks constituted 53 percent of starting major league outfielders and first basemen, but only 4 percent of pitchers and catchers; none were starting shortstops. Although Emmett Ashford had broken the big league color barrier for umpires back in 1966, and Art Williams had become the National League's comparable pioneer in 1973, by the end of the 1070s African Americans still constituted only one of the majors' sixty arbiters. As for the Baseball Hall of Fame, in 1977 a separate Negro Leagues Committee was dismantled and absorbed within the Veterans Committee after only seven years of remedial nominations. Symptomatic of baseball's entrenched backwardness, Calvin Griffith was caught in 1978 telling a local civic gathering that he had moved his franchise to Minnesota almost two decades earlier because "you have good, hard-working white people here."[63]

If baseball's resistance to the advancement of racial minorities remained so entrenched, it is all too easy to imagine how unprepared the industry, or even members of the players' union, was to acknowledge the rights and struggles of a gay ballplayer. In the late 1970s Glenn Burke became the first widely identified homosexual to reach the major leagues, although it seems certain that other "closeted" gay performers had preceded him. Burke joined Los Angeles in 1976 as a reserve outfielder, and although he did not openly proclaim his sexual orientation, the suspicions of other Dodgers led club executive Al Campanis to urge him to get married. Burke rejected the suggestion and was traded to Oakland, where he faced open harassment from manager Billy Martin. After Martin declared, "I don't want no faggots on this team," the outfielder retired in 1980 and "came out" in a magazine article two years later. Falling on hard times after his baseball exile, he contracted the AIDS virus and died at age forty-one. In an ironic, tragic postscript on baseball's, and America's, homophobic denial and neglect, Burke's old Dodger manager, Tommy Lasorda, subsequently lost his son at age thirty-three to AIDS-related pneumonia.[64]

Columnist Red Smith described the late 1970s in baseball as both "the best and worst of times." If the players emphasized the former, certainly the magnates stressed the latter. Lee MacPhail referred to the combination of salary arbitration and free agency as a "Catch-22" and a "whipsaw" that devastated club bottom lines and competitive prospects. The reality was far more ambiguous. What legitimately grated most on the owners was the fact that they had lost their principal form of monopsony power over big league workers and, therefore, industry cost control at the highest, wealthiest level. Rather than feeling in charge of the pace of growth in revenues and expenses, the owners now saw themselves on an acceler-

THE INFLATIONARY ERA

ating treadmill in which they ran faster just to stay in place competitively and faced greater risks of falling off with bad judgments.[65]

The magnates placed the blame for their heightened anxieties squarely on baseball's new industrial relations system and, in particular, the arbitration and free-agency processes. The big-money contracts and multi-year deals they generated, officials maintained, destroyed player incentive and led to excessive stays on the disabled list. The movement of players from old clubs crippled competitive balance and ripped apart the bonds between stars and specific communities. Escalating payrolls eroded profits and took away money needed to shore up the minors. Periodic labor strife with an emboldened Players Association not only caused economic disruptions but spilled over and infected other employee groups, most notably the umpires, and soured fans' romantic attachment to the sport.

How many of the owners' laments were true? Some studies actually indicated that the performance of players eligible for free agency dropped during their option year and improved during the first season with a new team. Others claimed that player statistics did decline in the first year after free agency, whether due to adjustment to the new team or league, reduced motivation, or simply advancing age. In any event blanket generalizations about the performance of free agents proved difficult to bear out. What probably created most of the disillusionment of fans and owners alike with free agents was that they had been paid huge sums without sufficient discrimination and then had been unrealistically expected to produce at heretofore unreached levels. Based on their previous statistics, some free agents were badly overpaid, often by the new breed of wealthy egotists who insisted on overriding the judgments of their personnel directors. Perhaps an even greater contributor to excessive expectations was the failure to recognize that baseball players, like athletes in other sports, tended to improve into their late twenties but then decline. Because of how the free-agency system had been structured, eligibles tended to be men who, after several minor league seasons and six major league years, had already reached their peak. They then found themselves in position to demand big contracts based on recent performances that likely represented their maximums, only to drop off after they signed deals as free agents. It was as if the magnates fantasized that big money could turn back the hands of time, only to become embittered when it did not. As for player shirking, the percentage of players spending time on the disabled list did rise from 14 percent in the mid 1970s to 21 percent by 1979, but that also owed to keener medical diagnoses and quicker assignments to the disabled list that prevented more serious, career-ending injuries. Players may have been likelier to go on the disabled list rather than jeopardize contract windfalls by "playing with pain," but general managers also did not want to risk permanent loss of their expensive long-term investments. Clubs also could still mandate examinations by their own physicians if they suspected their men of "jaking."[66]

The owners' lament that free agency crippled competitive balance was even less credible. It was true that in the new financial environment, money disparities persisted and widened between organizations, and likewise the means of affording the highest-priced talent. By 1979, while the Yankees fielded their $200,000-a-man lineup, Oakland's averaged only $41,000. But the all-too-frequent talent misjudgments of the big spenders undermined their ability to construct dynasties. In any event, the argument for competitive imbalance presupposed an earlier era of balance that simply had never existed. As Marvin Miller repeatedly pointed out, in the "good old days" four teams had won 66 percent of pennants between 1921 and 1964. Free agency *widened* slightly the on-field organizational oligarchy by making it harder for any one club to afford all the best talent. Whatever competitive impact free agency produced also was limited by the modest actual number of migrations by player "mercenaries." Ironically, under the old reserve system, since 1951 the annual average number of players a club lost to its rivals had stood at 4.7, and the figure *fell* slightly after the adoption of free agency. In short, under the new system rosters were slightly *more* stable than before, not less so.[67]

A few teams, most notably the small-market A's and Twins of the American League, did fall from the ranks of contenders. But previous eras had featured similar "weak sisters" that had conducted fire sales to salvage bottom lines. As a whole, big league revenues were soaring. Baseball continued to be a relative entertainment bargain despite the stereotyped assumptions about the impact of higher salaries. Adjusted for inflation, ticket prices actually fell in the 1970s. Hoping to generate larger gate attendance and broadcast fees, the long-lagging American League had injected more offense through the designated hitter rule in 1972. The junior circuit also led the way in constructing new stadiums and modernizing older ones, and in 1977 the clubs garnered an additional $7 million through entry fees from its two expansion franchises in Seattle and Toronto. The majors' switch in baseball manufacturers from Spalding to Rawlings, in materials from horsehide to cowhide, and in production facilities from the United States to Haiti, combined with expansion's effect on pitching depth to add even more scoring. In response big league attendance climbed from 30 million in 1973 to more than 43.5 million by 1979. Television revenue, $42 million in 1972, soared to $80 million by 1980. By the end of the 1970s, overall revenue approached the $300 million mark.[68]

Major league executives claimed red ink, but as baseball economist Andrew Zimbalist has since noted, such assertions were largely the product of owner "ledgerdemain." Club owners cited as losses, rather than returns on capital, player-depreciation costs and interest expenses on earlier loans taken out to purchase franchises. Although the IRS finally narrowed a decades-old tax shelter by limiting team player-depreciation claims to 50 percent of the club's purchase value, owners and accountants explored new forms of special treatment. Under their stadium deal with Milwaukee County, the Brewers paid $1.00 in rental fees for the team's first million admissions a year and just 5 percent on the next half-million. In 1977 the club drew only 1.1 million fans but also owed the county only $21,149 in rent. George Steinbrenner rewrote his Yankee Stadium lease to permit deduction of maintenance costs. As a consequence, rather than owing the city $850,000 in 1976, Gotham owed him $10,000. The next season, the club did pay, but only $170,681, less than 1.5 percent of its gross income.[69]

Even team payrolls still absorbed only 28 percent of revenues by 1979, albeit up from 18 percent five years earlier. Such increases only partially countered decades of penury. For three-quarters of a century, big league real wages had only risen an average of 2 percent a year and represented just 15 percent of the players' economic return to their clubs. Despite the new surge in salaries, if player-depreciation and interest deductions were eliminated from the owners' calculations of poverty, rather than losses the books would actually show profits of $3.1 million, $3.6 million, $6.1 million, $10.4 million, and $12.8 million in the last five years of the 1970s. Ironically, a strong case could be made that the increased interest in baseball *generated* by free agency's "hot-stove-league" signings and the changes to improve scoring and facilities had been a boon rather than a burden to baseball's finances. As endorsement of that theory, observers noted no decline in interest in buying franchises, and selling prices rose from an average of $5 million to nearly $13 million.[70]

Still, the owners poor-mouthed the state of their industry. They pointed to the fact that the number of minor leagues and teams remained at shrunken, albeit stable, levels. The wages in those circuits had risen, but at a more modest pace than those of brethren in the "big show." By 1979 the average AAA player earned $2,340 a month; a AA performer, $1,037; an A-level man, $666; and a rookie leaguer, only $584. Although the levels represented a decline in minor league payroll's share of industry revenues from 13 percent to 11 percent in the decade, the magnates pointed out their additional $1.5 million subsidy costs apiece to the minors and their escalating amateur signing amounts, symbolized by the $175,000 paid Bob Horner and the Tigers' $150,000 to Kirk Gibson. One experiment intended to generate lower-cost talent from the inner city, the Kansas City Royals' Baseball Academy, absorbed $2 million only to be abandoned. Hoping to reduce player procurement costs, in 1974 the owners agreed to chip in $118,000 each to a scouting collective, the Major League Scouting Bureau, while paring back individual operations, even though big league organizations carried but twenty scouts and paid them just $16,000 a year plus expenses.[71]

If the magnates had been willing to look in the mirror, they might have blamed their fiscal pressures not on excessive salaries but on inadequate revenue sharing. Income imbalance between clubs hardly represented a new issue, but the rising sums and the nature of their sources aggravated the problem. Ironically, the wider the revenue gap between the haves and the have-nots became, the harder it was for those with the money to part with more of it. By 1977 less than 19 percent of an average AL team's revenues, and only 12 percent of an NL team's, came from shared sources. Local broadcast revenue, the most rapidly growing and unshared source of income, by 1979 ranged from Montreal's $6.3 million to Kansas City's $0.5 million. Because of Oakland's poor attendance and small TV market, its share of income going to player salaries, despite its low payroll, nonetheless measured nearly 64 percent in 1980. Rather than solve their own problem, however, owners found it easier to seek solidarity by scapegoating the players' union.[72]

In one respect the owners' jeremiad against the impact of the Players Association on the industry was accurate — it had led to rising militancy by other groups of employees. In 1977 John Cifelli, the new head of the umpires' association, negotiated his membership's first comprehensive basic agreement with the major leagues. But a growing number of umpires concluded that although the pact secured modest gains of guaranteed four-man crews, higher salary and fringe benefits, and vague promises of tenure for veterans, on the whole it was a "sellout" that failed to address other key issues and locked them into its inadequate terms for five years. A movement to oust Cifelli led to his replacement by Richard G. "Richie" Phillips, who had been a founder of the NBA referees' union. According to the umpires' new counsel, the recent pact's salary increases failed even to keep pace with inflation. The unpopular deal also retained the leagues' unilateral power to fire umpires with only ten days' severance. Demanding removal of the dismissal policy and reopening of other issues, Phillips ordered an umpire work stoppage commencing on August 25, 1978. After one day, a federal district court forced the men in blue back to work, but the anger continued to simmer.[73]

Following their return to work and a round of unhelpful public broadsides from the commissioner questioning their integrity, the umpires secured an endorsement deal that netted the union $150,000 for bankrolling a new strike. Phillips garnered $50,000 as his own annual retainer, up from his predecessor's $12,500. With a strike fund to sustain them, the umpires agreed not to sign individual contracts for the 1979 season and not to report to spring training. The leagues retaliated by threatening firings, hiring replacement arbiters, and again seeking an injunction to force the regulars back to work. This time, however, Judge Joseph McGlynn refused, and all but two union members, Ted Hendry and Paul Pryor, launched a regular-season strike on Opening Day. Under pressure from their brethren, even Hendry and Pryor belatedly joined, only to be forced to return to work for another ten days to fulfill termination-notice requirements in their contracts. For a month and a half of the regular season, players and fans alike groused about the quality of the "scabs," while management officials, determined not to show weakness in advance of the next round of player-union talks, hung tough. Phillips retaliated by threatening NLRB intervention and outside mediation.[74]

On May 18 the two sides finally reached agreement on a three-year pact. Under its provisions all big league umpires would be paid on a fixed salary scale based on seniority. Starting pay was set at $22,000, and salaries ranged to a top level of $50,000 for twenty-year veterans. The average raise measured $7,500, and each umpire's daily expense money rose to $67. New language specifically barred the in-season firing of arbiters, and those released between seasons were guaranteed one full year's severance pay. The umpires also won two-week paid vacations during the season and forty-five days of guaranteed pay in the event of a player strike during the period of the contract. One provision opposed by the union but pushed through by the leagues permitted them to rehire any of the strike-replacement umpires via the promotion process or as needed to augment the big league population. The few scabs retained encountered immediate on-field hostility and off-field ostracism from their unwilling colleagues. At the same time, the verbal support given to the regular umpires during the strike by the players led to growing harmony between the two unions that alarmed management observers.[75]

Seeing the umpires' militancy as yet another indicator of rising labor defiance in their industry, baseball marshaled its resources for full-scale war in 1980 against the Players Association. With their 1976 agreement scheduled to expire at the end of 1979, owners who had suffered major losses to free agency now clamored for increased compensation in the form of other major leaguers. The magnates also intended to demand from the union, or impose it unilaterally after the old deal expired, a salary scale for pre-free-agency players and the elimination of salary arbitration. In an early sign of their displeasure with previous negotiations and their renewed determination to play hardball, they dismissed sixty-four-year-old John Gaherin despite his desire to remain for one more year. Reminiscent of their old paternalism toward players they discarded, the owners bestowed their ex-negotiator with a clock whose engraved plaque fell off, a gold pass to big league parks that he had no interest in, and hollow tributes that prompted him to recall the words of an Irish widow to her son at the wake: "For the love of God, Dinny, look in the casket and be sure it's your father they're talking about."[76]

Gaherin's replacement as PRC point man also signaled the owners' hard-line intentions. A search process conducted with the aid of an executive recruitment company produced C. Raymond Grebey from a list of three finalists. Forty-nine-year-old Grebey was not the most blatantly "union-basher" candidate; that distinction belonged to Jack Donlan, whom the NFL hired to lead its own antilabor campaigns from 1980 to 1991. Nonetheless, Grebey came from a company, General Electric, that carried the legacy of a take-it-or leave-it labor negotiating philosophy dubbed "Boulwareism." The candidate's apparent sophistication and learnedness also persuaded the owners that they had finally found a worthy adversary to Marvin Miller, whom they loathed, feared, yet grudgingly respected.[77]

Anticipating the worst as early as the winter of 1977–78, Miller and his young legal counsel Donald Fehr, a veteran of the Messersmith litigation, had advised the players to create a special fund from their licensing revenues for any future work stoppage. The magnates offered more indications of militance in 1979 by adopting a "gag rule" on themselves intended to prevent "loose-cannon" comments undermining their negotiators. Under the order a disciplinary committee consisting of three AL and three NL executives would impose fines of up to $500,000 on offenders. The owners also agreed to pool 2 percent of 1979 home gate receipts into a war chest and took out additional strike insurance. One last harbinger of renewed confrontation came with the death of the man who had used his clout in the past to scuttle lockouts, Dodger owner Walter O'Malley. With his patron no longer present to offer cover for another season-saving intervention, Bowie Kuhn invited Miller to dinner at the 21 Club and pleaded for union concessions on free agent compensation. "Marvin," the commissioner begged, "the owners need a victory." Replying that they would get one "over my dead body," Miller returned to his office and related the evening's events to Don Fehr. Grim-faced, the association's boss concluded, "We're in for a hell of a fight."[78]

CHAPTER 7 : THE EMPIRE STRIKES BACK

1980–1988

By 1980 the Players Association could look back at remarkable gains over fifteen years. Within the larger U.S. economy, however, union busting and forced givebacks had become a growing reality. The United Auto Workers alone had sacrificed $642 million in benefits as a consequence of the Chrysler bankruptcy. For their part, major league baseball players had won so much in rights and benefits that they now risked complacency and selfish internal divisions. Having won so much of what they had dreamed of more rapidly than they could have expected, big league players apparently had left merely to gain more of the same. By contrast, the owners were now the side seeking structural changes, the side needing to take the offensive. The new national television contract, which more than doubled the networks' payout to $47.5 million a year, served to ratchet up the stakes of victory or defeat in the magnates' minds.[1]

The players' agenda in 1980 was basic enough: a substantial pension boost, an increase in minimum salary to $40,000, and elimination of the five-year waiting period for repeater free agency. For the owners, however, the militant mantra had become "meaningful compensation" for free agent losses, in the form of major league players. Their negotiator Ray Grebey, noting that the average salary had risen $90,000 in just four years, endorsed the goal of forcing major givebacks. According to rumors, he also hoped to use a defeat of Marvin Miller as a personal springboard to the commissionership. But while Grebey agreed with the owners' objectives, he faulted them for lacking either strategic vision or tactical sense and for relying too much on league lawyers poorly versed in labor relations. He planned to deploy a few issues as stalking-horses, while pursuing his real agenda quietly and keeping his cards close to his vest. The pseudoproposals would include a salary scale on pre–free agent players and the elimination of salary arbitration, while the genuine objective was a major boost in free agent compensation.[2]

The new PRC negotiator's salary-scale proposal called for escalating limits from $40,800 for first-year men to $187,900 for six-year veterans. As one measure of the ridiculousness of the latter figure, star Boston outfielder and six-year man Jim Rice already drew a $700,000 salary. Barring the adoption of formal caps, Grebey demanded provisions requiring arbitrators to base pay rulings on players' seniority. He also insisted on barring multiyear pacts to players with four years' or less big league service. In exchange he offered to make anyone in the future with major league experience eligible for the pension and to raise the minimum salary to $25,000 the first two years of a deal and $28,500 afterward. Buried in the middle of this laundry list of positions was the plan requiring each club that signed a "ranking" free agent (one sought by a full eight clubs) to compensate the loser by swapping it a major leaguer. Each club participating in free agent bidding would be allowed to "protect" fifteen of its men from such a fate. Feigning an air of reasonableness, Grebey urged the players to "trust me"; disavowed any intent to gut free agency; and refused to use the blunt term "compensation" in public—instead, he called it "improved player selection rights." He claimed that even if his system had been in place, only seven players would have required compensation in each of the 1978–79 seasons, and only three in the 1980 market.[3]

If the PRC chief thought he could con the union, he was deeply mistaken. Under the existing free-agency rules, which provided compensation in the form of amateur draft picks, as of 1979 only 20 of these 149 first- or second-round amateur selections from 1975–77 had reached the majors as yet. This limited compensation had not caused any effective drag on free agent bidding. But a new scheme in which teams risked losing a proven major leaguer might pose a far more serious deterrent, consequently pulling down the pay of both free agents and arbitration eligibles. The magnates were now pressing the union to give its blessing to a system to protect the owners from themselves. Management's salary-scale proposal for younger players also put the association in the position of the magnates' fiscal guardian, for it would be the union, which provided salary information to players and agents, that would be in a position to discover and be expected to report any under-the-table deals made in violation of the scale.[4]

To Marvin Miller, Grebey's gambit represented nothing less than a personal challenge to the compensation system he had wrested, and he viewed his adversary's reassurances to the players as outright lies. Reinforcing his low opinion of Grebey was union research that revealed examples of their adversary's past rigidity and double-dealing. Player/activist Mark Belanger noted that his mother, an employee of General Electric in Pittsfield, Massachusetts, in 1969 during a bitter 102-day strike, warned him of the PRC chief's history of negotiating in bad faith. But Miller was not certain of the solidarity in his own ranks since the union's last major showdown of 1976. He also feared that the PRC proposal for immediate pension eligibility was a wedge intended to entice and split off young players not eligible for free agency. As a result, although Miller evoked the crisis in Iran in calling the Grebey compensation plan a foray at "taking hostages," he grudgingly signaled flexibility on an alternative compensation idea of additional monetary payments to teams losing free agents.[5]

Negotiations began in late January 1980 but remained stalemated by March. The union's executive board then approved a strike date of April 1. Grebey pretended conciliation by jettisoning the salary-scale stalking-horse, but he underscored his hard line on free agent compensation by claiming on CBS's "60 Minutes" program that twenty-one of twenty-six big league clubs were losing money. Miller called the assertion nonsense, and his player representatives called their opponent a liar to his face. Accelerating his own public relations offensive, Grebey then began regular press briefings and announced his acceptance of nonbinding intervention by Federal Mediation and Conciliation Service deputy director Kenneth Moffett. The union retaliated by offering to lift its April 1 strike deadline and continue talks on all issues save free agency while deferring the latter to a joint study panel for two years. When the PRC refused to budge, the union opted for a dose of "shock therapy" and authorized the April 1 stoppage halting the rest of the exhibition schedule. Although the union agreed to permit the regular season to start in the absence of a new agreement, it received its members' authorization to renew a strike on May 23 if no settlement had been reached.[6]

Under mediator Moffett's auspices, sessions continued, but each side merely challenged the other's positions and presented its own version to the media. With no progress to report in mid-April, Moffett recessed the talks until May 6 in hopes that the union's new strike deadline would spur movement. The PRC continued to demand direct free agent compensation in the form of a major leaguer from the signing team. Although the owner committee had accepted performance criteria rather than just the number of bidders as the basis for determining which free agents would require such compensation, it had set the "bar" so low that fully half of all free agent eligibles would fall into this premium category. The union countered with an exclusive performance standard and insisted player compensation come indirectly from a pool of unprotected big leaguers. As the crunch neared, Miller and top aide Don Fehr fretted about whether association solidarity would hold among its younger members in behalf of free-agency clout for their elders. One report indicated that thirteen of twenty-five Red Sox, including outfielder Dwight Evans, would not support a strike. When the union's leader asked his counsel for his judgment on whether support for the in-season stoppage would hold, the latter hesitated, then said, "Yes." Miller worriedly replied, "We'd better be right." [7]

On May 18 Moffett suspended the talks again for twenty-four hours. While union leaders pondered whether their ranks would stay firm, unbeknown to them the owners' wall began to crack. At the forefront of the management erosion was Edward Bennett Williams, the Democratic Party insider and famous Washington lawyer who had leveraged his finances to the hilt to buy the Orioles. Desperate to prevent a strike that would stop his badly needed revenue flow, Williams—along with Houston's John McMullen, who had spent heavily on free agents and stood to lose millions if the season and the Astros' pennant chances were scotched—pleaded with Commissioner Kuhn to break the deadlock. As he had been successfully prodded to do on previous occasions, Kuhn once more agreed to intervene and signaled a new role in the talks by personally appearing at the next bargaining session.[8]

A season-saving, stopgap deal was struck, but not without one last high-stakes game of "chicken." On the day before the scheduled player walkout, Grebey and his partners arrived an hour late to the morning bargaining session. When Marvin Miller decided to test their desire for a deal by floating a "softball" issue—whether to have the Joint Health and Safety Committee look into players' call for umpires to suspend games more quickly in case of bad weather—the owners surprisingly rejected the idea. Then NL president Chub Feeney launched into Miller for having directed Dodger players not to board airplanes for their upcoming series. After explaining that the instructions were merely in keeping with the requirements to implement a strike only hours away,

C. Raymond "Ray" Grebey and Marvin Miller
(Corbis/Bettmann-UPI)

the union head turned to Fehr and whispered resignedly, "They never believe it." Finally convinced of the association's intent to go through with its stoppage, management negotiators returned for the afternoon session with a 180-degree shift in attitude. Talks moved to Grebey's hotel room via a freight elevator to avoid the press, then to Moffett's suite with lawyers and other note-takers excused. Behind a closed bedroom door, Miller and his opposite number personally hammered out an interim deal while the mediator and aides played cards at a table in the next room.[9]

The stopgap package that emerged, a four-year basic agreement and pension pact, resembled the union's latest proposals. The two sides agreed to boost minimum salaries to $35,000 by 1984 and to raise the owners' pension contribution to $15.5 million a year. The free-agency compensation issue was deferred to a four-person study committee until the end of the year. Anticipating that the study committee's findings would serve as the starting point for last-ditch talks in early 1981, the

deadline for agreement on the issue was set for February 19. If no resolution was reached by then, the owners could try to impose their last
formal proposal, effective with the 1981–82 free agent class. The most
recent owner plan required big leaguer compensation for Type A free
agents—those sought by eight or more clubs and statistically ranking in
the top third of major league hitters and pitchers. Teams that signed free
agents could only protect their top fifteen men from the possibility of
being selected by clubs losing free agents. For signing Type B men, those
between the top third and half of major league performers, clubs could
protect eighteen players. In response, the union could either give in without a fight, launch a delayed strike after the 1982 season to overturn the
new system, or try to preempt compensation by declaring a formal objection to the plan by March 1 and commencing a strike no later than
June 1, 1981.[10]

The owners ratified the new pacts by a 21-5 margin; the players, by
tallies of 619-22 and 749-11. For the union, the deal represented a short
truce at best and a victory for no one on the central issue of free agent
compensation. But for Grebey, his need to be able to proclaim a win led
him to leak a memorandum to the Associated Press containing the assertion. In similar grandstanding fashion, Commissioner Kuhn appeared
on the "Today" show to take credit for management's latest "success" at
the bargaining table. A furious Miller, in turn, rejected the claims and
blasted Grebey's press release as "horribly inaccurate." Whatever the substance of the agreement, it was now unquestionably true that the self-
serving statements of Grebey and Kuhn had further poisoned an already
polluted bargaining well for round two. As a sign of the ill will, at a party
celebrating Ken Moffett's fiftieth birthday hosted by Baltimore owner Ed
Williams, Orioles player and union activist Doug DeCinces presented
the honoree a cake and a T-shirt. The latter bore pointed reference to
the phrase the union had come to loath: "Trust me."[11]

Despite the last-minute inking of a stopgap Basic Agreement, neither
the owners nor the players had any illusions about the cease-fire. While
the big leagues played out their 1980 season, in a disturbing premoni-
tion the Mexican League wrestled with its own labor conflict. In July the
Asociación Nacional de Beisbol struck in protest over its demands for
official recognition and player Vicente Peralta's firing for union activity.
The walkout forced cancellation of the schedule at mid-season and then
produced a 1981 campaign in which each side fielded skeleton circuits

and attendance plummeted. If leaders on each side of the major league impasse were paying attention, however, they did not show it. The four-man study group on free agency, consisting of players Sal Bando and Bob Boone and front-office executives Harry Dalton and Frank Cashen, produced nothing but dueling final reports.[12]

All signs pointed to a renewed bitter struggle in the spring. In October the NLRB ruled in the union's favor on its complaint about the unfair labor practices of the PRC for denying financial information. In November, the last season of free agency under the old rules, management's big spenders bid lavishly to lock up their players to multiyear deals and even extended pay guarantees to some in the event of a 1981 strike. Five of fourteen free agents garnered offers of better than $0.5 million, topped by Dave Winfield's ten-year Yankee pact with $1.4 million (unguaranteed) the first year. After stockpiling star talent, the magnates issued bold challenges to the union. Predicting association leader Miller's "Waterloo," George Steinbrenner proclaimed, "Marvin always waits for three or four owners to bolt. It won't happen this time." Miller defiantly rejoined that if the magnate felt so strongly about compensation for free agents, he should offer San Diego one of his players, or perhaps a racehorse, for Winfield.[13]

By the start of 1981 the owners had amassed a $15 million emergency pool for weaker clubs in the event of a strike. Their $50 million strike insurance fund, scheduled to kick in after the loss of 153 games, or less than two weeks into a season, provided $100,000 for each canceled contest up to a maximum of 500, or about 40 additional days. The union also had used the interim to shore up its own strike fund with another year's accumulated licensing money. After thirty days of pretend negotiations, the owners, as expected, announced the unilateral implementation of their compensation scheme effective February 19. The Players Association, in turn, agreed to play out the exhibition season but set a strike date of May 29. Even with the sword of a regular-season stoppage hanging over their heads, neither side expected a deal on their own terms, nor would either accept anything less. So deep had the mutual animosity grown between the PRC and the union that each appeared more eager to antagonize the other than attempt progress. Knowing that it irked the "buttoned-down" Grebey, player representatives deliberately "slummed" in jeans and sweatsuits and acted indecorously at bargaining sessions. The PRC head retaliated by deliberately addressing player attendees in a condescending manner and goading Miller with the hated nickname "Marv." Given the almost equal loathing that had festered between Miller and Bowie Kuhn, Kuhn determined once and for all to resist intervening. He accused the players of becoming "prisoners" of Miller's ego and knee-jerk hatred of management; the executive director returned the favor by labeling the commissioner an idiot with delusions of independence.[14]

When Miller toured spring camps to stage prestrike rallies, the open-air meetings drew taunts and disruptions from angry fans. But while grassroots public opinion favored the owners, "opinion-makers" had adopted a more pro-union viewpoint than the year before. Kuhn and other industry spokesmen issued dire laments on the fiscal health of baseball. "Unless we find oil under second base," Kuhn insisted, "we will never survive." Grebey joined the chorus by claiming that in 1980 the Orioles, the Cubs, and the Braves had lost from $53,000 to $1 million. Spotting an opening in the management poor-mouthing, Miller pounced. Although he indicated the union's willingness to accept compensation in the form of big league players for owners in principle, he now filed for another NLRB injunction on the grounds that while the owners had pleaded poverty, they had refused to provide the required supporting data to the union. In any collective bargaining negotiation in which management publicly asserted an "inability to pay," the refusal to share supportive information could be considered a "failure to bargain" justifying NLRB action.[15]

At first it looked as though the union's stroke might succeed in derailing the PRC compensation plan and save the 1981 season. NLRB general counsel William Lubbers upheld the grievance and sought a federal court injunction just twenty-four hours before the strike deadline. The action would have had the effect of extending the 1980 rules on free agent compensation and preventing a work stoppage for a year, during which a full hearing would take place before an NLRB administrative law judge. As the deadline neared, rifts again surfaced in the owner ranks. For the sin of opining to a reporter that the union was receptive to compromise and that a "macho test of wills" benefited no one, Milwaukee's Harry Dalton drew a $50,000 fine. Noting that similarly unauthorized owner statements *attacking* the players had not drawn "gag-order" fines, Miller sarcastically quipped, "I had always realized that the truth had a price, but I never realized it was that expensive." The leading management dove, Ed Williams, burned up the phone wires with pleas to Kuhn and PRC aide Barry Rona for a compromise, arguing that Miller would never allow his legacy to be tarnished through the erosion of his "monument," free agency. But Grebey and his hard-line allies on the PRC beat back Williams by comparing his "peace-at-any-price" attitude to that of Neville Chamberlain—in the process also revealing the light in which they viewed Marvin Miller.[16]

The injunction hearings led to a two-week suspension of the union's strike deadline. With the PRC unwilling to budge, any hopes for saving the season lay solely with the NLRB's petition before Judge Henry Werker. The judge possessed several options, including granting the injunction outright or denying it while finding the owners guilty of an "unfair labor practice," which would then change the legal status of any subsequent strike to make it possible for the players to win back wages and the owners to lose strike insurance coverage. Given the economic risks of the latter outcome, the magnates still might be forced to cut a deal to avoid a strike. But Nixon appointee Werker did neither. Discounting Grebey's poverty statements on the grounds that they had not been made at the bargaining table, and ignoring Kuhn's pleas because he was not an official bargaining participant, the judge found that no management violation had occurred. On June 10 Werker threw out the injunction request, ordered a strike delay for an additional forty-eight hours in hopes of a last-ditch deal, and theatrically declared, "Play ball!"[17]

Despite Werker's wishful proclamation, the substance of his ruling virtually guaranteed a lengthy work stoppage. Miller had offered to place all players listed on clubs' forty-man reserve rosters but not on the twenty-five-man active squads in an indirect compensation pool. But after the federal court decision, the PRC made it clear that it had no intention of budging from its entrenched position. On June 12 the player strike of 1981 commenced. Although an NBC poll claimed the public narrowly supported the owners, dove Ed Williams once more risked his colleagues' wrath by assisting Orioles players stranded in Seattle at the deadline to get home. Even in Baltimore, however, PRC strike directives barred the strikers from using club equipment and facilities, and pay was denied to all but those with guaranteed money. In contrast, coaches, managers, and administrative personnel were retained on full salary, and Commissioner Kuhn kept his $200,000 income while clubs furloughed stadium employees.[18]

On the basis of his own back-channel discussions with Belanger and DeCinces, Williams had concluded that Grebey had not only been guilty of disingenuousness toward the union; he had also failed to report accurately its positions back to the owners. Suspecting that the negotiator was misleading his employers in order to maintain his hard-line posture, Williams joined George Steinbrenner and Texas owner Eddie Chiles in renewing calls for Kuhn to intervene. Again the gambit backfired, as the commissioner and AL president Lee MacPhail also rebuked them, and the owners' executive council formally endorsed Grebey. Part of Kuhn's newfound reticence, besides his desire to punish Marvin Miller, lay in his injunction testimony, in which he had discounted his earlier comments on the industry's hardship on the grounds that he (Kuhn) did not represent it in labor matters. If Kuhn now entered the negotiations, the action would belie his earlier sworn statements and place the magnates in renewed legal jeopardy. Williams continued in his course despite his setback and the risk of further retribution, but a chastened Steinbrenner worried, "Soon they'll be sending Chiles and me to Lower Slobbovia."[19]

Grebey and PRC hard-liners remained convinced that because of the players' past contract gains, an extended strike would cost them too much for them to stay out. According to one PRC insider, bets on the duration of the holdout ranged only to a maximum prediction of five days. Major leaguers' losses varied from $181 a day for those at the minimum to Dave Winfield's $7,777. Militant owners also pointed to the loss of pension moneys that cancellation of the All-Star Game would cause. With both sides dug in, however, after only two hours of negotiation in the strike's first week mediator Moffett issued a halt to talks on June 20. The mediator labeled the impasse the most bizarre in all his twenty-two years of troubleshooting. Marvin Miller, tired of being blamed publicly as the obstacle to progress, and convinced at any rate that nothing would happen until management became convinced of the players' resolve, opted out of the sessions until July 1 and from the outside floated the threat of a rival league run by players in 1982 if no settlement was reached.[20]

By July 4 the strike had canceled over 250 games. As the All-Star break neared, the last thing industry hard-liners wanted was another "peace mission" by Ed Williams conveying an impression of owner wavering. But since PRC bylaws required a joint meeting of all the clubs if as few as three requested one, Williams rallied eight colleagues for a July 9 session. Grebey and his allies again succeeded in converting the meeting into a pep rally, but enough owners had become suspicious of being "left out of the loop" by their chief negotiator that Lou Hoynes began providing them with his own updates on the talks.[21]

Concern over Grebey soon escalated when owners learned he had not told them at their joint meeting about a new proposal by Ken Moffett to end the deadlock. The NLRB had even given its blessing to his offer, and because no government mediator would inject a proposal without up-front assurance that both sides would accept it as a basis for further discussion, Grebey's failure to inform the owners about it represented a deliberate withholding of information. The PRC negotiator personally dismissed Moffett's proposal for indirect free agent compensation as "written by the union" and feared owner awareness of it would give Williams and his doves fresh ammunition. Seeing the same potential, Miller tried to empower Moffett to impose his plan through binding arbitration, but Grebey blocked the gambit. With NLRB hearings on the union's spring failure-to-bargain complaint under way, but a decision unlikely for weeks or even months, the All-Star Game became the strike's next casualty.[22]

By July 12, 392 regular-season games had fallen by the wayside. Grebey tried to drive new wedges in the association membership by offering particular subgroups special "carrots." He proposed to make free agents with twelve years' service time, including Tom Seaver, Don Baylor, Johnny Bench, Ferguson Jenkins, and the Niekro brothers, exempt from compensation; then he extended the same offer to repeater free agents, including Reggie Jackson. Grebey also tried to lobby veterans claiming long multiyear deals to return to the ballfield, since they would never again be in position to seek free agency. In all these gambits the PRC chief was trying to pry away the veteran stars who were both the game's greatest attractions and clubhouse leaders. For his part, Miller employed umpires' union chief Richie Phillips as a messenger to dovish owners, especially Steinbrenner. Phillips's men had gotten their full paychecks on July 1, only to be ordered to return half the money because, in contrast to the preceding year, their contract only allowed them to receive thirty days' salary, rather than forty-five, in the event of a 1981 stoppage.[23]

Ed Williams once again injected himself into the impasse by combining with Houston's John McMullen to solicit Reagan administration labor secretary Raymond Donovan. Although the secretary lacked the power to impose a settlement, he hoped through widely publicized meetings to turn up the heat on both sides. After conferring with Miller and Grebey in Washington, the well-intentioned but ill-versed Donovan traveled to New York City to urge progress upon the parties and then moved the talks back to the capital. Probably the most important effect of the secretary's intercession, however, was his securing a pledge from both sides to stop talking to the media. For Miller the concession proved a rare tactical error, for he relied on friendly reporters from newspapers in different parts of the country to keep his scattered membership informed. Now players grew restive not only from lack of work and pay but from the news blackout. Others complained of the lack of shared sacrifice, pointing to more than one hundred comrades who still received salaries through individual strike protection pay clauses. On July 22 the *Los Angeles Times* carried antiunion comments by veteran Dodger second baseman Davey Lopes blasting the negotiations as a "circus" and assailing union officials for failing to communicate with the membership. The Boston press printed pitcher Dennis Eckersley's similar, blunt exhortation, "Screw the strike, let's play ball!" Fearing a meltdown of solidarity, Miller and his aides hastily broke off talks and scheduled regional "information sessions" to shore up support. One insider confessed later, "I believe ownership didn't know how close they were to causing huge cracks." Even Ed Williams now speculated that "Miller has lost control of his union."[24]

The 1981 showdown had reached its critical juncture. If player support for the strike suddenly collapsed and stars returned to work, not only would free agency crumble, but additional major givebacks, perhaps even the union's disintegration, would follow. If the regional rallies managed to restore the union's wavering solidarity, however, the sudden turn of events ironically might very well force a settlement on labor's terms. For if the two sides did not reach an agreement by August 1, thereby giving enough time for the minimum one hundred games necessary for a genuine regular season and playoffs based on them, the bulk of the national TV revenue the magnates counted on for their bottom lines would be lost. Also, at the end of the first week of August, the owners' strike insurance fund promised to run out. In short, if the players did not fold immediately, the odds suddenly would shift overwhelmingly in their favor.[25]

The Players Association held. At the union's regional meeting in Los Angeles, the maverick Lopes retracted his earlier criticism and endorsed its stance. Dissenters at other gatherings followed suit. With the owners suddenly back on the defensive, rumors quickly swirled of Grebey's imminent demotion or outright removal from the talks. The rumors gained still more credence when AL president MacPhail suddenly contacted Miller for a private discussion. The sixty-three-year-old veteran of multiple talks had hovered at the margins of the negotiations from the start, and as Grebey had persisted in his hard-line tactics, MacPhail had been "drafting and doodling" on his own plan for pooled rather than direct free agent compensation. With owners panicking and splintering into bickering factions, Commissioner Kuhn, lawyer Lou Hoynes, and NL compatriot Chub Feeney asked the AL leader to cut the best deal compatible with saving the season.[26]

MacPhail first defused a demand from AL doves for binding arbitration by letting them in on his clandestine meetings and expanded role. After similarly briefing NL magnates, on day fifty of the strike he arranged a bargaining session with Grebey, Miller, and Fehr at the senior circuit's offices with the imperative of "making a settlement." After a pro forma last attempt failed to budge Miller from pooled compensation and service time for strikers, within forty-eight hours the two sides reached agreement in the early hours of July 31. Miller stubbornly refused to shake the hand of the hated, and now discredited, Grebey, and in an aside to MacPhail, the union's Mark Belanger chastened the veteran executive to "never let this happen again."[27]

The fifty-day strike cost more than 700 major league games — over a third of the schedule — along with at least $30 million in player wages and $72 million in owner revenues on top of the $50 million insurance fund. Players at the minimum salary level had sacrificed $11,000 of their $32,500 incomes, while Dave Winfield had forfeited almost $390,000 of a $1.4 million contract. The average player lost $52,000. Club losses ranged from the Minnesota Twins' $1.6 million to the Dodgers' $7.6 million. An unforgiving Miller termed the entire confrontation "an exercise in terminal stupidity" by the owners. Don Fehr observed that the owners' provocation of the strike and Grebey's bad-faith bargaining "permanently colored the way I viewed people and their motives." Strictly speaking, the 1981 deal represented a slight retreat by the union. But compared with the owners' original aims, and with the string of management victories over organized labor in other industries, baseball's hard-liners had failed mightily. Elsewhere in America, in the months that followed, the United Mine Workers splintered into wildcat striking factions after losses at the bargaining table and forced givebacks. Striking air traffic controllers were fired en masse by President Ronald Reagan, and their union was devastated. But in baseball the PRC's Barry Rona could only describe, and defend the ratification of, his industry's new pact as "better than nothing."[28]

The fact that the final bargain paralleled the players' prestrike proposal of late May made the lengthy showdown all the more incomprehensible. Under the agreement, owners would protect the top twenty-four men on their rosters while making the rest available for a compensation pool for teams losing Type A free agents (those in the top one-fifth of players, based on performance criteria). Clubs refusing to bid on any free agents were allowed to protect an additional two men. Up to five clubs could exempt themselves entirely from the free agent process for all three remaining years of the Basic Agreement and thereby protect their entire forty-man squads. In exchange for the union dropping its failure-to-bargain case, the players received full service-time credit toward the pension as well as free-agency and arbitration eligibility. Given that the 1981 settlement ended in little more than a bloody stalemate, its main long-term consequences lay not in its specifics but in the escalated mistrust between the two sides and the continuing reality of the power of the players' union—a sharp counterpoint to the nation's dominant conservative trends.[29]

Marvin Miller viewed his successful defense of the free agent market in 1981 as a last hurrah before a well-earned retirement. Following the recommendations of a search committee formed after the strike's conclusion, Ken Moffett was chosen as executive director-elect. Once the former mediator took over formal reins of leadership on January 1, 1983, Miller assumed consultant duties to the union. The result was an unmitigated disaster.

In fairness to Ken Moffett, many of his troubles were owed to the legacy of the man he replaced. Marvin Miller had amassed perhaps the greatest record of accomplishment of any modern-day U.S. labor leader. Under the best of circumstances he was a hard act to follow. Escaping his shadow became even more problematic given his continuing presence in the union, including an office in association headquarters and a staff of protégés he had groomed. Miller understandably viewed the union as his personal creation, and accordingly he expected it to continue on the course he had charted—one rooted in the larger labor movement and openly suspicious and adversarial toward management. Such an outlook had been justified, and reinforced, by the union's past underdog battles with the industry over basic rights and benefits. But by 1983, primarily because of Miller, the union no longer was a supplicant but, instead, a powerful economic force dedicated mainly to preserving its many gains. Its changed status carried a new responsibility for nurturing the economic health of an industry that provided its members, albeit grudgingly, generous benefits. Miller's "chip-on-the-shoulder" persona had been right for the time, but with his retirement was that time past? In the view of his successor, the need for a new era of cooperation had been demonstrated by the bitter war of 1981. To Miller, by contrast, the bad faith demonstrated by management during the same struggle only underscored the naïveté of any change in the union's confrontational philosophy.[30]

Whatever Miller's faults, however, it remained that Moffett failed to show sufficient consideration to the man who had made the union what it was. By word and deed he gave credence to colleagues' growing fears that he was lazy and tied to a flawed philosophy. The executive director-elect got off to a bad start by claiming at the 1982 winter meetings that "no one ever wins" a labor showdown—a statement that suggested a lack of stomach for future battles and insufficient knowledge of or respect for the association's past. Once on the job, he quickly gained a reputation as a detached leader by delegating daily operations to aides he brought in from the outside while ignoring Don Fehr, the highest-ranking Miller holdover. In March 1983 Moffett committed another gaffe by making favorable comments on the reported results of the owners' TV negotiations, thereby undermining the union's ongoing lawsuit to force a participatory role in the same talks. A messy power play then unfolded in which Miller tried to dictate an anti-Moffett memorandum for distribution on union stationery, only to see it confiscated before it could be sent to the executive board or the membership. Moffett expelled his predecessor from union facilities and even had the office locks changed. Miller sent his memo to the union board anyway, accompanied by an attack on Moffett's attempt at censorship. Although Moffett "won" the battle by expelling Miller, the latter eventually won the war. After concerns over the successor's disengagement escalated and troubling whispers foretold management plans to steamroller him in upcoming negotiations, in the fall of 1983 the union's executive committee ousted Moffett.[31]

In the aftermath of the ouster, the Players Association brought back Miller for a three-week interim, then tabbed Don Fehr as its new leader. Even though he had served as Miller's loyal legal deputy for a half-dozen years, some succession frictions still arose. The old lion resented Fehr's unwillingness to back him vigorously during the earlier showdown with Moffett. In turn, the new leader quietly shared some of the perception of Miller as a restless retiree prone to second-guessing. Of more serious long-term consequence, as Fehr later admitted, was the fact that Miller had been such a hands-on workaholic that he had not built a strong union bureaucracy to carry on his multitude of roles. Under Miller and his series of legal counsels, the association had essentially been a two-man operation. If he now perceived his successors as inadequately prepared for the challenges ahead, or the membership too forgetful and complacent, he deserved his share of the blame. If Marvin Miller had been a Napoleon, Don Fehr promised to be more like an Eisenhower—methodical, smart, and hard working but less colorful. Would he prove merely a competent bureaucrat? The skills required of that were not unimportant, and the new executive director demonstrated his value in constructing a specialized staff operation appropriate to a mature union with a major voice in the baseball industry. In the arts of inspiration and public leadership, however, Fehr faced a steep learning curve. Partly in recognition of his need for help in the short term, as well as to ensure good relations with his old boss, Fehr kept Miller at his side for the upcoming basic agreement and pension talks in 1984–85.[32]

The issue that presented Fehr his most vexing early challenge, however, and which highlighted the union's renewed "public-be-damned," unflinching defense of its members, was drugs. Substance abuse had long been a problem in professional baseball, but it had grown sharply with player incomes and access to expensive, dangerous substances. In 1980, admissions of alcoholism by Los Angeles pitcher Bob Welch and Kansas City catcher Darrel Porter had drawn brief press attention, but more controversial was the arrest of Texas Rangers hurler Ferguson Jenkins at a Toronto airport for possession of marijuana, hashish, and cocaine. Following the pitcher's refusal to submit to interrogation by baseball investigators, his suspension by Commissioner Kuhn, and a union grievance, arbitrator Raymond Goetz overruled the commissioner on the grounds that Jenkins had justifiably feared compromising his court case by cooperation with baseball, and because Canadian authorities had deemed the offense trivial by allowing a no-contest plea without jail time.[33]

In response Kuhn had urged the clubs to create their own Employee Assistance Programs for player reporting and treatment, but his suggestion drew sparse reaction. He then had joined league presidents in establishing a policy that combined mandatory punishment for offenders with leniency for men who came forward voluntarily. In 1982 San

Diego suspended infielder Alan Wiggins for a month following his arrest for cocaine possession, and St. Louis outfielder Lonnie Smith volunteered for treatment of his habit. Two years later, however, the Padres received their own belated fine from the commissioner because they had continued to pay Wiggins's salary during his suspension. Dodger relief ace Steve Howe spent five and a half weeks in drug rehabilitation, then received a suspension for a relapse and returned to treatment in May 1983. Reactivated following a $50,000 fine, he appeared headed for the suspended list again July 16 after he showed up late for a game, but he was reinstated after a drug test the next day. On September 22 his non-appearance combined with a refusal to allow testing drew another suspension. The union filed a grievance but withdrew it when the commissioner agreed to transfer Howe to the inactive list, where he continued to accumulate service time. The unchastened abuser again tested positive for cocaine the day after Thanksgiving, forcing Kuhn to order him to the bench for the 1984 season.[34]

The biggest scandal in 1983, however, involved Kansas City Royals players Willie Wilson, Willie Aikens, Jerry Martin, and Vida Blue. For pleading guilty to charges of soliciting cocaine, the defendants received $5,000 fines and one-year prison terms reduced to three months for good behavior. Kuhn followed up by attempting to suspend them for 1984. Once more the Players Association took the unpopular step of filing a grievance to block the suspensions, and arbitrator Richard Bloch concurred that the punishments to Wilson and Martin were excessive and reinstated the players on May 15, 1984. The commissioner then cut Aikens's suspension similarly, but Blue remained under the stiffer initial penalty because of his purported role as the procurer of drugs for the others. Despite the Kansas City quartet's public humiliation, Atlanta pitcher Pasqual Perez garnered a one-month suspension and a one-year probation for cocaine possession and refusal to cooperate with baseball's inquiry. Once again at the union's request, arbitrator Bloch overturned the penalties, citing the lack of proof of cocaine *use* by Perez.[35]

One of the issues contributing to Ken Moffett's eventual downfall had been his own enthusiasm for a labor-management committee to draft guidelines for testing, treating, and punishing baseball's drug offenders. By contrast, Fehr viewed the drug controversy through a lens of skepticism of management motives and saw protecting his members' procedural rights and continued earnings as his priority. Accordingly, he vehemently opposed cooperation in any arrangements to help management regulate or police his membership's behavior. But while the union's legal positions frequently prevailed in arbitration, they provided no cover in the court of public opinion. In the five years up to the start of 1984, sixteen active players and a handful of former players and managers admitted to drug problems by either seeking treatment or being convicted on drug offenses. The ousted Moffett also struck back at those who had fired him by claiming the union knew that teams averaged four or five drug users each and that the FBI had uncovered cocaine use in clubhouses and even during games.[36]

In the face of public pressure, the association conceded to negotiations on an industry policy. Patterned after a plan adopted by the NBA, the Joint Drug Policy developed in 1984 applied to illegal hard drugs but not to marijuana or prescription substances such as amphetamines. Nor did it authorize mandatory random drug testing. Instead, a player voluntarily coming forward to seek help would receive no penalty for a first offense but would be subject to discipline for repeat instances. A club suspecting a player of drug abuse could approach him with its suspicions and request he seek treatment; if he denied the assertions or refused help for an acknowledged problem, the dispute would be adjudicated by a three-person medical panel. A player seeking treatment went on the inactive list but still received his full salary for thirty days, half-pay for another thirty if necessary, and the major league minimum after that if the team agreed to extend the treatment period. The union acknowledged the commissioner's right to suspend a player convicted in court of drug offenses, with accompanying penalties ranging from a one-year ban without pay to permanent ineligibility. Baseball could also punish performers who possessed or used illicit drugs on stadium premises with a suspension of up to one year. The union could still file an arbitration grievance, however, challenging any such action if it deemed the commissioner had exceeded his authority or violated a player's right to due process. The relative absence of harsh deterrents led many outside observers to view the new joint policy as more of a public relations stroke than a serious assault on the drug menace.[37]

If the Players Association's messy transition to a post-Miller era made it vulnerable to a new management offensive, however, the owners' own poststrike disorganization bought the union time. Bowie Kuhn and Ray Grebey became obvious direct casualties of the failure in 1981 to crush the players. The PRC negotiator, who once had hoped to succeed Kuhn, failed even to outlast him; Grebey was voted out by the magnates in April

1983 and replaced in the short term by Lee MacPhail. As for Kuhn, his controversial "split season" and jury-rigged playoff structure after the strike irked owners of clubs, notably Cincinnati and St. Louis, that possessed better overall records but were excluded from postseason play. With the desertion of these traditional supporters, by November 1982 anti-Kuhn factions in both circuits voted to deny him a new term. After a second repudiation the following spring, he finally announced his resignation, although he lingered on as a lame duck for another year and a half. On the PRC, Ed Fitzgerald not only stepped down as chair but left the industry. League presidents MacPhail and Feeney then oversaw a subsequent restructuring that reduced the panel's power relative to the next commissioner.[38]

Less obvious than the musical chairs in the commissioner's office and the PRC, but even more fundamental, was the continuing turnover in big league ownership ranks. As part of a trend that had preceded the advent of free agency, traditionalist owners with long-standing family or professional ties to the industry increasingly left it. Instead, by 1985 every major league club claimed backing from at least one outside corporate entity. In many cases the departed had been heirs to the Rickey philosophy of strong farm systems and paternalistic tightfistedness. While their views on labor relations had been archaic, their fortunes more limited, and their perspectives more parochial, their knowledge of the sport and their ability to assess playing talent arguably had been greater. By the early 1980s, the Wrigleys, Howsams, Griffiths, Finleys, and Veecks had almost disappeared in favor of newcomers with vaster financial resources and expansive egos to match. Following on the heels of George Steinbrenner and Ted Turner, the new breed included Eddie Einhorn and Jerry Reinsdorf of the White Sox, Steinbrenner protégé John McMullen in Houston, Levi Strauss magnate Walter Haas of Oakland, and corporate entities Taft Broadcasting for the Phillies and the Tribune Company and its WGN superstation for the Cubs.[39]

While a few customary names and perspectives remained, the industry's rising power brokers generally represented nonbaseball conglomerates and media empires that all too often demonstrated more impulsiveness than good sense in baseball decisions. Their steep learning curve and their ego-driven unwillingness to defer to the better judgment of seasoned subordinates made them "pigeons" for player agents in arbitration and free-agency processes. With pay negotiations in such inexperienced hands, combined with the fact that only eleven free agents of

1983–84 even qualified as Type A players, the free agent compensation adjustments of the 1981 agreement completely failed to restrain salaries. Owners continued to lavish expensive multiyear pacts on one-season "flashes-in-the pan" and aging eligibles, such as Yankee signees Dave Collins and Ed Whitson, who were likely to decline in performance.[40]

As player agent Randy Hendricks noted, one thing the "new blood" owners might have been expected to do to relieve their bottom lines was embrace fully, rather than in disadvantageous, piecemeal fashion, a fundamental shift from seniority-based to performance-based rosters. Salary arbitration and free agency both implicitly expressed this new philosophy, and yet as late as the 1980s, clubs refused to apply their own forms of performance-to-cost calculation for compensating payroll economies. Specifically, clubs continued to spend excessively on senior journeymen rather than conserve money for genuine stars and up-and-comers, and they refused to accept greater annual roster turnover through more rapid promotion of cheaper rookies. In fairness to the magnates, players' eligibility for salary arbitration after only two years in the big leagues put limits on the ability of clubs to maximize payroll economies through the use of more young players. After early routs at the arbitration table, the owners gradually realized their need for specialized expertise in that forum. Former Houston general manager Tal Smith became management's "hired gun" of choice in arguing its cases. Through 1980, players had won fifteen hearings and lost only eleven. Beginning in the 1982 postseason, however, the clubs began a seven-year string of victories. Even these results, however, came partly from the belated adjustment to more "realistic" (i.e., higher) bids. In 1983 alone, for example, the pay of arbitration "losers" climbed an average of 54 percent.[41]

From 1980 to 1984 the average major league salary jumped from $143,756 to $329,408. But minimums rose only $10,000, to $40,000, over the same span (see Appendix, Fig. 3). In the 1982 postseason alone, the number of major leaguers earning more than $750,000 doubled to thirty-eight. Big league payroll costs climbed 27 percent in 1980, 29 percent in 1981, 30 percent in 1982, 20 percent in 1983, and 13 percent in 1984. By 1984 the Yankees led with a payroll averaging over $450,000 a man, but even bottom-feeder Cleveland spent nearly $160,000 per player. In order for managers to maintain their on-field authority, their salaries had to be adjusted accordingly. By 1984 Tommy Lasorda topped the list at $330,000. The upward pull of the major league salary system also influenced the minors, with the levels closest to the big leagues affected the most. Average monthly pay at AAA level rose by over a third, to over $4,000, between 1981 and 1985. At AA, salaries increased more modestly from a little under $1,200 to about $1,500. A-level pay inched up from about $750 to $830, and rookie circuits climbed from a little over $600 to slightly more than $700.[42]

The owners subsequently claimed they lost $80 million in 1982, $66 million in 1983, and $41 million in 1984. In fact, the greater opportunities the clubs' new mega-sponsors gave for sheltering money meant that, with few exceptions, major league franchises could afford the salary escalation. The payroll rise had, however, cut into the profits the clubs otherwise might have realized from television. Attendance had held relatively steady, with 43 million fans in 1980 and from 44 to 46 million each year in 1982–84. But the 1980–83 national TV take had doubled to $190 million, representing $1.8 million per club per year. The new pact with ABC and NBC in the spring of 1983 promised to generate $1.125 billion over 1984–89, producing a fourfold increase in the clubs' annual take. As for local broadcast revenue, the fuel for George Steinbrenner's perpetual attempts to buy a world championship was the $6.7 million annually secured from the Yankees' deal with Sports Channel.[43]

Despite the growth in revenue sources, however, player salaries had risen as a share of big league moneys to over 40 percent. The handful of poorer clubs that could not cash in on the bonanza in local TV worried about their future ability to turn a profit and remain competitive with their richer brethren, and the well-heeled resented having to share any more of their growing gains with labor. Discouraged and frustrated at their PRC's failure to bully the Players Association into systemic changes protecting them from their own profligacy, the owners now desperately sought, as Lou Hoynes put it, a "man on a white horse" to save them from themselves and the union.[44] But to paraphrase the old adage, the magnates might have been wiser to be careful about what they asked for, because, to their eventual dismay, they got it.

As his middle name suggested, Peter Victor Ueberroth claimed a life story emblematic of a highflier of the Reagan era, complete with an instinct for self-promotion and an ability to stay a step ahead of the curve — or the posse. Ueberroth was born in Chicago in the late 1930s, but he grew up in California. There he attended San Jose State University, competed on the water polo team (he later claimed erroneously to have made

Peter Ueberroth
(National Baseball Hall of Fame Library, Cooperstown, N.Y.)

the U.S. Olympic team as an alternate), and financed his education by working as a traveling seed salesman and chicken-farm egg inspector. After graduating with a business degree, he went to work for go-go airline financier Kirk Kerkorian. By the late 1970s, and after Ueberroth had ventured out on his own, his First Travel Company had grossed $300 million annually. His burgeoning reputation in Southern California circles as a "can-do" executive led local promoters of the 1984 Los Angeles Summer Olympics to tab him as staff director of the event. Undeterred by the narrow vote of 9-8 that elected him, forty-seven-year-old Ueberroth acted according to the motto that "authority is 20 percent granted, 80 percent taken." Relentlessly squeezing costs and raising revenue to guarantee a profit, he pioneered the privatization of the Olympic Games through wholesale corporate sponsorships, and he basked in the subsequent glow of a $222 million gain and, aided by a Soviet-bloc boycott, a flood of American gold medals. Capping a triumphant twelve months, *Time* magazine named him its 1984 Man of the Year.[45]

Even before the conclusion of the 1984 Olympics, Ueberroth's notoriety had caught the attention of major league baseball. As a consequence of the industry's management reshuffling, fellow Californian and Oakland A's club official Roy Eisenhardt (Walter Haas's son-in-law) headed the executive restructuring committee, and Bud Selig, Ed Fitzgerald's former subordinate in Milwaukee, had assumed charge of the commissioner search. Since baseball had tried, with mixed success, a jurist, a politician, an ex-sportswriter turned league executive, and a corporate lawyer, many of the newer magnates wanted someone more like themselves. By contrast, the more traditional Selig preferred Yale president A. Bartlett Giamatti, but a messy strike by university employees compromised his availability. At the lobbying of San Francisco owner Bob Lurie, in March 1984 the search committee passed over Giamatti and White House aide James Baker in favor of Ueberroth. Playing "hard to get" to ensure the terms he wanted, the commissioner-in-waiting insisted on taking over only after the end of the Olympics, and he demanded a hefty salary increase, changes in the reelection process to permit reappointment by a simple majority of owners rather than three-quarters support from each league, and upgraded authority in the areas of marketing and labor relations. Ueberroth later explained of his power grab, "If you are trying to accomplish something, you should control as much of the environment as you can." By the time he took over in October 1984, he had gotten virtually all he had demanded.[46]

From the very outset of his five-year term, Ueberroth exuded the self-confident assurance, or delusion, dubbed commissioneritis—the belief that he could somehow serve the owners as well as act as a dispassionate advocate of the game's overall interest. Determined to become the puppet of no single owner or faction, as he deemed Bowie Kuhn had been to the O'Malleys, Ueberroth utilized direct flattery, covert informants, and periodic public surprises to keep both labor and management off balance and reacting to rather than challenging his position. His initial test came only two weeks into his tenure when the major league umpires threatened a walkout of the playoffs. The union's main concern centered on postseason eligibility and pay. Under their old contract, the men in blue drew $10,000 for League Championship Series employment and $15,000 for the World Series. The umpires wanted higher direct pay for postseason participants but also an enlarged pool for nonparticipants and a selection process based on rotation rather than a merit system they considered a subjective reward to management favorites. At first Ueberroth stayed out of the fray, but when a strike materialized, he interceded to arbitrate the dispute and gave the strikers most of what they wanted. The pay pool nearly doubled to $405,000 for 1984 and climbed to $465,000 and $525,000 over the next two years. After walking out of seven of the first eight playoff games, the umpires returned for the deciding fifth game of the National League Championship Series. Ueberroth also took advantage of the crisis to send an early signal of independence, replying to a press question on the owners' degree of engagement with the barb, "You can't find them. They're all out on their yachts." Peter O'Malley, traveling to Japan and seeing himself as the target of the salvo, angrily called the new chief executive but received no retraction. Ueberroth cared far less about O'Malley's good opinion than the public's, and the latter showered him with praise for "saving the integrity" of the fall classic.[47]

Ueberroth's handling of the umpire walkout displayed patterns consistent throughout his commissionership. To serve his masters' ultimate interests, he knew he had to produce stronger bottom lines, and to do that he needed both to squeeze labor costs and to generate greater revenues. But he also knew that he would be judged by the press and the public for his ability to prevent labor confrontations from disrupting the normal flow of pennant races and postseason games. In the larger scheme of things, therefore, he judged getting the regular umpires back to work more important both to baseball's larger economic health and to his own image than the relatively paltry sum the union demanded. Season-threatening collective bargaining confrontations with the players' union likewise would be viewed as not worth the ultimate financial or public relations cost. Ironically, the skepticism toward in-season labor showdowns echoed the earlier perspective of Walter O'Malley, deceased patriarch of the Dodgers' ruling family that parvenu Ueberroth hated so much.[48]

But if Ueberroth intended to eschew the overt hardball tactics the owners had previously tried, how could he produce the economies to bolster industry profits and his reputation with his employers? The old Basic Agreement and pension deals expired at the end of 1984 and the following March, respectively. The owners remained in a state of near-panic over their accelerating payrolls, but they had not stopped extending expensive long-term and even "lifetime" pacts to pending free agents. The magnates clearly had not the stomach nor the unity for another "scorched-earth" negotiation, and their dilution of the PRC's authority reflected the sentiments of a majority badly burned by the most recent such effort. Accordingly, Ueberroth set the tone for a friendlier negotiation by courting Miller and Fehr and catering to their contempt for his predecessor and some owners. As a goodwill gesture, he also suggested lifting suspensions Kuhn had imposed on ex-players Willie Mays and Mickey Mantle for ties to gambling casinos.[49]

After "softening up" the union, Ueberroth then launched a drumbeat dramatizing the industry's purported financial peril. The goal that lay behind the poverty pleas was retention of a larger share of the new TV bonanza rather than allocating traditional percentages to the pension plan. Management hoped to hold the player pension share of the annual broadcast fees to $15 million. Having failed to crack the hard nut of free agency in 1981, the magnates also hoped with Ueberroth's help to gain concessions to reduce the number of players eligible for arbitration. The aim was a one-year increase in the service time required for a player to become eligible for salary arbitration and a limit on arbitration raises to 100 percent. On the union side, Don Fehr faced his first negotiation as chief with the goals of repealing the free-agency player compensation provisions of 1981, maintaining the existing arbitration system, and securing a third of national TV moneys for the pension.[50]

As of February 1985 the talks had generated little progress. Frustrated owners attacked Fehr and the union on the issue of random drug testing, hoping to put them on the defensive. John McMullen urged association members to fire their leadership for maintaining their opposition to testing, and O'Malley's Dodgers attempted to insert drug-testing clauses into individual contracts in contravention of the Joint Drug Policy. When the union retaliated with a charge of unfair labor practice against management for its renewed but undocumented claims of poverty, PRC chief Lee MacPhail sold Ueberroth on the gambit of having the industry open its books to buttress its claims and in so doing torpedo the grievance. So deep was the magnates' penchant for secrecy, however, that they resisted releasing their financial statements. In May the commissioner forced the issue by threatening to release the figures on his own. MacPhail and Ueberroth then engaged in a "good-cop/bad-cop" dialogue with the union, with MacPhail demanding a payroll scheme with an overall freeze on salaries and pensions and Ueberroth secretly reassuring the union that the proposal was just "posturing." Knowing that Marvin Miller, in particular, viewed with disdain the NBA's recent adoption of a salary cap, Ueberroth hoped through his solaces that the baseball players would consider "softer" forms of restraint.[51]

If the commissioner thought his courtship would coax the union into accepting the industry's cries of poverty, he was sadly mistaken. Not only did association leaders term MacPhail's freeze call "pathetic," but they commissioned Stanford economist Roger Noll to examine the owners' claims. Noll concluded that rather than losing $27 million in 1984, baseball had ended up $25 million in the black. To conceal the reality, the owners had devised a multitude of bookkeeping tricks. The Braves had underreported their broadcast fees from parent company WTBS, while the Cardinals had assigned parking and concessions income to a separate Anheuser-Busch subsidiary. The Yankees had claimed Steinbrenner's real estate investments in Tampa and charitable contributions as a half-million dollars in club expenses. Other entries reflected wasteful management practices, such as Oakland's exorbitant marketing costs and Los Angeles's extravagant front-office payroll, four times the league average.[52]

The union expressed its distaste for an immediate showdown by voting to honor the All-Star Game, but it authorized an August 6 walkout date in the continued absence of a deal. The later date made a strike more palatable to the membership, since they would already have the bulk of their salaries, while the owners would still be awaiting roughly 80 percent of their national TV revenue. As the risk of yet another shutdown grew, so did the commissioner's desperation to avoid one. After one more Ueberroth interjection as "the voice of the fan" drew a rejoinder from Miller—"What fans elected him?"—on August 1 the commissioner urged the players to drop their strike deadline and endorse a $31 million pension offer halfway between the union and PRC positions. Each side would forfeit $1 million in either pension or profits for each day after August 10 they failed to reach a settlement, and the money sacrificed through delay would instead go to amateur baseball programs. At the same time, Ueberroth endorsed the owners' demand for a curb on salary arbitration by embracing monetary ceilings except for extraordinary young stars. An intimate of the commissioner confidentially insisted that the proposal was not self-serving public relations but reflected the latter's faith in his ability to cut a "napkin deal" with the union. The source pessimistically noted, however, "Marvin Miller doesn't do napkin deals."[53]

As the strike deadline neared, each side followed recent bargaining tradition and cut its negotiating teams to bare bones. But on the substance—its demands for a three-year threshold for arbitration and a limited pension offer—the PRC held firm. The owners gave the appearance of increasing the pension figure to $25 million annually, but it tied that sum to an aggregate payroll limit that reduced the amount by every dollar of salary increases over $13 million. Since player salaries alone were projected to rise as much as $34 million a year over the next four seasons, the union justifiably saw the PRC proposal as a massive de facto pension *cut*. Nonetheless, partly because of the propaganda offensive Ueberroth had orchestrated on the industry's financial picture and partly as a result of Fehr's public awkwardness in his first high-profile negotiation, it was the union that showed signs of wavering. Fehr himself—perhaps because he saw a grain of truth in the industry's laments—seemed willing to accept less than the usual percentage contribution for the pension, but he continued to resist giving back a year of arbitration eligibility. Miller strenuously argued against any givebacks on either issue, but key veterans, led by Bob Boone, came out in opposition to "going to the wall" for the sake of arbitration for two-year men. Turning around one of the union's long-held strictures, Boone condemned a strike to preserve the extra arbitration year on the grounds, "If 30 percent of the players don't want to strike, that's a losing proposition."[54]

One day before a walkout union leaders privately hesitated to risk, a panicked Ueberroth hinted at using his "best interests" powers to prevent it. His bluff, however, failed to delay the reckoning. On the first evening of the strike, the commissioner called Barry Rona to inform the PRC of his intention to give the talks one more day, but then seek binding arbitration to end the impasse. With some owners sensing the union's private weakness, the commissioner's untimely threat led one of them later to conclude, "We should have fired him right then." Ueberroth then coaxed Fehr into excluding the hard-line Miller from a bargaining session and instead meeting Rona alone. On the strike's second morning, the commissioner phoned MacPhail's apartment, where the negotiators had gathered, to reiterate that if no deal had been reached by 2:00 P.M., he would "walk down Fifth Avenue and take it all away from you." With Fehr anxious for a deal and Rona worried that intervention by Ueberroth would actually cost the owners ground, the two men hammered out a five-year pact in the bedroom. Twenty minutes after the deal had been consummated, Ueberroth barged into the scene to claim credit for the breakthrough.[55]

The union had relinquished a year of service time for salary arbitration effective with the fall 1986 class. Fehr also gave ground slightly on the criteria arbitrators were to use in their decisions. New language directed them to pay special attention to the salary levels of men of the same arbitration class and those of the year before. In another piece of economizing, clubs gained the right to limit their pre–August 31 active rosters to twenty-four men. The union consented to management's proposal to expand league championship series to the best of seven games (which led to a 40 percent increase in umpire postseason pay awarded by special arbitrator Richard Nixon), and it settled for pension contributions of $25 million for 1984, $33 million annually in 1985–88, and $39 million in 1989—figures representing only 18 percent of the available revenue pool. Increased benefit levels, averaging $13,593 a month and $91,000 a year for a ten-year man at age sixty-two by 1987, were applied retroactively to 1975 veterans; pre-1975 players received prorated amounts at 40 to 50 percent of full levels.[56]

For its part, the union won an increase in minimum salary to $60,000 and subsequent upward adjustments. It garnered an extra $5,000 and $3,500 a man for winning and losing World Series participants through receipt of 60 percent of the entire central fund. The owners also gave up their hard-won player compensation scheme for top-level free agents and permitted free agents to entertain offers from any clubs. As a gesture of good faith on their claims of hardship and a response to Fehr's compromise on the pension, Ueberroth and the owners promised to create a $20 million fund from their national TV bonanza to aid strapped smaller-market clubs. They also arranged to graduate each team's pension fund obligations on the basis of its attendance and the size of its local television market.[57]

Taken as a whole, the 1985 Basic Agreement represented a greater victory for the owners than had been won by all of the scorched-earth tactics in 1981. Ironically, like the SALT II pact between the United States and the Soviet Union, it was also a covenant honored by each side without either ever concurring on a formal written version. Almost immediately the two sides squabbled over the precise language of what they had agreed on in Lee MacPhail's apartment. One of the two men in the best position to clarify matters, Don Fehr, claimed temporary indisposition with diabetes-related complications. Because of both its method of conclusion and its content, the 1985 agreement also led to grumbling in the player ranks and pressure on their leadership for a harder bargain next time. Had Fehr been taken advantage of as leader of his first basic agreement negotiation, or had he gotten the best deal possible in view of the players' own affluence and divisions of interest? In a show of support, the association's executive board voted Fehr a hefty pay increase and cost-of-living adjustments boosting his salary to $0.5 million.[58] But time would prove whether Fehr's concessions had been justified in light of union and industry realities, or whether he had been a naive victim of bad faith from a man once more basking in public praise.

Although a few owners expressed dismay that the commissioner had not stood aside and let the players suffer the fate of the air traffic controllers, he soon revealed his reasons for not doing so. Ueberroth had been devising his own strategy for ratcheting down payrolls far more effectively than any feature in the new Basic Agreement. His approach would become known by one simple word: collusion. Ironically, a similar way of crippling bidding on free agents had been urged in the late 1970s by Walter O'Malley. Like the former Dodger owner, Ueberroth had no stomach for in-season labor confrontations and recognized the inadequate returns from collective bargaining. As one magnate put it, "The thing that was called collusion grew out of the failure to get what we wanted in 1985." The commissioner hinted at what was to come in an address at Cooperstown that same summer when he cited management's need to "stop asking the players to solve their financial problems." Collusion represented a different, unilateral approach.[59]

The owners had hinted at collusion in the early 1980s, but their disorganization and threats of union retaliation had preempted any follow-through. Detroit's John Fetzer had called for a "buddy system," resembling Alcoholics Anonymous, in which fellow magnates could keep waverers "on the wagon." When free agent activity briefly slowed after the troubled 1981 season, the Players Association had used the opportunity of congressional testimony to threaten legal retaliation, and bidding soon resumed. The next January, Marvin Miller blocked a scheme by the Angels to provide additional compensation to the Yankees for signing

THE INFLATIONARY ERA

Reggie Jackson. Miller also had set up a union panel to "assist" (that is, coordinate) agents' preparation of cases for arbitration eligibles. Owners fumed at this form of player collusion and voted in reply to require that clubs maintain assets-to-liabilities ratios of 60-40 based on a common franchise value average (a similar formula had been required of expansion teams since 1975). Since the regulation translated into a subtle form of salary cap, the union had filed suit against it in April 1983. When the magnates had won the case before arbitrator Richard Bloch, the union had dismissed him.[60]

Ueberroth unveiled his new version of collusion immediately after the 1985 season. Lee MacPhail first laid the statistical groundwork, warning his listeners, "The revenue from television is the anesthetic that has put the club owners to sleep." According to his calculations, the magnates retained an outlandish $45–50 million in multiyear contract obligations to players who were no longer even in the game. He argued that the performance of men receiving big free agent deals almost always declined, and that such players spent markedly more time on the disabled list. While not directly ordering his audience not to sign free agents, he urged the owners to fill more roster spots with minor league promotees rather than yielding to "unreasonable" demands from marginal veterans. MacPhail also prodded them to be "smarter" in salary arbitration and to commit firmly to the Basic Agreement reduction to twenty-four-man squads.[61]

On the heels of MacPhail's written strictures, at the owners' World Series meetings in St. Louis Ueberroth pressed even harder. With the operative motto "Just say no to free agency," he hectored the magnates for preferring $10 million losses and fleeting pennant hopes from free agency over middle-of-the-pack finishes with $4 million profits. When Kansas City's Avron Fogelman tried to justify his "lifetime pacts" to Royals stars, with Ueberroth's prodding colleagues ridiculed him. The commissioner went around the room grilling each club executive on his free agent bidding intentions for the upcoming off-season. Under his harsh scrutiny, all indicated they would refrain. At one point Ueberroth, well aware of the tenuous legal ground on which he was treading, asked Barry Rona and league counsels Lou Hoynes and Jim Garner to "stop this discussion at any point" if it violated Basic Agreement anticollusion provisions. When they did not, he concluded the session with the vague admonition, "You all agree we have a problem. . . . Go solve it."[62]

The commissioner kept up his pressure on the clubs' general managers at Tarpon Springs, Florida, in November. If they did not hold the salary line, he warned, he would "come down hard on sixty-forty." Again alluding only vaguely to the necessary methods, he cautioned, "Don't be dumb. . . . We have a five-year agreement with labor." Taking their cues from Ueberroth and supportive owners Bud Selig, Jerry Reinsdorf, and John McMullen, nine clubs formulated guidelines calling for the abolition of contracts longer than three years for star players, two years for pitchers, and one year for journeymen. Others went farther, pledging not to bid on any free agents even for limited-term pacts.[63]

Long after he left baseball, Ueberroth continued to maintain that his actions had not violated the collective bargaining prohibitions on collusion. Lee MacPhail insisted that only concerns for the "good of the game" had led the owners to refrain from bidding on free agents. Barry Rona was only slightly more candid, insisting that the clubs "independently" had come to recognize the need for "fiscal responsibility," and that their actions differed little from the Players Association and its agent allies. On the other side, Marvin Miller decried the collusion of the 1980s as a form of "game-fixing" every bit as shameful as the "Black Sox" scandal. What in retrospect is irrefutable is Don Fehr's assertion that collusion was a deliberate strategy to violate collective bargaining promises, and one that cast the negotiations immediately preceding it as examples of bad faith. Regardless of the later verdicts of arbitrators and writers, however, in the short run collusion worked. By February 1986 dismayed agents reported a precipitous drop in interest in free agent clients. In the previous year twenty-six of forty-six free agents had changed clubs, many for multiyear deals. Now only one player, catcher Carlton Fisk, received a reasonable offer (three years, $2.25 million) from a different team, the Yankees, only to see it abruptly withdrawn.[64]

Given New York's image as the flagship organization for big spenders, its sudden reticence spoke volumes about the scope of collusion. In 1986 eventually 29 of 33 men returned to their old clubs, and average pay for the class rose only 5 percent. All but 10 signed one-year deals, and only 4 garnered as much as three-year agreements. As another consequence of collusion, in contrast to the preceding two years, when clubs preemptively signed 75 players to multiyear pacts, now only 15 men secured them. Owing to the universal application of 24-man rosters, 26 major league jobs were cut at an additional estimated savings of $10 million in salary and other expenses. Because of the newfound savings, the owners ignored Lee MacPhail's additional advice to use more rookies, and their number on Opening Day squads fell from 73 to 67. The full effect of collusion remained to be felt, however, as the lower free agent settlements in 1986 would not have their ripple effects on arbitration awards until the next off-season. As a result the average salary still rose 11 percent to $412,520 and the number of player "millionaires" climbed to 55. But the clubs' share of revenue going to pay players remained unchanged from the year before.[65]

The Players Association quickly filed a grievance charging the magnates with collusive violations, but it was months before arbitrator Thomas Roberts could rule on the case and longer still, even with a union victory, before any damages could be assessed. Adding to Don Fehr's frustrations was the continuing fallout from yet another drug scandal that put the union even more on the defensive when it could ill afford it. During the 1985 season, spring indictments had culminated in a September federal trial in Pittsburgh involving former clubhouse caterer and cocaine distributor Curtis Strong. Twenty-one players either had provided testimony in exchange for immunity or had been implicated as drug users, including Dave Parker, Lonnie Smith, and Keith Hernandez. Ueberroth, with his keen eye for public relations, had already issued brash statements calling for air strikes against Colombian sites, demanding the testing of minor leaguers and front-office employees to shame the union for its refusal, and claiming that the cocaine cartel had targeted his family because of his strong stance. Raising the specter of hooked players throwing games to support habits, he had used the Pittsburgh trial to renew his calls for mandatory testing only to have Fehr rebuff him for undermining the Joint Drug Policy. Ueberroth then had appealed to individual players to consent to testing, while he imposed fines, community service, and random testing on the confessed player witnesses. At the same October meetings at which collusion had been hatched, the owners had followed the commissioner's lead on the drug issue by voting to suspend their joint policy with the union.[66]

On the heels of collusion, individual clubs now attempted to include clauses for random drug testing in new contracts. Just before Opening Day, Ueberroth used management's cancellation of the cooperative drug policy to justify ordering mandatory tests of major leaguers four times a year. Fehr immediately filed a grievance with arbitrator Roberts. On July 30 Roberts sided with the union and invalidated the testing clauses in hundreds of contracts on the grounds that they had not been the result of collective bargaining (under the Basic Agreement only *benefits* could be added to individual standard playing contracts without authorization through formal collective negotiations). Any voluntary regimen required the approval of, and would be administered through, the Players Association. When the owners then sought Roberts's immediate dismissal, Fehr suspected that the covert purpose of the firing was to delay or scuttle the union's pending collusion case through a kind of "Saturday night massacre." Such suspicions heightened when Ueberroth, who had made so much of baseball's drug problem, abruptly declared it "solved." The commissioner's sudden abandonment of the drug "hammer" also conveyed a new management confidence that collusion by itself had the union on the run. If the owners hoped that by firing Roberts they would derail the pending free-agency case, however, they were disappointed. The union filed another challenge over the timing of Roberts's dismissal, and in September another arbitrator reinstated him for the adjudication of what eventually became known as Collusion I.[67]

Despite the setback, by the end of 1986 Peter Ueberroth stood at the peak of his power. His sport did not face the prospect of another contentious labor negotiation for three years. Baseball's drug problem appeared to be fading. The surging profits from rising gate attendance, television, and collusion had tempered owner restlessness. Even Ted Turner had agreed, in exchange for the lifting of restrictions on Braves superstation telecasts, to pay his owner colleagues $30 million over five years in fees. On the marketing front Ueberroth had squeezed Gillette for a fourfold increase in All-Star Game rights to $1 million, and after it had balked, he had secured USA Today for the desired bounty. Under the auspices of his new Major League Baseball Properties licensing operation, he similarly inked the Equitable Life Insurance Company as backer of a series of old-timers' games, IBM as sponsor of tape-measure home runs, and Arby's as supporter of runs-batted-in awards. To keep its position as industry equipment supplier, Rawlings forked over $1 million, and Coca Cola likewise anted up for clubhouse soft drink rights. Thanks to Ueberroth's aggressive marketing, licensing revenue now stood 150 percent above 1984 levels. Overall, while twenty-one clubs had claimed losses in 1984, only four did now. In 1986 revenues jumped to $800 million and profits surged to $66.5 million, with the latter topping $100 million the next season.[68]

As collusion entered a second off-season, even Ueberroth's legal advisers Hoynes and Rona began to advocate allowing a few free agent bids to reduce the owners' legal risk. As Hoynes admitted, the player marketplace undeniably "looked cooked." But from hubris, greed, and the "fear of offending Peter," the magnates maintained a strict vigilance. Only unbroken collusion could explain the reticence toward the new class of free agents, for it was far stronger than the previous year's crop. The spurned now included notables Andre Dawson, Tim Raines, Lance Parrish, Willie Randolph, Bob Horner, Doug DeCinces, Brian Downing, Jack Morris, and Ron Guidry. So confident were the magnates in their newfound ability to constrain payroll that in order to boost revenues further they "juiced up" the baseball, despite the impact on player's offensive statistics. The 1987 season saw twenty-eight players hit thirty or more home runs apiece, and the NL's 1,824 round-trippers broke the old record set in 1970. The bulging profits also permitted the owners to boost the pay of field managers, with salaries for skippers rising to a range of $100,000 to $500,000; player/manager Pete Rose garnered $700,000.[69]

While management beamed, players and agents squirmed. Lacking any outside offers, and with host club Detroit willing only to submit his salary demand to arbitration, pitcher Jack Morris grudgingly agreed to the latter tack and received a one-year, $1.85 million contract. Other free agents became known as the "January 8 group" for rejecting the same option by that deadline. As a consequence, they were stranded, lacking outside contract offers yet prohibited from re-signing with their old clubs until May 1. By refusing to accept arbitration and opting to sit out, they risked their livelihoods to strengthen the union's case in a second grievance labeled "Collusion II." As agent Tom Reich bluntly put it, "For the guys who bought the program it was a bitch." One of them, Tiger catcher Lance Parrish, did sign before May 1 with a new club, Philadelphia, but for the same $800,000 plus $200,000 in incentives he had been paid the preceding year. Even then Phillies executive Bill Giles drew, first, private "reminders" of fiscal responsibility, then condemnations for "breaking ranks" from colleagues Selig and Reinsdorf. Ironically, management later used Giles's defiant action as proof of noncollusion against the union's lawsuit. In the case of Montreal's Andre Dawson, his agent, former union official Dick Moss, sought to expose the existence of collusion by having his client offer to sign a "blank contract" at whatever amount any other club offered. After discussions with Rona, Cubs general manager Dallas Green signed Dawson, who had made $1.5 million in 1986, at a ridiculously low figure of $500,000 with $200,000 in incentives.[70]

After the May 1 deadline the union filed its new grievance, and nearly all of the January 8 group re-upped with their former clubs at amounts far below their worth. Tim Raines, despite an NL batting championship and seventy stolen bases to his credit, received only a $100,000 raise. Catcher Bob Boone rejoined the Angels, and Rich Gedman returned to the Red Sox. Only Bob Horner journeyed elsewhere, opting to play in Japan for $2.25 million over three years. In a brazen parting shot at Gedman, Boston general manager Haywood Sullivan openly taunted, "You're thinking there's collusion going on. . . . Of course we talk, we talk all the time, and you talk to people all the time, too." When the owners' strict fiscal discipline also was extended to younger players, the danger of more lengthy holdouts grew. Ueberroth personally intervened in the case of star hurler Roger Clemens, and as a result, agent Randy Hendricks secured a contract for his client worth $1.7 million and $300,000 or more in incentives over two years.[71]

As a consequence of Collusion II, the pay of the 1987 free agent class *fell* 16 percent. Three-quarters of the group signed one-year deals. Only seven non–free agents garnered preemptive multiyear contracts. With two years of nonbidding having restrained the top values at each position, and salary arbitration now available only after three years of service, the average pay of two-year men plummeted 38 percent to under $192,000. Utilizing the rock-bottom free agent contracts as "markers" the clubs continued their new string of victorious arbitration "seasons" by winning sixteen of twenty-six cases. When salary arbitrator Glenn Wong ruled for management in all five cases before him, a frustrated Players Association's only recourse was to fire him. Amateur draft signees also felt the ripple effect of the newly restrictive pay environment and failed to break the $250,000 ceiling. For the first time in the modern history of the players union, its members' average pay declined, from $412,520 to $412,454. The number of on-field millionaires shrank by one, and the percentage of the clubs' revenue claimed by player pay dropped 5 percent.[72]

If the salary setbacks of 1987 were not troubling enough, the Players Association lost a case before the Supreme Court. The high court upheld the owners' right to exclude the union from direct profit sharing in all of the industry's television revenues, rejecting union arguments that state law protected the players' rights to grant or withhold their likenesses for such broadcasts. In the meantime, the costs to the union of prosecuting the first collusion case already reached $300,000, and Don Fehr personally deferred a quarter-million dollars in salary to help foot the bill.[73] Although it was not yet evident, however, the fortunes of the players, the owners, and the commissioner were about to take a sharp turn. Within a matter of months Ueberroth, not the union, found himself on the run, no longer leading a management charge but hustling out of town.

Even before the 1987 season had began, the Ueberroth era had started to lose luster. On the drug front, despite the commissioner's claims that baseball had rid itself of the scourge, former Cy Young Award winner LaMarr Hoyt pleaded guilty to possession charges and was fined and suspended for violating the "no second chances" policy. George Nicolau, Roberts's successor on all grievance cases save Collusion I, reduced the suspension to sixty days. The following October Hoyt flunked three tests for cocaine and was arrested in December and drew a one-year sentence on distribution charges. At the start of the 1987 season Mets star pitcher Dwight Gooden admitted to cocaine use after he had previously denied a drug problem. Alan Wiggins, implicated in cocaine abuse repeatedly in the past, received another suspension that summer; he later died of AIDS-related pneumonia in early 1991. Outfielder Otis Nixon also pleaded guilty of reduced charges during the season, and Texas owner Eddie Chiles's premature attempt to sign recovering addict Steve Howe drew a $250,000 fine.[74]

Although continued drug scandals cast a shadow on the Ueberroth era, they at least represented a public relations problem the commissioner shared with the union. The same could not be said for another damaging controversy that erupted in April: baseball's persistent racism. Ironically, within the major league playing force the sport had never been more diverse, and the pay gap between whites and nonwhites had narrowed tremendously. While the portion of African American players in the big leagues had leveled off at about 1 in 5, the number of Hispanics had continued to rise despite minor league quotas of 10 percent that restrained the annual number of visa holders to 520 a year. By the 1986 season 102 of 956 major leaguers claimed foreign citizenship, including 59 Latin Americans, 45 of whom were from the Dominican Republic alone. But positional stereotyping and the old-boy network within organizations still imposed a low ceiling on postcareer opportunities for men of color. In 1987 only 21 of 180 major league coaches were black or Hispanic, only 9 such men served as managers throughout Organized Baseball, and only 30 racial minorities (the aforementioned categories plus Asians) held administrative positions, out of 879 slots. The majors employed no African American trainers. Only 6 minority umpires worked in the minors, and there were *none* in the American League.[75]

Triggering baseball's embarrassing public confrontation with racism was Dodger executive Al Campanis's appearance on an ABC "Nightline" broadcast commemorating the fortieth anniversary of Jackie Robinson's major league breakthrough. To the shock of interviewer Ted Koppel and a national audience, Campanis attributed the lack of minority progress off the playing field to a "lack of necessities" that included desire and mental acuity. "How many quarterbacks do you have?" he posed. "How many pitchers do you have—that are black?" Campanis even echoed the old canard attributing the absence of black Olympic swimmers to their race's poor buoyancy. In the furor that followed, the Dodgers fired him, and the NAACP and Jesse Jackson announced boycotts of baseball. Ueberroth hastily recruited black sociologist Harry Edwards as a special assistant for minority affairs, and Edwards amassed a pool of minority candidates for forthcoming front-office jobs. By December 1988 Ueberroth claimed a fivefold increase in such hires, to 10 percent of the force, but virtually all the hires were in low-level positions. From April to November 1987, none of thirteen hires as managers, general managers, or club presidents were minorities. Finally, in late 1988 Houston named Bob Watson its general manager, and Bill White became NL president in early 1989.[76]

While the Campanis furor marred the start of the 1987 season, near the end of the same campaign came the initial verdict on Collusion I. Led by Players Association assistant counsel Lauren Rich, dubbed by colleagues the "mother of collusion" for her single-minded zeal, fifty-eight days of testimony culminated in a September 21 ruling by arbitrator Roberts in favor of the union. Roberts found that the owners and Ueberroth had blatantly violated Article XVIII-H of the Basic Agreement barring conspiracy to fix the player marketplace, and he declared all sixty-two players who had been free agents as of November 1985 eligible for individual damages. Seven plaintiffs, led by Kirk Gibson, also won rights to re-entry into the upcoming free agent market without abandoning their existing contracts—a "free bite" of the apple. Although actual damages were to be assessed later, the owners clearly faced a huge tab for their illegality. Union consultants Dan Durland and Paul Sommers estimated the lost wages of the winter 1985–86 class alone at $20–30 million, with the prospect of triple damages based on those claims.[77]

In fallout from the defeat on Collusion I, the magnates demoted their long-standing legal team of Willkie, Farr and Gallagher and its representative Lou Hoynes in favor of Chuck O'Connor and the Washington,

D.C., firm of Morgan, Lewis and Bockius. At O'Connor's urging, the clubs modified their methods of collusion. Instead of group rallies directly orchestrated by Ueberroth, under PRC auspices the magnates set up an "information bank" into which clubs could "deposit" their free-agency intentions and make "withdrawals" about those of others. To most observers, the new system that was intended to reduce the owners' legal jeopardy presented a distinction without a difference. From a practical standpoint, the new system also had serious flaws. Under the old process, face-to-face jawboning at group sessions had more effectively instilled "group-think." Now, without exposure to the same blunt forms of coercion, magnates dallied in reporting their bids to the bank or understated the terms offered.[78]

In a choice irony the very profits "hard" collusion had generated—$206 million on over $900 million in revenues—encouraged renewed profligacy. Peter O'Malley, a skeptic of collusion from the start, signed Kirk Gibson for three years at $4.5 million. Agents noted that clubs were at least offering raises to their free agents, although the rough uniformity of the amounts suggested continued price-fixing. The number of baseball millionaires resumed an upward march by fifteen, and salaries rose a modest 7 percent, while the number of rookies fell further, to fifty, on 1988 rosters. Signs of owners' decreasing confidence in their fiscal solidarity included imposing stricter balk rules, thereby aiding scoring without bolstering hitting statistics, and reinterpreting the strike zone to lower it and home-run totals. Round-trippers fell by fully 25 percent.[79]

Buoyed by the Collusion I initial verdict, the Players Association threw more resources into its Collusion II grievance before arbitrator Nicolau. The union also tightened the screws on agents it deemed had been too amenable to the owners' earlier price-fixing. The union spent an extra $1.3 million on the grievance cases and nearly $300,000 more on a new "agent certification" program, which required agents to renew their status annually, barred them from certification if they worked in a management capacity, and disallowed fees steep enough to drop a player's salary below the big league minimum. With few other standards explicitly spelled out, the new certification program left the clear impression that it was intended as a union warning to agents to be more vigorous henceforth in behalf of their clients.[80]

The 1988 season played out as a surreal "Indian summer" of on-field heroics and profit before the next drop of the arbitrator's hammer. In the Collusion II hearings, adjudicator Nicolau was posing, in the words of Don Fehr's brother Steve (an outside counsel to the union), "tougher questions than I was." In the meantime gate attendance climbed to nearly 53 million, and gross industry revenues rose to more than $1 billion. But on August 31, 1988, collusion received another massive blow. In an eighty-one-page ruling, Nicolau found that the magnates had violated the rights of another class of free agents. This time the number of affected men totaled seventy-nine, and fourteen received "second-look" free agency. Like Roberts, Nicolau had yet to decide on the total monetary damages from his finding, but the union estimated the direct harm at an additional $50–60 million, putting the two classes' combined wage losses at $70–90 million and potential damages at $270 million.[81]

The Nicolau ruling, for all intents and purposes, marked the end not only of collusion but of the Ueberroth reign. Though his term was not scheduled to expire until the end of 1989, shortly before the arbitrator's judgment the commissioner announced his decision to leave early. Before he departed, he had one last financial prize to present to his employers to ease the pain of their collusion damages. Owing to the 1983 TV deal and local bonanzas, such as George Steinbrenner's Madison Square Garden cable deal for twelve years at $500 million, broadcast revenue had pushed the share of industry income from gate and stadium earnings down more than 20 percent in the decade. But given the growing splintering of the television audience with the expansion of cable channels, Ueberroth had issued a pessimistic forecast for future deals. During the 1988 playoffs, in an effort to scare network suitors into higher bids, Ueberroth hinted at creating an industry-owned baseball channel or selling all the pending TV packages to a single network, leaving the rest high and dry. CBS then jumped at the invitation. The network bid a whopping $1.1 billion for rights to the All-Star Game, the World Series, and twelve regular-season contests from 1990 to 1993. Ueberroth also announced a second four-year, $100 million annual contract to ESPN for 175 cable telecasts. The two deals added up to a $14 million-per-club going-away present. After he delivered this bonanza, without looking back Peter Ueberroth left baseball to pursue new adventures.[82]

After a decade of Ray Grebey's union-busting forays and Ueberroth's salesmanship and duplicity, the baseball industry had gained a wider revenue stream and a short-term profit bubble at the cost of massive union ill will and pent-up cost pressures. The owners had won modest givebacks after a series of negotiations, but they had not fundamentally dismantled the payroll system that still promised to bedevil them. The piled-up profits would not be eaten up all at once. But the tenures of "Trust Me" Grebey and "Peter the Arrogant" had set back the industry's labor relations a generation. If player gains in the 1970s had laid the basis for a possible new relationship based on labor-management equality, the events of the 1980s had shattered any hope of partnership for years to come. Don Fehr put his view of the magnates bluntly: "I don't trust anything they tell me."[83] The seeds of baseball's greatest modern crisis had been sown by the magnates and the man to whom they had subordinated themselves as their savior.

CHAPTER 8 : ARMAGEDDON

1989–2000

The Ueberroth years were an era marked by illusions of easy profits and problems deferred. A self-promoting chief executive officer had boosted baseball's earnings but had been no more able to extend them over the long haul than his predecessors had been. Once more the magnates found themselves looking for a new leader and a new approach. Led by the deceptively even-tempered Bud Selig, ownership hard-liners on the PRC stared at the hefty price tag of collusion and yearned for someone who could not only evoke but somehow re-create the golden age of paternalism. They wanted a commissioner who could wax rhapsodic about the game's traditions, conjure up images of the old-fashioned integrity of Landis, and stay out of their way as they planned a new assault on the Players Association. In short, they wanted A. Bartlett Giamatti.

Bart Giamatti came across as a Renaissance scholar in a Red Sox cap. In real life he was both a romantic regarding the on-field game and a tightfisted conservative toward its economic relationships. Selig's 1983 attempts to woo Giamatti had been foiled by the labor troubles at Yale, but after weighing a Senate candidacy or a return to teaching, Giamatti had accepted the stepping-stone of the NL presidency in 1986. He had garnered the backing of Ueberroth through loyalty and shared experience on the corporate board of Coca-Cola, and in September 1988 he received the call to become "Peter the Great's" successor. He assumed his new duties and the $650,000 salary that went with them on April 1, 1989. Not yet fifty, but looking far older because of his portly build, full beard, and dull pallor caused by chain-smoking, Giamatti gave the impression of an old favorite professor conducting a seminar. Compared to Ueberroth he was far more the charmer and far less the dictator. Jerry

Reinsdorf pointedly noted of the previous regime, "We just got tired of Peter doing everything by himself." By contrast, Giamatti promised not to apply his "best interests" powers in a fashion that would interfere with the PRC's business.[1]

Giamatti painted an initial picture of administrative continuity, but the fact remained that Ueberroth had left a host of troubles. Despite their pending collusion damages, many owners had already rushed to spend the brand-new TV bonanza on salaries before it had even been received. As Reinsdorf's partner Eddie Einhorn put it, "We spent the money before the ink was dry on the contract." Adding to the spending spree was the availability of accumulated cash from past collusion and rising franchise values. Even before the start of the 1989 season, pitchers Orel Hershiser, Roger Clemens, and Dwight Gooden and infielder Cal Ripken claimed salaries over $2.4 million, and twenty men topped the $2 million mark. Salaries of players eligible for arbitration now resumed their upward march, rising by 70 percent, and overall pay went up 13 percent (see Appendix, Fig. 3). Scrambling to redraw the line, the owners tried to maintain a $350,000 maximum for first- and second-year men, but the Players Association only became more determined to push for restoration of arbitration eligibility for two-year veterans in the upcoming negotiations.[2]

Even before he entered baseball, Bart Giamatti had weighed in on behalf of more traditional player-management relations. In a 1981 "plague-on-both-your-houses" diatribe in the *New York Times,* he had assailed the idea of wealthy ballplayers striking and accused the union of a "1930s" mind-set, drawing a sharp rebuke from Marvin Miller. As NL president, he had been a willing participant in collusion. Now, in response to the restoking of labor-cost fires, the PRC's Barry Rona was urging the magnates to push for a salary cap with a pay-for-performance (PFP) scale for pre–free agents and the scrapping of salary arbitration. Having been thwarted at collusion, the owners were falling back on the failed hard-line bargaining strategies of the early 1980s. PRC leaders Selig and Reinsdorf now urged an industry lockout in 1990 to obtain their objectives. Even before he was formally sworn in as commissioner, Giamatti personally endorsed the lockout idea. Rejecting the more conciliatory line advocated by Chub Feeney and Lou Hoynes, he lined up former academic colleague Richard Levin to develop models for the pay-scale proposal.[3]

If events had unfolded differently, it is quite possible that Bart Giamatti would have presided over his own disastrous industry shutdown four years early. But other issues came to absorb his short tenure. Besides the collusion mess, Ueberroth had swept a variety of scandals under the rug, since they ran counter to the public image of a man who had "saved baseball." Among them, the problem of illicit income and its implications for the integrity of the game had never gone away despite Landis's crackdown in the 1920s. By the late 1980s, the curbing of legitimate earnings brought on by collusion combined with the boom in baseball cards and memorabilia merchandise pushed by both Ueberroth and the players' union to create the raw materials of disaster. The years 1986–90 became the modern-day period of greatest abuse of outside income opportunities, whether from unreported souvenir earnings or massive betting on sporting events that included baseball games. Several members of the 1986 World Champion New York Mets, for example, joined retirees of the "500 homer club" at a notorious Atlantic City trade show and subsequently tried to conceal the moneys garnered. Darryl Strawberry amassed more than a half-million dollars in such under-the-table payments over a five-year period. Eventually he, Rickey Henderson, and ex-stars Duke Snider and Willie McCovey paid huge fines or served jail time for tax avoidance.[4]

The baseball personality most wholeheartedly part of the memorabilia scene, however, had also engaged in reckless betting to the point of endangering himself and the integrity of the games he managed. Pete Rose, baseball's all-time hit leader, had retired as an active player in 1986 but remained in the game as the Reds skipper. Through transactions such as selling his own record-breaking bat, he amassed nearly $350,000 in unreported income. As for his gambling proclivities, as early as 1978 general manager Dick Wagner had worried that "Charlie Hustle" would "get his legs broken" by those to whom he owed big sums. On February 20, 1989, Rose was confronted by Commissioner Ueberroth with fresh gambling rumors. But the departing leader accepted Rose's denials at face value and reassured him, "There's nothing ominous and there won't be any follow through."[5]

If his predecessor had professed a lack of concern, Giamatti saw things differently. In Landis-like fashion he retained a lawyer friend and former mob prosecutor, John Dowd, to investigate Rose. In the manner of a baseball "special prosecutor," Dowd employed a twelve-man team that produced a 228-page report with 2,000 pages of exhibits at a cost of $3 million. The investigators found that their inquiries overlapped with an FBI probe into a drug and tax-evasion network that netted Dayton bodybuilder Paul Janszen. Janszen, a Rose "gopher" for two years, had fallen out with his hero over $44,000 he claimed the star owed him for unpaid gambling debts. Another "canary," bookie Ron Peters, claimed routine losses by Rose of $2,000 to $4,000 a game on 1986–87 baseball contests. If true, the charges dictated at least a one-year suspension. Worse still, additional evidence indicated that Rose had placed bets on his own team on fifty-two separate occasions. According to baseball law and precedent, the latter offenses under Rule 21(d) called for Rose's permanent ineligibility. While amassing $0.5 million more in unpaid debts to New York note holders, Rose also had borrowed $50,000 from a member of a cocaine transportation ring. When *Sports Illustrated* broke the story in a March 21, 1989, article, Giamatti directed Dowd to interview Rose over two days at a Dayton convent and authorized letting the accused see the evidence gathered against him. The commissioner hoped that an overwhelmed Rose would quickly throw himself on the "mercy of the court." According to Dowd, his boss wanted to work with the defendant on his gambling addiction while placing him under a two- to five-year suspension, after which he would be allowed to return to the game. But Rose refused to concede guilt, and Giamatti failed to recruit any former teammates and friends willing to intercede. Nor would the Players Association, citing Rose's present status as a member of management rather than the union.[6]

Given the massive evidence and Rose's mounting legal bills and tax liabilities, Giamatti still hoped to force the accused into accepting his terms. But before he could convene a formal hearing, Giamatti foolishly signed a mid-April letter to Ron Peters's sentencing judge urging leniency because of his cooperative and "truthful" testimony to baseball. Immediately, Rose's defenders asked how the new commissioner could have defended Peters's honesty unless he had already prejudged the outcome of the pending disciplinary hearing. Armed with new legal ammunition, the Rose legal team won a temporary restraining order from a Hamilton County, Ohio, judge. The case proceeded to the Ohio Supreme Court, the U.S. District Court, and finally the U.S. Court of Appeals. While the court battles dragged on, the two sides inched toward a deal. Giamatti offered Rose a ten-year ban, then seven years, then placement on the permanent ineligibility list but with permission to seek reinstatement after just one year. At the insistence of attorney Reuven Katz, Rose also secured a written statement from the commissioner's office making no explicit claim of baseball betting in exchange for his dropping the legal challenge to Giamatti's authority. The accused then signed the deal and immediately flew to a home shopping network to hawk more baseball wares.[7]

Within twelve hours after the deal, Giamatti violated the part of the agreement drawn up to protect Rose's public reputation. When asked at an August 24 press conference whether he believed that the defendant had bet on baseball, after brief hesitation the commissioner replied in the affirmative. The following April Rose was found guilty on separate federal income-tax evasion charges stemming from personal appearance and memorabilia earnings, for which he served a five-month prison term in Marion, Indiana, and paid a $50,000 fine. Nonetheless, if the commissioner expected public vindication for his strong stance in his lifetime, it would not come. Slightly over a week after his press conference on the Rose matter, Giamatti died of a massive heart attack at his Martha's Vineyard home. The magnates' "philosopher-king" had been snatched away on the eve of their next showdown with labor, without the chance to prove his mettle. Would they be able quickly to find another man as eloquent in projecting their nostalgic image of the game or as willing to subordinate himself to their efforts at restoring a lost economic order?[8]

With a fresh showdown pending over a 1990 Basic Agreement, hard-line owners who wanted a cooperative commissioner found themselves back to square one. In the wake of the Giamatti tragedy, the man apparently best able to ensure a smooth succession was the departed's right-hand man, Francis T. "Fay" Vincent Jr. As a student at Williams College, he had suffered a crippling back injury that permanently prevented him from walking without a cane. After contemplating entering the priesthood, Vincent instead had matriculated at Yale Law School. From there he pursued careers as a corporate lawyer, a Securities and Exchange Commission officer, and head of Columbia Pictures. Nudged out of the latter position, he landed on the Coca-Cola board and renewed friendships with fellow Eli Giamatti. The duo shared a bond based on a common love of Yale, literature, and baseball, although Vincent claimed loyalty to the rival of his friend's beloved Red Sox, the Yankees.[9]

Based on a Camelot-style idealization of Giamatti's brief reign and an understandable impulse to pick the man he presumably would have recommended, the magnates superimposed the deceased's characteristics onto Vincent and proclaimed him as heir-apparent. Peter O'Malley warned against such haste, suggesting appointment only of an acting commissioner until the owners concluded a more thorough search. Jerry Reinsdorf did seek reassurances of support from the chief-in-waiting for changes in the Landis-era Major League Agreement that would enable Vincent's dismissal before the end of his term if necessary. Vincent deflected the formality by reassuring the PRC's driving force that in such a case of owner "no-confidence" he would voluntarily step aside. (He later claimed that the resignation promise had been conditional upon facing a *criminal* conviction against him.) Vincent's show of calm decisiveness in suspending and restarting the 1989 World Series after the Bay Area suffered a major earthquake then strengthened his position enormously, and he soon secured his appointment without the "acting" limitation.[10]

Upon winning the commissionership Vincent quickly began to show troubling signs of the commissioneritis hard-liners dreaded. After pledging not to undercut the PRC's bargaining stance, he pushed out Barry Rona as lead negotiator in favor of Chuck O'Connor only a month after the World Series and three months before management's February 15 "deal-or-lockout" deadline. In another gesture worrisome to PRC hawks, Vincent hired as his deputy Steven Greenberg, the forty-year-old son of Hall of Famer Hank Greenberg and both a former player agent and a friend of Don Fehr. The new commissioner also displayed disturbing attentions to association "gray eminence" Marvin Miller, inviting him to lunch and attempting to demonstrate independence and humility.[11]

Reasonableness from the commissioner was the last thing the PRC's small-market majority wanted, given the renewed acceleration of player salaries (see Appendix, Fig. 3). Top pay roared past $3 million. Even Bud Selig had anted up to keep stars Robin Yount and Paul Molitor. Nine men exceeded the new plateau, while 29 made over $2 million and 150 topped $1 million. Again management lost a majority of arbitration cases, and even the ten "defeated" men saw their pay rise an average of $0.5 million. Payroll as a percentage of revenue now reversed three years of declines and rose to 43 percent. The ripple effects were also felt in higher draft prices and minor league costs. The latter salary and development prices, $143 million in 1989, jumped to $169 million. Minor league pay climbed by over $400 a month at AAA, $140 at AA, $100 at A, and $28 in rookie circuits, respectively, to $5,424, $1,763, $1,074, and $868. Signing bonuses for amateur draftees also jumped sharply. Ben McDonald smashed the unofficial $250,000 barrier with a $1 million pact, and Toronto paid John Olerud $575,000. The rising cost of player acquisition pushed the magnates to broaden the U.S. amateur draft to include Puerto Ricans and accelerated the rush into the rest of Latin America for teenage prospects outside the draft at costs of $3,000 to $25,000 in bonuses. In order to level the playing field for the Latino talent, each organization now received twenty-four nontransferable visas for allocation throughout its system.[12]

Rising percentages of revenue eaten up by labor costs would have irritated the magnates at any time, but in 1990 they also faced the formal sentence for their shortsighted foray into collusion. Arbitrator Thomas Roberts had released his initial penalty figure of $10.5 million back in September, but the Players Association had quickly submitted additional claims of over $16.5 million. As for the Collusion II damages, the owners had submitted a cost figure of not more than $12 million, but the union had called for $60 million. In addition to that pending ruling, arbitrator Nicolau also was soon expected to render an initial verdict on the 1988 "information-bank" class of free agents now dubbed Collusion III. Anticipating a total price tag from the three years in the $100 million range, the owners had begun stashing away marketing revenue for the purpose, with each team chipping in $2.7 million the first year alone.[13]

Under the gun, the PRC now returned to a strategy of overt confrontation with the players' union to secure a "predictable," and cheaper, salary system. Changes in the panel's membership had made it an even more militant body. Although on the surface the committee possessed a balance of three small-market owners and three titans, in truth the power lay with the former. Chairing the PRC was Selig, whose mild-mannered civic-mindedness and Paul Tsongas-style liberalism on social issues masked an old-fashioned economic agenda. Joining Selig in the PRC's small-market ranks were Houston's McMullen and Minnesota's Carl Pohlad. The three "rich" PRC owners included Reinsdorf, the Cardinals' Fred Kuhlmann, and the Mets' Fred Wilpon, but Reinsdorf actually was as hawkish as Selig and his compatriots. A Brooklyn-born tax-shelter lawyer turned Chicago real estate and partnership syndicator, the White Sox owner openly believed the industry should be run "for the owners, not the players or the umpires or the fans." The self-effacing Selig and the bellicose Reinsdorf seemed an odd couple at first, but their common Jewish heritage and shared economic aims strengthened their partnership while their opposing personalities meshed. Selig believed he needed severe payroll restraint and greater revenue equalization for his club to compete, but to get these he required support from someone influential in the big-revenue group. Reinsdorf, who also owned the

NBA's Chicago Bulls, wanted the payroll predictability he associated with that industry's salary cap, and his ego relished the role of strong-arming an intramanagement alliance to a decisive victory over the Players Association. Ironically, although his vision for the baseball economy differed starkly, in his combativeness, need for respect, and religious roots Reinsdorf resembled Marvin Miller.[14]

Led by Selig and Reinsdorf, the PRC prepared for a lockout by amassing a $170 million nest egg and securing a $130 million credit line with CitiBank. Determined to maintain an uncompromising position, the panel kept new negotiator O'Connor on a short leash. After a few "getting-acquainted" sessions with the union, the spokesman presented in broad outlines in December and more detail in early January the owners' salary-cap and PFP proposals. Under the schemes, player payroll would be limited to 48 percent of the majors' ticket and broadcast revenue. Union spokesmen quickly noted that the latter basis for calculating the cap made up only 82 percent of owners' gross revenues and excluded concessions and postseason income. If the latter were included in the calculation, the magnates' dollar figure actually represented less than 40 percent of the gross. As for PFP, association counsel Gene Orza dubbed it "rotisserie baseball for lawyers." It sought to eliminate both arbitration and maximum salary cuts in favor of a scale paying younger players according to their seniority and comparative performance in one of four positional groupings: starting pitchers; relief pitchers; outfielders, first and third basemen, and designated hitters; and catchers, second basemen, and shortstops. If the plan had been in place in 1990, the union pointed out, San Francisco first baseman Will Clark, who had just garnered a three-year deal at $3.75 million total, would have been able to get only half that amount. Not surprisingly, the scheme resembled Jerry Reinsdorf's ploy toward White Sox rookies in which he had pressured them to accept a standardized pay regimen in their first four seasons, thereby forfeiting a year of arbitration, or else provoke constant pay punishment from the club until they reached eligibility.[15]

Under the guise of "flexibility" the PRC claimed a willingness to bargain the precise pay levels under PFP. But because the owners refused to budge from their overall percentage cap, any boost in young players' pay would come at the expense of senior teammates and artificially restrict bids on free agents. When the union pointed out that the plan effectively crippled members' rights to negotiate individual contracts, the PRC tried to present that as a virtue by claiming it would therefore eliminate the need of players to pay agents. When the union asked the bottom-line question regarding whether the plan would result in more or less money overall to its members, O'Connor disingenuously claimed not to know. Having advocated a plan he claimed not to know the price of while his bosses demanded financial predictability, he then issued the shutdown threat if the union did not accept PFP by February 15. "Lockouts and strikes," he injected, "are what make people serious." Behind the scenes, however, O'Connor had warned the PRC not to proceed with the action unless it was prepared to see it through past Memorial Day.[16]

The Players Association had long anticipated the lockout gambit. Still stinging from his willingness five years earlier to give modest credence to the owners' poverty pleas only to be burned by collusion, Don Fehr described his side's attitude by 1990 as being "ready to shoot them all." As its own lockout insurance, the union had stashed away $80 million in licensing revenues and had counseled individual members engaged in contract negotiations to insist on "defensive" (guaranteeing pay in the event of an owner-initiated stoppage) or "neutral" (ensuring salary no matter the stoppage's origin) clauses. Hoping to chasten the PRC through a threat of its own, the union encouraged Dick Moss and an investor group featuring Donald Trump to initiate plans for a rival circuit called the Baseball League. At the top of the association wish list — representing a personal "line in the sand" for Fehr — was restoration of salary arbitration for two-year men. Other proposals called for a boost in minimum salaries to $100,000 and increases to $125,000 over four years, the restoration of the formula fixing owners' pension contributions to one-third of All-Star and postseason TV revenue, and the return of twenty-five-man rosters. As protection against a repetition of collusion, the union also demanded specific language requiring triple damages for any future violations. Although the sides managed to keep their early talks calm, Fehr underscored, "It's not shirts and skins. No one has trouble telling one side from the other."[17]

Despite the tough talk from both camps, each had reason to worry about internal dissension. Within the player force many well-heeled veterans without guaranteed money did not relish the prospect of losing fortunes because of a protracted stoppage over their juniors' pay levels. Gene Orza captured the union's dilemma when he noted, "Samuel Gompers said that the goal of unions is to create Republicans. Well, we've created a lot of Republicans." As for management, although hard-line control of the PRC seemed solid, within the broader fraternity big-market mavens were unenthusiastic about risking regular-season revenues for radical schemes, and others, like the Orioles' Eli Jacobs, required uninterrupted cash flows to finance heavily leveraged club purchases. As before, they could be expected to seek the commissioner's ear and his intercession to end any long-term deadlock. Bart Giamatti had pledged not to intervene and undercut the PRC's line, but Fay Vincent quickly gave indications that, regarding the labor negotiations, he drew his lessons from Bowie Kuhn.[18]

Hoping naively to secure both peace and a legacy as the labor relations commissioner, with a heady rush of commissioneritis Vincent forgot who the majority of his employers were. Courted by the doves soon after the lockout began, he responded by pressing Selig for the right to host a new round of bargaining, then after it was held, he conveyed his skepticism of the PRC stance, asserting to O'Connor, "I don't think we can get a revenue participation. . . . What's our fallback?" The commissioner then performed an end run around his negotiator by holding direct conversations with Fehr. Convinced even more of the futility of the PRC's demands, Vincent pulled them off the table and substituted his own four-year plan retaining the arbitration status quo and calling for a $39 million pension contribution; minimum salaries of $75,000, $125,000, and $200,000 in a player's first three seasons; an arbitration raise cap of 75 percent; and a joint study commission on revenue sharing and salary-cap issues with recommendations due in April 1991. When Vincent defended his interference by citing the approval of political columnist and Orioles stockholder George Will, a frustrated Jerry Reinsdorf blustered, "Who the f—— is George Will?"[19]

Privately PRC members conceded that the commissioner's action had left them to "fight over nothing." Scrambling to reconcile Vincent's agenda with the shambles of their own, they cobbled together a new set of demands that included the current salary arbitration structure with prohibitions on free agent or multiyear salary comparisons, elimination of limitations on salary cuts, and inclusion of the commissioner's pay minimums for one- to three-year men. The union refused to take the package seriously, and the next day Steve Greenberg phoned Orza to scuttle it, declaring, "Yesterday never happened." The commissioner then submitted a revised version of his original offer that boosted initial minimum salaries to $85,000 and pension contributions to $179.3 million over the four years of a deal. As PRC hawks soon bitterly noted, Vincent's interventions not only failed to produce a deal but led to prolonged stalemate.

Seeing the owners' side crumbling, Don Fehr viewed the new proposals merely as starting points for even more concessions, especially on salary arbitration eligibility. As for the PRC, it became even more determined not to allow such further humiliations, and it dug in. On February 25, ten days into the lockout, the two sides recessed.[20]

When talks resumed on March 6, the union suddenly lowered its eligibility demand on arbitration to the top half of two-year men according to service time. Agent Randy Hendricks had been lobbying both Fehr and Reinsdorf to compromise on the issue rather than jeopardize the regular season over a relative pittance. But when Vincent likewise chimed in urging management acceptance of a "token" number of additional eligibles for the sake of a deal, hard-liners bucked up and refused not only any rollback on the three-year requirement but also the idea of lifting the lockout in exchange for a union promise not to strike later in the year. Instead the PRC launched another attempt to "redirect Don [Fehr]," only to be end run again when the commissioner broke a fresh promise to stay out of the talks and covertly hosted the union executive director at Vincent's Greenwich home. However, not all the chaos had erupted on the management side. By mid-March writer Peter Gammons reported that union representatives Paul Molitor and Bob Boone opposed the leadership's demands on arbitration and were polling other members as a prelude to a public challenge. In Fehr's eyes the two men were guilty of pure selfishness, since Molitor had just inked his lucrative pact and Boone had signed a deal with Kansas City worth nearly $2 million. The leader called in Marvin Miller to deliver another group "history lesson," and the executive board then voted unanimously to endorse its negotiators' stance.[21]

The two sides now stood 43 players apart on the number of annual arbitration eligibles to be permitted under a new agreement, or fewer than 2 per team. The owners tried a last-ditch gambit to test union solidarity by removing a self-imposed "muzzle" on public statements and having individual magnates dare the union to permit a secret ballot on the PRC's latest position. When it failed, both sides inched toward a final compromise. Ironically, Reinsdorf now argued for the same token number of additional filers he had rejected when Vincent had urged it—the top 12 percent (or about 10 players) of two-year men according to service time. But now the PRC could claim credit for brokering the deal. Fehr countered with a proposal for the top 20 percent (16 to 17 players) of two-year men in 1991, 25 percent (21 to 22 men) in 1992, and 35 percent

(27 to 28 men) in 1993. With Hendricks again the go-between, the union lowered its bid to a flat 20 percent in each of the deal's last three years, and the PRC raised its offer to 15 percent. Late on March 18 the sides met at 17 percent, or 15 more eligibles per year, and announced the deal at a 1:15 A.M. press conference.[22]

Besides its "17 percent solution," the four-year 1990 Basic Agreement contained the restoration of rosters to twenty-five men, plans to admit two new expansion teams, boosts in minimum salary to $100,000 with cost-of-living adjustments, raises in postseason pay guaranteeing World Series winners nearly $2 million apiece and losers $1.3 million, and increased owner pension contributions to $55 million. A joint committee would study the economic state of the industry and issue its report in 1991. Direct language declared the owners liable for triple damages if they attempted to revive collusion during the pact's lifetime. A reopener clause permitted either side to begin new talks as early as the end of 1992. Because of the disruption of spring training caused by the lockout, an abbreviated, delayed exhibition season pushed the regular campaign and the postseason back one week each. Baseball now could enjoy labor peace until 1993, but in getting it Fay Vincent already had begun to lose his commissionership. Nor did anything in the deal promise to restrain the magnates' headlong rush to spend their TV surplus on salaries. The key actors on both sides knew that their latest test of strength had produced merely a "delay of game," not a final resolution.[23]

In many ways the rest of Fay Vincent's reign resembled the lame-duck days of Bowie Kuhn. PRC hawks had expected a compliant executive; they had gotten, instead, not only a meddler but a bumbling one. Barely six months into his job, Vincent had alienated the largest owner faction, the operators of small-market organizations. If winning them back seemed unlikely, at least Vincent might have been expected to make sure he did not lose the industry's big-money men. To retain their support he needed, at minimum, to show that his leadership would not endanger their particular interests, and he failed miserably.

In fairness to Vincent, many of the circumstances that led to his demise were either the product of others' mistakes or issues that defied easy solutions. At the front of the list was the high price of collusion. In September 1990 George Nicolau determined the overdue back wages for years two and three at $38 million and $64.5 million, respectively, bringing the remedial total for the entire collusion period to $113 million before any punitive damages. Rejecting their former leader Ueberroth's self-serving advice to fight it out in federal court, the magnates opted for closure in the form of a $280 million settlement. Each team's separate price tag was a hefty $10 million, and the industry's first installment of $120 million came on January 2, 1991, with subsequent $40 million payments on July 15, September 15, November 15, 1991, and April 15, 1992. The only comfort firebrands such as Jerry Reinsdorf could draw was the possibility that the players' new bonanza might further split them by widening the income disparities within their ranks.[24]

Magnifying management discontent was the acceleration of salaries in the aftermath of the 1990 collective bargaining deal. The owners quickly demonstrated how wrong Peter Ueberroth had been in assuming that baseball's new TV contract had generated more money than even they could spend. As "middle-class" owner Bill Giles claimed, "Baseball was basically a break-even situation going into 1990, and then we got all this money." In truth, since the 1970s, baseball payroll growth had been directly linked to the level of broadcast revenue. From 1971 to 1990, player salaries had risen 1,741 percent, while national TV money had gone up 1,742 percent. With TV helping to create $1.4 billion in industry revenue in 1990, the $3 million salary barrier was shattered only seven months after it was established. Creating an ominous trend that smaller markets followed at their peril, nine of the first ten contracts over $3 million were from big-market clubs. Fueled by the free agent markup, arbitration eligibles also won their biggest pay boosts in history to date. Overall, major league pay climbed 42.5 percent in two years to $851,000 by 1991, then jumped to over $1 million the next season (see Appendix, Fig. 3). Revenue percentages going to players' pay rose to 55 percent, while club profits contracted from $214.5 million in 1989 to under $100 million in 1991. As recently as 1976, big league players had made "only" eight times as much as the average U.S. worker. By 1991 the figure was forty-seven times greater.[25]

Belatedly the owners sought savings by trimming journeymen. Paul Molitor noted the new pattern and predicted, "The superstars will always be up there, but the average contract will probably level off quite a bit." But the magnates undercut their economizing efforts by paying ever-greater sums to amateur draftees. First-round bonus prices jumped 40 percent in 1990, 44 percent in 1991, and 35 percent in 1992. Frightened by the trend being driven by clubs with deep pockets and hardball tactics from agents such as Scott Boras, in the spring of 1992 the owners copied NHL policy and allowed drafting clubs to retain exclusive signing rights to high school picks for five years. But when Boras and the Players Association challenged the legality of the rule, arbitrator Nicolau agreed and threw it out. It remained true that once an amateur had been signed, an organization could control him in the minors for three and a half years, then another three as a major league optionee to an affiliate. Those outside reserve rosters—the "Rule 5" players—could be selected by rival teams in a special draft, but they had to be kept as big league actives through the next season or be returned to their old organizations. Nonetheless, major league magnates noted bitterly that while they subsidized the minors $270 million by 1990, a figure nearly matching their collusion bills, attendance in those circuits had hit a forty-year record of nearly 27 million fans. For as little as a $5,000 entry fee, some AAA clubs now claimed values exceeding $5 million.[26]

In a rush of self-pity, the big leagues threatened to pull out their props from the minors and create cooperative player development operations in the Sun Belt, but they stopped short. They did terminate fifty-nine working agreements. Under the pressure the minors accepted a new seven-year National Agreement that forced them to assume their clubs' travel expenses and pay ticket taxes to the majors of $750,000 in 1991 and $1.5 million, $1.75 million, and $2 million minimums, respectively, in 1992, 1993, and 1994. In turn the majors agreed to cover affiliates' player and umpire salaries, meal money, and equipment and included them in a $28 million annual licensing arrangement. The National Association successfully resisted magnates' demands for a "natural emergency" clause that permitted the majors to suspend minor league contracts and schedules in the event of a future big league work stoppage.[27]

Behind much of the panic in major league circles loomed the troubling new specter of sagging television ratings, reduced advertising revenue, and lower rights fees. Without the full national TV subsidy—one of the few sources of baseball revenue shared roughly equally—the smaller-market clubs feared for their ability to remain even as modestly competitive as they had been. Under its 1990 pact CBS had committed $265 million a year. But that fall's World Series proved a ratings disaster, and the network claimed losses of $100 million. Owing to the cancellation of spring training telecasts and the late start of the regular season because of the lockout, ESPN also found its 1990 revenues slashed. Nielsen surveys of twelve- to seventeen-year-olds showed a one-quarter drop-off in baseball viewership from 1989 to 1992, while professional football rose

16 percent and pro basketball, 31 percent. In 1991 CBS announced a $169 million quarterly loss from the baseball deal. After 1992 ESPN opted not to pick up the 1994–95 seasons, preferring a $13 million contract buyout to more rights fees.[28]

The gloomy television forecasts forced owners, especially those with poor local revenue streams, to focus intensely on the gap between the haves and have-nots. If the evenly shared industry moneys from national TV leveled off or declined in relation to other sources, the small markets faced disaster. While the Yankees generated an annual $50 million from their local cable contract, four clubs—Seattle, Kansas City, St. Louis, and Milwaukee—began 1992 without firm local TV deals of any kind. By 1991 the composite revenue gap between rich and poor clubs had grown to $60 million. The majors derived $615 million, roughly half their revenue, from broadcast sources, but fully $250 million of it did not have to be shared. National League teams with games on pay TV did remit a quarter of the revenue to visiting teams, and American League teams featured a 20 percent transfer. Under Ueberroth, "superstation" clubs that broadcast games nationally on cable had been allowed to retain local-station status by paying extra fees to their colleagues; $7.5 million in 1989, $10 million by 1991, and $15 million in 1993 came from Ted Turner's WTBS alone. But such amounts were a drop in the bucket compared with the income the superstations generated. In turn, local cable money-sharing was not only grossly inadequate but flawed in execution. The Los Angeles Dodgers, a lucrative franchise possessing a huge "free-TV" local contract worth $15 million a year, still received shared revenue. As for gate revenue, its level of distribution had scarcely been altered since the late nineteenth century. The National League extended about 5 percent to visiting clubs, and the American League offered a more generous 20 percent; but income from concessions and luxury boxes remained exempt.[29]

Describing the divisions of interest within owner ranks was not always simple. Some commentators portrayed the cartel as divided into three tiers: lower class, middle class, and upper class. But although a handful of teams consistently remained at opposite ends of the scale, others slid up or down with changes in ownership or success or failure in obtaining new stadiums. It is more accurate to say that at a given moment about ten clubs enjoyed big-market status, usually from the combination of a large fan base, a commensurate local TV deal, and an owner with deep pockets, increasingly in the form of a global entertainment or merchandise conglomerate. Exclusionary forms of revenue sharing at the top rung aggravated the gap with the have-nots. The Tribune Company and its WGN broadcast superstation, owners of the Chicago Cubs, in 1991 not only contracted to carry Cubs games but also a lesser number of White Sox, Angels, and Yankees contests. By 1993 the list included Phillies, Dodgers, and Colorado Rockies tilts as well. At the other extreme, clubs unable to find an immediate revenue bonanza, extravagant buyer, or politicians willing to fund a new stadium ignored fans and slashed costs, only to worsen on-field performance and their bottom lines. For these overmatched misers, their role model for success all too often seemed to be Seattle's George Argyros. In the fashion of a true corporate raider, Argyros bought the Mariners in 1981 and ran the club into the ground only to sell it in 1989 for an inflated price of $78 million and therefore avoid any share of the pending collusion damages.[30]

Because baseball clubs were entities whose on-field labor force constituted the main entertainment product, the hard fact was that they could not easily be "downsized" or "cost-squeezed" into profitable operation like a discount merchandising chain. New owners from that different world, such as Royals and Wal-Mart executive David Glass, learned the lesson the hard way. The clubs that escaped economic disaster to prosper for at least the immediate future, such as Baltimore, Cleveland, and Texas, usually did so by securing new stadiums whose multiple attractions resembled amusement parks and similarly generated broader revenue streams. But these investments also entailed risks, even when municipalities absorbed most of the construction costs, and whenever one franchise escaped poverty through the strategy, ironically it weakened further the competitive position of those unable to follow the same path. The number and power of small marketeers in industry councils therefore threatened to decline just as those flailing at the bottom needed help most. Not surprisingly, their demands for immediate action drew ever sharper.[31]

As owner squabbling increased, Fay Vincent appeared bent on self-destructively offending every constituency. Although few magnates held George Steinbrenner in high personal regard, the commissioner's arbitrary handling of his 1990 suspension and fine for entanglements with gambler-turned-extortionist Howard Spira not only cost Vincent New York's support in subsequent battles but planted due-process concerns in other owners' minds. League presidents Bill White and Bobby Brown resented the commissioner because of his clumsy interventions in areas they deemed under their authority, such as negotiations with the umpires. In early 1991 Vincent averted a continuing strike and use of replacement umpires beyond Opening Day by interceding to produce a new four-year pact. Its price tag, however, included a salary range of $61,000 to $175,000 and an additional third week of in-season vacation in exchange for the return to merit-based postseason assignments. When the commissioner presented the plan to the league presidents for their signatures, a furious White not only refused but nearly resigned on the spot. For its part, the Players Association, while welcoming any chaos in management ranks, soon had its own reasons to distance itself from Vincent. On the issue of player drug offenses, his continuation of Giamatti's moral crackdown and Landis-like arbitrariness quickly put him at loggerheads with the union. Vincent's 1991 ban on Lenny Dykstra for gambling associations, his sixty-day suspension of Otis Nixon for cocaine use, and especially his 1992 strong-arm attempt to ban pitcher Steve Howe permanently for more drug violations led to major dustups.[32]

With all of the underlying rumblings, three interrelated and controversial economic issues — expansion (and the distribution of its benefits and burdens), franchise realignment, and authority over future collective bargaining negotiations — sealed Fay Vincent's fate. As foreshadowed in the 1990 Basic Agreement, the National League had confirmed its intent to expand by two teams in 1993, its first increase since the 1960s. A four-person committee headed by president Bill White set the entry fees at $95 million per newcomer, even though only one team in history had as yet sold for so much. With the pot set so rich, the American League then insisted on a slice of the NL expansion pie. Although the senior circuit resented the demand, it knew that AL permission would be required for assigning the new teams to geographic markets, and if the two leagues failed to cut a deal, the power both to select the host cities and to set their fees would fall to Vincent. Accordingly, the National League offered 30 percent to its rivals. But the American League, believing that the commissioner would deliver a better deal, rejected it, only to receive 22 percent, or about $3 million per club, from Vincent. At the same time, each club in the junior circuit lost three players via a draft to both the Florida and the Colorado expansion teams. With the American League two clubs larger prior to the National League's additions, the plan meant that the junior circuit was being ordered to provide over half the men for the NL's new teams. Worse still, with the American League almost certainly part or all of the next round of expansion, Vincent decreed the future 50-50 split of such fees between the leagues. To the American League's beleaguered small-market clubs—including Bud Selig's Brewers—the commissioner's edict constituted a declaration of war.[33]

Vincent might have expected his decisions on expansion to earn him stronger backing from the National League's powerful interests. But in the case of that circuit's superstation clubs, the Braves and the Cubs, the commissioner already had managed to alienate them through separate efforts at "blackmailing" them into higher fees. Vincent proposed raising their annual obligations to $20–25 million, and for leverage he lobbied Congress to repeal the compulsory license, a federal regulation permitting television stations to extend signals nationwide without permission from or payment to program copyright holders. The commissioner intended to use the threat of this costly repeal to force the superstations to accept a new industry policy blacking out such games when they conflicted with a local club's telecasts. But the superstations utilized their lobbying clout to kill the plan in Congress, a result that effectively wedded a hatred of Vincent for his failed gambit to emboldenment at his political weakness.[34]

As for the issue of collective bargaining authority, Vincent's intercession in the 1990 negotiations had revived it with a vengeance. In November 1991 the owners sent him a clear "hands-off" message by hiring a new labor negotiator—their sixth in seventeen years—Richard Ravitch. The new hired gun, a descendant of a prominent Russian Jewish family, had graduated from Columbia University and Harvard Law School. His work history included positions as a multimillionaire real estate tax lawyer, a political fixer, and even a mayoral candidate. As head of New York City's public transit system from 1979–83 he had bumped heads with powerful municipal unions and survived an eleven-day subway strike. Hired at a salary of $750,000—$150,000 more than Vincent's—Ravitch lobbied for the commissioner's ouster from labor matters from the outset. Frustrating that goal was the seven-decades-old Major League Agreement prohibition of any diminution of a commissioner's power without his consent. The magnates also lacked the statutory authority to vote Vincent out earlier than the end of 1992. When Ravitch, through Selig, tried to persuade Vincent to accept reduction of his power via a dignity-saving cover story crediting the change to his initiative, the commissioner bluntly rejected the idea as "sedition."[35]

In an effort to save his job, Vincent belatedly reassured his skeptics that he would not repeat his 1990 meddling. At the PRC's June 1992 meeting, seven of nine members wanted to initiate formal action to remove him from labor matters. The lone dissenters were the Mets' Fred Wilpon and Houston's McMullen, only recently converted to Vincent's side because of the latter's endorsement of the demand for a new stadium. After successfully deflecting an official vote, the commissioner then foolishly provoked his hosts by "spinning" the meeting's events to USA Today's Hal Bodley. Bodley's article cast Vincent as a hero who had saved his office from a coup of a small handful of owners. Given the reality of growing opposition and the unshakeable resistance of virtually all the small-market hawks, Vincent's dimming hopes of survival lay in retaining the support of enough big marketeers, particularly those in the more traditionalist National League. But by crossing the powerful Cubs over realignment in the aftermath of his expansion edict, Vincent cut his last, fraying safety rope.[36]

On its merits, even Vincent critics such as Bill White supported the idea of realigning the expanding circuits into regional divisions. Vincent proposed moving the Cubs and the Cardinals to a western division that would receive expansion Colorado, while Atlanta and Cincinnati would "migrate" eastward to join Florida. Of the four teams being asked to shift, the Braves quickly agreed, seeing profits in more eastern telecasts on its schedule. The Reds' notorious cheapskate Marge Schott also went along when shown how the change would lower her club's travel costs. The Cardinals found little to gain but hesitated to oppose the scheme by themselves. WGN's Cubs, however, adamantly resisted the proposal for having an effect on its telecasts opposite that of the Braves and creating a greater number of West Coast games that would conflict with its lucrative evening news program. When the Mets joined in to deny the necessary unanimous consent, White urged Vincent to employ a 1976 Bowie Kuhn precedent and order another vote with a relaxed, three-fourths majority requirement. Ignoring the advice, the commissioner instead unilaterally tried to impose his plan, and the Cubs took him to court to block the edict.[37]

At a September owners meeting in Chicago convened by the league presidents, the magnates voted 18-9-1 (with the eccentric Schott abstaining) to approve a no-confidence resolution authored by Jerry Reinsdorf. The Mets' Nelson Doubleday, one of the commissioner's few remaining defenders despite his team's opposition to realignment, crudely vented his ire at Bill White for cooperating with the insurgents, spitting, "I guess the Jew boys [Reinsdorf and Selig] have gotten to you." After first signaling an intent to fight on by retaining Oliver North's defense attorney Brendan Sullivan, four days later Fay Vincent resigned. At a follow-up gathering in St. Louis, the owners' victorious majority celebrated, though exactly why seemed less certain.[38] In truth, with the opportunity to reopen the 1990 labor agreement just months away, those who wanted all-out war to wrest economic power back from the players' union were now in a better position to implement their strategy without interference. But would they be able to swallow the harsh medicine they now professed a renewed willingness to prescribe?

With Fay Vincent out of the way, Selig and Reinsdorf consolidated power. As executive council chairman, Selig assumed the posture of an acting commissioner. Reinsdorf took prominent positions on both a new restructuring committee circumscribing the future role of the baseball executive and a seven-member expansion panel. With the Twins' Carl Pohlad and new Astros owner Drayton McLane, the two power brokers led a clearly hawkish majority on the PRC. In a sop to the Mets' Wilpon, Selig tabbed him to chair the restructuring panel. The shuffling demonstrated that the hard-liners would no longer tolerate the existence of an independent-minded commissioner to interfere with them, and that Ravitch would be accountable to them alone in pushing an uncompromising proposal. As Reinsdorf explained the owners' plan for victory, "You do it by taking a position and telling them we're not going to play unless we make a deal, and being prepared not to play one or two years if you have to."[39]

In trying to ensure that their colleagues would stick together behind a hard-line stance, the leaders inadvertently made it harder for Ravitch to formulate an initial bargaining proposal. At the end of 1992, they pushed through a requirement that any specific collective bargaining stance, as well as ratification of any negotiated agreement, had to receive support from three-fourths of the clubs. It fell to Ravitch to find an opening package that such an owner "super-majority" would endorse. He soon realized that the small markets would not accept any deal lacking significant revenue sharing, and the big markets would not accept that provision unless the money came from somewhere other than their profits. Clearly the redistributed dollars would have to come from reductions in the expenses of the big-market clubs — in short, their player salaries. But Ravitch also found that because of the desperate need of small-market mavens for immediate cash, his original idea to secure owner consensus on a salary-cap proposal in advance of nailing down a revenue sharing scheme appeared "dead on arrival." Instead, the revenue sharing proposal would have to be forged first. The big markets registered their discontent not only by trying to minimize the amount shared, but also by requiring their poorer brethren to spend it, rather than bank it, by insisting that a minimum amount be spent by each team for payroll.[40]

Further complicating Ravitch's goal of creating a package reconciling a salary cap and revenue sharing was the work of the Economic Study Committee appointed under the 1990 Basic Agreement. As expected, each side's appointees—former Federal Reserve chairman Paul Volcker and the Rockefeller Foundation's Peter Goldmark for the owners, and labor law professor David Feller and Brookings Institution economist Henry Aaron for the players—drew opposing conclusions. After a year and a half of squabbling over the committee's membership, the group gathered testimony and released its report a year late. Where the panelists did appear to approach consensus, their findings were neither as dire as Ravitch needed nor as sanguine as Don Fehr would have preferred. The panel, while citing the positive impact of new stadiums such as Comiskey Park and Camden Yards, issued a vague plea for greater revenue sharing and a genuine labor-management partnership to "grow" the game. What the members could not agree on was whether necessary revenue sharing dollars should come from the players. Union appointee Aaron maintained, "A governance structure of clubs that is incapable of enforcing greater revenue-sharing is *the* problem. Unless that problem is addressed and solved, labor/management peace will never come to baseball."[41]

Despite the small-market pressure for a consensus on revenue sharing first, Ravitch—sensitive to the economic power the richer clubs could wield to sustain or disrupt his collective bargaining strategy—still sought the salary cap first. Through the fall he held meetings with the owners, predicted imminent financial gloom and doom in public, and solicited owner votes for early reopening of the labor deal. Leading the minority in opposition to an early restart of talks and pursuance of a hard-line strategy were Wilpon and the Orioles' Larry Lucchino, who argued that a lockout of the 1993 season would hurt most the very teams in greatest need of revenue. Instead they counseled individual club self-restraint to force a "market correction" in salary costs. Hoping to create roadblocks for Ravitch, Wilpon even used his position on the restructuring committee to threaten the restoration of a strong commissioner, to which the negotiator replied, "Over my dead body." Late in the year

Ravitch got his desired endorsement to reopen labor negotiations early by a razor-thin 15-13 margin. Helping to put him over the top was the owners' schizophrenic behavior toward salaries, which belied the notion that owners could discipline themselves and widened the competitive gap between the haves and the have-nots. Although cuts of journeymen led overall pay to rise only 5 percent, compared with 20 percent the year before, the number of millionaires climbed to 273, the ranks of men earning $2 million went up to 189, and top annual pay ascended to the $6.5 million range (see Appendix, Fig. 3). When financial officer Jeff White reported the owners' claims of $830 million in 1993 salary obligations, Ravitch ruefully noted that the real totals from actual contracts rather than the magnates' secondhand reporting stood fully $90 million higher.[42]

Following a series of get-acquainted lunches with Don Fehr, on January 9 Ravitch called for an accelerated schedule to negotiate a deal before spring training. The Players Association added the absence of any clear, formal owners' proposal with the hasty deadline and correctly came up with "lockout." The union leadership remained unmoved, for as it saw matters, if insufficient revenue sharing was the problem, the owners had the power to solve it themselves. Fehr viewed a cap on team payrolls as a nonstarter, particularly if, as expected, the revenue percentage limit management proposed would translate into an overall pay freeze or cut. Faced with solid union opposition and not having any detailed plan for discussion, Ravitch had no choice but to lift the lockout threat. If he hoped for the association's gratitude, he was mistaken. Fehr's only response was a terse "That's constructive."[43]

Despite the pro forma counterthreat of a player walkout on Labor Day if no progress was made, the collapse of the lockout gambit ensured an uninterrupted 1993 season. Unprecedented success at the gate, bolstered by the 7.5 million new fans in Florida and Colorado, nonetheless did not mollify the magnates in light of their dwindling broadcast revenues. While overall industry receipts rose to $1.9 billion and franchise values averaged over $100 million, the new TV package appeared unlikely to generate more than 50 percent of the previous pact's bounty. Adding uncertainty to even these modest projections was the fact that the new deal was an unusual joint venture between the majors and NBC, ABC, and ESPN that carried no guaranteed amounts but pledged baseball 85 percent of the first $140 million in advertising revenue garnered, 50 percent of the next $30 million, and 80 percent of any additional dollars. With

Donald Fehr
*(*The Sporting News*)*

effective marketing, the returns to the clubs might prove better than the early, pessimistic forecasts, but the industry's track record encouraged skepticism.[44]

Worries over the TV pact only buttressed renewed demands of small-market clubs for immediate adoption of a specific revenue sharing plan. In a preliminary gesture the owners agreed to share more financial information with one another. Serving as a warning of the poorer clubs' need for cash to compete was San Diego's mid-season fire sale of three stars, slugger Gary Sheffield and pitchers Bruce Hurst and Greg Harris. Attention now focused on the upcoming August meeting in Kohler, Wisconsin, a city with a troubled labor past that had included violent New Deal–era confrontations and the longest work stoppage in American history — an action by the United Auto Workers that lasted eight and a half years. Twenty-one votes were needed to adopt a revenue sharing formula, and it looked as though the clubs might take nearly as long as the auto workers had to reach a consensus. A few nouveau riche franchises with new stadiums, led by Cleveland, found themselves in the position of compromise brokers, and they called for a $65 million transfer. A ten-team bloc of big-market clubs, however, indicated the willingness to go only as high as $43 million. Small-marketeers understandably liked the numbers in the Cleveland plan but noted that from one year to the next they could swing back and forth between being payers and recipients. Jerry Reinsdorf provided a new wrinkle, extending subsidies over a longer period and allowing more gradual transitions from each category. This, however, proved less palatable to the big markets. In a pointed attack on the White Sox and its fellow defectors, the Cubs and the Braves, the other wealthy clubs boosted their bid to $54 million, but with the additional $11 million to come only from the three "traitors."[45]

With the owners at loggerheads over revenue sharing and any salary-cap proposal contingent on its resolution, about the only decision reached at Kohler was a new pledge not to lock players out of 1994 spring training. In response the union's Don Fehr removed all remaining possibility of a 1993 late-season strike. Although both sides worked ahead on other subjects, they knew that the main showdown had merely been delayed. In December five NL small-market clubs — Montreal, Pittsburgh, San Diego, Houston, and Florida — threatened a blackout of superstation games by giving the required year's notice of intent not to sign a leaguewide renewal. Although nine AL organizations seeking similar fees concessions and the sharing of luxury-box revenues failed to notify their colleagues in time to do the same, they promised to initiate a comparable roadblock for 1995. Haves, such as the Yankees, retaliated by threatening to expand their local cable coverage nationally into their rivals' markets, as well as to reject any proposed revenue sharing deal and to create a big-market-only TV network that would keep all revenues for its members.[46]

At the end of the year the 1990 Basic Agreement formally expired. With 1994 spring training only a month and a half away, the owners scrambled to piece together a revenue sharing plan in time for a salary-cap showdown with the players. Since the magnates had come within three votes of the necessary total in August, Richard Ravitch now successfully lobbied George W. Bush of Texas and Wayne Huizenga of the Marlins to his cause, but he still needed one additional supporter. The big marketeers were nowhere near as close to forging a majority behind an alternative and could only hope to block their adversaries. In Rosemont, Illinois, the two sides finally managed to agree to make any plan contingent on the prior implementation of a salary cap but could not concur on the plan itself. A week and a half later in Ft. Lauderdale, St. Louis's Stuart Meyer provided the basis for a breakthrough with a revenue sharing scheme featuring three levels of clubs rather than two. Teams with revenues over $50 million (the Mets, Yankees, Blue Jays, Dodgers, Red Sox, Orioles, Rockies, Cardinals, Phillies, and Braves) would pay; the middle tier (San Francisco, Oakland, Florida, Texas, Detroit, Cincinnati, the Cubs, the White Sox, Houston, and Cleveland) would neither give nor receive redistributed revenue at first; and eight clubs (Milwaukee, Montreal, Seattle, San Diego, Pittsburgh, Minnesota, Kansas City, and California) would qualify for aid on a sliding scale with a maximum of about $9 million going to the poorest. Since the American League already practiced more revenue sharing, NL titans stood to take the hardest hit under the compromise. As the scheme's author, the Cardinals insisted on being permitted to adjust the specifics of the revenue sharing formula to its benefit, and the two NL expansion clubs also brokered a three-year phase-in of their participation as payers. Not to be outdone, George Steinbrenner garnered a virtual veto over the choice of the next commissioner as his price of agreement. After wrangling for more than a year, however, the owners finally had secured a revenue sharing outline.[47]

Armed with their fragile consensus, the owners now girded for war with the Players Association. They postponed the search for a new commissioner and tabbed Selig as the sole authority to whom Ravitch would report. At the same time, hard-liners tried to ensure that they would control all future decisions on lockouts, expansion, realignment, or superstation issues by reversing decisions of a decade earlier and stripping such authority from the commissioner's "best interests" powers. They also reiterated the formal requirement of a three-fourths supermajority to approve any labor deal. Reinforcing owners' determination to hang tough toward the union were the continuing, albeit moderate, increases in salaries and, more pointedly, the comparatively greater success of other professional leagues possessing salary caps. The NBA had operated a 53 percent limit with "soft-cap" loopholes for a decade, and the NHL had adopted a 61.4 percent revenue-percentage maximum. During the preceding March, the NFL also had joined the ranks with a "hard" cap at a 64 percent level. But baseball could only continue its piecemeal economies on veterans, while due to continued escalation at the top end the aggregate pay rose to 58 percent of clubs' revenues. Thirteen players garnered

$5 million or more, thirty others exceeded $4 million, and seventy-seven more drew over $3 million. By the start of the season, payrolls ranged from San Diego's $13.5 million to the Yankees' $45 million, and reflecting a comparable salary disparity between players, despite a record mean of $1.185 million the median salary fell to $0.5 million (see Appendix, Fig. 3).[48]

By the end of March, management still had not presented a detailed bargaining proposal to the union. Given the owners' determination nonetheless to impose a salary cap and the union's equal fervor to resist one, the discussions took on all the appearance of a formality to a preemptive player strike. Setting aside a third of their $100 million licensing income for a strike fund, the union claimed — and Ravitch denied — that the magnates intended to suspend their minor league obligations and hoard the savings in the event of a walkout. The owners' negotiator then offered to share club financial data with the union on condition of confidentiality, only to join Selig to exploit the association's counterpromise not to discuss the data with the press by publicly floating the claim that eighteen teams had lost money over the past two years. When the season began with still no bargaining progress, the union turned up the heat. Fehr traveled to Congress to lobby for lifting the industry's antitrust exemption, and the association announced its intention to vote on a strike date at the All-Star break. Selig retaliated in a fashion by naming ex-umpire Steve Palermo a special assistant with the task of crafting proposals to speed up the game. Ostensibly such changes were intended to enhance spectator enjoyment, but the union suspected the real purpose was to reduce offense and thereby undercut salaries. Only in mid-June, a full five months after the owners' revenue sharing breakthrough, did Ravitch finally present a formal salary-cap proposal to the union. It called for a $1 billion major league payroll minimum and a maximum limited to 50 percent of revenues, the latter including moneys the players had separately generated from licensing deals. Club payrolls would have a ceiling of 110 percent of the previous year's big league average, and none could fall below 84 percent of the same mean. Salary arbitration would be replaced by a sliding scale tied to seniority, while free agency would be broadened to include four- and five-year men. Fehr pointedly noted that under the present system his members received 58 percent of revenue over and above any licensing income. The owners' plan, in contrast, he calculated would cost his men at least $1.5 billion over the seven-year lifetime of the contract.[49]

Three weeks later, with still no progress to report, when Ravitch attempted to spin the news by labeling the fruitless discussions "useful," Fehr scornfully replied that his adversary obviously had "taken a course in how to write press releases." The two sides tried to move ahead on side issues such as a proposed joint licensing program, the amateur draft, expansion, and international play. But industry promotional advertisements for the All-Star Game slighted the union by omitting its insignia from display. At the all-star break the players tentatively adopted an August 12 strike deadline, and after the season resumed, they issued a formal counteroffer. The union's largely status-quo proposal called for restoration of salary arbitration for all two-year veterans, minimum salaries in the $175,000 to $200,000 range, higher pension benefits for pre-1970 players, and another study panel for the revenue sharing and salary-cap issues. Resigned to the likelihood of a strike, however, Astros player representative Ken Caminiti spoke for the overwhelming majority of the membership when he stated, "When Don says go, we have to go."[50]

If there were any questions about the players' solidarity, the owners helped answer them through yet another foolish provocation. As part of an effort to deny funds to the union strike pool and hoard more for themselves, the owners refused to make a scheduled $7.8 million pension contribution. Furious players called for an immediate retaliatory strike, but representatives convinced them that the owners' action had been intended "to push our hot buttons to get us to go out earlier," and cost them more in-season pay. With each side apparently needing "to feel like it's screwing the other," as one anonymous owner put it, events slid toward the inevitable. Last-ditch union calls on management to generate more and better-distributed income by committing expansion club fees to revenue sharing, encouraging more teams to pursue pay-per-view ventures, raising visiting clubs' gate shares, tying the level of such re-allocations to the fortunes of the new Baseball Network, and creating a short-term fund for stopgap bailouts of failing clubs all fell on deaf ears. The talks broke off on August 10. Two days later, the 1994 player walkout began.[51]

Having provoked the players' strike, owners quickly implemented their planned countermeasures. Even inactive players on the disabled list—not technically guilty of walking off the job—lost pay and service credit. Clubs signaled their intentions for a long, bitter siege by refusing to pay for players' travel home or to provide facilities for the men to stay in shape in hopes of an early resumption. The magnates also rejected mediation offers from Clinton administration labor secretary Robert Reich. The union likewise had prepared for a prolonged war, and since members had already received ¹¹/₁₅ of their season salaries, it now arranged for additional twice-monthly drawings from the strike fund of up to $165,000 per man, starting on September 15. Each side launched a public relations offensive. Selig published a full-page "Dear Fans" letter in *USA Today* at a $70,000 cost, and the union released a study by Roger Noll again debunking the industry's poverty claims. Besides playing defense, the union also pursued two lines of attack. Fehr pushed again for Congress to lift the antitrust exemption, and the players endorsed the formation of a rival major league for 1995 run either by themselves or by a supportive set of investors that included their former lawyer Dick Moss. To lend credence to the latter threat, Marvin Miller urged the union to seek an NLRB failure-to-bargain ruling that would void all current player contracts and free all major leaguers for possible recruitment.[52]

The economic costs of the strike itself, however, provided the biggest incentive for serious bargaining. Although Selig continued to draw his $1 million salary, the Red Sox' John Harrington estimated that if the strike killed the rest of the season, his club alone would lose $14 million. Other teams reported similar looming disasters. For their part, the players would miss three full paychecks, with top earner Bobby Bonilla sacrificing $31,000 a day. The projected average individual's season loss stood at $300,000. Barry Bonds at least received a side benefit in having his monthly child-support obligations halved to $7,500. Among the few real beneficiaries were the minors, whose attendance rose 14 percent. Women's professional ball also benefited, with a new circuit earmarked for October 15 and the Colorado Silver Bullets barnstorming squad playing a forty-four-game schedule and paying salaries of up to $20,000.[53]

To save the postseason, both sides belatedly permitted intervention by Federal Mediation and Conciliation Service chairman John Calhoun Wells. Hopes rose when, in response to the restlessness of the Mets, the Rockies, and the Orioles, Selig reluctantly agreed to appoint a new six-member owner panel to participate in the talks. Unfortunately, the majority of the initial group remained hard-liners Reinsdorf, McLane, MacPhail, and Selig's daughter Wendy Selig-Prieb. A cynical Fehr predicted that the first bargaining session including the new panel would be a "management chorus of 'Solidarity Forever' and 'We Love Dick [Ravitch].'" Selig then reconstituted a more balanced team that retained his daughter, Reinsdorf, and Harrington but substituted the Braves' Stan Kasten, the Cardinals' Stuart Meyer, and the Rockies' Jerry McMorris. The latter's presence, in particular, heartened the players, since his Nation's Way Transport trucking company claimed a history of amity with the teamsters' union. McMorris sought to break the impasse by suggesting a new formula that would replace an absolute salary cap with a tax on clubs whose spending exceeded the average, along with a guaranteed minimum payroll to prevent hoarding of revenue sharing dollars. Although Fehr worried that the tax would still exert a serious drag on salaries, he did not reject it out of hand. On September 8, in a last-ditch counteroffer, the union endorsed tiny taxes on revenues and payrolls to transfer progressive amounts of money from the top sixteen clubs to the bottom ten. Although the owners' team rejected the specifics, Harrington confessed that he liked the concept, and Ravitch found himself shunted to the sidelines. Pressured by the signs of support for McMorris's efforts, Selig grudgingly delayed a season cancellation announcement for one week. But the same obstacles he and the three-fourths supermajority requirement had posed to any compromise remained. Even though the industry faced a $200 million loss from the continuation of the strike, Selig refused to lend his presence to the moderates' efforts to cut a deal and left for Milwaukee. After presiding over a conference call on September 14, the chief magnate announced the cancellation of the rest of the 1994 schedule, the playoffs, and the World Series.[54]

With the 1994 season terminated, what had been merely projections of huge losses now became realities. Major league cities dropped an average $91,000 a game in taxes, and businesses were out $641,000 in sales. The networks lost $3 million from each canceled TV broadcast, and Major League Baseball Properties sales sank 15 percent, with projections of another 25 percent drop in 1995. Net losses totaled $364 million, and fund estimates of red ink if the strike continued until June ran to $500–600 million. Some 1,250 ballpark employees per franchise lost their jobs. Other labor economies included pay and bonus cuts and even abandoning pension obligations to front-office retirees. Ironically, one day after Selig's cancellation announcement the NHL locked out its players, leaving Americans without either major professional sport until the hockey league reached a settlement in January. Nonetheless, baseball's opposing sides continued to carry out their mutually destructive vendettas. The owners' strategy called for declaring an impasse in

November if the players did not give in, followed by a unilateral imposition of the salary-cap scheme. The players also anticipated a deadlock and planned to file NLRB charges of unfair labor practices in pursuit of a federal court ruling blocking the magnates. All the while the strike would go on, and the clubs could be expected to try to break it by hiring replacement players. As reluctant picket Lenny Dykstra put it, "I knew this would be World War III, a real bloodbath. . . . And we ain't even seen the worst of it yet. Lots of players will crack. I support our position. But I'll admit I'm afraid." Each side also launched dueling lawsuits to intimidate the other, with the union seeking owner payment of the withheld pension contribution and the owners charging unfair practices by Mets players Bonilla, John Franco, and Scott Kamienecki for threatening wavering teammates.[55]

Under public pressure the two sides agreed to the appointment of new special mediator William J. Usery, former labor secretary during the Gerald Ford administration. But as preparation for declaring an impasse and imposing their last offer, the owners withdrew their previous carrots of a $1 billion minimum payroll and a 50-50 licensing split, revived the 50-percent-of-revenues pay cap and elimination of salary arbitration, and proposed a "luxury tax" with rates over 100 percent on all team payrolls over $34 million. The plan called for a 1 percent tax on pay $0.5 million or less above the threshold, another 1 percent for each additional half-million up to $5 million, and an extra 1 percent for each quarter-million above that. Based upon 1994 payroll figures, eight teams would owe $20 million or more each, with Detroit alone obligated for $46 million. Only seven clubs—including Selig's Brewers—would avoid taxation. The Players Association also noted that buried in the "fine print" was a definition of payroll used to determine the threshold that included not just salaries but also pension and health benefits, medical expenses, workers' compensation, payroll taxes, meal and travel expenses, postseason pay, and college scholarships. That meant that a $34 million starting point for taxes actually translated into a threshold based just on salary of only $29 million. The union counterproposed a 5 percent flat tax and a disingenuous 25 percent "secondary tax" on payrolls over $64 million when no clubs had even reached that figure. After rejecting the players' bid, the owners formally declared the impasse and announced the imposition of their cap. Although Usery continued to try to broker a deal, the stalemate ultimately would be broken only by the outcome of two outside battles. One was "replacement ball," in which the clubs' results at the turnstiles and on TV would either tighten or relax the financial nooses around the strikers. The other was the legal war in the NLRB and the courts, where the union would either win or lose its effort to stop implementation of the owners' scheme.[56]

In a controversial thrust that quickly backfired, the Players Association tried to undercut replacement ball by threatening to cut off union licensing and pension benefits to any participating coaches and players. But management proved to have a bigger headache, in the person of maverick Baltimore owner Peter Angelos. The wealthy lawyer had already proven himself a worthy successor to Ed Williams's legacy by voting against Selig's September cancellation declaration. With a mountain of debt from his purchase of the club and with Cal Ripken's consecutive-games streak in jeopardy, Angelos risked $50,000-a-day fines by refusing to participate in replacement games. Supporting him were the Mets' Wilpon and the Blue Jays' Paul Beeston, with the latter pointing out that Ontario labor laws prevented him from using scabs in home games. Adding to hard-liners' headaches, Labor Department certification of the strike meant that the Immigration and Naturalization Service was now required to deny visas to potential replacements who were not U.S. citizens. Pressing ahead anyway, clubs hired substitute players to spring training contracts at $188.50 a week and promised regular-season salaries of $115,000 to $200,000. But then the umpires, whose contract had expired at the end of 1994, also threatened a walkout. Richie Phillips demanded a 60 percent pay raise for his members and their severance money boosted to $0.5 million. With the umpires unwilling to extend a no-strike pledge, owners feared that they would have to initiate another lockout and hire replacement arbiters to call games featuring replacement players.[57]

As replacement ball crumbled, the owners received portents of bad news on the legal front. NLRB regional director Daniel Silverman delivered a report supporting the union's failure-to-bargain case, and general counsel Fred Feinstein was expected to recommend board endorsement of a formal complaint seeking an injunction. The owners' negotiating committee abruptly offered to make good on the $7.8 million pension payment and even dropped the recently renewed insistence on a specific percentage cap on salaries. Now they relied instead on a 75 percent luxury tax on payrolls of $35–44 million and 100 percent on higher amounts. Viewing the new offer as merely a gambit to undermine the NLRB complaint, the union tested the owners' good faith by lifting its prior directive against members signing individual contracts while the strike continued. To the association's anger, the magnates responded by abruptly substituting their own signing freeze. When a February 6 deadline for a settlement imposed by President Bill Clinton passed, mediator Usery offered his own nonbinding proposal for a 1996 luxury tax of 25 percent on combined payrolls and benefits over $40 million, rising in two or three years to 50 percent. The plan infuriated the union, as did the suggestion that any pension "overfunding" be transferred for other purposes. The proposal's "pro-management" tilt encouraged the owners to dig in their heels, direct lobbying efforts by President Clinton failed, and the administration then turned away to launch a futile attempt to legislate binding arbitration.[58]

Spring training began with frustrated bargainers on both sides again cranking up the rhetoric. The players inched down their proposed $59 million threshold for a 25 percent payroll tax to $54 million, a figure that still affected only two teams. An angry Reinsdorf threatened to unleash his favored union-busting attorney, Robert Ballow, and compared Fehr to suicidal cult leader Jim Jones. Both sides awaited the decision of the NLRB and the courts. On March 26 the labor panel authorized a request for an injunction restoring the 1994 system. With the prospect of an injunction that would destroy their leverage for major changes in the salary structure, the owners scrambled for the best preemptive deal they thought they could get. In a take-it-or-leave-it presentation, they demanded a 50 percent payroll tax with a $44 million threshold affecting eleven teams beginning in 1996, either the retention of past free agency and arbitration or the latter's phaseout with the former's lowering to four years, and team minimum payrolls of $30 million. Fehr countered with a 25 percent tax on payrolls over $50 million for three years but insisted on no tax in a deal's last year to ensure no carryover. Because the union's offer still taxed only six teams and promised to generate under $5 million, the owners voted to open the regular season with the replacements. But on March 31, 1995, federal district judge Sonia Sotomayor of New York granted the NLRB injunction and restored the old terms of the expired Basic Agreement. The union responded by voting to end their 232-day walkout and return to work. After April Fool's Day meetings, Selig announced that his side would not pursue a player lockout but would agree to open the season with the regulars on April 26.[59]

Having restored a real season, ironically the Sotomayor ruling caused the talks to bog down again. Now holding the upper hand, the union felt little pressure to offer additional compromises. In turn, even though management's strategy had collapsed, hard-liners still had the three-fourths ratification requirement to fall back on to block any settlement they viewed as unacceptable. While the negotiations muddled on, the umpires at least secured a deal. Another management hard line was shattered by an Ontario Labor Board verdict barring use of replacements in Toronto, and on May 1 the men in blue secured a five-year pact that boosted salaries to a $75,000–225,000 range; increased severance pay to $400,000; doubled All-Star Game money to $5,000, playoff bonuses to $15,000, and World Series pay to $17,500; provided all members $20,000 more; and put off for a year an arbitration dispute over 1994 postseason pay obligations. But even with both regular players and umpires back on the field, the 1995 season played out as a depressing, uncertain interregnum. Bill Giles noted, "The irony is that players don't like the idea of a drag on salaries, but they've already put the biggest drag on salaries ever created." If that was so, it was also true that small-market owners had not only failed to improve their position through their confrontational strategy, but they had interrupted existing revenue streams and made their situations worse. Based on prestrike projections, they estimated the aggregate toll of the war at more than a billion dollars. About the only victory they could claim was the death of the proposed rival circuit. The players put their losses at over $300 million, and the median salary, which had contracted to $400,000 in strike-shortened 1994, now fell further to $325,000. Off-season contracts for 1996 rose only 3 percent, and pay for men eligible for arbitration went up by its lowest percentage since the last collusion year of 1988 (see Appendix, Fig. 3).[60]

Announcement of new five-year national TV deals with Fox and NBC for $1.7 billion and with ESPN for $400 million finally offered a ray of sunshine to management spirits. An anticipated two-team expansion of the majors also projected an extra $150 million or more each in entry fees. The formal jettisoning of Richard Ravitch and his replacement with former New York City labor relations commissioner Randy Levine also raised hopes for a bargaining breakthrough. But while the prospect of more money presumably made a deal easier for some, to others it merely raised the stakes of the war. One omen of progress in the new year was the owners' crafting of an inaugural revenue sharing plan for the coming season despite the continued absence of any accompanying payroll cap or luxury tax. Another positive development was the union's cautious approval of interleague play.[61]

By the spring of 1996, the basic outlines of a deal that would combine revenue sharing, a tax on top-end payrolls, and retention of existing arbitration and free agency appeared to be emerging. By late June the two sides had agreed to a three-year luxury tax on payrolls preceded by a two-season, 2.5 percent individual salary levy. The gap over the size of the luxury tax had been shrunk to under 10 percent (39.5 percent or 30 percent), and disagreements over payroll thresholds had similarly narrowed. What now stood in the way of a long-overdue deal were the seemingly secondary issues of back service time for the strikers and extension of the luxury tax into the last year of the contract. Press reports then hinted at a deal extending through 2000 or 2001, with 1997–99 luxury taxes of 35 percent triggered at somewhere between $51 million and $59 million in club payroll. The adversaries still could not agree on whether all clubs over the threshold, or whether the smaller of either that total or the five top spenders, would pay luxury tax. Nor had they decided whether to sacrifice striker service time for a tax-free final period of the contract. When Levine and Fehr resolved both issues in the union's favor, however, the powerful Jerry Reinsdorf sided with the stubborn remnant of small-market hawks to block the tentative deal.[62]

Bud Selig aided his friend's obstinacy by refusing to endorse the tentative pact or call for an owner vote, even though he claimed to have the necessary twenty-one votes. Negotiator Levine bluntly warned the holdouts that rejection carried with it the loss of the $6-million-apiece revenue sharing the magnates had agreed on in March, as well as any hope of interleague play in 1997, early approval of expansion, luxury-tax restraint on payroll in 1997–99, or prevention of another destructive work stoppage next year. An unchastened Reinsdorf castigated the union for demanding service time and repeated his call to pull the deal off the table and issue a new ultimatum for either a hard cap or another shutdown. An early November owner vote ordered the deal reopened to demand that all teams over the threshold pay luxury tax and scrap tax-free status in 2001. What came next represented a sudden, remarkable reversal of fortune. The man who had successfully orchestrated the blocking of the Levine-Fehr deal, Jerry Reinsdorf, now managed to revive it through a profligate and duplicitous action. After successfully convincing his poorer colleagues to kill the pact because it did not commit *enough* rich clubs to paying them taxes long enough—and thereby saving *himself* from the same tax obligations—the White Sox owner turned around and escalated his payroll by signing controversial slugger Albert Belle to a $55 million

Jerry Reinsdorf
(National Baseball Hall of Fame Library, Cooperstown, N.Y.)

five-year contract. Outraged, the betrayed owners quickly reversed their votes and resuscitated the old deal by a 24-4 margin that even included Bud Selig's Brewers.[63]

The ratified deal, a five-year pact with a one-year extension at the union's option, included interleague play for 1997 and 1998, the addi-

THE INFLATIONARY ERA

Allan H. "Bud" Selig
(National Baseball Hall of Fame Library, Cooperstown, N.Y.)

tion of two clubs in 1998 and two more in 2002, pledges of cooperation to end baseball's antitrust exemption in labor matters, minimum salary increases to $200,000 by 1999, and service time for the strikers. A 2.5 percent tax on player salaries would be deducted from union licensing income in 1996 and 1997, and a 35 percent luxury tax would be assessed on a maximum of five payrolls, with thresholds of $51 million in 1997, $55 million in 1998, and $59 million in 1999; there would be no tax in 2000–2001. Escalating revenue sharing from the richest to the poorest thirteen clubs would begin at roughly $70 million the first year.[64] After nearly three years without a contract—and more than two years since the start of the most damaging work stoppage in baseball history—the 1996 Basic Agreement had finally become reality.

After the disasters of mid-decade, the baseball industry struggled to gain momentum. Aided by the new Arizona and Tampa Bay franchises, attendance finally regained the ground lost by 1997, and the Mark McGwire–Sammy Sosa home-run race in 1998 captivated the nation. Television ratings continued their downward trajectory, however, and licensing sales in 1997 remained at nearly a third lower than their peaks. The majors' new marketing chief, Greg Murphy, saw a prospective ten-year $325 million deal with Nike torpedoed by the magnates while George Steinbrenner struck a separate $95 million bargain with Adidas. The rogue contract led to the Yankee mogul's suspension from the executive council but also to an out-of-court settlement that left his deal intact. When another Murphy deal with Pepsi collapsed, the owners forced him to resign. A trial balloon in spring 1999 to display corporate patches on player uniforms was also punctured amid a chorus of public opposition. On the TV front, ESPN took baseball to court after the industry canceled its contract in anger over the network's bumping of broadcasts in favor of NFL matches, then the two sides made up with a contract extension.[65]

Salaries, which had dropped from a prestrike average of $1.17 million to less than $900,000 per man in 1994, also regained previous levels and climbed to nearly $1.4 million in 1998, almost reached $1.6 million in 1999, and approached $2 million by Opening Day of 2000 (see Appendix, Fig. 3). Despite the advent of revenue sharing and luxury taxes, the disparity between rich and poor clubs reached new heights. The Yankee payroll topped $90 million in 1999, experts predicted a $100 million top figure by 2000, and shortstop Derek Jeter inked a seven-year, $118.5 million deal with the pinstripers. With a few embarrassing exceptions, as the big spenders made fewer mistakes in utilizing superior resources, payroll differences played out on the diamonds. In 1996 the four teams that made the league championship series represented four of baseball's top five payrolls. By 1998 all eight playoff squads claimed total salaries over $48 million. In an effort to maintain at least the symbolism of authority over their player millionaires, clubs boosted the pay of their field managers and general managers. Joe Torre of the Yankees led the former by 2000 with a $3 million salary, while John Schuerholz of Atlanta topped the latter at $1.2 million. More than ever, poorer clubs such as Pittsburgh, Detroit, Seattle, Milwaukee, Minnesota, and Montreal depended on the willingness of host cities to construct new stadiums in order to compete. Wealthy owners such as Colorado's Jerry McMorris suggested consolidation and elimination of up to four weak franchises, a move certain to anger the players' union at the loss of one hundred regular-season jobs. *Fortune* writers listed fourteen big league clubs that lost money in 1998, while industry officials put the total at twenty-two. Intending to provide fresh avenues of capital, the owners belatedly agreed to let teams publicly sell stock, a move that ran counter to decades of tradition, given that publicly traded companies required open books. And in early 2000, the clubs relinquished their separate Internet marketing rights fees to the commissioner's office to be redistributed on an equal basis.[66]

With the industry's economic realities fundamentally unchanged by the bitter strike, administrative reshuffling continued. Bud Selig officially became commissioner in July 1998 after the magnates went through the motions of a search. Former Toronto executive Paul Beeston assumed supporting duties as industry president and number-two man, and Oakland's Sandy Alderson became executive vice-president for on-field operations. In January 2000 the magnates expanded Selig's "best interests" powers to include unilateral actions to maintain competitive balance, although the reality remained that any such actions, including increased revenue sharing or a salary cap, could not be imposed on the union but would have to be bargained. The owners also voted to phase out the positions of the league presidents in a further consolidation of power in the commissioner's office. Expansion and the advent of interleague play led to the permanent shift of Selig's Brewers to the National League and to more squabbling with the Players Association over the designated hitter. Former arbiter Steve Palermo's recommendation to speed up the game by calling "high strikes" met with stubborn refusals by the umpires that underscored their perception of common economic interest with players whose pay benefited from soaring offense. Hoping to tap into the foreign fan market, in spring 1999 Baltimore played a "home-and-home" series with the Cuban national team, and San Diego and Colorado opened their regular season in Monterrey, Mexico. In 2000 the Cubs and the Mets started their campaigns with a series in Japan.

Owners and players also embraced the general idea of a Dream Team like those of the NBA and NHL, but they struggled with reconciling such Olympic participation with pennant races, required aluminum bats, and tighter international restrictions on chemical substances.[67]

Baseball's escalating costs for player procurement and training led to the greater use of Pacific Rim and especially Hispanic players, and as demand drove acquisition costs higher, it triggered renewed management calls to globalize the amateur draft. When the magnates recommended a global draft with compensation caps averaging $400,000 for each player selected in the first five rounds, however, the union and player agents countered with demands to eliminate the draft entirely. By 1997 the majors included 89 Dominicans, 35 Venezuelans, and 26 Puerto Ricans, and 31 percent of Organized Baseball's 7,000 players required visas, including 1,343 Dominicans and 487 Venezuelans. Estimates projected that the Latin American share of the industry's player population would reach 35 percent by the year 2000. As the number of foreign players soared, the portion of African Americans, the previous, domestic source of cheaper big league talent, contracted to 14 percent by Opening Day of 1998, and nearly half of those players were already thirty years of age or older. Organizations also tried to recoup escalating procurement expenses by limiting minor league costs. By 1997, first-year pros still earned $850 a month, and only $575 after deductions; men at the AAA level took home $6,000; and a fortunate few were paid double that sum. Pay for minor league umpires ranged from a meager $9,000 to $17,000 a year, prompting them to seek NLRB union certification as the Association of Minor League Umpires. A new National Agreement continued the majors' guarantees of minor league player contracts but required the minors to assume costs for umpire development and equipment. The big leagues also continued to receive revenue from taxes on tickets, but in flat levies of 3.5 percent in 1998, 4 percent in 2000, and 4.5 percent by 2002.[68]

If owners found themselves wrestling with the same dilemmas they had before the strike, not all was rosy for the players' union. The 1994 action had set back salaries, and nothing in the aftermath addressed the growing disparity in pay between members that undermined solidarity. Since the union's philosophy essentially still advocated a free market for player services, stars flourished; but the ranks of entry-level earners grew, and the player "middle-class" shrank. Escalating incidents between players and umpires also represented a threat to the union's relationship with an important ally. When Roberto Alomar spit on arbiter John Hirshbeck late in the 1996 season and the union successfully delayed a suspension into the next season, umpires threatened a postseason walkout only to be blocked by a federal injunction. Subsequent demands for a player code of conduct with sure, swift penalties only generated "summit" meetings with players' union representatives, leading the men in blue to inject their own "no tolerance" policy of immediate expulsions. Ejections rose by 11 percent in 1997, but an arbitrator then ruled that suspended players still could draw full pay during their appeals. In yet another "successful" defense of a player facing disciplinary sanctions that created public relations nightmares, after Atlanta pitcher John Rocker's printed diatribes against minorities and foreigners drew a seventy-three-day suspension and a $200,000 fine from Commissioner Selig in early 2000, the union persuaded an arbitrator to reduce the sentence to two weeks and $500.[69]

The stalwart defense by the Players Association of its members' rights to due process also continued to create moral dilemmas and public relations problems regarding substance use. When the Angels tried to suspend Tony Phillips for cocaine possession, the union retaliated with a grievance that resulted in the player's reactivation with pay. Columnist Bob Nightengale noted that according to one unnamed All-Star, one-third of big leaguers used steroids, and others relied on creatine monohydrate to build strength without sufficient knowledge of its possible relation to dehydration, reduced energy, and higher frequency of muscle injuries. Disclosure of Mark McGwire's use of another muscle-enhancing product, androstenedione, threatened to mar his seventy-home-run milestone of 1998 and led to the authorization of a Harvard study of the substance's effects and risks. As for tobacco, a 1998 spring training survey showed that fully 59 percent of players examined showed mouth lesions, and 11 percent of those were serious enough to require biopsies. Estimates placed the proportion of big league "chewers" at between one-third and two-fifths. Despite the existence of a minor league ban since 1994, however, Don Fehr opposed a similar edict on his members, citing its unenforceability and players' freedom of choice. The union did agree to cooperate in a series of antitobacco public service announcements.[70]

In the aftermath of the nearly suicidal war between management and labor in the mid-1990s, the question facing both was whether they were ready to enter a new millennium of cooperation, or if they would be dragged into it only after another round of destructive conflict. The paternalistic past could not be re-created, but continuation of the unstable status quo in labor relations risked a baseball Armageddon that could destroy the entire industry. The two sides cooperated to back the Curt Flood Act of 1998, which ended the majors' antitrust exemption in labor negotiations. But Commissioner Selig continued to beat the drums of war by threatening strict enforcement of the old "60-40" rule and praising the NBA's 1999 postlockout victory of a rookie pay scale and a $14 million individual salary cap. Another signal of strife was the appointment of yet another study commission on industry economics that included outsiders Paul Volcker, Richard Levin, George Will, and former senator George Mitchell, but *no* union representatives. The most alarming portent, however, was a 1999 showdown with major league umpires triggered by the pending expiration of the arbiters' contract, a unilateral strike-zone edict by Sandy Alderson, a three-game suspension of Tom Hallion for an on-field altercation, and the aforementioned push to eliminate the league presidencies and, in so doing, centralize umpire control. At leader Richie Phillips's urgings, and reassured by his insistence that minor league umpires would decline to become scabs, the men in blue extended "resignations" effective September 2 (since their current contract, active until the end of the year, barred striking). Baseball called their bluff, however, by refusing to allow twenty-two of them to rescind their resignations and then hiring minor league replacements. The umpires' disaster precipitated a successful ouster vote against Phillips, decertification of the old union by dissidents, and its replacement by a new World Umpires Association. Both Phillips and his twenty-two involuntary retirees were left on the outside looking in, as the major leagues and their new umpire bargaining partners attempted to reconstruct talks aimed at a new contract.[71]

As professional baseball in the United States approached the new century, what would the future hold? A few long-term trends were obvious: the industry, like others, would become still more international, with the forces of globalization buffeting its franchises and labor markets, and the likely combination of both horizontal expansion and vertical contraction would carry unprecedented challenges to management and labor alike. Fundamental choices regarding baseball's acquisition and training of its playing labor also clearly loomed. The debate over the scope of the amateur draft would result in either the creation of a globalized process or an international free market for teenage players, requiring organizations to spend even more on scouts and youth "academies" around the world. Owners desperate to hold down their costs for player development and competitive bidding for talent would vigorously resist the latter, while agents and the players' union would press for it. One possible trade-off might prove to be the establishment, as in the NBA, of a global draft encompassing foreign amateurs and professionals but featuring a reduced number of rounds, lower eligibility ages, and the opportunity for youngsters to "test" their draft prospects and then withdraw if they chose. Such changes in the draft would likely accelerate the contraction of Organized Baseball's lower levels in the United States as they had existed since the 1920s and 1930s. Whether through negotiated agreement or international trade war conquest, the U.S. majors eventually were likely to seek control of a hierarchal global network with foreign "minor" leagues stretching from Canada and the Caribbean to Japan, and these circuits, along with college baseball and collective camps in Florida and Arizona, would effectively replace most of the U.S. farms. Although some additional minor leagues might still survive, they would have to operate as independent leagues, and most of the smaller circuits would disappear entirely. In other words, like much of U.S. industry at the end of the century, baseball stood at the precipice of transplanting its lower-wage segments abroad or eliminating many of them entirely as long as the majors' talent needs continued to be met.

Driving the globalization of the baseball industry as well was the growth of international communications, entertainment, and consumer product empires, symbolized by the Dodgers' $311 million purchase by media tycoon Rupert Murdoch. Because of the looming presence of these titans, regardless of whether the industry agreed to extend or expand its forms of revenue sharing, the problem of uncompetitive franchises was likely be addressed primarily by market forces — by the movement of teams to stronger markets, their purchase by richer buyers, or both. Even so, industry inequities of economic power and on-field success would remain, as entities able to spend as much as they pleased could still refuse to do so and choose to subject their fans to mediocrity while raking in the nongate sources of profit. Given such possibilities, the players' own interests might prove best served by agreeing to a new partnership in which labor peace and a formal coequal role in industry decisions was gained in exchange for accepting reasonable leaguewide minimum and maximum payrolls, letting individual salary negotiations take place within those parameters. The desire of twenty-first-century baseball's cartel for order and uniformity in labor processes that increasingly crossed national borders also could point to the formal recognition of an expanded Players Association as the official bargaining agent for all industry performers, not just U.S. major leaguers. The major league umpires' union could similarly expand its reach to encompass arbiters throughout the cartel and develop its own revenue sharing formula for each industry level. Baseball would gain greater economic predictability; the players, umpires, and owners would claim an even more explicit commonality of interest in maintaining industry prosperity; and the two internationalized unions would be in position to be able to extend protections of worker health, safety, and economic rights downward and outward across the globe. Baseball then could truly reverse much of its reactionary history and serve as a modern model of profitable yet responsible global enterprise.

Whether such cooperation eventually comes peacefully from bold steps by visionaries on both sides, or only after an even more destructive "next war," for the industry's sake it must come. Baseball's prospects in the brave new world of global entertainment competition depend in large measure on management's willingness to recognize its on-field employees as constituencies deserving not only respect but a seat in the boardroom. In turn, those whose labor provides the on-field product must not only look to guard hard-won gains, but to exercise the responsibility that goes with them to seek out enlightened cooperation for the common good. The baseball public still awaits unambiguous evidence that the two sides have finally learned from, and by so doing have jettisoned the self-destructive hatreds of, their contentious history, and are ready to move beyond the industry's traditional self-image as America's national pastime to pursue the goal of becoming the world's sport. No greater gift could the industry give to itself—or to all of us who avidly follow its on-field heroics, whether in the United States or anywhere youngsters dream of diamond fame and fortune.

APPENDIX

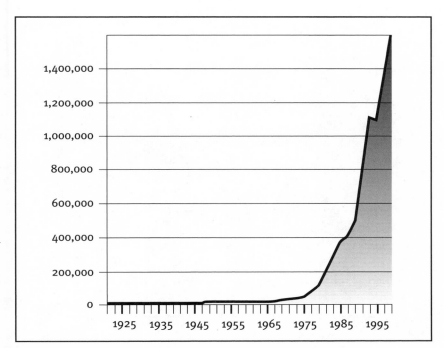

FIGURE I. Mean Major League Salary, 1921–1999, in Dollars

In the paternalistic era (1921–65), major league player salaries remained relatively flat, only to soar in the inflationary era (1966–present). Sources: House Judiciary Committee, *Study of Monopoly Power: Hearings before the Subcommittee on the Study of Monopoly Power of the Committee on the Judiciary,* serial no. 1, pt. 6, Organized Baseball, 82d Cong., 1st sess., July 30–October 24, 1951 (Washington, D.C.: Government Printing Office, 1952), 1610–11; Paul M. Gregory, *The Baseball Player: An Economic Study* (Washington, D.C.: Public Affairs Press, 1956), 95–96; Andrew Zimbalist, *Baseball and Billions: A Probing Look inside the Big Business of Our National Pastime* (New York: Basic Books, 1994), 85; and "Salaries" subject files, National Baseball Library, Cooperstown, N.Y.

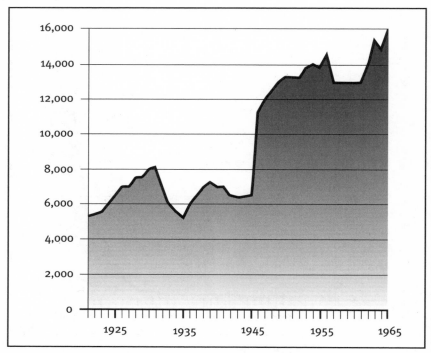

FIGURE 2. Mean Major League Salary, 1921–1965, in Dollars

In the paternalistic era, salaries rose steadily in the 1920s, only to plummet because of the Great Depression. After being frozen by wartime wage controls, pay shot up in 1946 — the year of the Mexican League raids on U.S. baseball talent, the establishment of the American Baseball Guild, and the collapse of controls — then inched upward from their new plateau over the next two decades. Sources: House Judiciary Committee, *Study of Monopoly Power: Hearings before the Subcommittee on the Study of Monopoly Power of the Committee on the Judiciary*, serial no. 1, pt. 6, Organized Baseball, 82d Cong., 1st sess., July 30–October 24, 1951 (Washington, D.C.: Government Printing Office, 1952), 1610–11; Paul M. Gregory, *The Baseball Player: An Economic Study* (Washington, D.C.: Public Affairs Press, 1956), 95–96; and "Salaries: General to 1970," Subject Files, National Baseball Library, Cooperstown, N.Y.

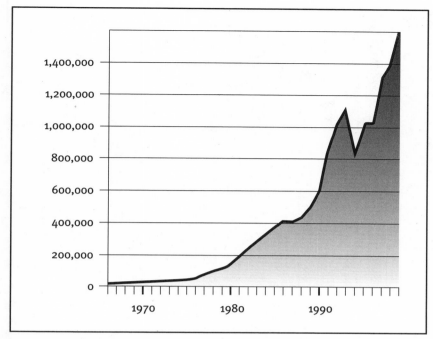

FIGURE 3. Mean Major League Salary, 1966–1999, in Dollars

In the inflationary era, player pay began to gather momentum in the late 1960s, as early Players Association negotiations brought minimum salary boosts. But the biggest jumps came from the combined effects of arbitration and free agency from 1977 on. Since then, the only brief slowdowns have been in the late 1980s, due to owner collusion against free agents, and in 1994, as a result of lost wages from that season's strike. Sources: Andrew Zimbalist, *Baseball and Billions: A Probing Look inside the Big Business of Our National Pastime* (New York: Basic Books, 1994), 85, and "Salaries" subject files, National Baseball Library, Cooperstown, N.Y.

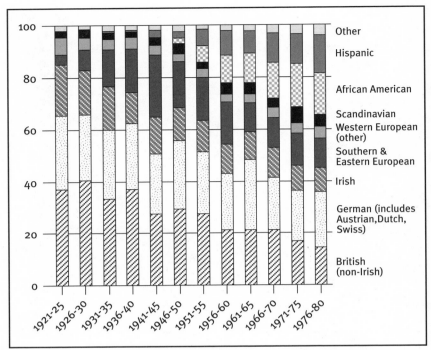

FIGURE 4. Ethnicity of Rookies (%), 1921–1980, by Five-Year Cohorts
The share of big league rookies with Western European backgrounds gradually diminished in the twentieth century, to be replaced first by Southern and Eastern European descendants in the 1930s and 1940s and then by African American and Hispanic players from the 1940s on. Today the latter two groups make up over a third of major league rookies, with the Hispanic percentage having overtaken that of African Americans. Source: Lee Allen Notebooks, National Baseball Library, Cooperstown, N.Y.

APPENDIX

NOTES

CHAPTER ONE

1. Robert L. Tiemann and Pete Palmer, "Major League Attendance," in *Total Baseball,* 3d ed., ed. John Thorn and Pete Palmer (New York: HarperCollins, 1993), 144–45; Bill Rabinowitz, "Baseball and the Great Depression," in *Baseball History,* ed. Peter Levine (Westport, Conn.: Meckler, 1989), 1:49–51.

2. Charles C. Alexander, *Our Game: An American Baseball History* (New York: Henry Holt, 1991), 137–39.

3. *Sporting News,* January 27, October 6, 27, November 10, 1921. For a general history of American labor in the 1920s, see Irving Bernstein, *The Lean Years: A History of the American Worker, 1920–1933* (Boston: Houghton Mifflin, 1960).

4. *Sporting News,* August 24, September 7, 14, 1922; Harold Seymour, *Baseball: The Golden Age* (New York: Oxford University Press, 1971), 355–56.

5. *Sporting News,* September 21, October 5, 12, 19, 26, November 2, 1922.

6. Ibid., November 2, 1922.

7. Ibid., December 21, 28, 1922, January 4, February 1, 1923.

8. Ibid., February 15, March 22, April 12, 1923; Lee Lowenfish, *The Imperfect Diamond: A History of Baseball's Labor Wars,* rev. ed (New York: Da Capo, 1991), 107–8.

9. David Q. Voigt, *American Baseball,* vol. 2, *From the Commissioners to Continental Expansion* (University Park: Pennsylvania State University Press, 1983), 222; Charles Stevens to Jim Gallagher, March 2, 1964, "Association of Professional Ball Players of America," Subject Files, National Baseball Library, Cooperstown, New York (henceforth, NBL).

10. *Sporting News,* February 5, December 24, 1925.

11. David Pietrusza, "The Continental League of 1921," *National Pastime* 13 (1993): 76–78.

12. Stephen D. Guschow, "The Exemption of Baseball from Federal Antitrust

Laws: A Legal History," *Baseball Research Journal* 23 (1994): 69–70; Seymour, *Baseball: The Golden Age,* 420.

13. For Landis's background, see David Pietrusza, *Judge and Jury: The Life and Times of Judge Kenesaw Mountain Landis* (South Bend, Ind.: Diamond, 1988), 1–172; J. G. Taylor Spink, *Judge Landis and Twenty-five Years of Baseball* (New York: Thomas Y. Crowell, 1947); Seymour, *Baseball: The Golden Age,* 367–68; and Ron Fimrite, "His Own Biggest Fan," *Sports Illustrated,* July 19, 1993, 76–80.

14. Seymour, *Baseball: The Golden Age,* 368–71.

15. Lowenfish, *Imperfect Diamond,* 113.

16. Clark Nardinelli, "Judge Kenesaw Mountain Landis and the Art of Cartel Enforcement," in Levine, *Baseball History,* 1:103–7; *Sporting News,* January 20, 1921, January 26, 1922.

17. G. Edward White, *Creating the National Pastime: Baseball Transforms Itself, 1903–1953* (Princeton, N.J.: Princeton University Press, 1996), 110–14.

18. *Sporting News,* March 31, 1921; Pietrusza, *Judge and Jury,* 173–94; Seymour, *Baseball: The Golden Age,* 324–34, 372–73; Alexander, *Our Game,* 130–34. For a detailed exposition of the "Black Sox" scandal and trials, see Eliot Asinof, *Eight Men Out: The Black Sox and the 1919 World Series* (New York: Holt, Rinehart and Winston, 1963).

19. Spink, *Judge Landis and Twenty-five Years of Baseball,* 109–11; Pietrusza, *Judge and Jury,* 241–53; Seymour, *Baseball: The Golden Age,* 375–77.

20. Alexander, *Our Game,* 133; Lowenfish, *Imperfect Diamond,* 110.

21. Nardinelli, "Judge Kenesaw Mountain Landis," 110; Spink, *Judge Landis and Twenty-five Years of Baseball,* 121–23.

22. *Sporting News,* October 9, 1924, January 15, 29, February 5, 12, 1925; Seymour, *Baseball: The Golden Age,* 378–82; Pietrusza, *Judge and Jury,* 262–83; Spink, *Judge Landis and Twenty-five Years of Baseball,* 129–45.

23. Seymour, *Baseball: The Golden Age,* 382–87, 391, 393–95; Pietrusza, *Judge and Jury,* 284–311; Spink, *Judge Landis and Twenty-five Years of Baseball,* 154–79.

24. Spink, *Judge Landis and Twenty-five Years of Baseball,* 180–84.

25. Ibid., 189–90.

26. Seymour, *Baseball: The Golden Age,* 389–91.

27. Robert W. Creamer, *Babe: The Legend Comes to Life* (New York: Simon and Schuster, 1974), 271, 281–82, 289.

28. *Sporting News,* October 27, November 10, 17, December 15, 1921, August 3, 10, 1922; Creamer, *Babe,* 236, 244–62; Edward G. Barrow with James M. Kahn, *My Fifty Years in Baseball* (New York: Coward-McCann, 1951), 135–36.

29. Creamer, *Babe,* 254, 292–93, 348–50; *Sporting News,* February 28, 1924, September 3, 1925; American League Office to Edward Barrow, May 23, 1927, in "Salaries: General to 1970," Subject Files, NBL.

30. Andrew Zimbalist, *Baseball and Billions: A Probing Look inside the Big Business of Our National Pastime* (New York: Basic Books, 1994), 11.

31. *Sporting News,* February 16, 1922; Gerald Astor, *The Baseball Hall of Fame Fiftieth Anniversary Book* (New York: Prentice-Hall, 1988), 130.

32. *Sporting News,* November 23, 1922, May 10, 1923, January 3, October 23, 1924, April 15, 1926; Seymour, *Baseball: The Golden Age,* 396; Robert Obojski, *Bush League: A History of Minor League Baseball* (New York: Macmillan, 1975), 22.

33. Spink, *Judge Landis and Twenty-five Years of Baseball,* 91–92, 97–98; White, *Creating the National Pastime,* 113–14.

34. *Sporting News,* January 4, December 13, 1923, January 24, March 6, August 7, 28, 1924, July 23, August 27, September 17, November 5, December 24, 1925, February 4, April 8, 1926, June 9, 1930; Paul M. Gregory, *The Baseball Player: An Economic Study* (Washington, D.C.: Public Affairs Press, 1956), 95; Voigt, *American Baseball,* 2:223; Seymour, *Baseball: The Golden Age,* 343, 346–47, 425.

35. American League Office to Edward Barrow, May 23, 1927, in "Salaries: General to 1970," Subject Files, NBL; *New York Times,* February 22, 1972; House Judiciary Committee, *Study of Monopoly Power: Hearings before the Subcommittee on the Study of Monopoly Power of the Committee on the Judiciary,* serial no. 1, pt. 6, Organized Baseball, 82d Cong., 1st sess., July 30–October 24, 1951 (Washington, D.C.: Government Printing Office, 1952), 1610; Creamer, *Babe,* 254, 348, 350; Paul M. Gregory, *Baseball Player,* 72.

36. House Judiciary Committee, *Organized Baseball: Report of the Subcommittee on the Study of Monopoly Power of the Committee on the Judiciary,* House Report no. 2002, 82d Cong., 1st sess. (Washington, D.C.: Government Printing Office, 1952), 109, and *Study of Monopoly Power,* 1610–12; Peter S. Craig, "Organized Baseball: An Industry Study of a $100 Million Spectator Sport" (B.A. thesis, Oberlin College, 1950), 112b; *Sporting News,* August 7, December 11, 1924, January 1, March 1, 1925.

37. *Sporting News,* January 27, February 24, March 17, 24, 31, April 7, May 5, June 9, 16, 1921; Seymour, *Baseball: The Golden Age,* 352, 391–92.

38. *Sporting News,* January 19, 26, February 16, March 9, 23, November 30, 1922, February 22, November 1, 1923, March 6, 1924; *Baseball Magazine,* January 1926, 353–54.

39. Bill Deane, "Awards and Honors," in Thorn and Palmer, *Total Baseball,* 3d ed., 278; *Sporting News,* February 16, March 16, 23, 1922, February 21, 1924; American League Office to Edward Barrow, May 23, 1927, in "Salaries: General to 1970," Subject Files, NBL.

40. *Sporting News,* October 20, 1921, October 29, 1925; Paul M. Gregory, *Baseball Player,* 109.

41. *Sporting News,* April 7, May 5, November 17, 1921; House Judiciary Committee, *Study of Monopoly Power,* 1612.

42. House Judiciary Committee, *Study of Monopoly Power,* 1366–71, 1612, 1614.

43. Lloyd Johnson and Miles Wolff, eds., *The Encyclopedia of Minor League Baseball* (Durham, N.C.: Baseball America, 1993), 89–91.

44. *Sporting News,* January 20, 1921; House Judiciary Committee, *Organized Baseball,* 60–61.

45. *Sporting News,* February 24, November 3, 17, December 15, 1921, December 21, 1922, November 1, December 27, 1923, November 20, 1924.

46. Ibid., December 22, 1921; Neil J. Sullivan, *The Minors: The Struggles and the Triumph of Baseball's Poor Relation from 1876 to the Present* (New York: St. Martin's, 1990), 80.

47. *Sporting News,* December 21, 1922, January 18, October 11, December 20, 1923, January 3, February 14, December 3, 1924.

48. Bob Hoie, "The Minor Leagues," in Thorn and Palmer, *Total Baseball,* 3d ed., 504; Seymour, *Baseball: The Golden Age,* 408–9.

49. *Sporting News,* December 22, 1921; Voigt, *American Baseball,* 2:218; Seymour, *Baseball: The Golden Age,* 353; Peter Levine, *Ellis Island to Ebbets Field: Sport and the American Jewish Experience* (New York: Oxford University Press, 1992), 109–13; Benjamin G. Rader, *Baseball: A History of America's Game* (Urbana: University of Illinois Press, 1992), 125; Lee Allen Notebooks, 1921–1929, NBL.

50. Donn Rogosin, *Invisible Men: Life in Baseball's Negro Leagues* (New York: Atheneum, 1985), 27–30, 39, 43–46, 50; Robert Peterson, *Only the Ball Was White* (Englewood Cliffs, N.J.: Prentice-Hall, 1970), 81–90, 101, 121; Richard Bak, *Turkey Stearnes and the Detroit Stars: The Negro Leagues in Detroit, 1919–1933* (Detroit: Wayne State University Press, 1994), 99–105, 182; Janet Bruce, *The Kansas City Monarchs: Champions of Black Baseball* (Lawrence: University Press of Kansas, 1985), 24–39, 57–67.

51. Richard C. Crepeau, *Baseball: America's Diamond Mind, 1919–1941* (Orlando: University Presses of Florida, 1980), 168; Bruce, *Kansas City Monarchs,* 44–45.

52. For a brief biographical sketch on Branch Rickey, see Seymour, *Baseball: The Golden Age,* 410–13. The best overall account of his life remains Murray Polner, *Branch Rickey: A Biography* (New York: Atheneum, 1982).

53. Polner, *Branch Rickey,* 78–83; Branch Rickey, "The Farm System," n.d., Branch Rickey Papers, box 13, Library of Congress, Washington, D.C. (henceforth, LC).

54. Polner, *Branch Rickey,* 83–95; Seymour, *Baseball: The Golden Age,* 413–20; *Sporting News,* January 25, 1923.

55. House Judiciary Committee, *Organized Baseball,* 64–65; Branch Rickey to Alan Rinzler, July 11, 1963, Rickey Papers, box 13, LC.

56. Spink, *Judge Landis and Twenty-five Years of Baseball,* 191–92, 195.

57. Polner, *Branch Rickey,* 110; Seymour, *Baseball: The Golden Age,* 418–20.

CHAPTER TWO

1. Harold Seymour, *Baseball: The Golden Age* (New York: Oxford University Press, 1971), 425; Charles C. Alexander, *Our Game: An American Baseball History* (New York: Henry Holt, 1991), 157–58; Dennis Bingham and Thomas R. Heitz,

"Rules and Scoring," in *Total Baseball,* 3d ed., ed. John Thorn and Pete Palmer (New York: HarperCollins, 1993), 2311.

2. House Judiciary Committee, *Organized Baseball: Report of the Subcommittee on the Study of Monopoly Power of the Committee on the Judiciary,* House Report no. 2002, 82d Cong., 1st sess. (Washington, D.C.: Government Printing Office, 1952), 75, and *Study of Monopoly Power: Hearings before the Subcommittee on the Study of Monopoly Power of the Committee on the Judiciary,* serial no. 1, pt. 6, Organized Baseball, 82d Cong., 1st sess., July 30–October 24, 1951 (Washington, D.C.: Government Printing Office, 1952), 1636; David Q. Voigt, "The History of Major League Baseball," in Thorn and Palmer, *Total Baseball,* 3d ed., 22–24; Bill Rabinowitz, "Baseball and the Great Depression," in *Baseball History,* ed. Peter Levine (Westport, Conn.: Meckler, 1989), 1:49–50; Peter S. Craig, "Organized Baseball: An Industry Study of a $100 Million Spectator Sport" (B.A. thesis, Oberlin College, 1950), 211.

3. House Judiciary Committee, *Organized Baseball,* 69; James Quirk and Rodney Fort, *Pay Dirt: The Business of Professional Team Sports* (Princeton, N.J.: Princeton University Press, 1992), 39, 56; Robert Obojski, *Bush League: A History of Minor League Baseball* (New York: Macmillan, 1975), 18; Andrew Zimbalist, *Baseball and Billions: A Probing Look inside the Big Business of Our National Pastime* (New York: Basic Books, 1994), 68.

4. Robert W. Creamer, *Babe: The Legend Comes to Life* (New York: Simon and Schuster, 1974), 350, 356, 369; Lawrence S. Ritter, *The Glory of Their Times* (New York: Vintage, 1985), 214, 273; Craig, "Organized Baseball," 115; Paul M. Gregory, *The Baseball Player: An Economic Study* (Washington, D.C.: Public Affairs Press, 1956), 72, 96; Lee Lowenfish, *The Imperfect Diamond: A History of Baseball's Labor Wars,* rev. ed. (New York: Da Capo, 1991), 120; Richard C. Crepeau, *Baseball: America's Diamond Mind, 1919–1941* (Orlando: University Presses of Florida, 1980), 177–80.

5. Paul M. Gregory, *Baseball Player,* 97–98; David Q. Voigt, *American Baseball,* vol. 2, *From the Commissioners to Continental Expansion* (University Park: Pennsylvania State University Press, 1983), 223; J. G. Taylor Spink, *Judge Landis and Twenty-five Years of Baseball* (New York: Thomas Y. Crowell, 1947), 203; House Judiciary Committee, *Study of Monopoly Power,* 1610–11; Zimbalist, *Baseball and Billions,* 87; Rabinowitz, "Baseball and the Great Depression," 53–54.

6. House Judiciary Committee, *Study of Monopoly Power,* 1371, 1374, 1610–14.

7. Alexander, *Our Game,* 165; Crepeau, *Baseball,* 182–83; Paul M. Gregory, *Baseball Player,* 17.

8. Spink, *Judge Landis and Twenty-five Years of Baseball,* 197–200; House Judiciary Committee, *Organized Baseball,* 67–68.

9. Murray Polner, *Branch Rickey: A Biography* (New York: Atheneum, 1982), 110–11; David Pietrusza, *Judge and Jury: The Life and Times of Judge Kenesaw Mountain Landis* (South Bend, Ind.: Diamond, 1998), 347–49.

10. Craig, "Organized Baseball," 155–57; Lowenfish, *Imperfect Diamond*, 118–19; Pietrusza, *Judge and Jury*, 349–51.

11. House Judiciary Committee, *Organized Baseball*, 68.

12. Ibid., 69–71.

13. *New York Times,* December 16, 1932; Spink, *Judge Landis and Twenty-five Years of Baseball,* 211.

14. Lloyd Johnson and Miles Wolff, eds., *The Encyclopedia of Minor League Baseball* (Durham, N.C.: Baseball America, 1993), 90–92.

15. Lee Allen Notebooks, 1930–1940, National Baseball Library, Cooperstown, New York (henceforth, NBL); Joseph A. Burger, "Baseball and Social Mobility for Italian-Americans in the 1930's" (unpublished paper, University of Scranton, 1987), in "Ethnic Background," Subject Files, NBL; Steven A. Riess, *City Games: The Evolution of American Urban Society and the Rise of Sports* (Urbana: University of Illinois Press, 1989), 106–7; Peter Levine, *Ellis Island to Ebbets Field: Sport and the American Jewish Experience* (New York: Oxford University Press, 1992), 119–20; Crepeau, *Baseball,* 164–67.

16. Allen Notebooks, 1930–1940, NBL; Riess, *City Games,* 88–89.

17. Robert Gregory, *Diz: The Story of Dizzy Dean and Baseball during the Great Depression* (New York: Penguin, 1992), 318.

18. Branch Rickey, "The Farm System," Branch Rickey Papers, box 13, Library of Congress, Washington, D.C. (henceforth, LC); House Judiciary Committee, *Organized Baseball,* 63–64, and *Study of Monopoly Power,* 987–1008; Frederick G. Lieb, *The St. Louis Cardinals: The Story of a Great Baseball Club* (New York: Putnam's, 1944), 84–86.

19. Polner, *Branch Rickey,* 109–10; Lowenfish, *Imperfect Diamond,* 116.

20. House Judiciary Committee, *Organized Baseball,* 72; Edward G. Barrow with James M. Kahn, *My Fifty Years in Baseball* (New York: Coward-McCann, 1951), 178–85; Frank Graham, *The New York Yankees: An Informal History* (New York: Putnam's, 1943), 187–88.

21. Voigt, *American Baseball,* 2:223; Paul M. Gregory, *Baseball Player,* 95–96; Alexander, *Our Game,* 360; 1930–31 and 1934–37 news clippings in "Salaries: General to 1970," Subject Files, NBL; *Fortune,* August 1937, 37–45, 112–16; *Literary Digest,* April 17, 1937; Craig, "Organized Baseball," 112b, 186; Rabinowitz, "Baseball and the Great Depression," 54; Robert Gregory, *Diz,* 307; Kenneth M. Jennings, *Balls and Strikes: The Money Game in Professional Baseball* (New York: Praeger, 1990), 214.

22. Bill Veeck, "The High Price of a Home Run," *Tropic,* April 2, 1972, in "Salaries, 1971–1973," Subject Files, NBL; Polner, *Branch Rickey,* 107.

23. Robert Gregory, *Diz,* 278–85, 304–12, 320, 340–42; Polner, *Branch Rickey,* 114.

24. Robert Gregory, *Diz,* 124; Paul M. Gregory, *Baseball Player,* 67–68.

25. Ritter, *Glory of Their Times,* 239; Robert Gregory, *Diz,* 362.

26. Voigt, *American Baseball,* 2:222; Paul M. Gregory, *Baseball Player,* 117.

27. Robert Gregory, *Diz,* 245–46; *Sporting News,* March 27, 1976.

28. Bill Deane, "Awards and Honors," in Thorn and Palmer, *Total Baseball,* 3d ed., 278, 288; Paul M. Gregory, *Baseball Player,* 38.

29. Larry R. Gerlach, "Umpires," in Thorn and Palmer, *Total Baseball,* 3d ed., 2245–46; Joseph Paparella interview, Albert B. Chandler Oral History Project, Special Collections, University of Kentucky Library, Lexington.

30. Craig, "Organized Baseball," 115–16; Voigt, *American Baseball,* 2:220–21.

31. Crepeau, *Baseball,* 156–57.

32. Spink, *Judge Landis and Twenty-five Years in Baseball,* 219–25; Gai Ingham Berlage, *Women in Baseball: The Forgotten History* (Westport, Conn.: Praeger, 1994), 73–77; Donn Rogosin, *Invisible Men: Life in Baseball's Negro Leagues* (New York: Atheneum, 1985), 181.

33. Bill Ballenberg, "Remembering Their Game," *Sports Illustrated,* July 6, 1992, 80–92; "Negro Leagues: Clippings, 1990–Present," Subject Files, NBL; Alexander, *Our Game,* 178–82; Jules Tygiel, "Black Ball," in Thorn and Palmer, *Total Baseball,* 3d ed., 491–92; Rogosin, *Invisible Men,* 5, 14, 77, 131; Robert Peterson, *Only the Ball Was White* (Englewood Cliffs, N.J.: Prentice-Hall, 1970), 93, 96, 101–2, 120.

34. Peterson, *Only the Ball Was White,* 95–98, 121, 152, 167; Janet Bruce, *The Kansas City Monarchs: Champions of Black Baseball* (Lawrence: University Press of Kansas, 1985), 83–90; Gerald Astor, *The Baseball Hall of Fame Fiftieth Anniversary Book* (New York: Prentice-Hall, 1988), 206–8; Jules Tygiel, *Baseball's Great Experiment: Jackie Robinson and His Legacy* (New York: Oxford University Press, 1983), 17–18.

35. Tygiel, *Baseball's Great Experiment,* 22.

36. Peterson, *Only the Ball Was White,* 132–40; Bruce, *Kansas City Monarchs,* 90–93.

37. Astor, *Baseball Hall of Fame,* 203; Peterson, *Only the Ball Was White,* 176–77; Arthur R. Ashe Jr., *A Hard Road to Glory,* vol. 1, *A History of the African-American Athlete, 1919–1945* (New York: Warner Books, 1988), 35–36; *Washington Post,* April 7, 1939.

38. Neil J. Sullivan, *The Minors: The Struggles and the Triumph of Baseball's Poor Relation from 1876 to the Present* (New York: St. Martin's, 1990), 202; Tygiel, *Baseball's Great Experiment,* 32–37; Crepeau, *Baseball,* 170–71; Rogosin, *Invisible Men,* 145.

39. Tygiel, *Baseball's Great Experiment,* 32–33.

40. Ford C. Frick, *Games, Asterisks, and People: Memoirs of a Lucky Fan* (New York: Crown, 1973), 94–95; Tygiel, *Baseball's Great Experiment,* 26–31; Rogosin, *Invisible Men,* 184, 193.

41. Tygiel, *Baseball's Great Experiment,* 33–34.

42. Frick, *Games, Asterisks, and People,* 49; Bob Feller, *Strikeout Story* (New York: A. S. Barnes, 1947), 61–67; Lowenfish, *Imperfect Diamond,* 120–22; Spink, *Judge Landis and Twenty-five Years of Baseball,* 226–32; Pietrusza, *Judge and Jury,* 352–58.

43. Obojski, *Bush League,* 23; Pietrusza, *Judge and Jury,* 359–61.

44. Spink, *Judge Landis and Twenty-five Years of Baseball,* 232–36; Polner, *Branch Rickey,* 99–100, 111–13; Sullivan, *Minors,* 111–13; Pietrusza, *Judge and Jury,* 361–62.

45. House Judiciary Committee, *Organized Baseball,* 71–74; Obojski, *Bush League,* 23; Pietrusza, *Judge and Jury,* 362–64.

46. Pietrusza, *Judge and Jury,* 364–66.

47. Spink, *Judge Landis and Twenty-five Years of Baseball,* 237–40; Pietrusza, *Judge and Jury,* 367–68.

48. Voigt, *American Baseball,* 2:147–48; Pietrusza, *Judge and Jury,* 368–70.

49. Spink, *Judge Landis and Twenty-five Years of Baseball,* 242.

50. House Judiciary Committee, *Study of Monopoly Power,* 1374, 1381, 1614, 1636; Alexander, *Our Game,* 168–69; Bill Felber, "The Changing Game," in *Total Baseball,* 1st ed., ed. John Thorn and Pete Palmer (New York: Warner Books, 1989), 261; Paul M. Gregory, *Baseball Player,* 89.

CHAPTER THREE

1. Richard Goldstein, *Spartan Seasons: How Baseball Survived the Second World War* (New York: Macmillan, 1980), 3; Richard C. Crepeau, *Baseball: America's Diamond Mind, 1919–1941* (Orlando: University Presses of Florida, 1980), 206–8; Bill Gilbert, *They Also Served: Baseball and the Home Front, 1941–1945* (New York: Crown, 1992), 20; Robert W. Creamer, *Baseball in '41* (New York: Penguin, 1991), 96, 122–36.

2. Crepeau, *Baseball,* 210–11; Creamer, *Baseball in '41,* 142; Red Smith interview, Albert B. Chandler Oral History Project, Special Collections, University of Kentucky Library, Lexington (henceforth, UKL); Franklin D. Roosevelt to Kenesaw Mountain Landis, January 15, 1942, A. B. Chandler Papers, Subject Files, box 162, Special Collections, UKL.

3. Paul M. Gregory, *The Baseball Player: An Economic Study* (Washington, D.C.: Public Affairs Press, 1956), 277–78; Crepeau, *Baseball,* 215; Gilbert, *They Also Served,* 32–33, 41–44, 57; Goldstein, *Spartan Seasons,* 10, 19–20.

4. Paul M. Gregory, *Baseball Player,* 193; Gilbert, *They Also Served,* 22, 74, 83–84; Goldstein, *Spartan Seasons,* 23–32, 155, 158.

5. Gilbert, *They Also Served,* 6, 113; Lee Allen Notebooks, 1940–1945, National Baseball Library, Cooperstown, New York (henceforth, NBL).

6. Goldstein, *Spartan Seasons,* xiii, 164–67, 197–99; Gilbert, *They Also Served,* 141; Allen Notebooks, 1940–1945, NBL.

7. Allen Notebooks, 1940–1945, NBL; Gilbert, *They Also Served,* 94, 117–18; Goldstein, *Spartan Seasons,* 187–90.

8. Gilbert, *They Also Served,* 170–74; Goldstein, *Spartan Seasons,* 200–222.

9. Paul M. Gregory, *Baseball Player,* 89, 98; House Judiciary Committee, *Study of Monopoly Power: Hearings before the Subcommittee on the Study of Monopoly Power of the Committee on the Judiciary,* serial no. 1, pt. 6, Organized Baseball, 82d Cong.,

1st sess., July 30–October 24, 1951 (Washington, D.C.: Government Printing Office, 1952), 1610–12, 1636; Simon Rottenberg, "The Baseball Player's Labor Market," *Journal of Political Economy* 64 (June 1956): 251.

10. David Halberstam, *October 1964* (New York: Villard, 1994), 19–20; Goldstein, *Spartan Seasons,* 146–51.

11. House Judiciary Committee, *Study of Monopoly Power,* 1381–85, 1610–16.

12. David Q. Voigt, *American Baseball,* vol. 2, *From the Commissioners to Continental Expansion* (University Park: Pennsylvania State University Press, 1983), 158; Gai Ingham Berlage, *Women in Baseball: The Forgotten History* (Westport, Conn.: Praeger, 1994), 133–43.

13. Gilbert, *They Also Served,* 89; Berlage, *Women in Baseball,* 143–49, 157.

14. Donn Rogosin, *Invisible Men: Life in Baseball's Negro Leagues* (New York: Atheneum, 1985), 18; Robert Peterson, *Only the Ball Was White* (Englewood Cliffs, N.J.: Prentice-Hall, 1970), 93; Arthur R. Ashe Jr., *A Hard Road to Glory,* vol. 1, *A History of the African-American Athlete, 1919–1945* (New York: Warner Books, 1988), 38–39.

15. Peterson, *Only the Ball Was White,* 97–98, 166; Monte Irvin and Effa Manley interviews, Chandler Oral History Project, UKL; Michael M. Oleksak and Mary Adams Oleksak, *Beisbol: Latin Americans and the Grand Old Game* (Grand Rapids, Mich.: Masters Press, 1991), 49; Rob Ruck, *Sandlot Seasons: Sport in Black Pittsburgh* (Urbana: University of Illinois Press, 1987), 174.

16. Rogosin, *Invisible Men,* 75; Peterson, *Only the Ball Was White,* 98, 120, 140, 153; "Negro Leagues: Newspaper Clippings, 1930–1960," Subject Files, NBL; Jules Tygiel, *Baseball's Great Experiment: Jackie Robinson and His Legacy* (New York: Oxford University Press, 1983), 20; Manley interview; Janet Bruce, *The Kansas City Monarchs: Champions of Black Baseball* (Lawrence: University Press of Kansas, 1985), 102.

17. G. Edward White, *Creating the National Pastime: Baseball Transforms Itself, 1903–1953* (Princeton, N.J.: Princeton University Press, 1996), 143–45.

18. Peterson, *Only the Ball Was White,* 122–23.

19. Rogosin, *Invisible Men,* 193; Tygiel, *Baseball's Great Experiment,* 30–31; David Pietrusza, *Judge and Jury: The Life and Times of Judge Kenesaw Mountain Landis* (South Bend, Ind.: Diamond, 1998), 405–30.

20. Accounts crediting Veeck with making some kind of offer to buy the Phillies with the intent of stocking the team with black ballplayers include Tygiel, *Baseball's Great Experiment,* 39–40; Bruce Kuklick, *To Every Thing a Season: Shibe Park and Urban Philadelphia, 1909–1976* (Princeton, N.J.: Princeton University Press, 1991), 145–46; and Bill Veeck interview, Chandler Oral History Project, UKL. In contrast, David Jordan, Larry Gerlach, and John Rossi, "A Baseball Myth Exploded," *National Pastime* 18 (1998): 3–13, asserts that no such offer was ever extended, and thus Landis and Frick did not have to block it. I suspect much of the disagreement is semantic—that Veeck made an offhand "offer" without

telling Nugent of the possibility of recruiting black players, and that Nugent did not "reject" it because the discussions never reached a formal stage. Veeck could therefore later remember making an offer, and since Nugent never followed up, he could harbor the suspicion it had been quashed at higher levels.

21. Peterson, *Only the Ball Was White*, 177–80.

22. Ibid., 184–85.

23. Tygiel, *Baseball's Great Experiment*, 42–46.

24. Albert B. Chandler interview, Chandler Oral History Project, UKL.

25. Lee Lowenfish, *The Imperfect Diamond: A History of Baseball's Labor Wars,* rev. ed. (New York: Da Capo, 1991), 125–28.

26. James B. Dworkin, *Owners versus Players: Baseball and Collective Bargaining* (Boston: Auburn House, 1981), 121–22.

27. House Judiciary Committee, *Organized Baseball: Report of the Subcommittee on the Study of Monopoly Power of the Committee on the Judiciary,* House Report no. 2002, 82d Cong., 1st sess. (Washington, D.C.: Government Printing Office, 1952), 161.

28. Gilbert, *They Also Served,* 259.

29. Goldstein, *Spartan Seasons,* 269–73.

30. Lowenfish, *Imperfect Diamond,* 129–36; Paul M. Gregory, *Baseball Player,* 163.

31. House Judiciary Committee, *Organized Baseball,* 76; Ford C. Frick, *Games, Asterisks, and People: Memoirs of a Lucky Fan* (New York: Crown, 1973), 120–22; Neil Sullivan, *The Minors: The Struggles and the Triumph of Baseball's Poor Relation from 1876 to the Present* (New York: St. Martin's, 1990), 217–19.

32. *Baseball America,* August 19–September 1, 1996; Peter S. Craig, "Organized Baseball: An Industry Study of a $100 Million Spectator Sport" (B.A. thesis, Oberlin College, 1950), 158–82; Oleksak and Oleksak, *Beisbol,* 50–51. One account of the trade war is John Phillips, *The Mexican Jumping Beans: The Story of the Baseball War of 1946* (Perry, Ga.: Capital, 1997).

33. House Judiciary Committee, *Organized Baseball,* 77–79; Stan Musial interview, Chandler Oral History Project, UKL.

34. Dworkin, *Owners versus Players,* 57–58; *New York Times,* July 27, 1946; Robert Broeg and Albert B. Chandler interviews, Chandler Oral History Project, UKL.

35. Paul M. Gregory, *Baseball Player,* 98; House Judiciary Committee, *Study of Monopoly Power,* 1610–12, 1636, and *Organized Baseball,* 109.

36. James Edward Miller, *The Baseball Business: Pursuing Pennants and Profits in Baltimore* (Chapel Hill: University of North Carolina Press, 1990), 12; House Judiciary Committee, *Organized Baseball,* 126; Red Smith, Joseph Paparella, and Albert B. Chandler interviews, Chandler Oral History Project, UKL; Larry R. Gerlach, "Umpires," in *Total Baseball,* 3d ed., ed. John Thorn and Pete Palmer (New York: HarperCollins, 1993), 2245.

37. Lowenfish, *Imperfect Diamond,* 139–41; Kenneth M. Jennings, *Balls and Strikes:*

The Money Game in Professional Baseball (New York: Praeger, 1990), 10–11; John Helyar, *Lords of the Realm: The* Real *History of Baseball* (New York: Villard, 1994), 10–11.

38. Paul M. Gregory, *Baseball Player,* 192; Dworkin, *Owners versus Players,* 18–19; Harold Seymour, "Unions Fail in Organized Baseball," *Industrial Bulletin,* April 1960, 11; Ralph Kiner interview, Chandler Oral History Project, UKL.

39. Lowenfish, *Imperfect Diamond,* 142–43.

40. Ibid., 144–46; Kiner, Musial, and Broeg interviews.

41. Craig, "Organized Baseball," 101–5; House Judiciary Committee, *Organized Baseball,* 174–75; Kiner and Al Lopez interviews, Chandler Oral History Project, UKL.

42. Lopez and Chandler interviews; Jennings, *Balls and Strikes,* 11–12.

43. Paul M. Gregory, *Baseball Player,* 192–93; House Judiciary Committee, *Organized Baseball,* 175; William O. DeWitt interview, Chandler Oral History Project, UKL.

44. Craig, "Organized Baseball," 101–2; Lowenfish, *Imperfect Diamond,* 147–50; Lopez interview.

45. *New Republic,* no. 115 (August 5, 1946): 134–36; Craig, "Organized Baseball," 103–5, 109–10; Chandler interview.

46. Paul M. Gregory, *Baseball Player,* 194; House Judiciary Committee, *Organized Baseball,* 175.

47. Craig, "Organized Baseball," 105–7.

48. Paul M. Gregory, *Baseball Player,* 196; Dworkin, *Owners versus Players,* 20–27; Craig, "Organized Baseball," 108; "Report for Submission to the National and American Leagues on 27 August 1946," Chandler Papers, Subject Files, box 162, UKL; Jennings, *Balls and Strikes,* 13.

49. *New York Times,* October 22, 1946; Paul M. Gregory, *Baseball Player,* 160–61, 198; James Quirk and Rodney Fort, *Pay Dirt: The Business of Professional Team Sports* (Princeton, N.J.: Princeton University Press, 1992), 186; Craig, "Organized Baseball," 138–42; House Judiciary Committee, *Organized Baseball,* 131–33, 164; Lowenfish, *Imperfect Diamond,* 151.

50. Broeg, DeWitt, and Marty Marion interviews, Chandler Oral History Project, UKL.

51. Craig, "Organized Baseball," 88–90; "Major League Baseball Pension Annuity and Insurance Plan, effective April 1, 1947," Chandler Papers, Subject Files, box 162, UKL.

52. Gilbert, *They Also Served,* 221; Oleksak and Oleksak, *Beisbol,* 53–54; Peterson, *Only the Ball Was White,* 186–87; Murray Polner, *Branch Rickey: A Biography* (New York: Atheneum, 1982), 144–176; Goldstein, *Spartan Seasons,* 265–67; Tygiel, *Baseball's Great Experiment,* 48–55; Frick, *Games, Asterisks, and People,* 95–96.

53. Tygiel, *Baseball's Great Experiment,* 45–48, 56–71.

54. Peterson, *Only the Ball Was White,* 188–90.

55. Tygiel, *Baseball's Great Experiment,* 76–79, 90–137, 160; Peterson, *Only the Ball Was White,* 191–97.

56. Tygiel, *Baseball's Great Experiment,* 80–85; House Judiciary Committee, *Study of Monopoly Power,* 483–84; Polner, *Branch Rickey,* 188–91; Chandler interview; "Report for Submission to the American and National Leagues on 27 August 1946," Chandler Papers, Subject Files, box 162, UKL.

57. Rogosin, *Invisible Men,* 199–201; Peterson, *Only the Ball Was White,* 198–200.

58. Oleksak and Oleksak, *Beisbol,* 54; David Faulkner, *Great Time Coming: The Life of Jackie Robinson from Baseball to Birmingham* (New York: Simon and Schuster, 1995), 152; Roger Kahn, *The Era, 1947–1957: When the Yankees, the Giants, and the Dodgers Ruled the World* (New York: Ticknor and Fields, 1993), 33–36; Tygiel, *Baseball's Great Experiment,* 164–70.

59. Faulkner, *Great Time Coming,* 153, 174.

60. Tygiel, *Baseball's Great Experiment,* 170–72.

61. Faulkner, *Great Time Coming,* 163–65; *USA Today,* February 28, 1997.

62. Peterson, *Only the Ball Was White,* 199; Kahn, *Era,* 46–50, 95–96; Tygiel, *Baseball's Great Experiment,* 193–94.

63. Frick, *Games, Asterisks, and People,* 97; Kahn, *Era,* 57–58; Tygiel, *Baseball's Great Experiment,* 187; Smith interview.

64. Kahn, *Era,* 40, 56, 60–61; Marion interview; Peterson, *Only the Ball Was White,* 200; Jennings, *Balls and Strikes,* 161–62.

65. Faulkner, *Great Time Coming,* 165–67; Chandler interview; Kahn, *Era,* 51–53.

66. Tygiel, *Baseball's Great Experiment,* 192–94, 201; Faulkner, *Great Time Coming,* 167–72.

67. Tygiel, *Baseball's Great Experiment,* 202–10; Faulkner, *Great Time Coming,* 172–77.

68. Allen Notebooks, 1945–1949, NBL; Rogosin, *Invisible Men,* 215; Quirk and Fort, *Pay Dirt,* 89–90; Peterson, *Only the Ball Was White,* 202; Tygiel, *Baseball's Great Experiment,* 211–250, 285; Faulkner, *Great Time Coming,* 182–90.

69. Kuklick, *To Every Thing a Season,* 147–48; George Weiss memorandum, ca. 1948, "Negro Leagues: Newspaper Clippings, 1930–1960," Subject Files, NBL; Kahn, *Era,* 187–90; Tygiel, *Baseball's Great Experiment,* 261; DeWitt interview; David Halberstam, *Summer of '49* (New York: William Morrow, 1989), 183–86.

70. Peterson, *Only the Ball Was White,* 201, 203; Berlage, *Women in Baseball,* 125; Bruce, *Kansas City Monarchs,* 116–19.

71. Gerald F. Vaughn, "George Hausmann Recalls the Mexican League of 1946–47," *Baseball Research Journal* 19 (1990): 59–63.

72. *Baseball America,* August 19–September 1, 1996; Dworkin, *Owners versus Players,* 58–59; Craig, "Organized Baseball," 158–60; House Judiciary Committee, *Organized Baseball,* 81–83, 115–16; Marvin Miller, *A Whole Different Ball Game: The Sport and Business of Baseball* (New York: Birch Lane Press, 1991), 176–77.

73. Goldstein, *Spartan Seasons,* 191–93; Paul M. Gregory, *Baseball Player,* 158–59; Craig, "Organized Baseball," 161–71; House Judiciary Committee, *Organized*

Baseball, 83–84, 135–37; Frederick Johnson and Danny Gardella interviews, Chandler Oral History Project, UKL.

74. Craig, "Organized Baseball," 171–77; Polner, *Branch Rickey,* 217; Lowenfish, *Imperfect Diamond,* 155, 164–67; Fred Saigh interview, Chandler Oral History Project, UKL.

75. Paul M. Gregory, *Baseball Player,* 89, 96; Craig, "Organized Baseball," 116–18; House Judiciary Committee, *Study of Monopoly Power,* 1610–14; Kahn, *Era,* 209; Lee Lowenfish, "What Were They Really Worth?," *Baseball Research Journal* 20 (1991): 81–82.

CHAPTER FOUR

1. Gai Ingham Berlage, *Women in Baseball: The Forgotten History* (Westport, Conn.: Praeger, 1994), 147–53; House Judiciary Committee, *Organized Baseball: Report of the Subcommittee on the Study of Monopoly Power of the Committee on the Judiciary,* House Report no. 2002, 82d Cong., 1st sess. (Washington, D.C.: Government Printing Office, 1952), 96, 108; Robert Obojski, *Bush League: A History of Minor League Baseball* (New York: Macmillan, 1975), 25; David Q. Voigt, "The History of Major League Baseball," in *Total Baseball,* 3d ed., ed. John Thorn and Pete Palmer (New York: HarperCollins, 1993), 29.

2. John Helyar, *Lords of the Realm: The Real History of Baseball* (New York: Villard, 1994), 62–63; House Judiciary Committee, *Study of Monopoly Power: Hearings before the Subcommittee on the Study of Monopoly Power of the Committee on the Judiciary,* serial no. 1, pt. 6, Organized Baseball, 82d Cong., 1st sess., July 30–October 24, 1951 (Washington, D.C.: Government Printing Office, 1952), 1636; Charles C. Alexander, *Our Game: An American Baseball History* (New York: Henry Holt, 1991), 221–22; Andrew Zimbalist, *Baseball and Billions: A Probing Look inside the Big Business of Our National Pastime* (New York: Basic Books, 1994), 14–16.

3. James Edward Miller, *The Baseball Business: Pursuing Pennants and Profits in Baltimore* (Chapel Hill: University of North Carolina Press, 1990), 52–54; Neil Sullivan, *The Minors: The Struggles and the Triumph of Baseball's Poor Relation from 1876 to the Present* (New York: St. Martin's, 1990), 235–39; Steven A. Riess, *City Games: The Evolution of American Urban Society and the Rise of Sports* (Urbana: University of Illinois Press, 1989), 248.

4. David Q. Voigt, *American Baseball,* vol. 3, *From Postwar Expansion to the Electronic Age* (University Park: Pennsylvania State University Press, 1983), 93; Helyar, *Lords of the Realm,* 76; Fred Saigh interview, Albert B. Chandler Oral History Project, Special Collections, University of Kentucky Library (henceforth, UKL).

5. Alexander, *Our Game,* 221; Zimbalist, *Baseball and Billions,* 57.

6. Helyar, *Lords of the Realm,* 13, 67; Voigt, *American Baseball,* 3:xix–xx, 58, 71, 88–91; James Quirk and Rodney Fort, *Pay Dirt: The Business of Professional Team Sports* (Princeton, N.J.: Princeton University Press, 1992), 39.

7. Paul M. Gregory, *The Baseball Player: An Economic Study* (Washington, D.C.: Public Affairs Press, 1956), 77, 96; House Judiciary Committee, *Organized Baseball,* 110; Ralph Andreano, *No Joy in Mudville* (Cambridge, Mass.: Schenckman, 1965), 140.

8. *New York Times,* February 2, 1950, and *Sports Illustrated,* May 16, 1960, in "Salaries: General to 1970," Subject Files, National Baseball Library, Cooperstown, New York (henceforth, NBL); *Sporting News,* March 24, 1973, in "Salaries, 1971–1973," Subject Files, NBL; *Sporting News,* May 25, 1974, July 8, 1978; *St. Louis Globe-Democrat,* August 21, 1978; and *St. Louis Post-Dispatch,* March 24, 1987, in "Salaries, 1974–1980," Subject Files, NBL; Kenneth M. Jennings, *Balls and Strikes: The Money Game in Professional Baseball* (New York: Praeger, 1990), 16.

9. Paul M. Gregory, *Baseball Player,* 109–11; Jennings, *Balls and Strikes,* 211–12.

10. Paul M. Gregory, *Baseball Player,* 111–14, 129–41; Ralph Kiner interview, Chandler Oral History Project, UKL.

11. Paul M. Gregory, *Baseball Player,* 98, 101–2, 160; House Judiciary Committee, *Organized Baseball,* 110, 118–26, and *Study of Monopoly Power,* 965, 1390.

12. James B. Dworkin, *Owners versus Players: Baseball and Collective Bargaining* (Boston: Auburn House, 1981), 60, 141; House Judiciary Committee, *Organized Baseball,* 161–70; Stephen R. Lowe, *The Kid on the Sandlot: Congress and Professional Sports, 1910–1992* (Bowling Green, Ohio: Bowling Green State University Popular Press, 1995), 19–21.

13. Ford C. Frick, *Games, Asterisks, and People: Memoirs of a Lucky Fan* (New York: Crown, 1973), 168–71; Voigt, *American Baseball,* 3:88–91; Jennings, *Balls and Strikes,* 216, 260; David Halberstam, *Summer of '49* (New York: William Morrow, 1989), 209.

14. Helyar, *Lords of the Realm,* 49–50; Voigt, *American Baseball,* 3:xxii, 59.

15. Quirk and Fort, *Pay Dirt,* 91–98; Zimbalist, *Baseball and Billions,* 35–36.

16. Paul M. Gregory, *Baseball Player,* 160–62; Dworkin, *Owners versus Players,* 62; Quirk and Fort, *Pay Dirt,* 189; Lee Lowenfish, *The Imperfect Diamond: A History of Baseball's Labor Wars,* rev. ed. (New York: Da Capo, 1991), 174, 186.

17. Lowe, *Kid on the Sandlot,* 23–29, 30–36.

18. Saigh interview; Paul M. Gregory, *Baseball Player,* 196.

19. Paul M. Gregory, *Baseball Player,* 67–68.

20. Charles W. Bevis, "A Home Run by Any Measure: The Baseball Players' Pension Plan," *Baseball Research Journal* 21 (1992): 65–67; Lowenfish, *Imperfect Diamond,* 183.

21. Paul M. Gregory, *Baseball Player,* 118–20.

22. W. Graham Claytor to Albert B. Chandler, September 19, 1950, A. B. Chandler Papers, Subject Files, box 162, UKL; Marty Marion interview, Chandler Oral History Project, UKL.

23. James Edward Miller, *Baseball Business,* 13.

24. Jennings, *Balls and Strikes,* 14; Paul M. Gregory, *Baseball Player,* 199–200.

25. Paul M. Gregory, *Baseball Player,* 201; Lowenfish, *Imperfect Diamond,* 185–88.
26. Paul M. Gregory, *Baseball Player,* 202–6; *Sporting News,* February 9, 1974, in "Unionism," Subject Files, NBL.
27. Jennings, *Balls and Strikes,* 14–15.
28. Lowenfish, *Imperfect Diamond,* 188–89.
29. Jennings, *Balls and Strikes,* 15–16.
30. Lowe, *Kid on the Sandlot,* 31–35; *Sporting News,* October 2, 1956, in "Unionism," Subject Files, NBL.
31. Jennings, *Balls and Strikes,* 16–17; Harold Seymour, "Unions Fail in Organized Baseball," *Industrial Bulletin,* April 1960, 8–14; Lowenfish, *Imperfect Diamond,* 190–91.
32. Bevis, "Home Run by Any Measure," 68; Curt Flood with Richard Carter, *The Way It Is* (New York: Trident, 1971), 115.
33. Paul M. Gregory, *Baseball Player,* 116–18; Charles Stevens to Jim Gallagher, January 29, March 2, 1964, in "Association of Professional Ball Players of America," Subject Files, NBL.
34. Quirk and Fort, *Pay Dirt,* 193; Zimbalist, *Baseball and Billions,* 17.
35. House Judiciary Committee, *Organized Baseball,* 109; Zimbalist, *Baseball and Billions,* 109–10; Gerald W. Scully, *The Business of Major League Baseball* (Chicago: University of Chicago Press, 1989), 48; James G. Scoville, "Labor Relations in Sports," in *Government and the Sports Business,* ed. Roger G. Noll (Washington, D.C.: Brookings Institution, 1974), 186.
36. Sullivan, *Minors,* 217–22; Paul M. Gregory, *Baseball Player,* 176–78; House Judiciary Committee, *Organized Baseball,* 143–45.
37. House Judiciary Committee, *Organized Baseball,* 146.
38. Sullivan, *Minors,* 227; James Edward Miller, *Baseball Business,* 53, 55.
39. Paul M. Gregory, *Baseball Player,* 163–64; Voigt, *American Baseball,* 3:55.
40. *New York Times,* February 2, 1950, and *Sporting News,* February 3, 1968, in "Salaries: General to 1970," Subject Files, NBL; Lance E. Davis, "Self-Regulation in Baseball, 1909–71," in Noll, *Government and the Sports Business,* 366; *Baseball America,* April 3–16, 1995; David Halberstam, *October 1964* (New York: Villard, 1994), 124, 220.
41. Sullivan, *Minors,* 254–55.
42. Obojski, *Bush League,* 29–31; James Edward Miller, *Baseball Business,* 55, 93, 103–4.
43. Davis, "Self Regulation in Baseball," 367; James Edward Miller, *Baseball Business,* 56–57, 104–6.
44. James Edward Miller, *Baseball Business,* 107–8.
45. Obojski, *Bush League,* 53–54; James Edward Miller, *Baseball Business,* 94.
46. Alexander, *Our Game,* 256; Davis, "Self-Regulation in Baseball," 367.
47. Lee Allen Notebooks, 1950–1965, NBL; "Cubans in Major Leagues" and "Negroes in Major League Baseball," in "Ethnic Background," Subject Files, NBL;

Milton Jamail, "Baseball's Latin Market," and Peter C. Bjarkman, "Hispanic Baseball Statistical Record," *National Pastime* 12 (1992): 84, 87; Aaron Rosenblatt, "Negroes in Baseball: The Failure of Success," *Transaction* 4 (September 1967): 52.

48. Jules Tygiel, *Baseball's Great Experiment: Jackie Robinson and His Legacy* (New York: Oxford University Press, 1983), 258–59, 285–95, 328; Halberstam, *Summer of '49,* 184–86; James Edward Miller, *Baseball Business,* 39–40, 66–67; Robert Peterson, *Only the Ball Was White* (Englewood Cliffs, N.J.: Prentice-Hall, 1970), 203.

49. Voigt, *American Baseball,* 3:53; Alexander, *Our Game,* 233; Tygiel, *Baseball's Great Experiment,* 296–97; Halberstam, *Summer of '49,* 183, 260, and *October 1964,* 55.

50. Michael M. Oleksak and Mary Adams Oleksak, *Beisbol: Latin Americans and the Grand Old Game* (Grand Rapids, Mich.: Masters Press, 1991), 45, 72–90; Rob Ruck, *Sandlot Seasons: Sport in Black Pittsburgh* (Urbana: University of Illinois Press, 1987), 188.

51. Halberstam, *October 1964,* 25, 53; David Faulkner, *Great Time Coming: The Life of Jackie Robinson from Baseball to Birmingham* (New York: Simon and Schuster, 1995), 216; Rob Ruck, *The Tropic of Baseball: Baseball in the Dominican Republic* (Westport, Conn.: Meckler, 1991), 68, 76; Roger Kahn, *The Era, 1947–1957: When the Yankees, the Giants, and the Dodgers Ruled the World* (New York: Ticknor and Fields, 1993), 327.

52. Faulkner, *Great Time Coming,* 234–35; Don Newcombe interview, Chandler Oral History Project, UKL; Tygiel, *Baseball's Great Experiment,* 316–18.

53. Tygiel, *Baseball's Great Experiment,* 319; Halberstam, *October 1964,* 59–60; Hank Aaron with Lonnie Wheeler, *I Had a Hammer: The Hank Aaron Story* (New York: HarperCollins, 1991), 123, 133–34, 146–47, 211–13, 230.

54. Lloyd Johnson and Miles Wolff, eds., *The Encyclopedia of Minor League Baseball* (Durham, N.C.: Baseball America, 1993), 93–96.

55. Tygiel, *Baseball's Great Experiment,* 270–83; Kahn, *Era,* 212; Aaron, *I Had a Hammer,* 70, 209–10; Halberstam, *October 1964,* 201.

56. Tygiel, *Baseball's Great Experiment,* 284; Aaron, *I Had a Hammer,* 71–79, 86–87.

57. Buzzy Bavasi with John Strege, *Off the Record* (Chicago: Contemporary Books, 1987), 69; Tygiel, *Baseball's Great Experiment,* 301; Aaron, *I Had a Hammer,* 52; Arthur R. Ashe Jr., *A Hard Road to Glory,* vol. 2, *A History of the African-American Athlete since 1946* (New York: Warner Books, 1988), 17.

58. Tygiel, *Baseball's Great Experiment,* 326; James Gwartney and Charles Haworth, "Employer Costs and Discrimination: The Case of Baseball," *Journal of Political Economy* 82 (1974): 874, 880; Aaron, *I Had a Hammer,* 204–5; Paul M. Gregory, *Baseball Player,* 39–40; *Sporting News,* June 24, 1996.

59. Faulkner, *Great Time Coming,* 231; Tygiel, *Baseball's Great Experiment,* 306–7; Scully, *Business of Major League Baseball,* 176–77; Halberstam, *October 1964,* 144.

60. Aaron, *I Had a Hammer,* 61; Halberstam, *October 1964,* 207; Flood, *Way It Is,* 80–85; Ruck, *Tropic of Baseball,* 83.

61. Allen Notebooks, 1950–1965, NBL; *Sporting News,* March 28, 1964.

62. Riess, *City Games,* 88–90; Allen Notebooks, 1950–1965, NBL.

63. Quirk and Fort, *Pay Dirt,* 220; James Edward Miller, *Baseball Business,* 78–84; Helyar, *Lords of the Realm,* 59–60, 68; Zimbalist, *Baseball and Billions,* 49.

64. James Edward Miller, *Baseball Business,* 91–92; Quirk and Fort, *Pay Dirt,* 157; Scully, *Business of Major League Baseball,* 54–55; Helyar, *Lords of the Realm,* 64–65.

65. James Edward Miller, *Baseball Business,* 132–35; Helyar, *Lords of the Realm,* 66–67.

66. Joseph Paparella interview, Chandler Oral History Project, UKL.

67. August J. Donatelli interview, Chandler Oral History Project, UKL; Larry R. Gerlach, "Augie Donatelli: Umpire and Union Organizer," in *Baseball History,* ed. Peter Levine (Westport, Conn.: Meckler, 1989), 1:1–11.

68. Donatelli interview.

69. Helyar, *Lords of the Realm,* 77.

CHAPTER FIVE

1. John Helyar, *Lords of the Realm: The* Real *History of Baseball* (New York: Villard, 1994), 16–18; Charles P. Korr, "Marvin Miller and the New Unionism in Baseball," in *The Business of Professional Sports,* ed. Paul D. Staudohar and James A. Mangan (Urbana: University of Illinois Press, 1991), 117, 119–21.

2. Marvin Miller, *A Whole Different Ball Game: The Sport and Business of Baseball* (New York: Birch Lane Press, 1991), 3–10; Korr, "Marvin Miller," 115–18; James B. Dworkin, *Owners versus Players: Baseball and Collective Bargaining* (Boston: Auburn House, 1981), 29–31; Lee Lowenfish, *The Imperfect Diamond: A History of Baseball's Labor Wars,* rev. ed. (New York: Da Capo, 1991), 195–96; Andrew Zimbalist, *Baseball and Billions: A Probing Look inside the Big Business of Our National Pastime* (New York: Basic Books, 1994), 75.

3. Marvin Miller, *Whole Different Ball Game,* 12–15.

4. Ibid., 19–32.

5. Helyar, *Lords of the Realm,* 19–21.

6. Ibid., 22; Marvin Miller, *Whole Different Ball Game,* 7, 9–10.

7. Korr, "Marvin Miller," 118–19; James Edward Miller, *The Baseball Business: Pursuing Pennants and Profits in Baltimore* (Chapel Hill: University of North Carolina Press, 1990), 142.

8. Marvin Miller, *Whole Different Ball Game,* 34–35, 47–48; Neil J. Sullivan, *The Dodgers Move West* (New York: Oxford University Press, 1987), 202; *Tampa Tribune,* April 1, 1966, in "Salaries: General to 1970," Subject Files, National Baseball Library, Cooperstown, New York (henceforth, NBL); Kenneth M. Jennings, *Balls and Strikes: The Money Game in Professional Baseball* (New York: Praeger, 1990), 20–21.

9. Marvin Miller, *Whole Different Ball Game,* 38–46, 52–54; Helyar, *Lords of the Realm,* 23–25; Curt Flood with Richard Carter, *The Way It Is* (New York: Trident, 1971). 160.

10. Marvin Miller, *Whole Different Ball Game,* 55–61; Lowenfish, *Imperfect Diamond,* 197–201.

11. Marvin Miller, *Whole Different Ball Game,* 65–67, 153; David Q. Voigt, *American Baseball,* vol. 3, *From Postwar Expansion to the Electronic Age* (University Park: Pennsylvania State University Press, 1983), 209–10; Jennings, *Balls and Strikes,* 21–22.

12. Marvin Miller, *Whole Different Ball Game,* 67–74; James Edward Miller, *Baseball Business,* 142–43; Korr, "Marvin Miller," 122–26.

13. Marvin Miller, *Whole Different Ball Game,* 91–92, 147–48.

14. Helyar, *Lords of the Realm,* 26–27.

15. Marvin Miller, *Whole Different Ball Game,* 74–78.

16. Charles W. Bevis, "A Home Run by Any Measure: The Baseball Players' Pension Plan," *Baseball Research Journal* 21 (1992): 68–69; Bowie Kuhn, *Hardball: The Education of a Baseball Commissioner* (New York: Times Books, 1987), 76–77; Marvin Miller, *Whole Different Ball Game,* 88–91; Jennings, *Balls and Strikes,* 22.

17. Korr, "Marvin Miller," 126–27; Kuhn, *Hardball,* 79.

18. Korr, "Marvin Miller," 122, 130; Helyar, *Lords of the Realm,* 28, 80–81.

19. Helyar, *Lords of the Realm,* 33, 82; Jennings, *Balls and Strikes,* 20.

20. Helyar, *Lords of the Realm,* 33.

21. Marvin Miller, *Whole Different Ball Game,* 95–96, 156–57; *Sporting News,* October 28, 1967, in "Salaries: General to 1970," Subject Files, NBL; Jennings, *Balls and Strikes,* 23.

22. Marvin Miller, *Whole Different Ball Game,* 159–61.

23. Ibid., 161–62; Helyar, *Lords of the Realm,* 29–31.

24. *Sporting News,* December 16, 1967, in "Salaries: General to 1970," Subject Files, NBL.

25. Helyar, *Lords of the Realm,* 36–38; *Sporting News,* December 16, 1967, February 3, 10, 1968, in "Salaries: General to 1970," Subject Files, NBL.

26. Marvin Miller, *Whole Different Ball Game,* 97–98, 163–64; Dworkin, *Owners versus Players,* 124–26; *Sporting News,* March 9, 1968; "Basic Agreement between the American League of Professional Baseball Clubs and the National League of Professional Baseball Clubs and the Major League Baseball Players Association, effective January 1, 1968," in "Players Association," Subject Files, NBL; Lee MacPhail, *My Nine Innings: An Autobiography of Fifty Years in Baseball* (Westport, Conn.: Meckler, 1989), 101; Gerald W. Scully, *The Business of Major League Baseball* (Chicago: University of Chicago Press, 1989), 34.

27. Korr, "Marvin Miller," 127; Marvin Miller, *Whole Different Ball Game,* 164–65; *Sporting News,* December 21, 1968, in "Salaries: General to 1970," Subject Files, NBL.

28. Marvin Miller, *Whole Different Ball Game,* 145–46, 148–49; Helyar, *Lords of the Realm,* 85; Lowenfish, *Imperfect Diamond,* 202–3; Zimbalist, *Baseball and Billions,* 79.

29. Marvin Miller, *Whole Different Ball Game,* 101–2, 165; Helyar, *Lords of the Realm,* 76–78, 92–93; James Edward Miller, *Baseball Business,* 140–41; Kuhn, *Hardball,* 34, 54–55.

30. Marvin Miller, *Whole Different Ball Game,* 98; Helyar, *Lords of the Realm,* 84; James Quirk and Rodney Fort, *Pay Dirt: The Business of Professional Team Sports* (Princeton, N.J.: Princeton University Press, 1992), 505; Zimbalist, *Baseball and Billions,* 48–49.

31. James Edward Miller, *Baseball Business,* 138–40, 146; Voigt, *American Baseball,* 3:113–14.

32. Marvin Miller, *Whole Different Ball Game,* 99–100, 166; Helyar, *Lords of the Realm,* 86–87; Jennings, *Balls and Strikes,* 24–26.

33. Marvin Miller, *Whole Different Ball Game,* 102–3, 166; Helyar, *Lords of the Realm,* 87–92.

34. Marvin Miller, *Whole Different Ball Game,* 104–5; Helyar, *Lords of the Realm,* 93–96; Bevis, "Home Run by Any Measure," 69; James Edward Miller, *Baseball Business,* 147–49; Kuhn, *Hardball,* 40.

35. Helyar, *Lords of the Realm,* 123–24.

36. Flood, *Way It Is,* 17; Lowenfish, *Imperfect Diamond,* 208–10; Marvin Miller, *Whole Different Ball Game,* 172–85; Helyar, *Lords of the Realm,* 102–4.

37. Flood, *Way It Is,* 194–95; Kuhn, *Hardball,* 74–83; Marvin Miller, *Whole Different Ball Game,* 187–91; Zimbalist, *Baseball and Billions,* 18.

38. Korr, "Marvin Miller," 131; James Edward Miller, *Baseball Business,* 183.

39. Helyar, *Lords of the Realm,* 107; Jennings, *Balls and Strikes,* 26–27.

40. Helyar, *Lords of the Realm,* 104–5, 108–9.

41. "Basic Agreement between the American League of Professional Baseball Clubs and the National League of Professional Baseball Clubs and the Major League Baseball Players Association, effective January 1, 1970," in "Players Association," Subject Files, NBL; Lowenfish, *Imperfect Diamond,* 211–12; Marvin Miller, *Whole Different Ball Game,* 214–15; Dworkin, *Owners versus Players,* 69, 126; Charles C. Alexander, *Our Game: An American Baseball History* (New York: Henry Holt, 1991), 273; Jennings, *Balls and Strikes,* 27–29.

42. Quirk and Fort, *Pay Dirt,* 158; Kuhn, *Hardball,* 54–55; Scully, *Business of Major League Baseball,* 54, 64–65, 72; *Sporting News,* February 28, June 9, 1970, in "Salaries: General to 1970," Subject Files, NBL; Zimbalist, *Baseball and Billions,* 85.

43. *Sporting News,* June 9, 1970, in "Salaries: General to 1970," and *Sporting News,* May 2, 1971, in "Salaries, 1971–1973," Subject Files, NBL.

44. *Sporting News,* May 3, October 11, 1969, July 4, 1970, in "Salaries: General to 1970," Subject Files, NBL: Zimbalist, *Baseball and Billions,* 80.

45. *Chicago Daily News,* August 30, 1970, in "Salaries: General to 1970"; *Christian Science Monitor,* September 11, 1973, *Sporting News,* February 27, May 29, 1971, in "Salaries, 1971–1973"; and *Sporting News,* December 12, 1970, in "Association of Professional Ball Players of America," all in Subject Files, NBL.

46. Lee Allen Notebooks, 1966–1970, NBL; "Some Facts about Major League Players, 1972," and "Negroes in Major League Baseball," in "Ethnic Background," Subject Files, NBL; Voigt, *American Baseball*, 3:258–59.

47. James Edward Miller, *Baseball Business*, 125–26; Scully, *Business of Major League Baseball*, 176–79; Marvin Miller, *Whole Different Ball Game*, 82; Helyar, *Lords of the Realm*, 35, 81.

48. Marvin Miller, *Whole Different Ball Game*, 108, 131–41; Voigt, *American Baseball*, 3:241.

49. Kuhn, *Hardball*, 69; Alexander, *Our Game*, 276.

50. *Sporting News*, December 20, 1969, May 9, 1970, in "Unionism," Subject Files, NBL.

51. James Edward Miller, *Baseball Business*, 146; *Sporting News*, February 22, 1969, in "Salaries: General to 1970," and *New York Daily News*, September 21, 1968, in "Unionism," Subject Files, NBL; August J. Donatelli interview, Albert B. Chandler Oral History Project, Special Collections, University of Kentucky Library, Lexington (henceforth, UKL); Larry R. Gerlach, "Augie Donatelli: Umpire and Union Organizer," in *Baseball History*, ed. Peter Levine (Westport, Conn.: Meckler, 1989), 1:10.

52. Dworkin, *Owners versus Players*, 275–76; *Sporting News*, February 22, 1969, in "Salaries: General to 1970," Subject Files, NBL; Voigt, *American Baseball*, 3:293–94.

53. *Sporting News*, March 7, 28, 1970, in "Salaries: General to 1970," Subject Files, NBL.

54. *Sporting News*, October 17, 1970, in "Unionism," Subject Files, NBL.

55. Kuhn, *Hardball*, 104–8; Marvin Miller, *Whole Different Ball Game*, 109, 203; Helyar, *Lords of the Realm*, 105; James Edward Miller, *Baseball Business*, 181–84; Jennings, *Balls and Strikes*, 29.

56. *Sporting News*, May 22, 1971, in "Salaries, 1971–1973," Subject Files, NBL; Marvin Miller, *Whole Different Ball Game*, 203.

57. Helyar, *Lords of the Realm*, 110; Marvin Miller, *Whole Different Ball Game*, 204.

58. James Edward Miller, *Baseball Business*, 184–85.

59. Marvin Miller, *Whole Different Ball Game*, 205–7; *New York Daily News*, May 20, 1972, and *New York Times*, May 21, 1972, in "Unionism," Subject Files, NBL.

60. Marvin Miller, *Whole Different Ball Game*, 208; Helyar, *Lords of the Realm*, 112.

61. Marvin Miller, *Whole Different Ball Game*, 210–12; Helyar, *Lords of the Realm*, 113–14.

62. Helyar, *Lords of the Realm*, 115–17; Jennings, *Balls and Strikes*, 30.

63. James Edward Miller, *Baseball Business*, 186–88; Marvin Miller, *Whole Different Ball Game*, 216–19.

64. Helyar, *Lords of the Realm*, 118–21.

65. Marvin Miller, *Whole Different Ball Game*, 220–22; Jennings, *Balls and Strikes*, 31–32.

66. Dworkin, *Owners versus Players,* 33; Lowenfish, *Imperfect Diamond,* 216; Zimbalist, *Baseball and Billions,* 119–20; Bevis, "Home Run by Any Measure," 69.

67. Scully, *Business of Major League Baseball,* 29–30.

68. Marvin Miller, *Whole Different Ball Game,* 366–67; Helyar, *Lords of the Realm,* 104.

69. Scully, *Business of Major League Baseball,* 31.

70. Dworkin, *Owners versus Players,* 64; Marvin Miller, *Whole Different Ball Game,* 192–94, 200–201; Lowenfish, *Imperfect Diamond,* 212–13.

71. Helyar, *Lords of the Realm,* 35, 123–24.

72. Lowenfish, *Imperfect Diamond,* 219.

73. Helyar, *Lords of the Realm,* 124–25.

74. Dworkin, *Owners versus Players,* 65–69; Marvin Miller, *Whole Different Ball Game,* 196–99.

75. Helyar, *Lords of the Realm,* 36; *Sporting News,* August 12, 1972, in "Salaries, 1971–1973," Subject Files, NBL.

76. Helyar, *Lords of the Realm,* 126–27.

CHAPTER SIX

1. James Edward Miller, *The Baseball Business: Pursuing Pennants and Profits in Baltimore* (Chapel Hill: University of North Carolina Press, 1990), 190.

2. Marvin Miller, *A Whole Different Ball Game: The Sport and Business of Baseball* (New York: Birch Lane Press, 1991), 110–11; Kenneth M. Jennings, *Balls and Strikes: The Money Game in Professional Baseball* (New York: Praeger, 1990), 32–33.

3. John Helyar, *Lords of the Realm: The Real History of Baseball* (New York: Villard, 1994), 132; Andrew Zimbalist, *Baseball and Billions: A Probing Look inside the Big Business of Our National Pastime* (New York: Basic Books, 1994), 20.

4. James Edward Miller, *Baseball Business,* 191.

5. *Sporting News,* January 6, 1973, in "Salaries, 1971–1973," Subject Files, National Baseball Library, Cooperstown, New York (henceforth, NBL).

6. *Sporting News,* January 6, 1973, in "Salaries, 1971–1973," Subject Files, NBL; James Edward Miller, *Baseball Business,* 192–93; Jennings, *Balls and Strikes,* 33–35.

7. Helyar, *Lords of the Realm,* 151–52.

8. *Sporting News,* March 3, 17, 1973, in "Salaries, 1971–1973," and *New York Times,* February 26, 1973, in "Players Association," Subject Files, NBL; Lee Lowenfish, *The Imperfect Diamond: A History of Baseball's Labor Wars,* rev. ed. (New York: Da Capo, 1991), 217–18.

9. *Sporting News,* March 17, 1973, in "Salaries, 1971–1973," Subject Files, NBL.

10. *Sporting News,* October 6, December 1, 1973, in "Salaries, 1971–1973," and *Sporting News,* February 16, 1974, and *New York Times,* March 24, 31, 1974, February 14, 1975, in "Salaries, 1974–1980," Subject Files, NBL: James Edward Miller, *Baseball Business,* 196; Gerald W. Scully, *The Business of Major League Baseball* (Chicago: University of Chicago Press, 1989), 36–37; Marvin Miller, *Whole Different Ball Game,* 373–76.

11. Helyar, *Lords of the Realm,* 153.

12. Ibid., 128–31; James Edward Miller, *Baseball Business,* 215–16; *New York Times,* January 30, 1974, in "Salaries, 1974–1980," Subject Files, NBL.

13. Marvin Miller, *Whole Different Ball Game,* 238.

14. Helyar, *Lords of the Realm,* 133–37; Marvin Miller, *Whole Different Ball Game,* 226–27. Hunter's career and confrontations with Charley Finley are related in Jim "Catfish" Hunter with Armen Keteyian, *Catfish: My Life in Baseball* (New York: McGraw-Hill, 1988).

15. Marvin Miller, *Whole Different Ball Game,* 111–12, 227–230; James B. Dworkin, *Owners versus Players: Baseball and Collective Bargaining* (Boston: Auburn House, 1981), 71.

16. *Sporting News,* October 26, 1974, in "Salaries, 1974–1980," Subject Files, NBL.

17. Helyar, *Lords of the Realm,* 138–40; Marvin Miller, *Whole Different Ball Game,* 113.

18. Marvin Miller, *Whole Different Ball Game,* 231–33.

19. *Sporting News,* January 25, 1975, in "Salaries, 1974–1980," Subject Files, NBL; Marvin Miller, *Whole Different Ball Game,* 233–35; Dworkin, *Owners versus Players,* 72–73.

20. Marvin Miller, *Whole Different Ball Game,* 237.

21. Helyar, *Lords of the Realm,* 141–50; Marvin Miller, *Whole Different Ball Game,* 225.

22. Marvin Miller, *Whole Different Ball Game,* 238–41; Helyar, *Lords of the Realm,* 153–54.

23. Marvin Miller, *Whole Different Ball Game,* 244.

24. Helyar, *Lords of the Realm,* 155–57; Bowie Kuhn, *Hardball: The Education of a Baseball Commissioner* (New York: Times Books, 1987), 154–72.

25. Marvin Miller, *Whole Different Ball Game,* 243; Helyar, *Lords of the Realm,* 158–59.

26. Marvin Miller, *Whole Different Ball Game,* 244.

27. Dworkin, *Owners versus Players,* 73.

28. Marvin Miller, *Whole Different Ball Game,* 245–48; Kuhn, *Hardball,* 157; Helyar, *Lords of the Realm,* 160.

29. Dworkin, *Owners versus Players,* 74–76; Lowenfish, *Imperfect Diamond,* 220.

30. Helyar, *Lords of the Realm,* 161–66.

31. Dworkin, *Owners versus Players,* 76–78.

32. Marvin Miller, *Whole Different Ball Game,* 248–51; Helyar, *Lords of the Realm,* 167–68.

33. *Sporting News,* January 17, 1976, in "Salaries, 1974–1980," Subject Files, NBL; Kuhn, *Hardball,* 160; Helyar, *Lords of the Realm,* 169–70.

34. Dworkin, *Owners versus Players,* 79–81; James Edward Miller, *Baseball Business,* 217–18.

35. Marvin Miller, *Whole Different Ball Game,* 252–53; Helyar, *Lords of the Realm,* 177.

36. Helyar, *Lords of the Realm,* 173.

37. Marvin Miller, *Whole Different Ball Game,* 255, 257.

38. Helyar, *Lords of the Realm,* 171–72.

39. Marvin Miller, *Whole Different Ball Game*, 258–59; James Edward Miller, *Baseball Business*, 217–20; Jennings, *Balls and Strikes*, 36–37; Helyar, *Lords of the Realm*, 173–74.

40. Marvin Miller, *Whole Different Ball Game*, 259–63.

41. Ibid., 269–71.

42. Ibid., 115; Kuhn, *Hardball*, 161–66; Jennings, *Balls and Strikes*, 37–38; Helyar, *Lords of the Realm*, 174–77.

43. Marvin Miller, *Whole Different Ball Game*, 264–66; Helyar, *Lords of the Realm*, 195.

44. James Edward Miller, *Baseball Business*, 221–24; Helyar, *Lords of the Realm*, 183. For an account of Oakland's collapse, see Tom Clark, *Champagne and Baloney: The Rise and Fall of Finley's A's* (New York: Harper and Row, 1976).

45. Kuhn, *Hardball*, 173–87; Lee MacPhail, *My Nine Innings: An Autobiography of Fifty Years in Baseball* (Westport, Conn.: Meckler, 1989), 135; Scully, *Business of Major League Baseball*, 27; Helyar, *Lords of the Realm*, 184–95.

46. Marvin Miller, *Whole Different Ball Game*, 377.

47. Ibid., 266–68; Jennings, *Balls and Strikes*, 38–39; Helyar, *Lords of the Realm*, 172–73, 195–97.

48. Charles W. Bevis, "A Home Run by Any Measure: The Baseball Players' Pension Plan," *Baseball Research Journal* 21 (1992), 69; Dworkin, *Owners versus Players*, 83–89.

49. Lowenfish, *Imperfect Diamond*, 263; Helyar, *Lords of the Realm*, 199–200.

50. Marvin Miller, *Whole Different Ball Game*, 282; James Edward Miller, *Baseball Business*, 225–30; Helyar, *Lords of the Realm*, 200–215.

51. Paul D. Staudohar, *The Sports Industry and Collective Bargaining*, 2d ed. (Ithaca, N.Y.: ILR Press, 1989), 2–5, 30, 192; James Quirk and Rodney Fort, *Pay Dirt: The Business of Professional Team Sports* (Princeton, N.J.: Princeton University Press, 1992), 13–14, 235–39; Dworkin, *Owners versus Players*, 98; James Edward Miller, *Baseball Business*, 252; *Sporting News*, March 31, 1979, in "Salaries, 1974–1980," Subject Files, NBL; Zimbalist, *Baseball and Billions*, 85; Scully, *Business of Major League Baseball*, 152; Jennings, *Balls and Strikes*, 41.

52. Staudohar, *Sports Industry and Collective Bargaining*, 35–36; Zimbalist, *Baseball and Billions*, 21, 87; Dworkin, *Owners versus Players*, 94–97, 113–17; Helyar, *Lords of the Realm*, 245; David Q. Voigt, "The History of Major League Baseball," in *Total Baseball*, 3d ed., ed. John Thorn and Pete Palmer (New York: HarperCollins, 1993), 42.

53. Dworkin, *Owners versus Players*, 143–71; Staudohar, *Sports Industry and Collective Bargaining*, 42–43; Helyar, *Lords of the Realm*, 290–92.

54. Dworkin, *Owners versus Players*, 133–34.

55. Ibid., 201–4, 207–8; Zimbalist, *Baseball and Billions*, 79–80; Marvin Miller, *Whole Different Ball Game*, 150–51.

56. Dworkin, *Owners versus Players*, 204–7, 209, 213–14; *Sporting News*, March 27, 1976, in "Salaries, 1974–1980," Subject Files, NBL.

57. Dworkin, *Owners versus Players,* 210–12.

58. Ibid., 218–28; David Q. Voigt, *American Baseball,* vol. 3, *From Postwar Expansion to the Electronic Age* (University Park: Pennsylvania State University Press, 1983), 274; *Sporting News,* October 26, 1974, in "Salaries, 1974–1980," Subject Files, NBL.

59. Dworkin, *Owners versus Players,* 213–14.

60. Marvin Miller, *Whole Different Ball Game,* 272–73, 276–79; *Sporting News,* August 10, 1974, in "Salaries, 1974–1980," Subject Files, NBL; Helyar, *Lords of the Realm,* 293–94.

61. James Edward Miller, *Baseball Business,* 263; Voigt, *American Baseball,* 3:258–60, 266; Lee Allen Notebooks, 1976–1980, NBL.

62. Allen Notebooks, 1971–1980, NBL; Rob Ruck, *The Tropic of Baseball: Baseball in the Dominican Republic* (Westport, Conn.: Meckler, 1991), 84–85; Alan M. Klein, *Sugarball: The American Game, the Dominican Dream* (New Haven, Conn.: Yale University Press, 1991), 37.

63. Hank Aaron with Lonnie Wheeler, *I Had a Hammer: The Hank Aaron Story* (New York: HarperCollins, 1991), 436–37; Voigt, *American Baseball,* 3:241–49; Scully, *Business of Major League Baseball,* 176–77; Bill Deane, "Awards and Honors," and Larry R. Gerlach, "Umpires," in Thorn and Palmer, *Total Baseball,* 3d ed., 298, 2246.

64. *USA Today Baseball Weekly,* October 5–11, 1994.

65. *New York Times,* December 30, 1979, in "Salaries, 1974–1980," Subject Files, NBL; MacPhail, *My Nine Innings,* 103; Helyar, *Lords of the Realm,* 290–91.

66. Zimbalist, *Baseball and Billions,* 93–94; Helyar, *Lords of the Realm,* 236, 245, 248–57.

67. *New York Times,* March 26, December 4, 1979, in "Salaries, 1974–1980," Subject Files, NBL; Staudohar, *Sports Industry and Collective Bargaining,* 198; Dworkin, *Owners versus Players,* 96–97, 99–101; Donald J. Cymrot, "Migration Trends and Earnings of Free Agents in Major League Baseball, 1976–79," *Economic Inquiry* 21 (October 1983): 545–56.

68. James Edward Miller, *Baseball Business,* 216, 253, 274; Quirk and Fort, *Pay Dirt,* 7, 133, 137–38, 158, 195, 220–22, 505; Marvin Miller, *Whole Different Ball Game,* 282, 285; MacPhail, *My Nine Innings,* 216; Helyar, *Lords of the Realm,* 221, 232; Charles C. Alexander, *Our Game: An American Baseball History* (New York: Henry Holt, 1991), 300–301; Zimbalist, *Baseball and Billions,* 36, 48–49; Scully, *Business of Major League Baseball,* 52–53, 65–67.

69. *Boston Herald American,* December 17, 1978, in "Salaries, 1974–1980," Subject Files, NBL; Quirk and Fort, *Pay Dirt,* 91–124; Zimbalist, *Baseball and Billions,* 34–35, 63–64; Scully, *Business of Major League Baseball,* 130–35; Steven A. Riess, *City Games: The Evolution of American Urban Society and the Rise of Sports* (Urbana: University of Illinois Press, 1989), 243.

70. *St. Louis Globe-Democrat,* March 3, 1979, in "Salaries, 1974–1980," Subject Files, NBL; *Philadelphia Inquirer,* August 14, 1994; Dworkin, *Owners versus Players,* 98; Quirk and Fort, *Pay Dirt,* 24, 196; James Edward Miller, *Baseball Business,* 253; Voigt, *American Baseball,* 3:133.

71. *Sporting News,* May 7, 1977, in "Salaries, 1974–1980," Subject Files, NBL; Voigt, *American Baseball,* 3:278, 280; Zimbalist, *Baseball and Billions,* 116; Helyar, *Lords of the Realm,* 244; *Baseball America,* February 3–16, 1997.

72. Staudohar, *Sports Industry and Collective Bargaining,* 181; Quirk and Fort, *Pay Dirt,* 505; Zimbalist, *Baseball and Billions,* 49–50, 57–59; Riess, *City Games,* 249–50.

73. Dworkin, *Owners versus Players,* 276–80; Voigt, *American Baseball,* 3:294–96.

74. *Sporting News,* March 24, 1979, and *New York Times,* April 15, 1979, in "Salaries, 1974–1980," Subject Files, NBL.

75. *New York Times,* July 31, 1994; Lowenfish, *Imperfect Diamond,* 221.

76. Helyar, *Lords of the Realm,* 216–17, 219; Marvin Miller, *Whole Different Ball Game,* 284.

77. Marvin Miller, *Whole Different Ball Game,* 276; Lowenfish, *Imperfect Diamond,* 227.

78. Jennings, *Balls and Strikes,* 41–42; Marvin Miller, *Whole Different Ball Game,* 280, 282, 285; James Edward Miller, *Baseball Business,* 252–53; Helyar, *Lords of the Realm,* 222.

CHAPTER SEVEN

1. John Helyar, *Lords of the Realm: The Real History of Baseball* (New York: Villard, 1994), 218–23; David Q. Voigt, *American Baseball,* vol. 3, *From Postwar Expansion to the Electronic Age* (University Park: Pennsylvania State University Press, 1983), 216; Andrew Zimbalist, *Baseball and Billions: A Probing Look inside the Big Business of Our National Pastime* (New York: Basic Books, 1994), 22.

2. James Edward Miller, *The Baseball Business: Pursuing Pennants and Profits in Baltimore* (Chapel Hill: University of North Carolina Press, 1990), 252; Kenneth M. Jennings, *Balls and Strikes: The Money Game in Professional Baseball* (New York: Praeger, 1990), 43–44.

3. James B. Dworkin, *Owners versus Players: Baseball and Collective Bargaining* (Boston: Auburn House, 1981), 91, 172; Marvin Miller, *A Whole Different Ball Game: The Sport and Business of Baseball* (New York, Birch Lane Press, 1991), 296; James Edward Miller, *Baseball Business,* 254–55; *New York Times,* December 7, 29, 1979, January 24, 25, 1980, and *Sporting News,* April 5, 1980, in "Salaries, 1974–1980," Subject Files, National Baseball Library, Cooperstown, New York (henceforth, NBL); "Comparison of 1978, 1979, and 1980 Reentry Drafts under Current Compensation Rule and Proposed Formula," undated manuscript, in "Players Association," Subject Files, NBL; Lee Lowenfish, *The Imperfect Diamond: A History of Baseball's Labor Wars,* rev. ed. (New York: Da Capo, 1991), 228.

4. *New York Times,* February 26, 1980, in "Salaries, 1974–1980," Subject Files, NBL; Charles C. Alexander, *Our Game: An American Baseball History* (New York: Henry Holt, 1991), 313; Zimbalist, *Baseball and Billions,* 87.

5. Helyar, *Lords of the Realm,* 224; Lowenfish, *Imperfect Diamond,* 226–27.

6. Marvin Miller, *Whole Different Ball Game,* 290–91, 196–97; Jennings, *Balls and Strikes,* 45–47; James Edward Miller, *Baseball Business,* 255–56; Lowenfish, *Imperfect Diamond,* 228–29.

7. *Sporting News,* March 1, April 5, 1980, in "Players Association," Subject Files, NBL; Helyar, *Lords of the Realm,* 225–26.

8. Helyar, *Lords of the Realm,* 226–28.

9. Lowenfish, *Imperfect Diamond,* 230–31.

10. "Memorandum of Agreement, May 23, 1980," in "Players Association," Subject Files, NBL; Jennings, *Balls and Strikes,* 49; Charles W. Bevis, "A Home Run by Any Measure: The Baseball Players' Pension Plan," *Baseball Research Journal* 21 (1992): 69.

11. Helyar, *Lords of the Realm,* 229–30.

12. *Sporting News,* July 26, 1980, and *New York Times,* August 13, 1981, in "Unionism," Subject Files, NBL; Helyar, *Lords of the Realm,* 258; Marvin Miller, *Whole Different Ball Game,* 291–92; Dworkin, *Owners versus Players,* 92–93; Lowenfish, *Imperfect Diamond,* 233.

13. *Sporting News,* November 15, 1980, in "Salaries, 1974–1980," Subject Files, NBL; Marvin Miller, *Whole Different Ball Game,* 295–97; James Edward Miller, *Baseball Business,* 257; Jennings, *Balls and Strikes,* 50–51; Dworkin, *Owners versus Players,* 85; Lowenfish, *Imperfect Diamond,* 234–36.

14. Helyar, *Lords of the Realm,* 259–61; Bowie Kuhn, *Hardball: The Education of a Baseball Commissioner* (New York: Times Books, 1987), 3, 331–65; Marvin Miller, *Whole Different Ball Game,* 293–95; Lee MacPhail, *My Nine Innings: An Autobiography of Fifty Years in Baseball* (Westport, Conn.: Meckler, 1989), 173–78; Dworkin, *Owners versus Players,* 28.

15. *New York Times,* December 14, 1980, in "Salaries, 1974–1980," and *Sporting News,* May 30, 1981, in "Salaries, 1981–1987," Subject Files, NBL; Marvin Miller, *Whole Different Ball Game,* 287–88.

16. Helyar, *Lords of the Realm,* 261–3; Marvin Miller, *Whole Different Ball Game,* 292; James Edward Miller, *Baseball Business,* 258–59; Lowenfish, *Imperfect Diamond,* 237.

17. *New York Times,* July 9, 1981, in "Salaries, 1981–1987," Subject Files, NBL; Jennings, *Balls and Strikes,* 52–53; Marvin Miller, *Whole Different Ball Game,* 288–90.

18. Marvin Miller, *Whole Different Ball Game,* 198–99; *USA Today,* August 11, 1994.

19. Jennings, *Balls and Strikes,* 54; Helyar, *Lords of the Realm,* 264–65; James Edward Miller, *Baseball Business,* 260–61; Kuhn, *Hardball,* 4; Lowenfish, *Imperfect Diamond,* 238–39.

20. Helyar, *Lords of the Realm,* 268–73; Marvin Miller, *Whole Different Ball Game,* 299–301; James Edward Miller, *Baseball Business,* 261; Voigt, *American Baseball,* 3:347.

21. Helyar, *Lords of the Realm,* 273–76; Lowenfish, *Imperfect Diamond,* 242.

22. Jennings, *Balls and Strikes,* 55.

23. Marvin Miller, *Whole Different Ball Game,* 310, 379; *New York Times,* July 15, 1981, in "Salaries, 1981–1987," Subject Files, NBL.

24. Jennings, *Balls and Strikes,* 56; Helyar, *Lords of the Realm,* 277–81; Marvin Miller, *Whole Different Ball Game,* 311–13; *Sporting News,* February 20, 1982, in "Salaries, 1981–1987," Subject Files, NBL; Lowenfish, *Imperfect Diamond,* 243–44.

25. Randal A. Hendricks, *Inside the Strike Zone* (Austin, Tex.: Eakin Press, 1994), 21.

26. *Sporting News,* August 15, 1981, in "Salaries, 1981–1987," Subject Files, NBL; Jennings, *Balls and Strikes,* 57; Helyar, *Lords of the Realm,* 281–84; Marvin Miller, *Whole Different Ball Game,* 313–15; Lowenfish, *Imperfect Diamond,* 245.

27. Helyar, *Lords of the Realm,* 285–87; Marvin Miller, *Whole Different Ball Game,* 286, 316; Lowenfish, *Imperfect Diamond,* 246.

28. Jennings, *Balls and Strikes,* 58; Helyar, *Lords of the Realm,* 289; *New York Times,* August 16, 1981, in "Players Association," Subject Files, NBL.

29. Marvin Miller, *Whole Different Ball Game,* 317.

30. Jack Sands and Peter Gammons, *Coming Apart at the Seams: How Baseball Owners, Players, and Television Executives Have Led Our National Pastime to the Brink of Disaster* (New York: Macmillan, 1993), 47–50; Paul D. Staudohar, *The Sports Industry and Collective Bargaining,* 2d ed. (Ithaca, N.Y.: ILR Press, 1989), 26; Lowenfish, *Imperfect Diamond,* 249.

31. Marvin Miller, *Whole Different Ball Game,* 320–27; Jennings, *Balls and Strikes,* 60; Lowenfish, *Imperfect Diamond,* 250–51.

32. Marvin Miller, *Whole Different Ball Game,* 327–29; Helyar, *Lords of the Realm,* 323–24; Sands and Gammons, *Coming Apart at the Seams,* 51; Hendricks, *Inside the Strike Zone,* 22; Staudohar, *Sports Industry and Collective Bargaining,* 27; David A. Kaplan, "The Players' Main Man," *New York Times Magazine,* October 29, 1989, 46–50, 54–56, 101; *Sporting News,* August 8, 1994.

33. Jennings, *Balls and Strikes,* 143–46, 148–49; Dworkin, *Owners versus Players,* 134–35; Staudohar, *Sports Industry and Collective Bargaining,* 45–47; James Edward Miller, *Baseball Business,* 263–64; Lowenfish, *Imperfect Diamond,* 254.

34. Lowenfish, *Imperfect Diamond,* 255.

35. Sands and Gammons, *Coming Apart at the Seams,* 52–54.

36. *Sports Illustrated,* March 26, 1984; Jennings, *Balls and Strikes,* 60; Staudohar, *Sports Industry and Collective Bargaining,* 26–27, 200; MacPhail, *My Nine Innings,* 183–89.

37. Jennings, *Balls and Strikes,* 149–50; Sands and Gammons, *Coming Apart at the Seams,* 25–26, 55; Staudohar, *Sports Industry and Collective Bargaining,* 47–48.

38. Jennings, *Balls and Strikes,* 89–90; Helyar, *Lords of the Realm,* 287–88; Marvin Miller, *Whole Different Ball Game,* 319; Lowenfish, *Imperfect Diamond,* 247; Staudo-

har, *Sports Industry and Collective Bargaining,* 22–24; MacPhail, *My Nine Innings,* 153–57, 181–83; James Edward Miller, *Baseball Business,* 281. For Kuhn's extended view of his firing, see Kuhn, *Hardball,* 366–440.

39. *Business Week,* August 12, 1985; *USA Today,* November 20, 1996; Jennings, *Balls and Strikes,* 74–76; Helyar, *Lords of the Realm,* 232, 308–9; Sands and Gammons, *Coming Apart at the Seams,* 26–37.

40. Helyar, *Lords of the Realm,* 245–57, 292–308; Staudohar, *Sports Industry and Collective Bargaining,* 37–38; *New York Times,* February 4, 1983, in "Salaries, 1981–1987," Subject Files, NBL.

41. Hendricks, *Inside the Strike Zone,* 44, 183–88, 229–30; *Sporting News,* March 7, 1983, in "Salaries, 1981–1987," Subject Files, NBL; Jennings, *Balls and Strikes,* 201; Staudohar, *Sports Industry and Collective Bargaining,* 42–44; James Edward Miller, *Baseball Business,* 262–63, 266.

42. *New York Times,* January 15, 1984, in "Salaries, 1981–1987," Subject Files, NBL; *USA Today,* May 11, 1993; Jennings, *Balls and Strikes,* 213; Staudohar, *Sports Industry and Collective Bargaining,* 30, 32; David Q. Voigt, "The History of Major League Baseball," in *Total Baseball,* 3d ed., ed. John Thorn and Pete Palmer (New York: HarperCollins, 1993), 50; Zimbalist, *Baseball and Billions,* 85, 116.

43. Jennings, *Balls and Strikes,* 61; Staudohar, *Sports Industry and Collective Bargaining,* 19, 180–81; James Quirk and Rodney Fort, *Pay Dirt: The Business of Professional Team Sports* (Princeton, N.J.: Princeton University Press, 1992), 505; James Edward Miller, *Baseball Business,* 274–75.

44. Zimbalist, *Baseball and Billions,* 48–49; Helyar, *Lords of the Realm,* 289.

45. Helyar, *Lords of the Realm,* 310–13. Ueberroth provides his own early life story in Peter Ueberroth, *Made in America* (New York: William Morrow, 1985).

46. Sands and Gammons, *Coming Apart at the Seams,* 35–39.

47. Ibid., 40–42; Lowenfish, *Imperfect Diamond,* 255–56.

48. Helyar, *Lords of the Realm,* 320–21.

49. Jennings, *Balls and Strikes,* 62; Helyar, *Lords of the Realm,* 314, 318–19, 324; Marvin Miller, *Whole Different Ball Game,* 335, 385–87; Sands and Gammons, *Coming Apart at the Seams,* 43–44; Staudohar, *Sports Industry and Collective Bargaining,* 36–37, 55.

50. Sands and Gammons, *Coming Apart at the Seams,* 61–62; Hendricks, *Inside the Strike Zone,* 15–16.

51. Helyar, *Lords of the Realm,* 325–26; Staudohar, *Sports Industry and Collective Bargaining,* 16, 24, 55; Zimbalist, *Baseball and Billions,* 23–24, 64.

52. Staudohar, *Sports Industry and Collective Bargaining,* 56–57; Gerald W. Scully, *The Business of Major League Baseball* (Chicago: University of Chicago Press, 1989), 131–35.

53. Jennings, *Balls and Strikes,* 62–64; Helyar, *Lords of the Realm,* 326–28; Marvin Miller, *Whole Different Ball Game,* 388–89; Lowenfish, *Imperfect Diamond,* 256.

54. Marvin Miller, *Whole Different Ball Game,* 336–37; Lowenfish, *Imperfect Diamond,* 257–58.

55. Marvin Miller, *Whole Different Ball Game,* 335, 389; Sands and Gammons, *Coming Apart at the Seams,* 63.

56. Jennings, *Balls and Strikes,* 65; Marvin Miller, *Whole Different Ball Game,* 338; Hendricks, *Inside the Strike Zone,* 187–88; Staudohar, *Sports Industry and Collective Bargaining,* 54; Lowenfish, *Imperfect Diamond,* 259; Bevis, "Home Run by Any Measure," 69–70.

57. Marvin Miller, *Whole Different Ball Game,* 339; Hendricks, *Inside the Strike Zone,* 19; Staudohar, *Sports Industry and Collective Bargaining,* 57; *Sporting News,* December 9, 1985, in "Salaries, 1981–1987," Subject Files, NBL; Lowenfish, *Imperfect Diamond,* 258.

58. Jennings, *Balls and Strikes,* 66–67; Marvin Miller, *Whole Different Ball Game,* 345; Lowenfish, *Imperfect Diamond,* 260–61; Kaplan, "Players' Main Man," 54.

59. Helyar, *Lords of the Realm,* 331.

60. Ibid., 337; *New York Times,* February 6, 1983, in "Salaries, 1981–1987," Subject Files, NBL; Scully, *Business of Major League Baseball,* 25, 39–40, 153.

61. Helyar, *Lords of the Realm,* 329–31; Sands and Gammons, *Coming Apart at the Seams,* 57–58, 63; Hendricks, *Inside the Strike Zone,* 142–44; *USA Today,* March 25, 1986, in "Salaries, 1981–1987," Subject Files, NBL; Zimbalist, *Baseball and Billions,* 24.

62. Helyar, *Lords of the Realm,* 322, 332–34; Marvin Miller, *Whole Different Ball Game,* 391–92; Sands and Gammons, *Coming Apart at the Seams,* 67–68; Lowenfish, *Imperfect Diamond,* 267.

63. Hendricks, *Inside the Strike Zone,* 144–45.

64. Jennings, *Balls and Strikes,* 192; Helyar, *Lords of the Realm,* 334–37; Sands and Gammons, *Coming Apart at the Seams,* 80; Hendricks, *Inside the Strike Zone,* 7–8; James Edward Miller, *Baseball Business,* 315–16; Scully, *Business of Major League Baseball,* 162.

65. Jennings, *Balls and Strikes,* 201, 213; Helyar, *Lords of the Realm,* 338–40; Sands and Gammons, *Coming Apart at the Seams,* 64, 69; Staudohar, *Sports Industry and Collective Bargaining,* 30, 42–43; "Major League Baseball Player Relations Committee Press Release, April 15, 1986," in "Salaries, 1981–1987," Subject Files, NBL; Zimbalist, *Baseball and Billions,* 24–25, 85; Scully, *Business of Major League Baseball,* 49; *USA Today,* May 11, 1993.

66. *New York Daily News,* June 1, 1985, in "Salaries, 1981–1987," Subject Files, NBL; Jennings, *Balls and Strikes,* 150–52; Helyar, *Lords of the Realm,* 341–42; Sands and Gammons, *Coming Apart at the Seams,* 45, 56; Staudohar, *Sports Industry and Collective Bargaining,* 48–49; Lowenfish, *Imperfect Diamond,* 261–63; Stephen S. Hall, "Scandals and Controversies," in Thorn and Palmer, *Total Baseball,* 3d ed., 209.

67. *Albany Times-Union,* January 12, 1986, and *USA Today,* June 5, 1986, in "Salaries, 1981–1987," Subject Files, NBL; Jennings, *Balls and Strikes,* 153; Helyar, *Lords of the Realm,* 342–43; Sands and Gammons, *Coming Apart at the Seams,* 65.

68. Helyar, *Lords of the Realm,* 315–17; Staudohar, *Sports Industry and Collective Bargain-*

ing, 19; Quirk and Fort, *Pay Dirt,* 15–16, 57, 124; Zimbalist, *Baseball and Billions,* 57, 64, 68; Scully, *Business of Major League Baseball,* 128–34.

69. Helyar, *Lords of the Realm,* 344–47; Voigt, "History of Major League Baseball," 51; Scully, *Business of Major League Baseball,* 72, 190; *New York Times,* May 8, 1994; *USA Today,* May 1, 1996.

70. Helyar, *Lords of the Realm,* 348–58; Sands and Gammons, *Coming Apart at the Seams,* 69–76; Hendricks, *Inside the Strike Zone,* 146–51; Zimbalist, *Baseball and Billions,* 25.

71. *Kansas City Star,* March 6, 1987, in "Salaries, 1981–1987," Subject Files, NBL; Helyar, *Lords of the Realm,* 359–60; Sands and Gammons, *Coming Apart at the Seams,* 79; Hendricks, *Inside the Strike Zone,* 67–73, 78–101; Scully, *Business of Major League Baseball,* 41.

72. *Sporting News,* April 20, December 21, 1987, in "Salaries, 1981–1987," and *New York Times,* November 3, 1987, in "Salaries, 1988– ," Subject Files, NBL; Sands and Gammons, *Coming Apart at the Seams,* 127–28; Zimbalist, *Baseball and Billions,* 85; Scully, *Business of Major League Baseball,* 162; *Sports Illustrated,* June 14, 1993; *USA Today,* May 11, 1993.

73. Staudohar, *Sports Industry and Collective Bargaining,* 59; *Sporting News,* November 6, 1989, in "Players Association," Subject Files, NBL; Lowenfish, *Imperfect Diamond,* 266–67.

74. Jennings, *Balls and Strikes,* 146–47, 154; Scully, *Business of Major League Baseball,* 14; Hall, "Scandals and Controversies," and Joseph M. Overfield, "Tragedies and Shortened Careers," in Thorn and Palmer, *Total Baseball,* 3d ed., 210, 230.

75. Rob Ruck, *The Tropic of Baseball: Baseball in the Dominican Republic* (Westport, Conn.: Meckler, 1991), 191; Alan M. Klein, *Sugarball: The American Game, the Dominican Dream* (New Haven, Conn.: Yale University Press, 1991), 50, 56–57; also *New York Times,* May 4, 1987; New York *Daily News,* April 19, 1987; *USA Today,* May 1, 1991; and Brent Staples, "Where Are the Black Fans?," *New York Times Magazine,* May 17, 1987, 27–32, 56, all in "Racism/Minorities," Subject Files, NBL.

76. Jennings, *Balls and Strikes,* 169–73; Sands and Gammons, *Coming Apart at the Seams,* 136; James Edward Miller, *Baseball Business,* 309–10; Scully, *Business of Major League Baseball,* 171–79; also *Albany Times-Union,* May 7, 1987; *USA Today,* March 29, 1988, June 13, 1991; *Sport,* March 1992, 93–95; *Sporting News,* April 20, 1987; "Major League Baseball Employment Statistics, Office of the Commissioner, December 3, 1990," all in "Racism/Minorities," Subject Files, NBL.

77. Major League Arbitration Panel, Thomas T. Roberts, chr., Barry Rona, and Donald M. Fehr, *In the Matter of Arbitration between Major League Baseball Players Association and the Twenty-Six Major League Baseball Clubs, Grievance No. 86-2,* September 21, 1987, in "Salaries, 1981–1987," Subject Files, NBL; Jennings, *Balls and Strikes,* 193–95; Hendricks, *Inside the Strike Zone,* 174–75; Quirk and Fort, *Pay Dirt,* 197; Dan Durland and Paul M. Sommers, "Collusion in Major League

Baseball: An Empirical Test" (Middlebury College working paper), 7, in "Salaries, 1988– ," Subject Files, NBL.

78. Helyar, *Lords of the Realm,* 360–63; Hendricks, *Inside the Strike Zone,* 8.

79. Sands and Gammons, *Coming Apart at the Seams,* 81; Hendricks, *Inside the Strike Zone,* 151–64; *New York Times,* March 17, 1988, and *Sporting News,* November 14, 1988, in "Salaries, 1988– ," Subject Files, NBL; MacPhail, *My Nine Innings,* 233–34; Scully, *Business of Major League Baseball,* 49, 54; *USA Today,* May 11, 1993.

80. Jennings, *Balls and Strikes,* 97; Zimbalist, *Baseball and Billions,* 81.

81. Jennings, *Balls and Strikes,* 196–98; Hendricks, *Inside the Strike Zone,* 175; Staudohar, *Sports Industry and Collective Bargaining,* 17; Quirk and Fort, *Pay Dirt,* 149, 197; *New York Times,* March 17, 1988, in "Salaries, 1988– ," Subject Files, NBL.

82. Jennings, *Balls and Strikes,* 69, 90–92; Helyar, *Lords of the Realm,* 364–82, 387; Sands and Gammons, *Coming Apart at the Seams,* 81–82, 89–91; Staudohar, *Sports Industry and Collective Bargaining,* 180; James Edward Miller, *Baseball Business,* 313–14; *USA Today,* December 15, 1989, in "Salaries, 1988– ," Subject Files, NBL; Zimbalist, *Baseball and Billions,* 48–49.

83. Marvin Miller, *Whole Different Ball Game,* 390, 392; Helyar, *Lords of the Realm,* 343; Kaplan, "Players' Main Man," 54.

CHAPTER EIGHT

1. Jack Sands and Peter Gammons, *Coming Apart at the Seams: How Baseball Owners, Players, and Television Executives Have Led Our National Pastime to the Brink of Disaster* (New York: Macmillan, 1993), xii, 93; John Helyar, *Lords of the Realm: The Real History of Baseball* (New York: Villard, 1994), 387–94; Marvin Miller, *A Whole Different Ball Game: The Sport and Business of Baseball* (New York: Birch Lane Press, 1991), 402.

2. Helyar, *Lords of the Realm,* 413; Kenneth M. Jennings, *Balls and Strikes: The Money Game in Professional Baseball* (New York: Praeger, 1990), 201–4, 220; Andrew Zimbalist, *Baseball and Billions: A Probing Look inside the Big Business of Our National Pastime* (New York: Basic Books, 1994), 64; Randal A. Hendricks, *Inside the Strike Zone* (Austin, Tex.: Eakin Press, 1994), 103–5, 197–98; *Albany Times-Union,* February 16, April 5, 1989, and *Sporting News,* April 24, 1989, in "Salaries, 1988– ," Subject Files, National Baseball Library, Cooperstown, New York (henceforth, NBL); *USA Today,* May 11, 1993, August 17, 1994; *Sport,* March 1993, 35.

3. Marvin Miller, *Whole Different Ball Game,* 394, 400–401; Jennings, *Balls and Strikes,* 90–91, 174; Helyar, *Lords of the Realm,* 395–97.

4. *USA Today,* December 9, 1994; *USA Today Baseball Weekly,* January 17–23, 1996.

5. Helyar, *Lords of the Realm,* 400–401. A good overview of the Pete Rose scandal is James Reston Jr., *Collision at Home Plate* (reprint, Lincoln: University of Nebraska Press, 1997).

6. Stephen S. Hall, "Scandals and Controversies," in *Total Baseball,* 3d ed., ed. John

Thorn and Pete Palmer (New York: HarperCollins, 1993), 206–7; *USA Today Baseball Weekly*, January 17–23, 1998; Helyar, *Lords of the Realm*, 401–3.

7. *USA Today Baseball Weekly*, January 17–23, 1998; Helyar, *Lords of the Realm*, 403–5; Marvin Miller, *Whole Different Ball Game*, 395–97.

8. Jennings, *Balls and Strikes*, 92.

9. Helyar, *Lords of the Realm*, 397–99; Sands and Gammons, *Coming Apart at the Seams*, 93.

10. Helyar, *Lords of the Realm*, 406–11.

11. Ibid., 412–13; Marvin Miller, *Whole Different Ball Game*, 403.

12. *USA Today*, January 30, April 23, 1990, in "Salaries, 1988– ," Subject Files, NBL; Lee Lowenfish, *The Imperfect Diamond: A History of Baseball's Labor Wars*, rev. ed. (New York: Da Capo, 1991), 273; Steve Mann and David Pietrusza, "The Business of Baseball," in Thorn and Palmer, *Total Baseball*, 3d ed., 568; *USA Today*, May 11, 1993; Zimbalist, *Baseball and Billions*, 116; *Sporting News*, June 18, 1990; *Sport*, March 1993; *Sports Illustrated*, June 14, 1993; *Baseball America*, February 3–16, 1997; Rob Ruck, *The Tropic of Baseball: Baseball in the Dominican Republic* (Westport, Conn.: Meckler, 1991), 69; Alan M. Klein, *Sugarball: The American Game, the Dominican Dream* (New Haven, Conn.: Yale University Press, 1991), 57–59.

13. Paul D. Staudohar, "Baseball Labor Relations: The Lockout of 1990," *Monthly Labor Review*, October 1990, 32; Jennings, *Balls and Strikes*, 195–98; Hendricks, *Inside the Strike Zone*, 8; *Sport*, March 1993.

14. Staudohar, "Baseball Labor Relations," 34; *Sporting News*, September 26, 1994; *USA Today Baseball Weekly*, August 21–27, 1996; Hendricks, *Inside the Strike Zone*, 10; Sands and Gammons, *Coming Apart at the Seams*, xiii–xiv.

15. Staudohar, "Baseball Labor Relations," 33; Helyar, *Lords of the Realm*, 413–14; Marvin Miller, *Whole Different Ball Game*, 353.

16. Lowenfish, *Imperfect Diamond*, 274; Hendricks, *Inside the Strike Zone*, 10–15.

17. Helyar, *Lords of the Realm*, 414–16; Staudohar, "Baseball Labor Relations," 33; *Sporting News*, August 21, November 6, 1989, in "Players Association," Subject Files, NBL; Lowenfish, *Imperfect Diamond*, 269, 274–75; Gerald W. Scully, *The Business of Major League Baseball* (Chicago: University of Chicago Press, 1989), 42; Sands and Gammons, *Coming Apart at the Seams*, 161–62; *New York Times*, March 2, 1989, in "Salaries, 1988– ," Subject Files, NBL.

18. *Sporting News*, August 8, 1994.

19. Staudohar, "Baseball Labor Relations," 34; Sands and Gammons, *Coming Apart at the Seams*, 176; Helyar, *Lords of the Realm*, 416–18; Hendricks, *Inside the Strike Zone*, 15–16; Marvin Miller, *Whole Different Ball Game*, 354–55.

20. Lowenfish, *Imperfect Diamond*, 276; Hendricks, *Inside the Strike Zone*, 16–18.

21. Helyar, *Lords of the Realm*, 418–19; Hendricks, *Inside the Strike Zone*, 19–25.

22. Helyar, *Lords of the Realm*, 420–23; Hendricks, *Inside the Strike Zone*, 25–31; Marvin Miller, *Whole Different Ball Game*, 355–62.

23. Staudohar, "Baseball Labor Relations," 35; Zimbalist, *Baseball and Billions,* 26.

24. Sands and Gammons, *Coming Apart at the Seams,* 5–6; Marvin Miller, *Whole Different Ball Game,* 399–400.

25. *USA Today,* November 7, 1995; Sands and Gammons, *Coming Apart at the Seams,* 7–8, 90–91, 103, 115; Helyar, *Lords of the Realm,* 364, 455–58; James Quirk and Rodney Fort, *Pay Dirt: The Business of Professional Team Sports* (Princeton, N.J.: Princeton University Press, 1992), 210–11; Zimbalist, *Baseball and Billions,* 64, 78–81; *USA Today,* August 17, 1994.

26. Zimbalist, *Baseball and Billions,* 75, 105–6; Hendricks, *Inside the Strike Zone,* 183–85, 317–18; Quirk and Fort, *Pay Dirt,* 235; *Sporting News,* March 9, 1992, in "Salaries, 1988– ," Subject Files, NBL; Sands and Gammons, *Coming Apart at the Seams,* 101, 134, 197; *Sports Illustrated,* June 14, 1993; *Baseball America,* February 3–16, 1997.

27. Zimbalist, *Baseball and Billions,* 114–16; *USA Today,* July 7, 1994.

28. Helyar, *Lords of the Realm,* 496; *USA Today,* November 7, 1995; Mann and Pietrusza, "Business of Baseball," 569; *Sports Illustrated,* May 17, 1993.

29. Sands and Gammons, *Coming Apart at the Seams,* 115, 199; Zimbalist, *Baseball and Billions,* 48–50, 57; Hendricks, *Inside the Strike Zone,* 324; Helyar, *Lords of the Realm,* 462, 494–97, 521–24; Quirk and Fort, *Pay Dirt,* 505.

30. Sands and Gammons, *Coming Apart at the Seams,* 105–17.

31. Mann and Pietrusza, "Business of Baseball," 37; Sands and Gammons, *Coming Apart at the Seams,* 106, 116–17, 239–47; Helyar, *Lords of the Realm,* 451–54, 497.

32. Marvin Miller, *Whole Different Ball Game,* 382–83, 407–12; Helyar, *Lords of the Realm,* 423–42, 481, 498–506; Zimbalist, *Baseball and Billions,* 45; Hall, "Scandals and Controversies," 207, 210, 214; Hendricks, *Inside the Strike Zone,* 38–40; Sands and Gammons, *Coming Apart at the Seams,* 181, 193–96.

33. Helyar, *Lords of the Realm,* 463–69; Zimbalist; *Baseball and Billions,* 45.

34. Hendricks, *Inside the Strike Zone,* 56; Helyar, *Lords of the Realm,* 490–91.

35. *Sporting News,* August 8, 1994; *USA Today,* November 20, 1991; Sands and Gammons, *Coming Apart at the Seams,* xv–xvi, 178–80; Hendricks, *Inside the Strike Zone,* 55; Helyar, *Lords of the Realm,* 471–79; Zimbalist, *Baseball and Billions,* 60; Hall, "Scandals and Controversies," 201–2.

36. Helyar, *Lords of the Realm,* 479–88.

37. Sands and Gammons, *Coming Apart at the Seams,* 190–91, 198–99; Hendricks, *Inside the Strike Zone,* 34–38; Helyar, *Lords of the Realm,* 488–92; Zimbalist, *Baseball and Billions,* 45.

38. Hendricks, *Inside the Strike Zone,* 56–59; Helyar, *Lords of the Realm,* 492–95, 506–17; Hall, "Scandals and Controversies," 202.

39. Sands and Gammons, *Coming Apart at the Seams,* 206–7; Hendricks, *Inside the Strike Zone,* 298–99; Helyar, *Lords of the Realm,* 517; *Sporting News,* September 19, 1994.

40. Hendricks, *Inside the Strike Zone,* 290; Helyar, *Lords of the Realm,* 518–19.

41. Hendricks, *Inside the Strike Zone*, 318–29; Zimbalist, *Baseball and Billions*, 212, 217.

42. Helyar, *Lords of the Realm*, 519–21, 527; Zimbalist, *Baseball and Billions*, 215; *USA Today*, July 27, December 7, 1993.

43. Helyar, *Lords of the Realm*, 525–528; Zimbalist, *Baseball and Billions*, 215–18; Hendricks, *Inside the Strike Zone*, 4–5.

44. *USA Today*, July 14, 1993; Helyar, *Lords of the Realm*, 528–33, 553; Hendricks, *Inside the Strike Zone*, 293–98; *Sports Illustrated*, May 17, June 7, 1993.

45. Hendricks, *Inside the Strike Zone*, 291; Helyar, *Lords of the Realm*, 534–45; Zimbalist, *Baseball and Billions*, 212.

46. Hendricks, *Inside the Strike Zone*, 298–301; *USA Today*, August 16, 1993; Helyar, *Lords of the Realm*, 524–25, 546–47.

47. Hendricks, *Inside the Strike Zone*, 301–5; *Sporting News*, January 17, 1994.

48. Hendricks, *Inside the Strike Zone*, 306–9; *Sporting News*, August 8, 1994; *USA Today*, April 5, August 17, 1994; *Wall Street Journal*, April 4, 1994.

49. Zimbalist, *Baseball and Billions*, 27; *Utica Observer-Dispatch*, July 21, 1994; *USA Today Baseball Weekly*, July 6–13, 1994; *USA Today*, April 7, July 7, August 5, 1994; Hendricks, *Inside the Strike Zone*, 312–16; "Address by Donald Fehr, National Press Club Luncheon, April 5, 1994"; *New York Times*, July 7, 1994.

50. *New York Times*, July 9, 19, 20, 31, 1994; *USA Today*, July 18, 19, 25, 28, 1994; *USA Today Baseball Weekly*, July 20–26, 1994; *Philadelphia Inquirer*, August 13, 1994.

51. *USA Today*, August 4, 5, 9, 10, 12, 1994.

52. Ibid., August 25, 1994; *Sporting News*, September 19, 1994.

53. *USA Today*, April 13, August 17, 18, 23, September 14, 22, 23, November 2, 1994; *USA Today Baseball Weekly*, September, 14–20, 1994; *Sporting News*, September 12, 1994.

54. *USA Today*, August 19, 22, 31, September 1, 7, 8, 9, 12, 14, 1994; *Sporting News*, August 29, 1994; *New York Times*, September 10, 1994; *Chicago Tribune*, September 10, 1994.

55. *USA Today Baseball Weekly*, September 21–27, October 5–11, November 2–15, 1994, September 25–October 1, 1996; *Sporting News*, September 26, October 10, 31, 1994; *Sports Illustrated*, October 3, 10, 1994; *USA Today*, September 23, 28, 29, 30, October 6, 20, November 1, 2, 7, December 17, 28, 1994, March 31, 1995; *New York Times*, October 30, 1994.

56. *USA Today*, October 14, 19, 20, November 1, 4, 9, 11, 16, 17, 18, 28, December 1, 8, 9, 12, 13, 14, 15, 16, 19, 21, 23, 1994; *New York Times*, October 18, 23, 1994; *USA Today Baseball Weekly*, October 19–25, November 16–29, 1994; *Sporting News*, December 26, 1994.

57. *USA Today*, December 27, 29, 1994, January 6, 12, 16, 17, 18, 19, 31, February 1, 1995; *Sports Illustrated*, March 6, 1995; *USA Today Baseball Weekly*, January 11–24, 1995; *Sporting News*, January 16, 1995.

58. *USA Today*, December 28, 1994, January 17, 31, February 1, 2, 7, 8, 9, 1995.

59. Ibid., February 10, 17, 20, 21, 22, 23, 27, March 3, 6, 7, 13, 14, 16, 20, 21, 22, 27,

28, 29, 30, April 3, 1995; *New York Times,* February 12, 27, March 5, 12, April 2, 1995; *Sports Illustrated,* March 13, 20, 1995; *USA Today Baseball Weekly,* March 1–7, 1995; *Sporting News,* March 13, 27, 1995.

60. *Sporting News,* April 10, November 13, 1995; *USA Today Baseball Weekly,* April 12–18, April 26–May 2, May 10–16, 24–30, August 9–15, September 20–26, 1995; *USA Today,* April 4, 5, 12, 13, 14, 19, 20, 21, 27, May 1, 2, 4, June 23, August 11, November 1, 29, 1995, February 21, April 5, 1996; *Sports Illustrated,* April 10, July 10, December 4, 1995; *New York Times,* April 3, 1995; *Baseball America,* October 16–29, 1995.

61. *Sporting News,* May 15, 1995, April 1, 1996; *USA Today,* June 9, July 12, September 19, October 25, November 7, 17, 1995, February 20, 22, March 5, 20, 1996; *Baseball America,* April 15–28, 1996; *USA Today Baseball Weekly,* August 16–22, September 20–26, November 1–7, December 6–12, 1995, January 17–23, February 19–March 3, 1996.

62. *USA Today,* March 27, May 10, June 25, July 19, August 2, 7, 12, 13, 15, 22, 27, September 5, 1996; *Sporting News,* July 22, 1996; *USA Today Baseball Weekly,* May 27–June 9, August 14–20, 21–27, 1996; *New York Times,* August 18, 1996.

63. *USA Today Baseball Weekly,* September 11–17, September 25–October 1, October 2–8, 16–22, 23–29, October 30–November 5, November 6–12, 13–19, 20–26, December 4–10, 1996; *USA Today,* September 11, 12, 25, October 28, 29, November 6, 8, 13, 14, 20, December 10, 13, 1996; *Sporting News,* November 4, 1996; *Baseball America,* November 11–24, 1996.

64. *Baseball America,* December 23, 1996–January 5, 1997.

65. *USA Today Baseball Weekly,* April 2–8, November 20–25, 1997, May 12–18, August 26–September 1, 1998, April 7–13, 1999; *USA Today,* April 3, July 25, October 3, November 14, 1997, March 3, April 2, 1998; *Baseball America,* January 5–18, January 19–February 1, 1998, May 31–June 13, 1999.

66. *USA Today,* June 26, September 12, October 1, November 21, 1997, December 18, 1998, April 6, November 10, 1999; *USA Today Baseball Weekly,* August 6–12, September 24–30, November 26–December 2, December 24–30, December 31, 1997–January 6, January 21–27, May 20–26, 1998, January 26–February 1, February 9–15, April 5–11, 2000; *Baseball America,* December 8–21, December 22, 1997–January 4, 1998; *Business Week,* December 15, 1997; *Sporting News,* January 19, 1998; *New York Times,* November 22, 1998.

67. *Sporting News,* June 1, 1998; *USA Today Baseball Weekly,* March 5–11, 12–18, July 30–August 5, October 22–28, 1997, March 25–31, 1998, January 26–February 1, 2000; *USA Today,* May 14, June 17, July 24, September 16, October 14, 1997, January 19, 1999; *Business Week,* August 11, 1997; *Baseball America,* November 10–23, 1997, January 19–February 1, August 17–30, 1998, December 21, 1998–January 3, October 18–31, 1999.

68. *Baseball America,* January 6–19, February 3–16, February 17–March 2, April 14–27, April 28–May 11, May 12–25, June 23–July 6, July 7–20, August 4–17, Septem-

ber 1–14, 15–28, October 27–November 9, November 24–December 7, 1997, December 22, 1997–January 4, January 19–February 1, March 2–15, March 30–April 12, May 11–24, 1998; *USA Today Baseball Weekly,* April 2–8, June 11–17, December 24–30, 1997, April 22–28, 1998, January 12–18, 2000; *USA Today,* April 15, September 29, 1997, February 27, 1998; *Sporting News,* April 6, 1998.

69. *USA Today Baseball Weekly,* January 29–February 4, February 12–18, March 5–11, 1997; *USA Today,* February 5, September 12, October 1, December 12, 1997, March 2, 2000.

70. *USA Today Baseball Weekly,* August 27–September 2, 1997, April 8–14, November 4–10, 1998; *USA Today,* February 6, April 1, August 24, 1998.

71. *USA Today Baseball Weekly,* October 14–20, November 4–10, December 16–22, 1998, January 13–19, 20–26, March 17–23, July 28–August 3, September 1–7, 15–21, November 10–16, December 1–7, 8–14, 1999, January 12–18, January 26–February 1, February 9–15, March 29–April 14, 2000; *Sports Illustrated,* December 21, 1998; *USA Today,* December 18, 1998, March 26, July 15, August 6, December 16, 17, 1999.

BIBLIOGRAPHIC ESSAY

As is true of other industries, baseball has provided sparse documentation of its business history. Secrecy has reigned, and although material is more plentiful for recent decades, even this data is selective and prone to manipulation. For the paternalistic era of the 1920s to the 1960s, among the few manuscript collections of management figures are the August "Garry" Herrmann Papers at the National Baseball Library in Cooperstown, New York; the Branch Rickey Papers at the Library of Congress in Washington, D.C.; and the papers of Commissioner Albert B. "Happy" Chandler in the Special Collections at the University of Kentucky, Lexington. Among the most valuable archival materials for baseball authors are three alternative sources: the Lee Allen Notebooks at the National Baseball Library, containing demographic information on each big league rookie class to 1980; the Subject Files, a collection mostly of press clippings on a range of topics, also at Cooperstown; and the Chandler Oral History Collection at the University of Kentucky, Lexington, an impressive compilation of interview tapes and transcripts by archivist Bill Marshall.

For the paternalistic era, government hearings, documents, and reports help fill the gaps. The most famous are the products of Congressman Emanuel Celler's subcommittee, titled *Study of Monopoly Power: Hearings before the Subcommittee on the Study of Monopoly Power of the Committee on the Judiciary,* serial no. 1, pt. 6, Organized Baseball, 82d Cong., 1st sess., July 30–October 24, 1951 (Washington, D.C.: Government Printing Office, 1952), and *Organized Baseball: Report of the Subcommittee on the Study of Monopoly Power of the Committee on the Judiciary,* House Report no. 2002, 82d Cong., 1st sess. (Washington, D.C.: Government Printing Office, 1952). Other inquiries include the U.S. Senate's Subcommittee on Antitrust, Monopolies, and Business Rights of the Committee on the Judiciary, *Organized Professional Team Sports: Hearings,* 85th Cong., 2d sess., July 1958 (Washington, D.C.: Government Printing Office, 1958); *Professional Sports Antitrust Bill, 1964: Hearings,* 88th Cong., January 30, 31,

February 17, 18, 1964 (Washington, D.C.: Government Printing Office, 1965); *Professional Sports Antitrust Immunity: Hearings,* 97th Cong., 2d sess., 1982 (Washington., D.C.: Government Printing Office, 1983), and 99th Cong., 1st sess., 1985 (Washington, D.C.: Government Printing Office, 1985); *Sports Programming and Cable Television,* 101st Cong., 1st sess., 1989 (Washington, D.C.: Government Printing Office, 1991); and *Baseball's Antitrust Immunity: Hearings,* 102d Cong., 2d sess, 1992 (Washington, D.C.: Government Printing Office, 1992); House Committee on Education and Labor, *Hearings: Labor Relations in Professional Sports,* 92d Cong., 2d sess., March 1972 (Washington, D.C.: Government Printing Office, 1972); House Select Committee on Professional Sports, *Inquiry into Professional Sports: Hearings* and *Final Report,* 94th Cong., 2d sess., 1976 (Washington, D.C.: Government Printing Office, 1976); and House Subcommittee on Monopolies and Commercial Law, Committee on the Judiciary, *Antitrust Policies and Professional Sports: Oversight Hearings, 1981–82,* 97th Cong., 1st and 2d sess., July 14, 15, 16, 1982 (Washington D.C.: Government Printing Office, 1984). Given the central importance of baseball's antitrust exemption, court cases also are crucial in understanding the industry's history. They include *National League of Professional Baseball Clubs v. Federal Baseball Club of Baltimore,* 269 Fed. 681 (D.C. Cir. 1921); *Federal Baseball Club of Baltimore v. National League of Professional Baseball Clubs,* 259 U.S. 200 (1922); *Gardella v. Chandler,* 79 F.Supp. 260 (S.D.N.Y., 1948), 172 F.2d 402 (2d Cir.1949); *Martin v. Chandler,* 174 F.2d 917 (2d Cir. 1949); *Gardella v. Chandler,* 174 F.2d 919 (2d. Cir. 1949); *Toolson v. New York Yankees,* 101 F.Supp. 93 (S.D. Cal. 1951), 200 F.2d 198 (9th Cir. 1952), and 346 U.S. 356 (1953); and *Flood v. Kuhn,* 407 U.S. 258 (1972).

Contemporary press coverage constitutes a vital, albeit time-consuming, source for the historian. Serving as an essential publication of record is the *Sporting News.* For the paternalistic era *Baseball Magazine* also was helpful, along with issues of *Fortune, Literary Digest, Nation, New Republic, North American Review, Outlook,* and the *Progressive.* For the inflationary era the most useful publications were *USA Today Baseball Weekly, Baseball America, Baseball Digest, Inside Sports, Sport,* and *Sports Illustrated,* supplemented by *Business Week, Ebony, Forbes, Jet, Newsweek, Time,* and *U.S. News and World Report.* Newspapers included the *New York Times* and, for recent economics coverage, *USA Today* and the *Wall Street Journal.*

Autobiographies of prominent players and management officials further assist, although their focus usually is on-field exploits. For the earlier era helpful memoirs are Jim Brosnan, *The Long Season* (New York: Harper and Brothers, 1969); Roy Campanella, *It's Good to Be Alive* (Boston: Little, Brown, 1959); Ty Cobb and Al Stump, *My Life in Baseball: The True Record* (New York: Doubleday, 1961); Bob Feller, *Strikeout Story* (New York: A. S. Barnes, 1947); Hank Greenberg with Ira Berkow, *Hank Greenberg: The Story of My Life* (New York: Times Books, 1989); Kirby Higbe with Martin Quigley, *The High Hard One* (New York: Viking, 1967); Rogers Hornsby with Bill Surface, *My War with Baseball* (New York: Coward-McCann, 1962); Monte Irvin with James A. Riley, *Nice Guys Finish First* (New York: Simon and Schuster,

1996); Stan Musial and Bob Broeg, *The Man Stan: Musial, Then and Now* (St. Louis: Beltway Press, 1977); Leroy "Satchel" Paige, *Maybe I'll Pitch Tomorrow* (Garden City, N.J.: Doubleday, 1962); Jackie Robinson with Alfred Duckett, *I Never Had It Made* (New York: Putnam's, 1972); and Ted Williams with John Underwood, *My Turn at Bat* (New York: Simon and Schuster, 1969).

Player remembrances from the modern era have tended to be more candid. The best of these include Hank Aaron with Lonnie Wheeler, *I Had a Hammer: The Hank Aaron Story* (New York: HarperCollins, 1991); Dick Allen and Tim Whitaker, *Crash* (New York: Ticknor and Fields, 1989); Don Baylor with Claire Smith, *Don Baylor: Nothing but the Truth* (New York: St. Martin's, 1989); Jim Bouton, *Ball Four* (New York: World, 1970); Roger Clemens with Peter Gammons, *Rocket Man: The Roger Clemens Story* (Lexington, Mass.: Stephen Greene, 1987); Don Drysdale, *Once a Bum, Always a Dodger* (New York: St. Martin's, 1990); Curt Flood with Richard Carter, *The Way It Is* (New York: Trident, 1971); Bob Gibson with Lonnie Wheeler, *Stranger to the Game: The Autobiography of Bob Gibson* (New York: Penguin, 1996); Keith Hernandez, *If at First* (New York: McGraw-Hill, 1986); Jim "Catfish" Hunter with Armen Keteyian, *Catfish: My Life in Baseball* (New York: McGraw-Hill, 1988); Reggie Jackson with Mike Lupica, *Reggie* (New York: Villard, 1984); Sandy Koufax with Ed Linn, *Koufax* (New York: Viking, 1966); Bill Lee and Dick Lilly, *The Wrong Stuff* (New York: Viking, 1984); Sparky Lyle and Peter Golenbock, *The Bronx Zoo* (New York: Crown, 1979); Denny McLain with Dave Diles, *Nobody's Perfect* (New York: Dial, 1975); Mickey Mantle and Herb Glick, *The Mick* (New York: Doubleday, 1985); Willie Mays and Lou Sahadi, *Say Hey: The Autobiography of Willie Mays* (New York: Simon and Schuster, 1988); Cal Ripken Jr. and Mike Bryan, *The Only Way I Know* (New York: Penguin, 1997); Frank Robinson and Barry Stainback, *Extra Innings* (New York: McGraw-Hill, 1988); Pete Rose and Roger Kahn, *Pete Rose: My Story* (New York: Macmillan, 1989); Willie Stargell and Tom Bird, *Willie Stargell* (New York: Harper and Row, 1984); Bob Welch and George Vescey, *Five O'Clock Comes Early* (New York: William Morrow, 1982); and Dave Winfield with Tom Parker, *Winfield: A Player's Life* (New York: Norton, 1988). Arbiter Ron Luciano offers a similarly open portrait in *The Umpire Strikes Back* (New York: Bantam, 1982).

Nonperformers, from managers, owners, league presidents, and commissioners to union officials and agents, have given accounts with varying degrees of candor. For the paternalistic era the reader should consult Edward G. Barrow with James M. Kahn, *My Fifty Years in Baseball* (New York: Coward-McCann, 1951); Buzzie Bavasi with John Strege, *Off the Record* (Chicago: Contemporary Books, 1987); Leo Durocher, *Nice Guys Finish Last* (New York: Simon and Schuster, 1975); Ford C. Frick, *Games, Asterisks, and People: Memoirs of a Lucky Fan* (New York: Crown, 1973); John J. McGraw, *My Thirty Years in Baseball* (New York: Boni and Liveright, 1928); Connie Mack, *My Sixty-six Years in the Big Leagues* (Philadelphia: John C. Winston, 1950); Effa Manley and Leon Hardwick, *Negro Baseball* (Chicago: Adams Press, 1976); and Bill Veeck with Ed Linn, *Hustler's Handbook* (New York: Putnam's, 1965) and *Veeck—As in Wreck* (New York: Bantam, 1963). Recent diarists include Jerry Colangelo with Len Sherman, *How You Play the Game: Lessons for Life from the Billion-Dollar Business of Sports* (Watertown, Mass.: Amacom, 1999); Bowie Kuhn, *Hardball: The Education of a Baseball Commissioner* (New York: Times Books, 1987); Lee Mac-Phail, *My Nine Innings: An Autobiography of Fifty Years in Baseball* (Westport, Conn.: Meckler, 1989); Tom Monaghan with Robert Anderson, *Pizza Tiger* (New York: Random House, 1986); and Peter Ueberroth, *Made in America* (New York: William Morrow, 1985). Marvin Miller offers his perspective on the Players Association in *A Whole Different Ball Game: The Sport and Business of Baseball* (New York: Birch Lane Press, 1991), and agent Randal A. Hendricks weighs in on the state of labor-management relations in *Inside the Strike Zone* (Austin, Tex.: Eakin Press, 1994).

Much of the best baseball scholarship being written is in the area of biography. Player histories include Frank Dolson, *Jim Bunning: Baseball and Beyond* (Philadelphia: Temple University Press, 1998); Charles C. Alexander, *Ty Cobb* (New York: Oxford University Press, 1984); Robert Gregory, *Diz: The Story of Dizzy Dean and Baseball during the Great Depression* (New York: Penguin, 1992); William Brashler, *Josh Gibson: A Life in the Negro Leagues* (New York: Harper and Row, 1978); Alexander, *Rogers Hornsby: A Biography* (New York: Henry Holt, 1996); Henry Thomas, *Walter Johnson: Baseball's Big Train* (Lincoln, Neb.: Bison Books, 1995); David Faulkner, *Great Time Coming: The Life of Jackie Robinson from Baseball to Birmingham* (New York: Simon and Schuster, 1995); Arnold Rampersand, *Jackie Robinson: A Biography* (New York: Alfred A. Knopf, 1997); Jules Tygiel, *Baseball's Great Experiment: Jackie Robinson and His Legacy* (New York: Oxford University Press, 1983); Michael Sokolove, *Hustle: The Myth, Life, and Lies of Pete Rose* (New York: Simon and Schuster, 1990); and Robert W. Creamer, *Babe: The Legend Comes to Life* (New York: Simon and Schuster, 1974). For umpire collective biographies, see Larry R. Gerlach, *The Men in Blue* (New York: Viking, 1980), and James M. Kahn, *The Umpire Story* (New York: Putnam, 1953).

Biographies of premodern management figures are Eugene Murdock, *Ban Johnson: Czar of Baseball* (Westport, Conn.: Greenwood, 1986); David Pietrusza, *Judge and Jury: The Life and Times of Judge Kenesaw Mountain Landis* (South Bend, Ind.: Diamond, 1998); J. G. Taylor Spink, *Judge Landis and Twenty-five Years of Baseball* (New York: Thomas Crowell, 1974); Charles C. Alexander, *John McGraw* (New York: Viking, 1988); Don Warfield, *The Roaring Redhead: Larry MacPhail, Baseball's Great Innovator* (South Bend, Ind.: Diamond, 1987); James Overmyer, *Queen of the Negro Leagues: Effa Manley and the Newark Eagles* (Lanham, Md.: Scarecrow Press, 1998); Arthur Mann, *Branch Rickey* (Cambridge, Mass.: Riverside Press, 1957); Murray Polner, *Branch Rickey: A Biography* (New York: Atheneum, 1982); and Robert W. Creamer, *Stengel: His Life and Times* (New York: Simon and Schuster, 1984). Accounts of latter-day figures include Peter Hernon and Terry Gainey, *Under the Influence: The Unauthorized Story of the Anheuser-Busch Dynasty* (New York: Simon and Schuster, 1991); James Reston Jr.'s look at A. Bartlett Giamatti and the Pete Rose case, *Collision at Home Plate* (reprint, Lincoln: University of Nebraska Press, 1997); Gail De George, *The Making of a Blockbuster: How Wayne Huizenga Built a Sports and Entertainment Empire from Trash, Grit, and Videotape* (New York: John Wiley, 1996); William Shawcross, *Murdoch: The Making of a Media Empire* (New York: Touchstone, 1997); Dick Schaap, *Steinbrenner* (New York: Putnam's, 1982); Porter Bibb, *Ted Turner: It Ain't As Easy As It Looks* (New York: Crown, 1993); Robert Goldberg and Gerald Jay Goldberg, *Citizen Turner: The Wild Ride of an American Tycoon* (New York: Harcourt Brace, 1995); and Evan Thomas, *The Man to See: Edward Bennett Williams, Ultimate Insider, Legendary Trial Lawyer* (New York: Simon and Schuster, 1991). Group portraits are Jerome Holtzman, *The Commissioners: Baseball's Midlife Crisis* (Raleigh, N.C.: Total Sports, 1998); Don Kowet, *The Rich Who Own Sports* (New York: Random House, 1977); and Harold Parrott, *The Lords of Baseball* (New York: Praeger, 1976).

Any listing of general baseball histories should include Charles C. Alexander, *Our Game: An American Baseball History* (New York: Henry Holt, 1991); Lee Allen, *The American League Story* (New York: Hill and Wang, 1962) and *The National League Story* (New York: Hill and Wang, 1961); Joseph Durso, *Baseball and the American Dream* (St. Louis, Mo.: Sporting News, 1986); Bill James, *The Bill James Historical Baseball Abstract* (New York: Villard, 1986); Benjamin G. Rader, *Baseball: A History of America's Game* (Urbana: University of Illinois Press, 1992); Steven A. Riess, *City Games: The Evolution of American Urban Society and the Rise of Sports* (Urbana: University of Illinois Press, 1989); Harold Seymour, *Baseball: The Golden Age* (New York: Oxford University Press, 1971); Robert Smith, *Baseball* (New York: Simon and Schuster, 1970); Ted Vincent, *Mudville's Revenge: The Rise and Fall of American Sport* (New York: Seaview, 1974); David Q. Voigt, *American Baseball*, vol. 2, *From the Commissioners to Continental Expansion* (reprint, University Park: Pennsylvania State University Press, 1983), and vol. 3, *From Postwar Expansion to the Electronic Age* (University Park: Pennsylvania State University Press, 1983); and G. Edward White, *Creating the National Pastime: Baseball Transforms Itself, 1903–1953* (Princeton, N.J.: Princeton University Press, 1996). The two main major league statistical compendiums are the *Baseball Encyclopedia* (New York: Macmillan, 1969–) and John Thorn and Pete Palmer, eds., *Total Baseball* (New York: Warner Books, 1989–), with the latter also featuring a changing lineup of historical essays in each edition.

Less comprehensive but offering important detail are team, period, and oral histories. For the paternalistic years see Eliot Asinof, *Eight Men Out: The Black Sox and the 1919 World Series* (New York: Holt, Rinehart and Winston, 1963); Red Barber, *1947: When All Hell Broke Loose in Baseball* (Garden City, N.Y.: Doubleday, 1982); Robert W. Creamer, *Baseball in '41* (New York: Penguin, 1991); Richard C. Crepeau, *Baseball: America's Diamond Mind, 1919–1941* (Orlando: University Presses of Florida, 1980); Bill Gilbert, *They Also Served: Baseball and the Home Front, 1941–1945* (New York: Crown, 1992); Richard Goldstein, *Spartan Seasons: How Baseball Survived the Second World War* (New York: Macmillan, 1980); Peter Golenbock, *Bums: An Oral History of the Brooklyn Dodgers* (New York: Putnam, 1984) and *Dynasty: The New York Yankees, 1949–1964* (Englewood Cliffs, N.J.: Prentice-Hall, 1975); David Halberstam, *Summer of '49* (New York: William Morrow, 1989) and *October 1964* (New York: Villard, 1994); Donald Honig, *Baseball between the Lines* (New York: Coward-McCann, 1976) and *Baseball When the Grass Was Real* (New York: Coward-McCann, 1975); Roger Kahn, *The Era, 1947–1957: When the Yankees, the Giants, and the Dodgers Ruled the World* (New York: Ticknor and Fields, 1993); Bruce Kuklick, *To Every Thing a Season: Shibe Park and Urban Philadelphia, 1909–1976* (Princeton, N.J.: Princeton University Press, 1991); William Marshall, *Baseball's Pivotal Era, 1945–1951* (Lexington: University Press of Kentucky, 1999); Eugene Murdock, ed., *Baseball between the Wars: Memories of the Game by the Men Who Played It* (Westport, Conn.: Meckler, 1992) and *Baseball Players and Their Times: Oral Histories of the Game, 1920–1940* (Westport, Conn.: Meckler, 1991); John Phillips, *The Mexican Jumping Beans: The Story of the Baseball War of 1946* (Perry, Ga.: Capital, 1997); Lawrence S. Ritter, *The Glory of Their Times* (New York: Vintage, 1985); Ritter and Honig, *The Image of Their Greatness,* 2d ed. (New York: Crown, 1984); Neil J. Sullivan, *The Dodgers Move West* (New York: Oxford University Press, 1987); Frederick Turner, *When the Boys Came Back: Baseball and 1946* (New York: Henry Holt, 1996); and the G. P. Putnam series of team histories of the late 1940s and early 1950s by Lee Allen, Frank Graham, Shirley Povich, and others.

In recent years the Negro Leagues have spawned a rich literature. Besides other individual memoirs and biographies cited above, the list includes Dick Clark and Larry Lester, eds., *The Negro Leagues Book* (Cleveland, Ohio: Society for American Baseball Research, 1994); Robert Peterson, *Only the Ball Was White* (Englewood Cliffs, N.J.: Prentice-Hall, 1970); Mark Ribowsky, *A Complete History of the Negro Leagues, 1884 to 1955* (New York: Birch Lane, 1995); Donn Rogosin, *Invisible Men: Life in Baseball's Negro Leagues* (New York: Atheneum, 1985); and Art Rust Jr., *"Get That Nigger Off the Field!"* (New York: Delacorte, 1976). Oral histories include John B. Holway, *Black Diamonds* (Westport, Conn.: Meckler, 1989); Holway, *Blackball Stars* (Westport, Conn.: Meckler, 1988); Holway, *Voices from the Great Negro Baseball Leagues* (New York: Dodd, Mead, 1975); and Brent Kelly, *Voices from the Negro Leagues* (Jefferson, N.C.: McFarland, 1998). Other works on individual teams and cities are Richard Bak, *Turkey Stearnes and the Detroit Stars: The Negro Leagues in Detroit, 1919–1933* (Detroit: Wayne State University Press, 1994); James Bankes, *The Pittsburgh Crawfords: The Lives and Times of Black Baseball's Most Exciting Team* (Pittsburgh: W. C. Brown, 1991); Janet Bruce, *The Kansas City Monarchs: Champions of Black Baseball* (Lawrence: University Press of Kansas, 1985); Paul Debono, *The Indianapolis ABC's* (Jefferson, N.C.: McFarland, 1997); and Rob Ruck, *Sandlot Seasons: Sport in Black Pittsburgh* (Urbana: University of Illinois Press, 1987). On women's professional leagues and players, see Gai Ingham Berlage, *Women in Baseball: The Forgotten History* (Westport, Conn.: Praeger, 1994), and W. C. Madden, *The Women of the All-American Girls Professional Baseball League: A Biographical Dictionary* (Jefferson, N.C.: McFarland, 1997).

Since the 1970s, studies of recent big league teams, cities, and eras have paid more attention to economic issues. The best single account of baseball's off-field agonies during the past four decades is John Helyar, *Lords of the Realm: The Real History of Baseball* (New York: Villard, 1994). Among other studies are Tom Clark, *Champagne and Baloney: The Rise and Fall of Finley's A's* (New York: Harper and Row, 1976); Bob Costas, *Fair Ball: A Fan's Case for Baseball* (New York: Broadway Books, 2000); John Feinstein, *Play Ball: The Life and Troubled Times of Major League Baseball* (New York: Villard, 1993); Bruce Markusen, *Baseball's Last Dynasty: Charlie Finley's Oakland A's* (Indianapolis: Masters Press, 1998); James Edward Miller, *The Baseball Business: Pursuing Pennants and Profits in Baltimore* (Chapel Hill: University of North Carolina Press, 1990); Larry Millson, *Ballpark Figures: The Blue Jays and the Business of Baseball* (Toronto: McClelland and Stewart, 1987); Peter Richmond, *Ballpark: Camden Yards and the Building of a Dream* (New York: Simon and Schuster, 1993); Dave Rosenbaum, *If They Don't Win It's a Shame: The Year the Marlins Bought the World Series* (Tampa, Fla.: McGregor, 1998); Jack Sands and Peter Gammons, *Coming Apart at the Seams: How Owners, Players, and Television Executives Have Led Our National Pastime to the Brink of Disaster* (New York: Macmillan, 1993); and Len Sherman, *Big League, Big Time: The Birth of the Arizona Diamondbacks, the Billion-Dollar Business of Sports, and the Power of the Media in America* (New York: Pocket Books, 1998).

Owing to, and adding to, the modern awareness of baseball's industrial relations, an impressive book literature on the sport's economics, law, and labor history has emerged in the past quarter-century. Predecessors of this generation of studies are Peter S. Craig, "Organized Baseball: An Industry Study of a $100 Million Spectator Sport" (B.A. thesis, Oberlin College, 1950); Paul M. Gregory, *The Baseball Player: An Economic Study* (Washington, D.C.: Public Affairs Press, 1956); and Robert W. Smith, "The Business Side of Baseball" (M.A. thesis, Princeton University, 1948). General treatments of baseball's modern economics include John Fizel, Elizabeth Gustafson, and Lawrence Hadley, eds., *Sports Economics: Current Research* (New York: Praeger, 1999); Brian Goff and Robert Tollison, eds., *Sportometrics* (College Station: Texas A&M University Press, 1990); Jerry Gorman and Kirk Calhoun, *The Name of the Game: The Business of Sports* (New York: John Wiley, 1994); James Quirk and Rodney Fort, *Pay Dirt: The Business of Professional Team Sports* (Princeton, N.J.: Princeton University Press, 1992) and *Hard Ball: The Abuse of Power in Pro Team Sports* (Princeton, N.J.: Princeton University Press, 1999); Gerald W. Scully, *The Business of Major League Baseball* (Chicago: University of Chicago Press, 1989); Paul Sommers, ed., *Diamonds Are Forever: The Business of Baseball* (Washington, D.C.: Brookings Institution, 1992); Paul D. Staudohar and James A. Mangan, eds., *The Business of Professional Sports* (Urbana: University of Illinois Press, 1991); and arguably the best, Andrew Zimbalist, *Baseball and Billions: A Probing Look inside the Big Business of Our National Pastime* (New York: Basic Books, 1994). Analyses of particular issues are Roger I. Abrams, *The Money Pitch: Baseball Free Agency and Salary Arbitration* (Philadelphia: Temple University Press, 2000); Dean Baim, *The Sports Sta-*

dium as a Municipal Investment (Westport, Conn.: Greenwood, 1992); Joan Chandler, *Television and National Sport: The U.S. and Britain* (Urbana: University of Illinois Press, 1988); Dale Hoffman and Martin Greenberg, *SportsBiz: An Irreverent Look at Big Business in Pro Sports* (Champaign, Ill.: Leisure Press, 1989); David Klatell and Norman Marcus, *Sports for Sale: Television, Money, and the Fans* (New York: Oxford University Press, 1989); Roger G. Noll and Andrew Zimbalist, *Sports, Jobs, and Taxes: The Economic Impact of Sports Teams and Facilities* (Washington, D.C.: Brookings Institution, 1997); Gerald W. Scully, *The Market Structure of Sports* (Chicago: University of Chicago Press, 1995); and David Whitford, *Playing Hardball: The High-Stakes Battle for Baseball's New Franchises* (New York: Doubleday, 1993).

A comprehensive account of baseball's tumultuous labor history is Lee Lowenfish, *The Imperfect Diamond: A History of Baseball's Labor Wars,* rev. ed. (New York: Da Capo, 1991). Other book-length works on the industry's labor-management relationship include Richard Armstrong, "The Unionization of Baseball" (B.A. thesis, Princeton University, 1947); Robert C. Berry, William B. Gould IV, and Paul D. Staudohar, *Labor Relations in Professional Sports* (Dover, Mass.: Auburn House, 1986); Michael R. Blankshain, "The Labor Market in Major League Baseball" (B.A. thesis, Princeton University, 1978); James B. Dworkin, *Owners versus Players: Baseball and Collective Bargaining* (Boston: Auburn House, 1981); Kenneth M. Jennings, *Balls and Strikes: The Money Game in Professional Baseball* (New York: Praeger, 1990); and Paul D. Staudohar, *The Sports Industry and Collective Bargaining,* 2d ed. (Ithaca, N.Y.: ILR Press, 1989). On the related issues of baseball's relationship to the law and government oversight, see Roger I. Abrams, *Legal Bases: Baseball and the Law* (Philadelphia: Temple University Press, 1998); Robert B. Berry and Glenn M. Wong, *Law and Business of the Sports Industries,* vols. 1 and 2 (Dover, Mass.: Auburn House, 1986); John Daly, ed., *Pro Sports: Should the Government Intervene* (Washington, D.C.: American Enterprise Institute, 1977); Arthur T. Johnson and James H. Frey, eds., *Government and Sport: The Public Policy Issues* (Totowa, N.J.: Rowman and Allenheld, 1985); Stephen R. Lowe, *The Kid on the Sandlot: Congress and Professional Sports, 1910–1992* (Bowling Green, Ohio: Bowling Green State University Popular Press, 1995); Jesse W. Markham and Paul V. Teplitz, *Baseball Economics and Public Policy* (Lexington, Mass.: Lexington Press, 1981); Roger G. Noll, ed., *Government and the Sports Business* (Washington, D.C.: Brookings Institution, 1974); Paul Porter, *Organized Baseball and the Congress* (New York: Major League Baseball, 1961); Lionel S. Sobel, *Professional Sports and the Law* (New York: Law-Arts Publishers, 1977); Gary Uberstine, ed., *Law of Professional and Amateur Sports* (New York: Clark Boardman, 1988); and Ray Yasser, ed., *Sports Law: Cases and Materials* (Lanham, Md.: University Presses of America, 1985).

One overdue spinoff of baseball scholarship is the attention being paid to the minors. General works are Arthur Johnson, *Minor League Baseball and Local Economic Development* (Urbana: University of Illinois Press, 1993); Lloyd Johnson and Miles Wolff, eds., *The Encyclopedia of Minor League Baseball* (Durham, N.C.: Baseball America, 1993); Robert Obojski, *Bush League: A History of Minor League Baseball* (New York: Macmillan, 1975); and Neil J. Sullivan, *The Minors: The Struggles and the Triumph of Baseball's Poor Relation from 1876 to the Present* (New York: St. Martin's, 1990). An important new study of the racial desegregation of the minors is Bruce Adelson, *Brushing Back Jim Crow: The Integration of Minor League Baseball in the American South* (Charlottesville: University Press of Virginia, 1999). Histories of individual circuits include Bill O'Neal, *The American Association: A Baseball History, 1902–1990* (Austin, Tex.: Eakin Press, 1990); O'Neal, *The International League: A Baseball History, 1884–1991* (Austin, Tex.: Eakin Press, 1991); O'Neal, *The Pacific Coast League* (Austin, Tex.: Eakin Press, 1990); O'Neal, *The Texas League: A Century of Baseball, 1888–1987* (Austin, Tex.: Eakin Press, 1987); Jim L. Sumner, *Separating the Men from the Boys: The First Half-Century of the Carolina League* (Winston-Salem, N.C.: John F. Blair, 1994); and Paul J. Zingg and Mark D. Medeiros, *Runs, Hits, and an Era: The Pacific Coast League, 1903–58* (Urbana: University of Illinois Press, 1994).

If the baseball industry's book literature has grown by leaps and bounds, the same also can be said of scholarly journals and articles. Leading publications on the history of baseball and of sports are the *Journal of Sport History*, the *Baseball Research Journal*, the *National Pastime*, and *SABR's by the Numbers*, the latter trio issued by the Society for American Baseball Research. Other annual compilations are *Baseball History* and the *Cooperstown Symposium on Baseball and the American Culture*, both from Meckler Publishing. For article treatments in economics and law journals of past labor-management negotiations and confrontations, see Thomas H. Bruggink and David R. Rose Jr., "Financial Restraint in the Free Agent Labor Market for Major League Baseball: Players Look at Strike Three," *Southern Economic Journal* 56 (April 1990): 1029–43; Lawrence DeBrock and Alvin Roth, "Strike Two: Labor-Management Negotiations in Major League Baseball," *Bell Journal of Economics* 12 (Autumn 1981): 413–25; T. Gilroy and P. Madden, "Labor Relations in Professional Sports," *Labor Law Journal* 27 (December 1977): 768–76; Erwin G. Krasnow and Herman M. Levy, "Unionization and Professional Sports," *Georgetown Law Journal* 51 (1962–63): 749–82; Robert McCormick, "Baseball's Third Strike: The Triumph of Collective Bargaining in Professional Baseball," *Vanderbilt Law Review* 35 (October 1982): 1131–69; Alvin E. Roth, "Further Thoughts from the Power of Alternatives: An Example from Labor-Management Negotiations in Major League Baseball," *Negotiation Journal*, October 1985, 359–62; and Paul D. Staudohar, "Baseball Labor Relations: The Lockout of 1990," *Monthly Labor Review*, October 1990, 32–36.

A massive periodical literature since the 1970s has been generated on the issues of the reserve, arbitration, and free agency. A select list of works includes James R. Chelius and James B. Dworkin, "Free Agency and Salary Determination in Baseball," *Labor Law Journal* 33 (August 1982): 539–45; Peter S. Craig, "Monopsony in Manpower: Organized Baseball Meets the Anti-Trust Laws," *Yale Law Journal* 62 (March 1953): 576–639; Donald J. Cymrot, "Migration Trends and Earnings of Free Agents in Major League Baseball, 1976–79," *Economic Inquiry* 21 (October 1983):

545–56; Christopher Drahozel, "The Impact of Free Agency on the Distribution of Playing Talent in Major League Baseball," *Journal of Economics and Business* 38 (May 1986): 113–22; James B. Dworkin, "Salary Arbitration in Baseball: An Impartial Assessment after Ten Years," *Arbitration Journal* 41 (March 1986): 63–70; James Hill and William Spellman, "Professional Baseball: The Reserve Clause and Salary Structure," *Industrial Relations* 22 (Winter 1983): 1–19; Kenneth Lehn, "Property Rights, Risk Sharing, and Player Disability in Major League Baseball," *Journal of Law and Economics* 25 (October 1982): 343–66 and "Information Asymmetrics in Baseball's Free Agency Market," *Economic Inquiry* 22 (September 1984): 37–44; Henry J. Raimundo, "Free Agents' Impact on the Labor Market for Baseball Players," *Journal of Labor Research* (Spring 1983): 183–94; Simon Rottenberg, "The Baseball Player's Labor Market," *Journal of Political Economy* 64 (June 1956): 242–58; Gerald W. Scully, "Pay and Performance in Major League Baseball," *American Economic Review* 64 (December 1974): 915–31; Paul M. Sommers and Noel Quinton, "Pay and Performance in Major League Baseball: The Case of the First Family of Free Agents," *Journal of Human Resources* (Summer 1982): 426–36; Paul D. Staudohar and Edwin W. Smith, "The Impact of Free Agency on Baseball Salaries," *Compensation Review* 3 (1981): 46–55; and Glenn M. Wong, "A Survey of Grievance Arbitration Cases in Major League Baseball," *Arbitration Journal* 41 (March 1986): 42–62.

Book-length works on the industry's ethnic and racial composition include Arthur R. Ashe Jr., *A Hard Road to Glory,* vol. 1, *A History of the African-American Athlete, 1919–1945,* and vol. 2, *A History of the African-American Athlete since 1946* (New York: Warner Books, 1988); Peter Levine, *Ellis Island to Ebbets Field: Sport and the American Jewish Experience* (New York: Oxford University Press, 1992); Bernard Postal, Jesse Silver, and Roy Silver, *Encyclopedia of Jews in Sports* (New York: Bloch, 1965); and Harold Seymour, *Baseball: The People's Game* (New York: Oxford University Press, 1990). The modern-day rise of Hispanic players also is spawning an impressive literature, including Roberto Gonzalez-Echevarria, *The Pride of Havana: A History of Cuban Baseball* (New York: Oxford University Press, 1999); Alan M. Klein, *Sugarball: The American Game, the Dominican Dream* (New Haven, Conn.: Yale University Press, 1991); John Krich, *El Beisbol* (New York: Atlantic Monthly Press, 1989); Michael M. Oleksak and Mary Adams Oleksak, *Beisbol: Latin Americans and the Grand Old Game* (Grand Rapids, Mich.: Masters Press, 1991); Samuel Regalado, *Viva Baseball! Latin Major Leaguers and Their Special Hunger* (Urbana: University of Illinois Press, 1998); and Rob Ruck, *The Tropic of Baseball: Baseball in the Dominican Republic* (Westport, Conn.: Meckler, 1991). Articles on latter-day race discrimination in baseball include James Gwartney and Charles Haworth, "Employer Costs and Discrimination: The Case of Baseball," *Journal of Political Economy* 82 (July–August 1974): 873–82; James Hill and William Spellman, "Pay Discrimination in Baseball: Data from the Seventies," *Industrial Relations* (Winter 1984): 103–12; Marshall H. Medoff, "A Reappraisal of Racial Discrimination against Blacks in Professional Baseball," *Review of Black Political Economy,* Spring 1975, 259–68; Robert G. Mogull, "Salary Discrimination in Major League Baseball," *Review of Black Political Economy,* Spring 1975, 269–79; Anthony H. Pascal and Leonard A. Rapping, "The Economics of Racial Discrimination in Organized Baseball," in *Racial Discrimination in Economic Life,* ed. Pascal (Lexington, Mass.: Lexington Books, 1972), 119–56; Aaron Rosenblatt, "Negroes in Baseball: The Failure of Success," *Transaction* 4 (September 1967): 51–53; and Gerald W. Scully, "Economic Discrimination in Professional Sports," *Law and Contemporary Problems,* Winter–Spring 1973, 67–84.

INDEX

238, 247, 254, 279–80, 285–86, 290, 299, 301
Atlanta Crackers, 135
Autry, Gene, 192, 207

Baker, James, 244
Ball, Phil, 38, 46
Ballow, Robert, 293
Ballparks, 111, 138, 165, 217, 277, 282, 285
Baltimore Orioles, 25, 30, 51, 124, 126, 152, 158, 161, 175, 187, 195, 203–4, 225, 227, 229–30, 271, 277, 282, 289, 292, 299
Bando, Sal, 204, 228
Bankhead, Sam, 76
Banks, Ernie, 131
Barber, Red, 96, 115
Barber, Steve, 124
Barlick, Al, 140–41
Barnstorming, 5, 13, 18–19, 33, 55, 60, 76, 92, 211
Barrow, Ed, 26, 51
Barry, Rick, 180, 197
Bartelone, Phil, 65
Bartholomay, Bill, 176
Basic Agreements: of 1968, 157–58, 166, 189; of 1970, 164–70, 179, 189; of 1973, 186–87, 191, 196, 199–202; of 1976, 206, 209–12; of 1980, 226–27; of 1981, 234–35, 246; of 1985, 249–53; of 1990, 273, 278, 282, 285, 293; of 1996, 296–98
Bavasi, Buzzie, 114, 156, 188, 192
Baylor, Don, 168, 204–7, 232
Beeston, Paul, 292, 299
Belanger, Mark, 224, 230, 234
Belle, Albert, 295
Bench, Johnny, 232
Bennett, Fred, 46
Benswanger, William, 60, 79–80, 89–91
Bentley, Jack, 25, 30
Berger, Sy, 159
Berra, Yogi, 113, 115
"Best interests of baseball" powers, 13, 164, 204, 263, 286, 299
Bishop, Max, 44

Blackmun, Harry, 181
"Black Sox" scandal, 5, 7, 12–14, 16, 252
Blades, Ray, 61
Blefary, Curt, 158
Bloch, Richard, 238, 251
Block, Cy, 114
Blue, Vida, 204, 238
Blue Ridge League, 38, 51
Bodley, Hal, 280
Bonds, Barry, 289
Bonham, Ernie, 118
Bonilla, Bobby, 289, 291
"Bonus babies," 63–64, 84, 104, 126–29
Bonuses: incentive, 24–26, 55–56, 135; amateur draftees' signing, 218, 167–68, 274
Boone, Bob, 168, 201, 228, 248, 256, 272
Boras, Scott, 274
Bostic, Joe, 81
Boston Braves, 24, 51, 91, 126–27
Boston Red Sox, 4, 24, 44, 71, 80, 94, 104, 120, 130–31, 174, 177, 191, 204, 207, 223, 225, 256, 266, 286, 289
Bouton, Jim, 154–55, 179
Bowman, Bob, 50
Bragan, Bobby, 98–99
Bramham, Walter, 65
Branca, Ralph, 102
Breadon, Sam, 35, 38, 62, 65–66, 92, 94, 101, 132
Brennan, William, 181
Brewer, Chet, 80
Brock, Lou, 136
Brooklyn Dodgers, 5, 24, 60, 65, 70–71, 81, 95–104, 109, 113, 115, 125–27, 130
Brosnan, Jim, 178
Broun, Heywood, 10, 58
Brown, Bobby, 277
Brown, Jimmy, 90–91
Brown, Willard, 102
Brubaker, Otis, 147
Bruton, Bill, 133
Bunning, Jim, 146, 148
Burger, Warren, 181
Burke, Glenn, 214

8, 216–17, 228, 241–42, 247, 250, 252,
266, 276–77, 285–87, 298–99
Nicolau, George, 257, 259–60, 268, 273,
275
Niekro brothers, 232
Nightengale, Bob, 302
Nixon, Otis, 257, 278
Nixon, Richard, 148, 151, 174, 180–81,
230, 249
Nixon, Russ, 161
Noll, Roger, 247, 289
Northeast Arkansas League, 65
Northern League, 63, 65
North Texas League, 34
Nugent, Gerry, 79–80
Nuxhall, Joe, 72

Oakland Athletics, 162, 175, 185, 187–91,
200, 203–4, 207, 214, 216, 218, 240, 244
O'Connell, Jimmy, 15–16, 30
O'Connor, Chuck, 258–59, 267, 269–71
O'Connor, Leslie, 24, 47, 65–66, 81, 92,
116
O'Doul, Lefty, 42
Olerud, John, 267
Oliva, Tony, 198
Oliver, John, 196–99
O'Malley, Peter, 245–46, 259, 266
O'Malley, Walter, 109, 115, 120, 132, 149,
157, 159, 174, 176, 183, 185–86, 193, 195,
203–4, 221, 244–45, 250
O'Neill, Buck, 136
Orsatti, Ernie, 52–53
Orza, Gene, 269–71
Owen, Mickey, 71, 85, 105–6
Owners: turnover in, 41, 111, 218; back-
grounds of, 111, 154–56, 200, 240;
factions among, 174, 218, 239–40, 242,
249, 267–68, 270–71, 273, 276–77,
281–86, 289–90, 294–96, 298–99, 303

Pacific Coast League, 30–31, 37, 65, 77,
80, 84–85, 92, 113, 125–26
Padgett, Don, 51
Pagan, Jose, 132

Paige, Satchel, 60, 77–78, 96–97
Palermo, Steve, 287, 299
Palmer, Jim, 161, 202
Panama Professional Baseball League,
105
Papanella, Joseph, 140
Pappas, Milt, 158
Parker, Dan, 58
Parker, Dave, 253
Parker, Wes, 175
Parrish, Lance, 255
Parrott, Harold, 98
Partlow, Ray, 98
Pasquel, Jorge, 76, 85–86, 195
Paulette, Eugene, 13
Pegler, Westbrook, 58
Pelekoudas, Chris, 140
Pennock, Herb, 26, 101
Pensions: major league player, 4, 6–8,
55, 88, 92–95, 117–24, 146, 149, 151–
53, 155, 159–62, 166, 172–77, 184, 186,
202–3, 206, 209–10, 222–24, 226, 231,
237, 246–49, 270–71, 273, 287, 292–93;
umpire, 87, 140–41, 171
Peoples, Nat, 135
Pepper, George Wharton, 9
Peralta, Vicente, 227
Perez, Pasqual, 238
Perry, Gaylord, 192
Perry, Jim, 175
Pesky, Johnny, 70–71
Peters, Ron, 265
Philadelphia Athletics, 16, 38, 44, 51, 91,
104, 126
Philadelphia Phillies, 15, 24, 51, 62, 79,
82, 100–102, 104, 113, 119, 127, 130, 132,
146, 162, 175–76, 178–79, 192, 240, 255,
277, 286
Phillips, Richie, 219, 232, 302
Phillips, Tony, 301
Piedmont League, 58
Pitman, Eduardo Quijano, 105
Pitts, Alabama, 58
Pittsburgh Crawfords, 59–60
Pittsburgh Pirates, 15, 31, 37–38, 57, 60,